Meaning and Humour

How are humorous meanings generated and interpreted? Under-standing a joke involves knowledge of the language code (a matter mostly of semantics) and background knowledge necessary for making the inferences to get the joke (a matter of pragmatics). This book introduces and critiques a wide range of semantic and prag-matic theories in relation to humour, such as systemic functional linguistics, speech acts, politeness, and Relevance Theory, emphasis-ing not only conceptual but also interpersonal and textual mean-ings. Exploiting recent corpus-based research, it suggests that much humour can be accounted for by the overriding of lexical priming. Each chapter's discussion topics and suggestions for further reading encourage a critical approach to semantic and pragmatic theory. Written by an experienced lecturer on the linguistics of the English language, this is an entertaining and user-friendly textbook for advanced students of semantics, pragmatics and humour studies.

ANDREW GOATLY is a professor in the Department of English at Lingnan University, Hong Kong.

KEY TOPICS IN SEMANTICS AND PRAGMATICS

'Key Topics in Semantics and Pragmatics' focuses on the main topics of study in semantics and pragmatics today. It consists of accessible yet challenging accounts of the most important issues, concepts and phenomena to consider when examining meaning in language. Some topics have been the subject of semantic and pragmatic study for many years, and are re-examined in this series in light of new developments in the field; others are issues of growing importance that have not so far been given a sustained treatment. Written by leading experts and designed to bridge the gap between textbooks and primary literature, the books in this series can either be used on courses and seminars or as one-stop, succinct guides to a particular topic for individual students and researchers. Each book includes useful suggestions for further reading, discussion questions, and a helpful glossary.

Forthcoming titles:

The Semantics of Counting by Susan Rothstein

Modification by Marcin Morzycki

Game-Theoretic Pragmatics by Anton Benz

Imperatives by Mark Jary and Mikhail Kissine

Metaphor by David Ritchie

Meaning and Humour

ANDREW GOATLY

CAMBRIDGE
UNIVERSITY PRESS

CAMBRIDGE UNIVERSITY PRESS
Cambridge, New York, Melbourne, Madrid, Cape Town,
Singapore, São Paulo, Delhi, Mexico City

Cambridge University Press
The Edinburgh Building, Cambridge CB2 8RU, UK

Published in the United States of America by
Cambridge University Press, New York

www.cambridge.org
Information on this title: www.cambridge.org/9780521181068

First published 2012

Printed in the United Kingdom at the University Press, Cambridge

A catalogue record for this publication is available from the British Library

Library of Congress Cataloging-in-Publication Data

Goatly, Andrew, 1950–
  Meaning and humour / Andrew Goatly.
    p.   cm. – (Key topics in semantics and pragmatics)
  ISBN 978-1-107-00463-4 (Hardback) – ISBN 978-0-521-18106-8 (Paperback)
  1. Discourse analysis.   2. Wit and humour–History and criticism.
3. Semantics (Philosophy)   4. Pragmatics.   5. Inference.   I. Title.
  P302.7.G63 2012
  401′.41–dc23

                                                        2011037330

ISBN 978-1-107-00463-4 Hardback
ISBN 978-0-521-18106-8 Paperback

To my family: past, present [and future?]

For me humor studies is fundamentally an interpretive exercise. It is an attempt to say what people are talking about even when they don't say so themselves. It is an attempt to wrest meaning – sometimes significant meaning – from ludicrous and seemingly discountable expressions. (Oring 2003: 146)

Contents

Figures

Tables

Illustrations

Acknowledgements

Thanks are particularly due to the following. To John Ng, my most interesting and best final year supervisee in the English Department at Lingnan University, whose project inspired this present work. To Salvatore Attardo, who was something of a mentor to me in the area of linguistically oriented humour studies. He made many admirable suggestions for improving the relatively humourless first draft. If I express minor disagreements with him in this book, then I do so at my own risk. To Connor Ferris with whom I first taught a course on Semantics and Pragmatics at The National University of Singapore, for his clear analytical thinking and association of semantics with humour. To my many students in Singapore and Hong Kong to whom I have attempted to teach semantics and pragmatics and whose responses have informed this work, especially to those students and colleagues who read the penultimate draft and made useful suggestions, notably, Mandy Wong and Melanie Mussett.

Helen Barton from Cambridge University Press and the copy-editor, Steve Barganski, for their admirable efficiency. And my wife, Mathanee, on whom I tested jokes and who kept me fed, and plied with tea and coffee while I was labouring to give birth to this book, never thinking it was misconceived.

And whatever Force or Being it was who distinguished animals from humans with a sense of humour.

Acknowledgements are also due to the following publishers for permission to use material, either free or at great expense: 'Yorkshire and China so easy to confuse' (29 April 2001) by Jo Bowman reproduced by permission of *South China Morning Post*; 'Product Recall – New Labour', 'Olympic Drug Shock', and 'Teenager Smoked Pot and Had Too Much to Drink' reproduced by kind permission of *Private Eye* magazine; extract from *The Best of French and Saunders* by Dawn French and Jennifer Saunders published by Heinemann (copyright © Dawn French and Jennifer Saunders 1991) reproduced by kind permission of United Agents (www.unitedagents.co.uk) on behalf of Dawn French and Jennifer Saunders; 'She picks up your rubbish' by permission of Singapore Press Holdings; advert for Anglia Building Society 1986 reproduced by permission of Nationwide Building Society.

Every effort has been made to contact other copyright holders for permissions, but without success. The publisher would be pleased to hear from any copyright holders that they were unable to communicate with.

And not to forget the Pope and Sarah Palin ...

Typographical conventions

- *italics* for word-form as type
- //slants for phonological form as type
- 'single inverted commas' for meaning
- "double inverted commas" for words as token
- SMALL CAPS for lexemes
- *asterisk** after the initial uninflected part (stem) of a lemma
- [+ CAPS IN SQUARE BRACKETS] for componential features of meaning
- * before grammatically unacceptable sentences
- * at the end of lemmas
- ^ for 'followed by'

1   Introduction

1.1.   ABOUT THIS BOOK

1.1.1.   Why write this book?

Anyone interested in semantics and pragmatics, the way meanings are coded in language and produced or interpreted in context, notices that jokes exemplify various kinds of ambiguity or risk to meaning. Of particular interest, as an object of study, is the question of what knowledge is necessary in order to understand a joke. This might be knowledge of the language code (a matter mostly of semantics) or background knowledge for making the inferences necessary for getting the joke (a matter of pragmatics). Teaching semantics and pragmatics over the years, I realised that jokes can be analysed by using semantic and pragmatic theory, an attempt which prompts one to question and develop theory when the joke is difficult to explain. But the converse is also true: jokes might be a useful way into teaching semantics and pragmatics.

At the most banal level the present book uses jokes as a peg on which to hang theoretical concepts, but it aims to achieve more than that. At least jokes might function as a mnemonic – helping students remember the theoretical concepts through remembering and enjoying the joke. Moreover, for students for whom English is not a first language, humour might be a useful pedagogic tool in developing competence (O'Mara, Waller and Todman 2002). "The use of humour in the classroom has been shown (e.g. Ziv 1979) to increase ease of learning and to be a good pedagogical resource overall (Gentilhomme 1992)" (Attardo 1994: 211). But most crucially, distinct from other books in the series *Key Topics in Semantics and Pragmatics*, it explores the interface between humour theory and linguistic theories of various kinds, especially the pragmatic Relevance Theory, and the psychologically tinged corpus/text-linguistic theory known as priming theory. It does, however, exploit other linguistic approaches quite eclectically, touching on systemic functional linguistics, speech act theory, conversational analysis and genre theory. I hope that, above all in Chapter 11, it might contribute to linguistic theory in its own right.

One of the advantages of using jokes as an introduction to the study of meaning is that jokes are authentic texts, whereas many semantics and pragmatics textbooks use made-up examples. There has been a minor revolution in linguistics since computers facilitated the storage of large text corpora, and the interrogation of these corpora with concordancing software for collocational data. Originally the scientific study of meaning was undertaken in the tradition associated with the twentieth century's most famous linguist, Noam Chomsky, where data consisted of the intuitions of an ideal native speaker. However, this tradition has been challenged, since the 1980s, with an approach which takes real recorded textual evidence more seriously. Jokes and humorous narratives belong in the category of authentic texts. Nevertheless, many are as short as the traditional made-up examples in semantic textbooks (none quoted in this book is more than one page long).

In step with these developments in linguistic theory, this book, though beginning by introducing basic traditional categories in semantics and pragmatics, extends to recent text-oriented theories. In particular, it progresses towards a discussion of the work of the late John Sinclair on collocation and the theory of lexical priming that Michael Hoey (2005) has recently built upon it. The semantic notion of ambiguity comes under scrutiny, along with an exploration of the extent to which ambiguity is present in most authentic texts, and whether it is rather artificial in humour. Moreover, by the use of judicious discussion topics, the book persists in challenging traditional semantic and pragmatic approaches, and, further, ends with a critique of Hoey's text-based theory itself.

This book is designed for advanced undergraduates or students on taught post-graduate courses in English language, (applied) linguistics or the philosophy of language. It attempts to provide a comprehensive overview of theories of different kinds of meaning and how they are encoded or implied in texts. It could therefore be a core textbook for courses in semantics and pragmatics. However, the jokes and activities, in particular, provide a resource to be used selectively in other linguistics courses, such as discourse analysis, morphology or even phonology. It should also be of use to students of humour studies, and less specifically of cultural studies, communication studies, and stylistics.

1.1.2. What's in this book?

The book consists of eleven chapters. After this introduction, Chapter 2 locates the study of meaning within the language system at a level above phonology. Looking downwards it illustrates the contribution of phonology to meaning through malapropisms, dyslexic jokes, etc. At the lowest meaningful level it considers the inflectional and derivational morphology of words. And looking up a level beyond the word it considers multiple-word lexical items – semi-fixed expressions, compounds of various classes, and idioms. From a humour standpoint it explores how jokes blur and problematise the boundaries of linguistic units operating at different levels, for instance by re-analysis.

Chapter 3 concerns sense, logical or conceptual meaning, as expressed in grammar. It concentrates on two areas, the meanings of modification of the noun phrase and the meanings of the clause, following, respectively, work by Ferris (1993) and by Halliday (1985/1994). It explains the different kinds of modification, such as ascription, association, and the overlapping categories of classifiers and epithets, as well as considering the ambiguities in the scope of modification. As for the clause, it introduces the various semantic categories of process types and participants, with a power hierarchy of these participants, and gives a brief example of critical linguistic analysis using these. It proceeds to a discussion of nominalisation and passivisation, and their consequences for introducing gaps into meaning. The concentration on the meaning of the clause allows scope for the illustration of syntactic ambiguity as a resource for humour.

Chapter 4 deals with areas traditionally the staple for semantics, the sense, or conceptual meaning, of lexis. It considers the logical basis of conceptual meaning by introducing the basic sense relations of synonymy, entailment, inconsistency, contradiction and tautology. It discusses semantic ambiguity based on homophony, homography and polysemy, and different forms of presupposition. It deals with meaning oppositions – complementarity, multiple-incompatibility, polar oppositions, converses, transitivity and symmetry, and meaning relations such as meronymy and hyponymy. The role of componential analysis and selection restrictions in this logical approach to meaning is demonstrated. However, it questions the psychological validity of this logical approach, and considers vagueness and fuzziness, prototypes, radial categories and family resemblances. Throughout it exemplifies lexical and sense relation ambiguities as used in humour, especially puns.

Chapter 5 introduces other kinds of meaning besides the conceptual: reflected, connotative, affective and social meanings. Particular emphasis is given to affective meaning, where we explore emotive lexis, evaluation and appraisal, and amplification through rhythmic repetition and syntactic parallelism; and to social meaning, which includes not only the dialectal, age and status meanings of lexis, but also the interpersonal meaning expressed by grammar through mood and modality. It illustrates humour dependent on stylistic mixing, and stresses humour's interpersonal functions.

Chapter 6 concentrates on the kinds of meaning associated with language use in textual and generic contexts. It covers collocational meaning, thematic meaning – the ordering of information in the clause and the role of intonation in establishing focus and contrast – and the cohesive relations within texts. An introduction to genre and register provides a way of tying together all aspects of meaning and locating them in a social context. A major section surveys the literature on different genres of jokes (humour) and their similarities to narrative, as well as genre-mixing as a humour resource. The chapter ends with a critique of stable de-contextualised notions of meaning, giving evidence for this critique with a brief excursus into varieties of meaning change.

Chapter 7 considers metonymy and, more importantly, metaphor and their role in meaning and humour. This is a pivotal chapter between semantics and pragmatics; conventional metaphors have become de-motivated and incorporated into semantics, whereas original metaphors are more dependent on pragmatic inferencing for their interpretation. First, the chapter explores the role of deletion in metonymy and the consequent ambiguities in genres, such as headlines, with their abbreviated grammar. It then discusses the distinction between original and conventional metaphors. After a sketch of experientialist theories of conceptual metaphor, data from the author's database *Metalude* illustrates conceptual metaphor themes and their role in jokes and humour. Metaphorical elaboration in texts is also explored – literalisation, extension and mixing. The chapter ends with thorough discussion of the commonalities and differences between jokes, irony and metaphor.

Chapter 8 shifts from semantics into pragmatics. It focuses initially on the boundaries of semantics and pragmatics, outlining degrees of motivation in relation to symbols, indexes and icons. In this context it explores the notion that central to humour is a kind of language play which attempts a re-motivation of the linguistic sign. The chapter next delineates the different kinds of reference and the variability of reference according to place, person and time in deixis. The chapter's main focus is speech act theory, the conditions and categories of direct and indirect speech acts, and their participation in larger text structures as analysed in conversational analysis. The chapter ends with a critique of the theory and the problems in applying it to discourse. The chapter exemplifies referential and speech act category ambiguities and infelicitous speech acts as a source of humour.

Chapter 9 continues the introduction to pragmatic theory with a focus on inferential pragmatics. It explains Paul Grice's (1975) co-operative principle, how maxims are observed in standard implicature, or how they are broken through violation, flouting, opting out, suspension and infringement, with jokes providing examples. It discusses and questions the claim that joking violates the co-operative principle. The end of the chapter stresses the need for interpersonal pragmatics and politeness theory, introducing the politeness principle and theories of face, and discussing humour in the context of modesty and banter.

Chapter 10 is based on an extension to Gricean theory – Relevance Theory (Sperber and Wilson 1986/1995). Topics include vagueness and the explication of propositions, propositional attitude, contextual effects and processing effort, the role of different kinds of knowledge in deriving implicatures, and the storage of knowledge in schemas. This provides an opportunity to explore script/schema opposition theories of humour. Another aspect of Relevance Theory delineated here is the theory of echoic utterances, including the reporting of speech, the use of proverbs, allusions and other kinds of intertextuality. The echoic theory of irony is discussed and extended.

Chapter 11 summarises theories of text-linguistics including the role and importance of collocation, and the relationship between meaning, information and predictability. It focuses on Hoey's priming theory and its hypotheses, especially the idea that different, potentially ambiguous meanings of the same word-form have different collocational, thematic and semantic profiles, with the result that in their context and co-text these word forms are often not ambiguous. Hoey (2005) hypothesises that humour is often achieved by these profiles or "primings" being over-ridden to create an unlikely meaning. The last chapter tests this hypothesis by examining examples of jokes dependent on the different kinds of ambiguity covered throughout the book, and investigating whether concordance data indicate that the least predictable un-primed meaning is essential to the ambiguity. Such exemplification constitutes a sort of summary of the areas of semantics and pragmatics covered in previous chapters. The chapter continues with a critique of Hoey's new theory, both in its own right, and in its ability to account for and extend the script-opposition theories of humour.

Besides summarising different kinds of linguistic humour, the last chapter also represents the climax of the book in terms of an exploration into linguistic theories of humour. While numerous references are made to the particular insights of linguistically based humour theory throughout the first ten chapters, the last chapter makes space for a more coherent discussion of theories of humour as incongruity, liberation and control, and hints at how they might be integrated into semantic and pragmatic theory.

1.2.   SEMANTIC TYPOGRAPHY

Before beginning a book to do with meaning, it is important to establish typographical conventions in order to avoid the kind of ambiguity exploited in the following joke:

> Beware of tennis players – love means nothing to them. (Tibballs 2006: 540)

This could be paraphrased either as

> Tennis players are short on emotional commitment to sexual relationships.

or

> Tennis players use the word *love* to mean 'zero'.

The ambiguity depends upon the fact that language can either be used to make a statement about the world beyond language or be mentioned in order to make a statement about language itself. This is known as **the use–mention distinction**. So in "love means nothing to them", "love" is either involved in describing the sexual mores of tennis players, a **use**, or has its own meaning described, i.e. 'nothing', a **mention**. In this latter case the language employed to describe the meaning is called **metalanguage**, and the bit of language described is known as **object language**.[1]

In order to distinguish between uses and mentions this book employs typographical conventions. The "use" meaning of the joke will not need to employ any special typography, just as it is presented above. But according to the typography adopted here, the "mention" meaning of the joke would appear as

> Beware of tennis players – *love* means 'nothing' to them. (Tibballs 2006: 540)

Single inverted commas are used for the meaning, and italics are used for the word-form as **type**, which constitutes some kind of generalisation about the many individual uses or **tokens** of the word-form.[2] To understand this **type–token distinction**, look at the coins in your pocket. If you have three 2p pieces, four 5p pieces and one 10p piece, how many coins do you have? You have three coin types and eight coin tokens. Or refer back to the first sentence of Section 1.1.1, where there are twenty-seven word forms as types and thirty-one as tokens.

The following humorous sentence from a newspaper uses the typographical convention for mentioning tokens, i.e. double inverted commas:

> Miss Charlene Mason sang "I will not pass this way again," giving obvious pleasure to the congregation. (Tibballs 2006: 495)

The ambiguity here is quite subtle. Firstly, if you quote what is said, or in this case sung, it counts as a mention, because the statement made cannot be attributed to you, only to the person making the statement. However, the added subtlety in this case is that, when Miss Mason performs, what she sings is in fact also a mention by her: she is not actually stating that she herself will not pass this way again. However, the joke depends upon pretending that she is stating this, that her utterance is a use, the implication being that she sang so badly the congregation is mightily pleased she will never return.[3]

A further convention concerning word-forms is useful when distinguishing the phonetic form from the written or graphic form.

> Waiter, waiter, why is my steak so small?
> Well, sir, that's what we call a minute steak.

The ambiguity here cannot be represented in print by spelling: we need a phonetic representation of the different sounds of the word-form as type, distinguished typographically by slants, e.g. /mɪnɪt/ meaning 'a period of 60 seconds'; /maɪnjuːt/ meaning 'very small'.

So far we have been dealing with words or word-forms. But, in the study of meaning it is often useful to think of a category even more abstract than the word as type, which lies behind various word-forms. This is the **lexeme** or **lexical item**. The following joke depends upon not only a use–mention distinction, but also the fact that the mention may be of the lexeme rather than just the word-type.

> A blonde went to the library and chose a book called HOW to HUG. It turned out to be volume seven of the Oxford English Dictionary. (after Tibballs 2006: 533)

The blonde mistakes a dictionary – which is metalanguage and object language throughout – for a manual on embracing. HOW and HUG in small caps in fact represent lexemes listed in the dictionary. Under the headword or lexeme HUG, one can find various types of word-forms, *hug*, *hugs*, *hugging*, *hugged*, all instances of the same lexeme, and examples of tokens of their uses. For instance, in the Oxford English Dictionary we have

> **1661** *LOVELL Hist. Anim.* Introd., The love of apes is such towards their young, that they often kill them by hugging them. *c***1705** *POPE Jan. & May* 1813 He hugg'd her close, and kiss'd her o'er and o'er. **1841** *DICKENS Barn. Rudge* xli, Dolly . . . threw her arms round her old father's neck and hugged him tight.

When searching for all the inflected forms of the same lexeme in a corpus one often uses the uninflected form or the initial part of the word, which is called the **lemma**. This is represented by its italicised type followed by an asterisk, e.g. *hug**.

There is one more notation we will use.

> On the whole men are more violent than animals. But women aren't.

This joke, if you can call it that, depends upon an ambiguity in the meaning of the word *man*. We might think "men" in the first sentence refers to humans in general. But the second sentence indicates that it only refers to the male members of humankind. The meaning of *man* has one more component of meaning than we at first thought, which we call a componential feature. So at first we think of the meaning of *man* as [+HUMAN], but reading on we add another feature [+HUMAN, +MALE].

To sum up, the typographical conventions employed in this book to distinguish object language, language as mention, and to describe it metalinguistically are:

> *italics* for word-form as type
> //slants for phonological form as type
> 'single inverted commas' for meaning
> "double inverted commas" for word-form as token
> SMALL CAPS for lexemes
> *asterisk** after the initial uninflected part of a word form type for lemma
> [+CAPS IN SQUARE BRACKETS] for componential features of meaning

Activity 1.1

Analyse the following four jokes in terms of the confusion between language use and language mention, employing the concepts of 'metalanguage' and 'object language'. Write your answers using the typographical conventions introduced above (if handwritten you may want to use <u>underlining</u> instead of *italics*).

    a. To some – marriage is a word … to others – a sentence. (Ng 2005: 13)
    b. What's orange and sounds like a parrot? A carrot.
    c. He walked with a pronounced limp. Pronounced L-I-M-P. (Alexander 1997: 53)
    d. That girl speaks 18 languages and can't say no in any of them.
       (Tibballs 2006: 658)

Comment

a. (i) To some *marriage* is a word …
    (ii) To some [marriage] is a sentence.
    In the first clause "marriage" is object language, a mention, and "is a word" is metalanguage describing it. The second clause has to be a use: some people feel imprisoned or punished by marriage. The joke depends upon the ambiguity of *sentence*, which represents two lexemes: SENTENCE$_1$, 'punishment handed down by a court' or SENTENCE$_2$, 'a linguistic unit comprising one or more clauses'. Since *sentence* in this second meaning is a metalingual term, and "sentence" occurs after "word", which can only have a metalingual meaning, we first access the metalingual SENTENCE$_2$ and are then forced to reject it.

b. This example, too, plays on the use–mention distinction. As a mention focussing on form *a carrot* /ə kærət/ sounds like *a parrot* /ə pærət/. As a use a carrot is orange.

c. (i) pronounced limp
    (ii) pronounced /l/ /ɪ/ /m/ /p/
    The first occurrence of "pronounced limp" is a use, with "pronounced" representing the meaning 'very noticeable'. The second puns on the meaning of a different lexeme, 'uttered' or 'said'.

d. This joke is slightly more complicated. "Say no" as a use means 'refuse'. But "say no" as a mention cannot really be represented as "say *no*", since the form of the object language will only be *no* in English not the girl's other seventeen or eighteen languages. It must mean, therefore, 'say the word with the equivalent meaning to the English word-form *no*'. With this focus on meaning rather than form, perhaps the best notation is:

That girl speaks 18 languages and can't say 'no' in any of them (Tibballs 2006: 658).

The theme of use-versus-mention will be revisited in Chapter 10 where we discuss echoic utterances in relation to the pragmatic Relevance

Theory. But the metalingual function is often important in jokes. And it is worth locating jokes in relation to this and other language functions. To do this we can make use of Jakobson's model of communication.

1.3. JAKOBSON'S MODEL OF COMMUNICATION AND THE METALINGUAL FUNCTION

Jakobson, a linguist of the Prague school who later lectured at MIT, advanced a model in which an act of communication involves six elements: addresser, addressee, context (topic and setting), message, contact (medium and channel) and code (see Figure 1.1) (1960: 353).[4] Briefly, an **addresser** (for example, a speaker), who has some **channel** for physical sense contact (air through which sound waves can travel) linking her/him with the **addressee** (the hearer), and a productive **medium** for creating a physical sign (the speech apparatus of mouth, lips, tongue, vocal cords etc.), selects items from the **code** (the language as system), and combines them into a **message** concerning a particular topic in a particular social and physical setting – the **context**. The addressee, who has a receptive medium (the auditory apparatus), and a knowledge of the code, receives the message and decodes it.

The power of Jakobson's model lies in its incorporation of different functions of language (given in italics in Figure 1.1). Although, he claims, all these six elements are necessary for communication, different communicative functions place emphasis on different elements: on the addresser for the **expressive** function; on the addressee for the **conative** function – an attempt to affect the actions of the addressee; on context for the **referential** function, where what is at stake is the description of the world; on contact for the **phatic** function – which is

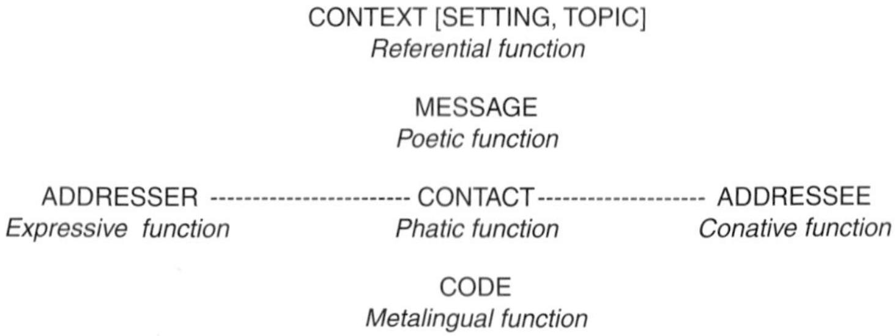

CONTEXT [SETTING, TOPIC]
Referential function

MESSAGE
Poetic function

ADDRESSER ----------------------- CONTACT -------------------- ADDRESSEE
Expressive function   *Phatic function*   *Conative function*

CODE
Metalingual function

Figure 1.1. Jakobson's model of communication

either physical or psychological (e.g. saying "1, 2, 3, 4, testing" to check a sound system, or meaningless greetings such as "Hallo!" or "Hi!"); on the message for the **poetic** function, where the important issue is the artful patterning of the text (e.g. "I like Ike", the slogan in General Eisenhower's election campaign (Jakobson 1960: 357)); and on the code for the **metalingual** function, when language is used reflexively to talk about language.

We remarked on the metalingual element in jokes since, like the object language referred to by metalanguage, many of them are mentions rather than uses. Moreover puns, for example, draw attention to a coincidence of form, and their metalingual aspect has long been recognised in humour research (Attardo 1994: 147). Furthermore, rather than a referential or conceptual function, jokes tend to have an interpersonal or even phatic function, being designed to establish or strengthen social relations through exploiting an affective element – expressing and provoking emotion. They may also fulfil a poetic function (Norrick 1993: 16–17, 162). For Jakobson the defining strategy of the poetic function was projecting the paradigmatic axis, the vertical axis of choice from the code, on to the syntagmatic axis of combination in the message. "I like Ike", for example, projects the choices of the /aɪ/ phoneme onto each successive syllable of the clause. Chiaro (1992) mentions Sherzer's claim that jokes do the same. The joke (c) above not only chooses an item from the paradigm of forms which represents two meanings. It also syntagmatically develops these two meanings in the most obvious way by repetition on the syntagmatic axis. The following joke is similar, though lacking complete identity of form, and the projection is also semantic: 'breakdown', 'fatigue', 'anguish'.

> – What are the first two stages before complete metal breakdown?
> – Metal fatigue and metalanguage.

In sum, humour highlights the non-referential functions or non-conceptual meanings of language. This is one reason that this textbook, unlike many textbooks in semantics, if not pragmatics, gives weight to non-conceptual meanings, notably in Chapters 5 and 6.

1.4.   AN INTRODUCTORY FRAMEWORK: FORM, MEANING, WORLD

To facilitate the discussion of meaning relations and kinds of ambiguity, a simple, if not simplistic, diagram will be useful (Figure 1.2).[5]

Figure 1.2. A simple diagram for forms, meanings and the world

The first column shows the spoken and written forms of a word as type, observing the typographical conventions already introduced. In the second column are the meanings attached to those forms by linguistic conventions more or less shared by members of a language community. (I have specified this meaning through componential features.) Generally speaking, this relationship between form and meaning has been regarded as arbitrary. That is to say, there is no intrinsic reason or motivation for using *house* for a building in which people live. The fact that French uses the form *maison* for the same meaning, and other languages use forms like *dom* (Russian), *bâan* (Thai) points to this **arbitrariness**. There are, nevertheless, attempts, as part of the humorous enterprise, to provide spurious cross-linguistic **motivation**: "What do Frenchmen have for breakfast?" "Huite heures-bix."

While columns 1 (F) and 2 (M) are internal to language (so that when language is used to describe them they are objects of metalanguage), column 3 represents the world external to language. A simple account would suggest that forms in column 1 via their meanings in column 2 are used to refer to objects, qualities, relations and processes in column 3, the world.

Discussion

Can the columns Meaning and World actually be so easily separated as Figure 1.2 suggests? Do worlds always exist independent of meanings? The linguist Benjamin Lee Whorf claimed:

> We dissect nature along lines laid down by our native languages. The categories and types we isolate from the world of phenomena we do not find there because they stare every observer in the face; on the contrary the world is presented in a kaleidoscopic flux of impressions which has to be organised by our minds – and this means largely by the linguistic systems in our minds. We cut

nature up, organize it into concepts, and ascribe significances as we do, largely because we are parties to an agreement to organize it in this way – an agreement that holds throughout our speech community and is codified in the patterns of our language (Whorf 1956: 212ff.).

So does the system of meanings in column 2 partly determine the world we observe in column 3?[6]

The following joke depends on the assumption that the two columns internal to language and the world exterior to it can be confused: "Waiter, there's a needle in my soup?" "Sorry, madam, that was a typographical error" (Alexander 1997: 24). I doubt this implies that a typographical error in columns 1 and 2 – the wrong form *ee* instead of *oo* – was decoded by the cook who then proceeded to put needles not noodles into the soup. Rather it seems to be some fantastic suggestion that a mistake internal to language magically produces mistakes in the world.

The two aspects of the meaning of **word-forms**, **sense** (M) and **reference** (→W), are, in this model, quite distinct, in column 2 and 3 respectively. Senses and referents are in a many-to-many relationship. One can use the same word-form and its sense to refer to many different referents in the world, and the same referent in the world can be referred to by many different word-forms/senses. The philosopher Frege established the difference between sense and reference with the example of *the morning star* and *the evening star*. In terms of semantics (sense) these seem to be opposite. In terms of reference they are identical: they both refer to Venus (which, to confuse matters is not actually a star, but a planet!). Compare "Greengrocer, do you have any aubergines?" "No, Madam, but we have some nice eggplants".

These examples show the same thing can be referred to by many different noun phrases: "Bill", "Chelsea's father", "Hillary's husband", "the only Democratic president to be re-elected for a second term", "the leader of the US who used the Oval Office for sex" etc. etc. Conversely, the same noun phrase with the same semantic meaning can be used to refer to different things on different occasions. "The chair" could refer to the one I am sitting on writing this in front of the computer in my study, or the one you are sitting on reading this.

The following extract from the beginning of Henry James' novel *A Portrait of a Lady* exemplifies the many-to-many relationship between word-form/meaning and referent. The word-forms referring to Ralph Touchett are in bold, those referring to his dog in italics. Most of these illustrate **elegant variation**, the tendency (especially with novelists like James) to use different words and phrases to point to the same referent. But notice, too, the use of the same form *hands* in sentences 2 and 4 to refer to Ralph's and the young woman's hands, and *master* to refer to different referents in sentences 6 and 7: Ralph, the master of the dog, and Ralph's father, the master of the house.

> (1) While this exchange of pleasantries took place between the two, **Ralph Touchett** wandered away a little, with his usual slouching gait, his hands in his pockets and *his little rowdyish terrier* at his heels. (2) His face turned towards the house, but his eyes were bent musingly on the lawn; so that **he** had been **an object of observation** to a person who had just made her appearance in the ample doorway for some moments before **he** perceived her. (3) His attention was called to her by the conduct of *his dog*, who had suddenly darted forward with a little volley of shrill barks, in which the note of welcome, however, was more sensible than the note of defiance. (4) The person in question was a young lady, who seemed immediately to interpret the greeting of *the small beast*. (5) *He* advanced with great rapidity and stood at her feet, looking up and barking hard; whereupon, without hesitation, she stooped and caught *him* in her hands, holding *him* face to face while *he* continued his quick chatter. (6) **His master** now had had time to follow and to see that *Bunchie*'s new friend was a tall girl in a black dress, who at first sight looked pretty. (7) She was bareheaded as if she was staying in the house – a fact that conveyed perplexity to **the son of its master**, conscious of that immunity from visitors which had for some time been rendered necessary by the latter's ill-health.
> (Henry James, *Portrait of a Lady*. Penguin Books, 1963 [1881], p. 15)

Activity 1.2

What noun phrases, excluding pronouns, are used in this passage to refer to the woman whom Ralph encounters? What effect does this elegant variation have?

Comment

- "a person who had just made her appearance in the ample doorway for some moments before he perceived her" (sentence 2)
- "the person in question" (sentence 4)
- "a young lady" (sentence 4)
- "Bunchie's new friend" (sentence 6)
- "a tall girl in a black dress" (sentence 6)

I suppose the effect of this elegant variation is to see the woman from different perspectives, perhaps the changing perspective of Ralph – the initial senses of the referring terms do not indicate sex, for example, and the youth of the female does not become apparent until Ralph approaches her. The first phrase in sentence 6 defines her in relation to Ralph's dog.

One interesting aspect of Figure 1.2 concerns names. Although names may have had some kind of sense originally, in practice they are simply forms used to refer to single individuals in column 3, rather like ID numbers. Unlike words with sense they, ideally, have a one-to-one correspondence with referents. (This accounts for the anomaly in "The plays were not written by Shakespeare, but by someone else of the same name", and in the joke "Why is there only one Eiffel Tower?" "Because it eats its babies" (Oring 2003: 13).)

Names skip over column 2. Consequently, even if you call your daughter Joy or Serena, there is no guarantee that she will bring you happiness or remain calm in a crisis. If you enter a classroom full of students none of whom you know, and the lecturer asks you to go and stand by the whiteboard, you use your knowledge of the sense of whiteboard (column 2) to pick out the likely referent. If, on the other hand, you are asked to sit by Monica then you will be at a loss, since Monica has no sense to guide you to the likely referent.

Nevertheless, some jokes pretend that names have a sense, or draw attention to the fact that in other contexts the same word-form can be used as a common noun. The jazz musician Chubby Checker named himself as a synonym of Fats Domino, a famous musician of the previous generation. We might manufacture an irony from the prelate of Manila being called Cardinal Sin (Blake 2007: 66–7). There is even a semi-humorous theory known as nominal determinism, the hypothesis that your name may determine your career. I noticed how many dentists in Singapore are called Chew/Chiu or Yap, and the waitress in my university canteen is called Amy Sup. (And yet, alas, Desmond Tutu missed out on ballet.)

It is not quite true that names in their non-humorous uses are entirely devoid of sense, ignoring column 2 of Figure 1.2. If all but one of the students in this room were identifiably male, then you would be able to pick out Monica, as most Western names seem to be coded for gender. In multi-cultural contexts, such as Singapore, one might recognise some students and their names as of a particular ethnic origin, for instance of Malay (Islamic) background, and others as Indian, and others as Chinese. There are also names reserved for pets, such as *Fido* (dog), *Tiddles* (cat), though *Polly* and *Rex* are ambiguous between female human/parrot and male human/dog.

Do all words refer? Traditionally reference is seen as to "things" using noun phrases, rather than properties by adjectival phrases, or processes by verbs. However, there is no reason in principle to limit the notion of reference in these ways (Searle 1969: 118). One might even suggest that conjunctions like *because* and prepositions like *to* refer to logical relationships or direction. This still leaves us with words such as the articles *the* and *a/an*, which hardly seem to refer at all. I imagine that one reason the following joke seems absurd is due to this fact:

> "What do Alexander the Great and Winnie the Pooh have in common?"
> "The same middle name."

Here we have two names with unique reference, and the article *the* is equated with them despite having no referent.

A further reason is that since names only refer, by-passing sense, they potentially carry a great deal of encyclopaedic information based on their referents, which, in this particular case, presents a stark contrast: a general who was a brilliant strategist and brave warrior, and the rather timid bear of little brain.

Activity 1.3

Explain, in terms of the columns of Figure 1.2, the following unintentionally humorous headline referring to Clinton's recommendation to his vice-president of the White House intern named Dickey.

CLINTON PLACES DICKEY IN GORE'S HANDS

Comment

As Bucaria points out (2004: 288), DICKEY in upper case is ambiguous as between a name, which has no sense, and a common noun meaning an article of clothing ('bow-tie' or 'false shirt-front') or, perhaps, even 'penis'. The first meaning skips column 2 in our figure, but the second meaning involves sense in column 2. The ambiguity is possible because headlines, being capitalised, cannot use upper/lower case to make the proper/common distinction. Are such ambiguities more common in German where all nouns are capitalised?

1.5.   DEFINING THE WORD AND OTHER LEXICAL CONCEPTS

This brings us to the question of how we define a word. There is an operational definition, which one uses, for example, in counting words for an assignment. This defines the **orthographic word**, a sequence of letters separated from the rest of the text by white space or punctuation. The emphasis on orthographic form in writing/print is simpler than a definition in speech, because, to some extent, the concept of the word is a product of literacy.

Shifting to grammatical/semantic criteria, a **word** has been defined as the smallest form that can meaningfully stand alone as a sentence, for example in an answer to a question or on a public notice. There are several problems with this definition, however.

Activity 1.4

Which of the following orthographic words does not pass the test of the smallest meaningful unit that can stand alone?

(1) *come*   (2) *yesterday*   (3) *slowly*   (4) *to*   (5) *over*   (6) *yours*   (7) *your*   (8) *candlestick*
(9) *the*

Comment

One can imagine an imperative sentence consisting of "Come!" and dialogues in which *yesterday, slowly, yours, over* (at least as an adverb) and, possibly, *to* might be answers to a question ("Does the up train go to London or from London?" "To."). However, it is impossible to think of language uses (rather than mentions) in which *your* and *the* pass this test. Moreover, though *candlestick* can stand alone, it is not a minimal or smallest unit of meaning, being divisible into *candle* and *stick*, which are both orthographic words and pass the semantic/grammatical stand-alone test. The conclusion must be that the orthographic definition and the minimum meaningful stand-alone unit test may give different results.

Not only do word compounds like *candlestick, strawberry, blackbird, flyover* and *waterbed* fail this test, despite being orthographic words, we also sense that they are single lexical items because they have idiosyncratic semantics; their meanings cannot be predicted from their parts. They are the realisation of the more abstract concept of lexeme, or lexical item (1.2).

The same is true of **phrasal compounds**, where a lexical item is constituted by more than one orthographic word, e.g. *water buffalo, water polo, water table, water down, in hot water* etc. Hyphenation and abbreviation (sometimes as acronyms) are orthographic clues to the existence of lexemes realised by more than one orthographic word. For example, compare *PR* (*public relations*), *pub* (*public house*) and *orange-juice* (*orange juice*) with *public telephone* and *orange jacket*. In the first three the potential for abbreviation and hyphenation indicate that the phrases in parentheses are phrasal compounds, whereas the latter two are free phrases.

A phonological equivalent of these graphological clues is sometimes found in stress patterns: if a phrase comprising more than one word-form only takes a single major stress then it likely represents one lexeme: compare 'or.ange juice with 'or.ange 'jack.et.

Activity 1.5

1. Which of these two-word (orthographic word) pairs constitutes one lexical item and which is made up of two lexical items? Say why you think so. What kind of further evidence might be useful in helping you decide?
   a. On the forest floor I saw this remarkable *baby bug*.
   b. He likes to go for walks in the *baby buggy*.
   c. He poured *water down* my neck.
   d. He has *watered down* these proposals so that they are unrecognisable.
   e. Dogs must not be let loose on the *public highway*.
   f. The initial *public offering* (IPO) of these shares will take place in August.
   g. He sent me *back copies* of the magazine.
2. Explain why this unintentionally humorous classified ad might not be humorous in spoken form:

   Four poster bed. 101 years old. Perfect for antique lovers. (Tibballs 2006: 499)

Comment

1. (b), (d) and (f) are likely phrasal compounds, that is single lexemes, while (g) is ambiguous. Stress patterns – one major stress – might help us with (d), (b) and the disambiguation of (g), while the single lexemes in (b) and (g) could also be hyphenated. In (f) the abbreviation is a good indicator that we have one lexeme.
2. One might suggest that in spoken form stress patterns would disambiguate the meanings: an 'tique 'lo vers 'lovers who are antique'; an 'tique lo vers 'people who love antiques'.

We can sum up, with the help of Table 1.1, the difficulties when the three definitions of word (orthographic word, minimal meaningful stand-alone unit, and lexical item) do not coincide.

We noted that articles and possessive adjectives, e.g. *the* and *your*, do not pass the stand-alone meaningful unit test, suggesting this is because they cannot on their own refer to the world. This fact reflects the traditional distinction between **lexical words** and **grammatical** or **function words**, which do not represent lexemes. In step with this, function words convey little if any information because they are more frequent and predictable. The more predictable an item of code, the less information it carries. So *the* in "Can you close the door please" conveys relatively little information compared with the *door* in the same sentence. Considering this phenomenon in

Table 1.1. *The application of the three definitions of word*

Example	Orthographic word	Lexical item	Stand-alone as minimal free form
cat	Yes	Yes	Yes
penknife	Yes	Yes	No
in hot water	No	Yes	No
the	Yes	No	No

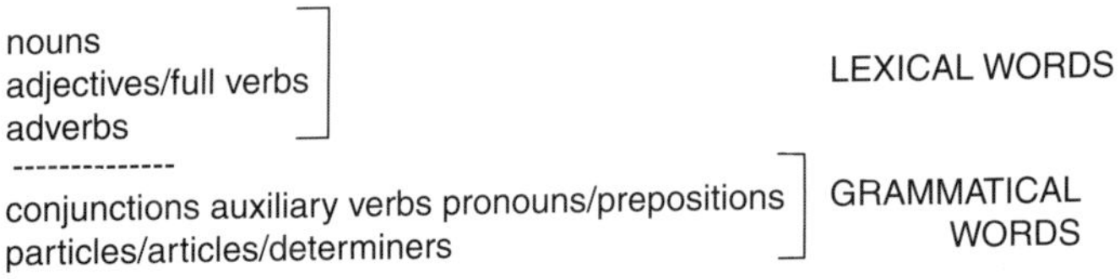

```
nouns
adjectives/full verbs                         LEXICAL WORDS
adverbs
--------------
conjunctions auxiliary verbs pronouns/prepositions   GRAMMATICAL
particles/articles/determiners                          WORDS
```

Figure 1.3. Lexical and grammatical words and word-class

relation to Figure 1.2, we note that, because they have no precise meaning or sense, and are not designed to refer, function words carry little information, and only count as orthographic words. This accounts for the anomaly behind the following joke: "Which of the following is the odd one out? Greed, envy, malice, anger and kindness?" "'And.'" (Critchley 2002: 19). They do, however, convey grammatical information, and when omitted in the telegraphic style of headlines tend to create ambiguities.

The distinction between grammatical and lexical words is reflected in word-class. This is probably best viewed as a scale rather than an absolute distinction: the number of different nouns in European languages[7] is higher than verbs, which in turn is higher than adverbs, so, theoretically, nouns carry more information than adverbs. Moreover, adverbs and prepositions often share the same word-form, e.g. *up, through, over, on,* suggesting they inhabit the borderline of lexical and grammatical words.

Grammatical words, being more frequent and predictable, occur in texts of every genre, while the most lexical of lexical words – nouns, verbs and adjectives – may be restricted to very specific genres and registers within highly specialised fields of human activity. And these fields may be adding new lexical words continuously, in contrast with the rarity of adding new grammatical words. The problem is that new words run the risk of failing to communicate if the language user is not acquainted with their sense. In this case they may function rather like the name of someone you don't know – without sense and also without reference. "You know about Euthanasia in Switzerland?" "No, what happened to her?"

A final question worth considering is under what circumstances we can claim that we are dealing with the same word. We can think of formal identity, column 1 in Figure 1.2. But we may want to give more weight to semantic identity in column 2. For example, we have already noted that the same lexeme (defined by meaning) may be represented by differently inflected word-forms. Or we could take into account syntactic or word-class identity. Is *catch*, in the following two sentences, the same word, given that it represents different word-classes?

He managed to catch the ball. It was a difficult catch.

There is a problem in establishing what we mean by identity in each case, the formal, the lexical-semantic and the grammatical. I suppose we accept that the following word-forms are the same, even though in different fonts:

Willow   *Willow*   `Willow`

Handwriting is less standardised than fonts, however, and spelling may be variable. Accents or pronunciations vary considerably and may also indicate different dialectal meanings: the difference between the pronunciation of *corn* in south-east England (/kɔːn/) and the southern US (/kɑːn/) matches a difference in meaning: 'cereals in general, including wheat, barley, rye etc.' and 'sweet-corn, maize'.

The problem with the semantic criterion is deciding whether words are so intimately related in meaning one should count the meaning as identical. For example, does *shake* in "the dog was shaking himself after his swim in the pond" and "the child was shaking with fear" represent the same lexeme or not? If I use a word in a one-off metaphor "the inverted cauldron of the Blue Mosque's dome" does *cauldron* maintain its normal lexical sense and simply have an unconventional referent, or has its sense or meaning changed to make it a new lexical item? Similarly, while *catch* in the example above might represent two different words because of word-class difference, despite referring to an identical process, in the case of *cocoon* the noun and the verb clearly have a quite distinct literal and metaphorical meaning, 'sheath of silk or fibre spun by a caterpillar' and 'protect a vulnerable person by isolating them', respectively. Moreover, how delicate a division in

sub-categories of word-class should we make? Just as slight cha
pronunciation may correlate with different meanings, so may c......
in sub-categories of word-class from, for example, transitive to intransitive. *Stagger* as intransitive verb means 'walk unsteadily', whereas
stagger transitive usually means 'surprise extremely' ("I was staggered
by the numbers of AIDS victims") or 'arrange at intervals in time or
space' ("The Beatles and Rolling Stones staggered the release dates
of their singles").

Activity 1.6

Does the word-form *egg* in the following joke represent the same lexeme for the
man and the girl? Is there a difference in sense which would suggest a
different lexeme, or simply a difference in reference?

After picking up a girl in a club a Romeo was desperate to get her to stay the
night. She clearly wasn't interested, but he wouldn't give up. "Say, honey," he
asked suggestively, "How do you like your eggs in the morning?" She looked at
him and replied coldly, "Unfertilised." (Tibballs 2006: 524)

Comment

I don't know! I suspect that the woman's understanding of the
word *egg* 'ovum' is a different lexeme from the *egg* which refers to
chicken eggs.

1.6. HUMOUR, AMBIGUITY AND INCONGRUITY

To end this chapter, I need to introduce in summary form the
theory of humour underpinning this book, and which I elaborate in
Chapter 11. There are many theories of humour, including superiority theory, in which the inferiority of the targets of jokes and the
superiority of those who create and understand them might be highlighted, and the relief or liberation theory based on the psychothera-
peutic notions of repression. More linguistically oriented theories of
humour, however, have built on these two theories by highlighting
the idea of ambiguity and bi-sociation, to develop an incongruity
theory (for the standard exposition, see Suls 1972). I take **incongruity**
to be the major technique for producing humour, though it does not
explain the functions or purposes of humour in the way other theories attempt.

Ambiguity has been long recognised as essential for most kinds
of humour, going back as far as Raskin (1981, 1985). "Deliberate

ambiguity will be shown to underlie much, if not all, of verbal humour" (Ritchie 2004: 40). Koestler's bi-sociation theory of humour builds on this insight to stress the incongruity necessary for humour: "the perceiving of a situation or idea, L, in two self-consistent but habitually incompatible frames of reference" (quoted in Ritchie 2004: 46–7).

Attardo, after Raskin, elaborated this notion of incompatible frames, aka scripts or schemas, into a fully-fledged theory of verbal humour. Essential to humour, for him, is the overlapping of opposed scripts (Attardo 2001: 17–19, 24). A **script** or, as I prefer, **schema** is the form in which we store stereotypical knowledge about events and actions in the world. For example, in the first joke in this book, "Beware of tennis players – love means nothing to them", two schemas are activated, one of tennis and tennis players, and another of human relationships. We can see how "love means nothing to them" is ambiguous. Although its spoken form is identical in column 1 of Figure 1.2, it has two meanings in column 2. One of these refers metalinguistically to the meaning of the form *love*, and the other refers out into column 3, the world, as a generalisation about the interpersonal behaviour of tennis players, via the sense of the idiom *means nothing to* 'is not important to'. I suspect the latter meaning is the more salient, especially in a written form without the typographical conventions indicating a metalinguistic statement.

Attardo suggests that, in its simplest structure, a joke includes a **set-up**, an **incongruity** and a **resolution** (Attardo 2001: 39). Crucial in this structure is a **disjunctor** (or **punchline**), a textual element that introduces the incongruity and forces a switch from the schema made most salient in the set-up. There also has to be a **connector** which functions as a bridge between these schemas to achieve a "resolution". The two schemas (scripts) have to be incongruous with each other. "By forcing the hearer/reader to backtrack and reinterpret the text, or by forcing him/her to produce a new and incompatible ... interpretation of the text, the punch line cannot be integrated into the narrative it disrupts (which is the one that has set up the first script)" (Attardo 2001: 83).[8]

How would this apply to the tennis-player joke? The first line "Beware of tennis players" strongly activates the schema (script) of tennis. The punchline or disjunctor "Love means nothing to them" probably activates most strongly the schema (script) of casual sexual relationships, which is incompatible with the tennis schema and creates an incongruity. We therefore have to backtrack and interpret this meaning as a reason to beware of tennis players. But we also fit the second sentence into a schema for tennis players, in order to account for its activation in the set-up, by accessing the metalingual meaning. So the second sentence also functions as a connector. We end up with two schemas into both of which, because it is ambiguous, the disjunctor/connector fits, though these schemas remain opposed or incongruous with each other. Thus the disjunctor, in this case, functions as both a signal to switch schemas and a form with ambiguous meanings which links them, a connector. Another, perhaps more obvious example of disjunctor and connector being realised by the same form would be "case" in the ambiguous headline DRUNK GETS NINE MONTHS IN VIOLIN CASE (Bucaria 2004: 292).

The importance of these theories is that they stress the reliance of humour on defeated expectations. Exactly how texts create expectations semantically and pragmatically through context and co-text is therefore crucial to the understanding of humour. Defeated expectations may be triggered at various linguistic levels – the lexical (Chapters 2, 4 and 5) and grammatical (Chapter 3), or the level of register and genre (Chapter 6).[9] Our discussion of schema opposition and (partial) resolution of incongruity will illuminate not only semantic theories at these levels, but also pragmatic processes (Chapters 8, 9 and 10). As this textbook proceeds to systematically consider semantics and pragmatics, it will incorporate some of the insights of incongruity theories of humour, before attempting in the final chapter (Chapter 11) to integrate semantic/pragmatic and text-linguistic theory with humour theory.

1.7.   SUMMARY

In this chapter I explained the content and purpose of the book, introduced various typographical conventions, and suggested a simple model for thinking about word-forms, their sense and the world they refer to. I then discussed how a word might be defined, the differences between lexical and grammatical words, and the problems in deciding when two tokens of a word are the same word. I also gave a short synopsis of the incongruity theory of humour with its implication that ambiguities of various kinds are central to humour and jokes. I will be elaborating on this theory in its relation to various semantic and pragmatic concepts as the book proceeds. In particular in Chapter 11 I will develop incongruity theory in relation to the discourse or text theory known as lexical priming.[10]

Discussion

To what extent is the use–mention distinction a watertight one? Is it particularly problematic with regard to quotations? How does it relate to plagiarism? You may wish to read Goffman, and Holquist on Bakhtin in the readings below as a stimulus to this discussion.

Suggested Readings

- Read Lyons (1977: 1–25) on the use–mention distinction, object language, type and token, and lexemes. His principled discussion of homonymy and polysemy (Lyons 1977: 550–69) is most relevant perhaps to Chapter 4, but nevertheless explores the question of when two words are the same word.

- Goffman's essay 'Footings' (1981: 124–59) makes more subtle distinctions than simply between use and mention. He introduces the concept of three different kinds of speaker/addresser: (1) principal, the original creator of the message, who is committed to and takes ultimate responsibility for it; (2) author, who is not the originator/principal but selects the message created by a principal; and (3) animator, simply the mouthpiece of a message selected and created by others. (His discussion of these speakers in relation to reporting of speech is relevant to my Chapter 10.)

- Holquist (1990, especially 40–66) gives a sound overview of Bakhtin's theory of dialogism, which challenges the use–mention distinction. This theory is equally relevant to echoic utterances, discussed in Chapter 10.

- Katamba (2005: 10–29) provides a basic discussion of what might be meant by the word "word", while chapters 3 and 4 are relevant to my Chapter 2. A slightly more advanced discussion of the same areas from a diachronic or etymological perspective point of view can be found in Durkin (2009), chapters 2 and 4.

2 Meaning in the language system: aspects of form and meaning

In this chapter we explore the lower and upper boundaries of words as meaningful units, and how humour might depend upon the ambiguity or the shifting of these boundaries. In order to discuss such boundary confusions we need to establish the different levels of linguistic analysis.

2.1. LEVELS IN THE LANGUAGE SYSTEM

We are familiar with the idea that language as a system operates at many different levels stretching from the phonemic/graphemic (sound/writing) level at one end to the sentential at the other. It has boundaries at both ends, the phonetic/graphetic at a lower level and speech act combinations and register/genre at the upper level. The different levels of language can be simplistically described as follows:

Phonemes/Graphemes – Morphemes – Words – Phrases – Clauses – Sentences

According to this model, a sentence comprises one or more clauses, a clause one or more phrases, a phrase one or more words, a word one or more morphemes and a morpheme one or more phonemes. It is theoretically possible, therefore, for a sentence to comprise only one phoneme, for instance, the reply in this dialogue:

"Who killed Cock Robin?"
"I."

However, for more versatility in language we exercise the option of "or more" to lengthen this chain of combinations. A more typical sentence is: "The romantic short story she was reading would have a happy ending". We can analyse this as in Figure 2.1 (confining full analysis to the first clause).

Since we identified ambiguity in a general sense as a critical feature of humour, it is worth noting how it works at the various linguistic

```
SENTENCE: The romantic short story she was reading would have a happy ending.
    2 CLAUSES: The romantic short story...would have a happy ending
                 She was reading [a romantic short story]
         3 PHRASES: (1) the romantic short story
                    (2) would have
                    (3) a happy ending
          (1) 4 WORDS (a) the
                      (b) romantic
                      (c) short
                      (d) story
          (2) 2 WORDS (a) would
                      (b) have
          (3) 3 WORDS (a) a
                      (b) happy
                      (c) ending
            (1)(a) 1 MORPHEME    (i) the
            (1)(b) 2 MORPHEMES (i) roman-
                               (ii) –tic
            (1)(c) 1 MORPHEME    (i) short
            (1)(d) 1 MORPHEME    (i) story
            (2) 2 MORPHEMES      (i) will
                               (ii) –d (past tense)
            (2)(b) 1 MORPHEME    (i) have
            (3) 1 MORPHEME       (i) a
            (3)(b) 1 MORPHEME    (i) happy
            (3)(c) 2 MORPHEMES (i) end
                               (ii) –ing
             (1)(i)    2 PHONEMES    /ð/ /ə/
             (1)(b)(i) 5 PHONEMES    /r/ /ou/ /m/ /æ/ /n/
             (1)(b)(ii) 3 PHONEMES   /t/ /ɪ / /k/
             (1)(c)(i) 3 PHONEMES    /ʃ/ /ɔ:/ /t/
             (1)(d)(i) 4 PHONEMES    /s/ /t/ /ɔ:/ /r/ /ɪ /
                               etc., etc.
```

Figure 2.1. Linguistic levels in the sentence

levels: the graphemic/phonemic – morphological – word – phrase – clause – sentence. As Ritchie (2004: 41) points out:

> Ambiguity is described in terms of two representational levels: one at which the item has a single representation, and one at which it has multiple representations. Thus *read* and *red* [both /red/] would be *phonetic-lexical* ambiguous, and also *phonetic-orthographical* or *phonetic-morphological* ambiguous if these levels were present in the assumed framework. In general, if the levels are totally ordered, as they usually are in linguistics, then if an item is 'M-N ambiguous' where M and N indicate levels, it will also be 'M-K' ambiguous for any level K which is higher than N.

Consider, for example, the spoken joke "What's black and white and red/read all over?" "A newspaper". According to our framework, this phonemic identity (one representation) at the lowest level produces a morphological ambiguity (two representations) at the next level, an ambiguity that is inherited throughout all the remaining levels. So, ascending through these levels, we have ambiguous words, phrases, clauses and sentences.

This chapter also explores how this simplistic framework is complicated by the category of word, and what counts as a lexical item. Some lexical items are made up of more than one word-form, as in phrasal verbs, some indeed are made up of more than one phrase, as in idioms like *kick the bucket*. Even proverbs, often of more than one clause, can function rather like a lexical item. For example, *don't count your chickens before they are hatched* resembles the meaning of the single word *over-optimism*. Many examples of humour in this chapter depend on playing with these levels and exploiting the elasticity of the lexeme-level boundaries in order to create extra ambiguity.

2.2. PHONOLOGY/GRAPHOLOGY

We start from the bottom up, where one or more **phonemes** constitutes a morpheme. Phonemes are beyond the limits of semantics, since it is the **morpheme** which is defined as the minimal meaningful unit. Nevertheless, because morphemes are constituted by phonemes, phonemes must contribute to meaning. This fact lies behind the familiar phenomenon of the **minimal pair**, a pair of word-forms representing distinct meanings but differing in only one phoneme/grapheme. Minimal pairs are used to test whether a phonetic difference is also a phonemic difference. For instance, the phonetic difference between the *l* in *love* and *bottle* (light and dark /l/) is not a phonemic difference: pronouncing *love* using the dark *l* of *bottle* would not change the meaning of the word-form *love*. By contrast, the distinction between /i/ and /i:/ is certainly a phonemic one for English: *i* and *ea/ee/ie/ei* are usually the graphemes concerned. Consider how "peace on earth" would suffer from a confusion of these phonemes. Or take the phoneme distinction /z/ /ʒ/:

> What do you get when an epileptic falls into a lettuce patch?
> Seizure salad. (Tibballs 2006: 541)

Joke books commonly include humorous typos (mistakes with regard to graphemes), malapropisms (where the speaker is confused about the correct word-form) and spoonerisms (which exchange initial consonant phonemes). These are examples of involuntary performance mistakes rather than intentional humour (see Attardo 2003), and may involve change in order (metathesis), transposition, omission, addition and substitution (Alexander 1997: 23ff.). All these mistakes seem frequent in everyday talk, and may indicate the order of the psycho-linguistic processes involved in lexical selection and production (Alexander 1997: 29).

One interesting series of typos is the following:

> Our paper carried the notice last week that Mr Shaw is a defective in the police force. This was a typographical error. Mr Shaw is really a detective in the police farce. (*Ely Standard*, Tibballs 2006: 492)

Mrs Malaprop in Sheridan's *The Rivals*, who gave her name to **malapropism**, described another character as "the pineapple [pinnacle] of politeness". The more inventive malapropisms tend to make more than one error. Consider:

> *At the doctor's*
> Maggie: I've forgotten to take my contradictive pills.
> Doctor: You're ignorant.
> Maggie: That's right. Three months.

Spoonerisms (one kind of metathesis[1]), such as "You have tasted a worm and must leave by the town drain", have provided the formula for joke types known as **spooneristic conundrums**:

> – What's the difference between a cosmetic surgeon and a school inspector?
> – A cosmetic surgeon tucks up your features. (Andy Bond)

Discussion

> Ritchie suggests that the distinctive feature of malapropisms (which distinguishes them from, for example, puns) is that the uttered word is a genuine form of the language but has no connection to the context, whereas the correct word would have: as when a boxer said "I'm only a prawn in the game", when he should have said "pawn" (Ritchie 2004: 117). Is this true in the examples of typos, malapropisms and spoonerisms above? And, if not, why not?

Phonemes are the constituents of morphemes, just as morphemes are the constituents of sentences. This is known as the **double articulation** of language (Martinet 1960: 22–7) and is what makes it such a flexible and open-ended instrument for communication. Double articulation makes possible two levels of ordering, so that the ordering of phonemes determines the meaning of the morpheme, just as the ordering of morphemes affects the meaning of the clause:

Phonemes	Morpheme		Morphemes	Clause
top	: pot	::	John hit the ball : the ball hit John

The fact that the order of phonemes/graphemes makes such a difference to meaning is exploited in dyslexic jokes like: DYSLEXIA LURES, KO:

- What do you get if you cross an insomniac, an agnostic and a dyslexic?
- Someone who's up all night wondering if there's a dog. (Tibballs 2006: 592)

2.3. MORPHOLOGY: AFFIXATION

Phonemes, therefore, both through minimal pair contrasts and through ordering, contribute to the smallest meaningful unit, the morpheme.

If a morpheme can stand on its own as an orthographic word then it is a **free morpheme**, but if not, a **bound morpheme**. In the morphemic analysis in Figure 2.1, -TIC, in "romantic", -D (PAST TENSE) in "would", -ING in "ending" and "reading" are bound morphemes. We observe that the second bound morphemes have a different function in *romantic* and *ending* from their function in *would* and *reading*. *Romance* and *end* represent different lexemes from *romantic* and *ending*. But *will* and *would*, *read* and *reading* are pairs of words representing the same lexemes WILL and READ respectively. Traditionally, we identify the former kind of suffix as derivational and the latter as inflectional.

In English, **inflectional** suffixes are added to the ends of words to indicate tense or person or number (Table 2.1). The un-suffixed

Table 2.1. *Inflectional suffixes*

			Tense	Person	Number
call	+	inflectional suffix -s	= *calls*	present	3rd	singular
call	+	inflectional suffix -ed	= *called*	past		
call	+	inflectional suffix -ing	= *calling*	continuous		
dog	+	inflectional suffix -s	= *dogs*			plural

form (stem) and the suffixed form in these cases are different forms of the same lexeme/lexical item.

By contrast, when affixes are added to a word-form to form a new lexeme they are **derivational**. They may be suffixes:

govern	+	-ment	=	government
cream	+	-y	=	creamy

or prefixes:

count	+	re-	=	recount
happy	+	un-	=	unhappy

or both

help	+	-ful	+	un-	=	unhelpful

And so they may be applied recursively:

nation	+	-al	=	national
national	+	-ise	=	nationalise
nationalise	+	-ation	=	nationalisation
nationalisation	+	de-	=	denationalisation

As the new lexeme criterion for derivation gives a circular definition, we can appeal to six other criteria for making the inflection–derivation distinction (Bauer 1983: 22–8).

1. Inflectional affixes involve few variables in a closed system, e.g. for marking number, person and tense. They cannot easily be added to. By contrast derivational affixes can be added to, e.g. -aholic, -ician, -gate seem to be relatively new derivational suffixes in English, e.g. workaholic, chocaholic, shopaholic; mortician, clinician, beautician; Irangate, troopergate, etc. Mc- is an interesting new prefix, meaning something like 'low quality, inferior (because privatised?)', modelled, presumably, on a re-analysis of McDonald's, giving us words like McJob, McGod, McHealthcare (Blake 2007: 60–1).

2. An inflectional suffix can indicate agreement between subject and verb. When the subject is plural it takes an -s, and when the subject is singular in present tense third person the verb takes an -s. For example, "the duck feeds" or "the ducks feed". Hence the possibility of jokes dependent on ambiguities between plural noun and third person singular: "Time flies like an arrow. Fruit flies like bananas."

3. When derivational and inflectional suffixes occur together, the derivational are closer to the root, the free morpheme to which

the affixes are added. For example, *reactions* can be analysed into the morphemes *act* + *re-* + *-ion* + *-s*. In this case *re-* + *-ion* are next to the root, the free morpheme *act*, and are hence derivational. While the *-s* is further away from *act* and is therefore inflectional.

4. If the word-form including affixes can be replaced by a simple one-morpheme word, this suggests derivational morphology. For example *unhappy* could be replaced by *sad*, indicating that *un-* is derivational rather than inflectional.

5. Inflectional suffixes are substitutable within a syntactic frame. If the suffix can be substituted with another suffix when word-forms occur in isolation (outside a sentence), then it is inflectional. For example, the inflectional suffix *-s* in *covers, tickles, walks, shows* can be replaced with *-ed* in all four cases; but the derivational suffix *-let* can only be added to *cover*, and *-ish* can only be applied to *tickle*.

Activity 2.1

Discuss the following joke in terms of inflectional and derivational suffixes:

"What's a baby pig called?"
"A piglet."
"So what's a baby toy called?"
"A toilet."

6. An overlapping criterion is that derivational suffixes are less **productive** than inflectional ones. Productivity is measured by the number of new words a suffix is used to form. The joke in Activity 2.1 depends on making the derivational suffix *-let* more productive than it actually is, by fixing it to the noun *toy*. Although this criterion holds in general, derivational suffixes vary enormously in terms of productivity. For example, *-er* and *-ing* apply widely to verbs to make nouns meaning 'someone who Xs' or 'the process/event in which something/someone Xs', e.g. "Mary is a *teacher*" and "The *sinking* of the Titanic". Or there are very productive derivational suffixes which turn nouns into adjectives.

Activity 2.2

"What's brown and sticky?"
"A stick."

How does this joke depend upon the productivity of the denominal adjectival suffix *-y*?

Comment

So productive is this suffix that, in informal contexts, it can be applied to almost any noun to mean 'like an X'. (Another meaning is 'full of/covered with'.) Although the dictionary meaning of *sticky* relates to the verb *stick*, meaning 'adhere', the productivity of the denominal suffix enables the joke meaning, and a switch from the excretion schema to a more innocent one.

Productive derivational suffixes like *-y* can produce such **nonce words**, newly invented on an ad hoc basis, but not all of them will be adopted by speakers of the language and be added to the dictionary, that is, become **lexicalised**. So the lexicalised form, *sticky*, derives from the lexeme STICK 'adhere easily', whereas the meaning 'like a stick' is a nonce meaning, created on the spot and un-lexicalised.

At the other extreme are derivational suffixes that are no longer productive: *-en* meaning either 'made of' or 'the colour of' is only found in a handful of word-forms, *golden*, *leaden*, *ashen*, *wooden*, and cannot produce nonce forms.

Consider the words of a cartoon joke in which a politician is making his resignation speech:

> I decisioned the necessification of the resignatory action/option due to the dangerosity of the trendflopping of foreign policy away from our originatious careful coursing towards consensivity, purposity, steadfastnitude, and, above all, clarity (Jeff MacNelly, quoted in Ross 1998: 46).

This seems to achieve humour by the ungrammatical use of most derivational suffixes, apart from the last, demonstrating the selectivity about the bases they attach to.

7. The last distinguishing feature is that inflectional affixes produce semantically regular results, whereas derivational suffixes produce less predictable meanings. The inflectional *-ed* regularly produces the meaning 'past'. The derivational prefix *de-* might be expected to give a negative meaning to the free morpheme it precedes. But the joke "'Is Bach still composing?' 'No, madam, he's decomposing'" illustrates this is not the case. Take a more complex example. One could predict that *-ment* combines with *appoint* to produce a predictable meaning as in *govern* + *-ment*. And indeed one lexeme, APPOINTMENT$_1$, has such a predictable meaning: "We appointed a Professor from Melbourne to the post. It turned out to be a disastrous appointment." But the same word-form, *appointment*, also represents a different lexeme, APPOINTMENT$_2$, as in "Can I make an appointment to see the dentist?" In this case the meaning of the

lexeme APPOINTMENT₂ cannot be predicted from the meaning of the lexeme APPOINT. Similarly *dis-*, a derivational prefix meaning 'reverse, negate', might in theory combine with *appoint* in a semantically predictable way as in *disrobe*. Hence the joke:

> "What do you call it when a celebrity cancels a show?"
> "A disappointment."

Activity 2.3

Explain how the semantic unpredictability and semi-productivity of derivation contributes to these jokes.

1. To write with a broken pencil is pointless. (Ng 2005: 17)
2. Girls who don't get asked out as often as their friends could feel out-dated. (Ng 2005: 15)

Comment

In (1) there is no reason in principle why *pointless* should not mean 'without a point' in the literal sense 'without a sharp end'. But its semi-productivity means this meaning has not been lexicalised, while the metaphorical meaning 'futile' has. Even more so in (2), *outdate* could mean 'be invited on dates more than', just as *outrun* means 'run faster than' or *outplay* 'play better than'. In fact this would be the more predictable meaning than the lexicalised one, 'out of date, unfashionable'. The lexicalised or salient meaning will, of course, activate a schema which clashes with the set-up.

We have discussed the morphemic analysis of words using the metalanguage *affix, suffix, prefix, derivation* and *inflection*. But it is useful to have some extra metalanguage: *root, stem* and *base* (Bauer 1983: 20–2). A **root** is a form that is not further analysable – what we have left when all affixes (bound morphemes) have been removed from the word-form, for example *act* is the root of *reactions*. A **stem** is the part of the word-form which remains when all inflectional suffixes have been removed, so *reaction* is the stem of *reactions*. We also need a term for parts of words which are neither stems nor roots, for instance, *react* is neither the root nor stem of *reaction*: a **base** is a form to which affixes of any kind can be added. All roots and stems will also be bases.

2.4.   RE-ANALYSIS AND FOLK-ETYMOLOGY

The history of the vocabulary of a language furnishes many examples of **re-analysis** of words to make them seem more motivated, that is, to connect them with existing lexical knowledge. This seems particularly likely with bound morphemes which could quite logically appear to be free morphemes with prefixes attached, such as *unkempt, dishevelled, uncouth, repeat*:

> I presented myself well at the interview, peating myself clearly. My hair was kempt, my clothing shevelled, and I feel I made a couth impression.

Attardo (1994: 132) refers to this phenomenon as "metanalysis", and cites the back-formation *gruntled* from *disgruntled*. It can apply to suffixes too: "If it's feasible, let's fease it".

In other cases loan words are given a spurious motivation by "identifying" a phonetic sequence in the loan word with a morpheme existing in the borrowing language. *Écrevisse* ('shrimp') was borrowed into English from French, but became naturalised in English, through phonetic modification of the *visse* into *fish*, as *crayfish*. This analysis, according to folk etymology, posits an existing morpheme *fish* as part of the borrowed word, even though shrimps are not a type of fish. Such folk-etymology can become a resource for humour (Attardo 1994). Some people, jocularly, analyse *asparagus* into *sparrowgrass* to give it extra motivation. These are cases of inventing non-existent morphemes or **pseudo-morphs** in borrowed words.

Activity 2.4

Explain the following joke, using the terminology of morpheme and pseudo-morph.

"What do you do with a wombat?"
"Play wom." (Nash 1985: 143)

Comment

The above borrowings and their re-analysis depend upon the folk belief that one morpheme is in fact composed of two morphemes. Some kinds of humour, like the *wombat* joke, pretend the same. The pseudo-morphology is apparent since no one knows what *cray* and *wom* mean.

In cases where the pseudo-morphs are free morphemes they can be represented as separate words in written form:

> The pen is
> Mightier than
> The penis.

Or their spoken form may represent them as separate words.

What do you call a woman with one leg? Eileen. (I lean)
What do you call a man with no shins? Tony. (Toe knee) (Carr and
Greeves 2006: 68)

Activity 2.5

Explain the (pseudo-) morphology in the following joke.

If a beefburger is made of beef what is a hamburger made of?

Comment

There is no morpheme *ham* corresponding to the 'cured pork thigh'
meaning of *ham* in *hamburger*; rather it originally referred to a type
of food originating in Hamburg. However, the new lexical items, *beefburger*, *veggieburger*, *cheeseburger*, *fishburger* etc. suggest that *hamburger*
has been re-analysed as though *X-burger* means 'type of snack
consisting of a sliced bun filled with X'. In this process of analysis
the original morpheme boundaries have shifted.

Similar re-analysis explains the new words *chocoholic* and *shopaholic*,
produced by analogy from *alcoholic*. To accurately preserve the morpheme boundaries these analogical formations would have had to take
the form *shopic* or *chocic/chocolatic*, but *-ic*, with its general role as a suffix
for converting nouns into adjectives/nouns is presumably not distinctive enough to convey the meaning 'addiction'. Whether the new morpheme is *-aholic* or *-holic* is doubtful, as the model for the analogy is not
alcaholic but *alcoholic* (though this would not matter in speech).

The present Pope, as a former enforcer of Church discipline, was
called "God's rottweiler". He later became known, more kindly,
perhaps, as a "German shepherd", though others refer to him as a
"mastiff". All these dogs are addicted to chasing felines, so it's no
surprise he's a cat-holic.

There are examples of re-analysis where the morpheme boundaries
shift, without much sense of a new morpheme being created. The word
helicopter is now often abbreviated as *'copter* (or through phonetic
change as *chopper*). This suggests a re-analysis of the original *helico-*
('spiral') + *pteros* ('wing') into *heli* + *copter*, no doubt driven by the rarity
of the phonetic combination [p] + [t] in syllable initial position in
current English. Some humour can depend upon similar re-drawing.
I rather like the following riddle with its chains of re-analysis:

– How is a lazy dog like a sheet of writing paper?
– A lazy dog is a slow pup; a slope up is an inclined plane; and an ink-
 lined plane is a sheet of writing paper (Alexander 1997: 31).

A related kind of word-formation leading to re-analysis occurs when a morpheme or word-form is assigned a different meaning as a bound morpheme (suffix). For instance, on the analogy of *Watergate*, the scandal over the burglary at the Watergate building precipitating the resignation of President Richard Nixon, *-gate* is now a suffix (bound morpheme) meaning 'political scandal', cf. Reagan's *Irangate*, Clinton's *Whitewatergate* and, more topically, Palin's *troopergate*.[2] The result is that a bound morpheme may have a different meaning from a for-mally identical free morpheme, and the resulting ambiguity can be humorously exploited, when the context triggers the wrong meaning:

> A termite walked into a bar and asked, "Is the bar tender here?" (Tibballs 2006: 57) (Cf. the bound morpheme *-tender* 'someone who looks after'.)

> I've got a stepladder. A very nice stepladder, but it's sad that I never knew my real ladder. (Carr and Greeves 2006: 41) (cf. the bound morpheme *step-* 'related through remarriage of a parent')

The word-play about nicknames for the present Pope includes the word *mastiff*. Not only is a mastiff a fierce dog, conforming to the schema for metaphors used of the Pope, but the word-play might involve some erroneous morphemic analysis. *Mass* means the celebration of the Eucharist within this context, but *-tiff* could be an abbreviation of *pontiff*, a title for the Pope originally from the Latin *pontifex* 'bridge-maker'. The same kind of re-analysis is at work in the following joke, but without abbreviation: the first four phonemes of *pina colada*, the name of a cocktail, are phonetically identical to that of the second morpheme in *subpoena*. This coincidence of form as part of the con-nector is a way of reflecting the two occupational schemas of bartend-ing and the law.

> Did you hear about the bailiff who moonlighted as a bartender? – He served subpoena coladas. (Tibballs 2006: 58)

When combinations like this involve parts of lexical items they pro-duce or evoke **portmanteau** words or **blends**, which Lewis Carroll popularised in the nonsense poem 'Jabberwocky': *slithy* (*slimy* + *lithe*), *chortle* (*snort* + *chuckle*), *galumph* (*gallop* + *triumph*) etc. These are the equivalent of dvandva compounds (2.5.1), though others like *affluenza* signal a metaphorical relationship (affluence is a disease).

All the above examples of jokes involving re-analysis support the contention "humorous use of language may require mappings between linguistic levels (e.g. the phonetic and morphological) which are not part of any conventional linguistic analysis of the text" (Ritchie

2004: 34). This mixing of levels is taken to extremes in the humorous trick children play on their parents by asking them to read out "If you see Kay ..." (Blake 2007: 42). This exploits a confusion between the word level and the graphological level, through the pronunciation of the name for the graphemes F, U, C and K.

Activity 2.6

Abbreviations in "netspeak", the language of internet chat (Crystal 2001), often seem to involve creative, if not semi-humorous examples of re-analysis and pseudo-morphology. What examples can you find from your chat/e-mails? Or how, for example, would you characterise the title of David Crystal's book "txtng: the gr8 db8"?

2.5.   COMPOUNDS, COLLOCATIONS AND IDIOMS

So far our discussion of morphology has emphasised the use of affixes, bound morphemes, for purposes of inflection and derivation. But, as Table 1.1 shows, orthographic words can comprise two free morphemes, e.g. *candlestick*, and lexical items can comprise more than one orthographic word, e.g. *public house*. These are traditionally referred to as **word compounds** and **phrasal compounds** respectively. Besides their orthographic differences, they may be distinguished by the criterion of single primary stress, e.g. *wheelchair, armchair, blackbird, orange-juice* have one primary stress, while *public house, double glazing, banana split, run over* have two.

A more difficult distinction is that between phrasal compounds (compound lexemes) and free phrases. Free phrases are regular in terms of phonology, syntax and semantics. Compounds tend to be irregular in syntax and semantics. The following humorous ambiguity depends upon treating the same collocation as either a free phrase ('stand to show respect for') or a phrasal compound ('tolerate'):

> The court will now stand for Judge Schnorrer. And if you'll stand for him, you'll stand for anything (Alexander 1997: 48).

And this disparaging remark about the author Ian Fleming draws attention to the fact that, although as part of free phrases *on* and *off* have opposite meanings, in the phrasal verb compound with *get ... with* they do not:

> The trouble with Ian is that he gets off with women because he can't get on with them (Ross 1998: 18).

Concordancing software (e.g. *Wordsmith* or *Collins Wordbanks Online*) can access data for deciding whether a sequence of word-forms is a free phrase or a phrasal compound. It does so by searching a corpus to produce concordance lines listing all the tokens of a particular word-form, the key-word, in its context (KWIC). Consider the lines below for the key-word *bug*.

```
 1. ver par 930721 Bears floored by flu bug A FLU epidemic has savagely disrup
 2. 29 September 1992 A PERSISTENT flu bug claimed full-back Lee Martin last
 3. r Kevin Kennedy, 32, was hit by a flu bug during an appearance at a shoppin
 4. imon Trump 06 December 1991  A FLU bug forced Princesses Diana and Beatr
 5. der. He's now back at home but a flu bug has added a few problems to his ca
 6. ed several regulars, victims of a flu bug, in the camp, but apart from a lor
 7. e public. Di and Bea get dose of flu bug; Princesses Diana and Beatrice B
 8. ress Julie Goodyear fell ill as a flu bug swept across the country. Scriptw
 9. 10 January 1992 THE A-Beijing flu bug that brought President Bush to his
10. was nothing more than the sort of flu bug that has hit many other Americans
11. circumstances. First he caught the flu bug that ravaged the Stuttgart Open ar
12. arkably, caused by a usually mild flu bug that in the spring of 1918 went go
13. es, such as colds, flu and 'any other bug that is doing the rounds". If the
14. often called influenza, the flu, the bug, the wog, or, in doctor language,
15. thousand times faster than a mild flu bug.) This is probably the route taken
16. d Huddersfield from the A-Beijing flu bug, which has already caused havoc in
17. n, 75, is suffering from the flu-type bug which hit Julie Goodyear and Barb
```

The semantic and syntactic regularity here means that *flu* could be replaced by *typhoid*, *laryngitis* or *gastro-enteritis*, evidence that *flu bug* is a free phrase rather than a phrasal compound. Moreover, as lines 13, 14 and 17 indicate, the phrase can be split up so that the forms *flu* and *bug* are not adjacent. Contrast this with:

. mily Columbia Tristar, PG, out now). Bug-eyed Christopher Lloyd has shaved his

. g his legend and it is the image of a bug-eyed, brain-frazzled Barrett that fla

. and the regular treat of seeing Ken-a bug-eyed mass of madness in a donkey jack

. cleaning everything up and absolutely bug-eyed with tiredness. Saturday, 24 Aug

. fiction writers: little green men and bug-eyed monsters – BEE EE ems – might ex

. e coming down to sit in the basement, bug-eyed in gas masks that gave us all th

. d that he is a lying, yellow-bellied, bug-eyed Tory toad?" John Major leapt up,

. g, belching, bellyaching, blubbering, bug-eyed fat bloke has been sane up till

. familiar costumes of Henson's fluffy, bug-eyed, melon-slice grins and animate t

. performances, notably Borgnine at his bug-eyed best. 7 Bob Mccabe FRANTIC Di

. d caught a close friend staring at me bug-eyed, wondering if I had lost my mind

. windows above the sink with a look of bug-eyed horror – Bloody hell. Who is

. ws – it's jigaboo time – or (later on) bug-eyed, leering, jive-ass, pimpmobile g

. nd. The baddies make a fine pairing – bug-eyed, snarling criminal genius Tommy

. aughter. A big dog was licking Joey's bug-eyed face. I left the show on; I can'

. in which I was to visit them; and so, bug-eyed from twelve sleepless hours on t

. on man, I love you); and synchronised bug-eyed sweating in stupid T-shirts. We'

. misspent youth, and an homage to the bug-eyed world of '60s trash movies such

. cial center. John and Bill and I were bug-eyed in wonderment. We were not then o

. Danny De Vito and Joe Piscopo with bug-eyed, screaming energy. Keitel came

Although in theory *bug-eyed* could be replaced by *bug-eared*, *bug-mouthed*, *bug-footed* etc., these forms rarely occur, if at all, and, moreover, the phrase appears as an uninterruptible syntactic unit. Whether it is a word compound rather than phrasal compound is doubtful – the hyphenation suggests a word compound, but the double stress not.

Activity 2.7

By considering these concordance lines, work out what you think *bug-eyed* means.
Does it simply mean 'with eyes like a bug' or something more specific?

Comment

Collocational evidence in the concordance lines suggests that *bug-eyed*
probably highlights the bulging nature of the eyes (as in 5, 7 and 9)
usually as a result of strong emotion (3, 8, 11, 12, 19, 20) or tiredness
(4, 16). This suggests that the compound is not entirely predictable in
terms of semantics.

Leech (1983: 225–7) suggested that compound lexemes undergo
semantic **petrifaction**, rather like fossils: they both shrink in meaning
and become solidified, relatively stable. So *orange juice*, which could
theoretically have a wide meaning as 'juice associated with orange/
oranges in some way or other', e.g. 'juice that is orange in colour', in
practice, and as a compound, has the narrower, stabler meaning 'juice
made from oranges'. *Baby milk*, on the other hand, has acquired the
precise and solid meaning 'artificial milk formula for feeding babies'
rather than 'milk made from babies'! (Compare also *crocodile skin bag*
and *handbag*.) But consider this ambiguous headline: POPE LAUNCHES
TALKS TO END LONG DIVISION, where *long division* in its compound
meaning (e.g. what is 24,693 divided by 58?) seems to be unintentionally suggested instead of the free phrase.

However, often the borderline between free phrases and phrasal
compounds is unclear. Semantically their meanings may be more or
less predictable. Consider these examples of phrases incorporating the
form *wedding*.

1. *wedding present*
2. *wedding cake*
3. *wedding reception*
4. *wedding list*
5. *white wedding*
6. *shotgun wedding*

1 conveys a quite predictable meaning 'present given on the occasion of a
wedding to the bride and groom', not very different from *Christmas present*
'present given on the occasion of Christmas'. 2 is also reasonably predictable, 'cake eaten at a wedding', cf. *Christmas cake* 'cake eaten at Christmas'.
3 is less predictable, 'reception' being rather ambiguous, and the meaning 'meal eaten to celebrate a wedding' is more elusive. 4 and 5, *wedding
list* and *white wedding*, incorporate a mass of encyclopaedic cultural

information, making them rather idiosyncratic: 'list of wedding presents requested from invitees by the bride and groom', 'wedding in which the bride wears white (as a symbol of the bride's virginity? and which is normally held in church?)'. Contrast the latter with the equally idiosyncratic *white Christmas* 'Christmas period in which snow is lying on the ground'. Lastly 6, *shotgun wedding*, means/meant something like 'wedding in which the bridegroom is forced to marry the bride because he has made her pregnant (as if forced to do so by her father threatening him with a shotgun)'. Or in the case of Bristol Palin, perhaps the mother!

Activity 2.8

How would you order the following four phrases, putting the freest first, and the more compound last? Use semantic predictability or idiosyncrasy as your main criterion.

1. *country house*
2. *greenhouse*
3. *new house*
4. *public house*

Comment

I suggest the order

a.   *new house*, free phrase, where syntactic substitutability is evidently possible – *new car*, *new bicycle*, *new TV*, etc. meaning 'an X that is new' in all cases.

b.   *country house*, where the word *country* might preserve its normal meaning, but where the house is not an ordinary house: 'mansion (usually owned by the aristocracy) located in the countryside'.

c.   *public house*, where neither the usual meanings of *house* or *public* give much clue to the meaning 'building open to the public for the purpose of buying and consuming alcoholic beverages, pub'.

d.   *greenhouse* is even more opaque, since the construction is neither a house, nor is it green, but rather means 'a building made of glass for growing plants inside' (Lyons 1977: 534–550).

Concordance lines for the phrase *wet blanket* give interesting data. Several of the meanings clearly instantiate a petrified and lexicalised metaphorical meaning – 'someone who spoils other people's fun by being negative and complaining'. Notice that even with this petrified meaning the first example makes the phrasal compound discontinuous, destroying its syntactic unity.

PETRIFIED METAPHOR

```
Zag: Oh go away you big wet studenty blanket type person. Get an opinion

ut me off. He seemed a bit of a wet blanket." Last was Conservative Mark Bish

a lad on the track and a bit of a wet blanket off it, at least publicly. Issue

Minister David Hamill proved a wet blanket on a visit to Canberra last week

around them. Who wants to be a wet blanket? Perhaps the most disturbing mix
```

Other examples seem to metaphorically extend this petrified meaning, by re-applying it to laws and other circumstances which prevent fun or enjoyment:

RELATED TO PETRIFIED METAPHOR

```
n the year since then, the long wet blanket of the law has smothered the life o

to European standards. Even the wet blanket of physical restrictions on exports

road speed, even at Australia's wet blanket 100kmh.Combining ABS brakes with ne

yesterday as heavy rain threw a wet blanket over other traditional Easter bank
```

The last example seems ambiguous between the 'spoiling fun' meaning and the quite normal use of *blanket* as a metaphor for layers of fluids or clouds:

OTHER METAPHORS/SIMILES

```
p like a mountain thrusting the wet blanket of the fog skyward. It was there fo

els treat the oceans as a dull, wet blanket, which does nothing for their preci
```

Lastly there are literal meanings:

LITERAL MEANINGS

```
s way in, would cover me with a wet blanket. With the thermometer well down the

ry care. Staff wrapped her in a wet blanket and an ambulance was called but she

electric blanket. Do not use a wet blanket; and switch off each morning. They

ch Apocalypse by hiding under a wet blanket in a concrete shelter annexed to th
```

In the last two groups *wet blanket* seems to be a free phrase, since it could be replaced by "wet covering" or "wet layer" or "wet sheet".

2.5.1. Semantic classes of compound nouns

Traditionally, four kinds of compounds have been defined semantically (Bauer 1983: 30). With **endocentric** compounds the meaning is a hyponym of the second noun head, as in *penknife, water-jug, dog collar*, which mean particular kinds of knife, jug and collar. By contrast, in **exocentric** compounds the meaning is not hyponymically related to the (second) noun head, as, for example, *egghead, sea-cucumber*. At the other extreme, in **appositional** compounds, the meaning is a hyponym of both first and second nouns, so that it is quite difficult to decide which is the head, for instance, *sofa bed, lady doctor*. In **dvandva** compounds neither noun is the head semantically – they mean a mixture or combination of both, for example, *handlebar, Cadbury-Schweppes*. One might posit a further class of compounds which are **pre-endocentric** such as *cotton-wool*, where the meaning is a hyponym of the first noun 'cotton that resembles wool'.

Activity 2.9

1. What semantic class of compounds are the following: *city state, roof garden, fuel oil, cab-driver, houseboat, blue-green, water-chestnut, Labradoodle, dogleg*?
2. Explain the ambiguity in this joke, in terms of endocentric and exocentric compounds:
    Old cartoonists never die – they just go into suspended animation.

Comment

1.
Unproblematically appositional: *city state, fuel-oil*.
Unproblematically endocentric: *roof garden, cab-driver*.
Unproblematically exocentric: *water-chestnut, dogleg*.
Dvandva: *blue-green*. *Labradoodle*, meaning a 'labrador-poodle cross' is actually a blend rather than a compound; perhaps blends are particularly suitable for dvandva semantics.

Houseboat is problematic. Could *houseboat* be dvandva: the bottom part is a boat, and the top a house? Or endocentric 'a kind of boat used as a house'? Or appositional: both a boat and a house? Probably it is not a house by any normal definition, so it's likely endocentric.

2. *Suspended animation* means 'a state almost like death, achieved by making the bodily processes of a person or animal work much more slowly than normal'. It is probably exocentric, not endocentric, since *animation* no longer has the sense 'bodily processes that give life to a body'. The pun depends upon the now current meaning of *animation* 'the process of making animated computer games, movies or cartoons', prompting a free phrase meaning.

2.5.2. Idioms

It is difficult to make any theoretical distinction between compounds and idioms. One definition could be "Any lexical item whose form comprises more than one minimal free form (word), where these forms can represent separate lexical items in other environments." This definition equally applies to the compound lexemes just discussed.

However, there is a circularity in this definition, because how do we know they are a lexical item? To help, two of the three criteria for distinguishing compounds from free phrases can be applied to idioms, namely:

1. semantic idiosyncrasy/opaqueness of meaning
2. syntactic substitutability or invariance

Opacity or unpredictability of meaning, which may explain the interest in idioms among non-native learners of English, applies to varying degrees. I imagine that people unfamiliar with the following idioms would find it easier to guess the first meaning than the last.

throw out the baby with the bathwater	'foolishly dispense with what is important or necessary along with the unimportant or unnecessary'
drop a brick	'make a tactless remark'
get cold feet	'have second thoughts, become reluctant or cautious'
kick the bucket	'die'

Proverbial idioms are relatively predictable semantically, since the literal meaning of the clause is related to the proverb's meaning as an instance of a general rule: *Don't count your chickens before they are hatched* – 'don't anticipate a successful result before you are sure of it'; *look before you leap* – 'consider carefully before you decide to take an irrevocable risky action'.

Syntactic substitutability seems to apply to idioms just as to compounds: you cannot have *kicked the pail* (*bucket*), *to be in the kennel* (*doghouse*), though you can have limited substitution with *he dropped a clanger* (*brick*), and I recently encountered "tubby feline" as a playful alternative to *fat cat*. However, syntactic unity applies less clearly to idioms than it does to noun compounds, and is highly variable, correlating, perhaps, with opaqueness. For example adjunction, insertion, permutation and extraction apply variously across the three idioms just mentioned (Table 2.2).

Table 2.2. *Degrees of syntactic invariance in idioms*

Adjunction	? he kicked the bucket very quickly	he dropped a brick very carelessly	he's in the doghouse as punishment
Insertion	*he kicked the horrible bucket	he dropped an enormous brick	he's in the marital doghouse
Permutation	*the bucket was kicked	a brick has been dropped	————
Extraction	*the bucket was what he kicked	*a brick was what he dropped	the doghouse is where he is

The concordance lines below from COBUILD WordsOnline give some evidence for the above intuitions –

Kicked the bucket:

Evidence for adjunction:

> Needless to say, England's finest took one look at this modern-day Robin Askwith and collectively kicked the bucket.

Evidence that other syntactic variation attracts the non-idiomatic free phrase meaning:

- A minute later there was a loud clang as the bucket was kicked and a boy rushed out.
- The victim stood on a bucket, put a noose around his or her neck, and then kicked away the bucket.

Dropped a brick:

Evidence of permutation to the passive/past participial adjective:

> A pity that last Saturday's game at Arsenal could not have been restarted with a dropped ball. That would have spared the FA <u>one dropped brick</u> in these weird, post-Hod, times.

Evidence of permutation to a postmodified definite noun phrase, plus extraction:

> I WENT off David Seaman in a big way when I learnt that he signed his autographs "Safe Hands". My dear chap, surely that's for others to say. Yesterday, Safe Hands <u>dropped the brick of his life</u> in a career not unacquainted with <u>bricks</u>.

In the doghouse:

Evidence of adjunction:

McCarthy agreed readily, even though it meant he would miss his brother's wedding, at which he was due to be best man, and knew he would be in the "doghouse" with his wife, Fiona.

Evidence of insertion:

- Banca d'Italia is in the central bankers' doghouse for investing in LTCM, the hedge fund that went belly up.
- For Germany's Gerhard Schröder, still in the White House doghouse after his anti-war election campaigning last September, the blackballing continues.

Evidence of extraction:

Once it emerges from the doghouse, India expects to get more attention and respect from America than it ever got during the cold war.

Similarly, truncation (which might overlap with extraction) seems to apply to idioms and proverbs more frequently than to compounds, presumably because they are longer:

the last straw that broke the camel's back → the last straw
people in glasshouses shouldn't throw stones → people in glasshouses

On the other hand the compound public house is abbreviated to pub and acronyms are common abbreviations of phrasal compounds, e.g. scuba for self-contained underwater breathing apparatus.

Carter (2004: 130–2) gives several examples of "pattern re-forming" of idioms in everyday speech and in the media, how they may be transformed, truncated and alluded to: "I always wanted to go [retire] when I retained the odd marble" (cf. lose your marbles 'become senile'), "That sounds like the wag the dog syndrome to me" (cf. let the tail wag the dog 'let the least important part control the more important'). Various brands of humour play with idioms and proverbs by truncation and addition, either by giving them abnormal endings, and/or combining two which share a common word-form:

- People who live in glasshouses should undress in the dark. (cf. . . . shouldn't throw stones)
- The recently appointed President is proving to be the new broom that sweeps the dirt under the carpet. (Combining the new broom that sweeps clean and sweep the dirt under the carpet.)

Idioms, and even more proverbs, tend to be echoic utterances (see 10.6–8).

2.5.3. Idioms and their paraphrases

It is a matter of some debate whether idioms and their paraphrases have exactly the same conceptual meaning, convey the same idea. (They probably have quite different stylistic or interpersonal meanings in terms of formality.) A clue to the fact that they may not is found in their different selection restrictions (4.7). I suggest the following acceptability judgments for the idiomatic meaning of *kick the bucket* and its paraphrase *die.*

the old man kicked the bucket	the old man died
*the sheep kicked the bucket	the sheep died

Moreover, research by Gibbs seems to confirm that different features of conceptual meanings are salient with metaphorical idioms compared with their literal paraphrases. For instance, *blow your stack*, *hit the roof/ ceiling*, *flip your lid* all mean, roughly, 'to express violent anger'. But they mean more than this: subjects in an experiment demonstrated a common set of interpretations based on an underlying conceptual metaphor:

- pressure (stress) causing the action;
- lack of control over the pressure once it builds up;
- unintentional release (especially with *blow your stack*);
- irreversibility of the action.

Gibbs claims that these more precise meanings are based on the schema of heated fluid building up pressure and exploding from a container, a conceptual metaphor or metaphor theme (7.3ff.) (Gibbs 1992). But maybe this is true only of relatively transparent metaphorical idioms. And perhaps the experimental conditions induced the subjects to think more carefully about the literal meaning of the idioms than they would under "normal processing conditions", which, incidentally, do not apply to jokes either.

By the definition given above idioms tend to be non-compositional, relatively unpredictable from the meaning of their parts, though these word-form parts do have a meaning in other contexts. It is as though in the idiom the word-forms are reduced to sub-morphemic status, equivalent to the phonemes comprising a morpheme. This suggests the analogy:

phoneme : morpheme :: word-form : idiom

In *kick the bucket* none of the meanings of the word-forms taken in isolation contributes to the meaning, and because of this unpredictability the succession of orthographic words actually represents a single lexeme KICK THE BUCKET. Consequently, there is an inherent ambiguity in the sequence of word-forms that make up an idiomatic phrase – they may attract the meanings they have as a non-idiomatic phrase, "As he was trying to milk it, the cow kicked the bucket".

This ambiguity is exploited for humour, in much the same way as re-analysis of compounds and false folk-etymologies or pseudo-morphs:

Activity 2.10

Explain how the idiomatic and literal meanings are exploited in the following:

a. "Listen, honey, you and I were meant for each other."
   "Save your breath for your inflatable date." (Tibballs 2006: 524)
b. A man went to see a psychiatrist. "Doctor, I'm having that same dream again."
   "Which one?" "The one where I'm into sadism, necrophilia and bestiality."
   "I should forget it," said the shrink. "You're flogging a dead horse." (Tibballs
   2006: 548)

Comment

In (a) *save your breath*, as a connector, has two meanings. First the idiomatic meaning 'don't waste any effort by saying anything'. Second, in the co-text of the following "inflatable" the more literal meaning is evoked, 'keep your breath for later use', as breath is needed to blow up an inflatable doll, "inflatable date" being the disjunctor.

In (b) the set up, "sadism" activates the literal meaning of "flogging", "necrophilia" of "dead", and "bestiality" of "horse".

In other cases the idiom (or proverb), opaque or not, can have its parts re-motivated into morphemes:

> Give him an inch and he'll take a yard →
> If you give some managers an inch they think they're a ruler.
> (Ng 2005: 38)

Or the coincidence in the word-forms comprising an idiom can be exploited to suggest meaning relations; in the following case identity of form expresses near antonymy of meaning:

> "You know heads turn when they see your face."
> "And stomachs turn when they see yours." (Tibballs 2006: 523)

Alternatively, as we saw with the re-analysis of compounds, one morpheme may be deliberately misidentified:

> How do you kill a vicious circus?
> Go for the juggler. (cf. the idiom *go for the jugular*)

2.6. SUMMARY

This chapter considered the way meanings are built up from phonemes into morphemes, morphemes into words through derivation and inflection, and words into compounds and idioms, showing that orthographic word boundaries and the boundaries of forms representing lexical items are quite variable. Various humorous effects can depend upon mistakes in phonology/graphology, the deliberate re-analysis or wrong analysis of these lexical words, or the ambiguity between phrasal compounds and idioms and free phrases. I suggested traditional tests to distinguish derivation from inflection, and free phrases from phrasal compounds and idioms. I also distinguished semantically various classes of noun compounds.

Discussion

Idioms and proverbs appear to occur relatively infrequently in real conversation. (You may test this by listening carefully to conversations you can overhear.) And yet foreign learners of English seem very keen to learn them. I suggested this was something to do with their semantic opacity. But, do you think there are any other explanations for this fascination?

Suggested Readings

- Bauer (1983: chapter 2) is an excellent introduction to the basic distinction between inflection and derivation. The present chapter relies heavily on Bauer's criteria. He also includes a discussion of difficult and exceptional cases that resist consistent application of these criteria.
- Carter (1998: chapter 3) surveys the ways in which word-forms form semi-fixed and fixed expressions, with a catalogue of the latter.
- Lyons (1977: 513–50) performs a thorough and painstaking analysis of the semantics of compounds and idioms.
- Plag (2003: chapter 3) is an accessible account of productivity. Particularly interesting is the idea that the more familiar we are with a word the less we are aware of its parts, and the less likely to decompose it into its constituent morphemes as we process it. This point is of importance to priming theory, Chapter 11, where we see the tendency for resisting decomposition spreading into

collocation. Our present chapter gives examples of the resistance to this tendency through decomposition and pseudo-morphology.

- Alexander (1997), Ross (1998: chapter 2) and Blake (2007: chapters 4–6, 10) provide many examples of the different levels of language at which ambiguity and errors can occur and be exploited for humorous purposes.

3   Semantics and conceptual meaning of grammar

Geoffrey Leech (1981) categorised meanings in a taxonomy, which, though somewhat dated, is still extremely useful. He distinguished conceptual, connotative, social, affective, reflected, collocative and thematic meanings. This chapter is about the conceptual meaning of grammar, Chapter 4 about the conceptual meaning of lexis, and Chapters 5 and 6 about the other kinds of semantic meaning. **Conceptual meaning** may be defined as logical meaning, the meaning used to convey ideas in order to describe the world.

In mainstream North American generative linguistics, which has followed Noam Chomsky, syntax was regarded as autonomous, and semantics was modelled as a separate component. Partly as a result, perhaps, semantics, at least in its infancy in modern linguistics, tended to concentrate on lexical meaning. However, in other models of grammar, such as Construction Grammar (Goldberg 1995, Croft 2001), Case Grammar (Fillmore 1968, 1982) and (Systemic) Functional Grammar (Halliday and Matthiessen 2004), insights have been developed about the meaning of grammar. This book is too short to explore all aspects of grammatical meaning, but confines itself to the meanings of noun modifiers (Ferris 1993) and clausal elements (Halliday 1985/1994).

3.1.   THE MEANING OF MODIFICATION (BASED ON FERRIS 1993)

Modification is one way of adding to entities extra information about their properties. Ferris makes a primary distinction between equation and qualification. **Equation** occurs when the referent of one noun phrase is the equivalent of the referent of another, and will allow reversal:

1. The Prime Minister, David Cameron.
1a. David Cameron, the Prime Minister.

or

   2. David Cameron is the Prime Minister.
   2a. The Prime Minister is David Cameron.

Qualification is the introduction of an element the speaker believes relevant to the identification/description of an entity, but without the equivalence associated with equation:

   3. The green bottles.
   4. The bottles are green.

There are two kinds of qualification, **ascription** and **association**. The distinction is clear in Ferris's examples, association in (5) and (6), and ascription in (7) and (8).

   5. A meteorological expert
   6. Romantic novelists
   7. French wine
   8. A reliable student

The test for ascription is whether the phrases can be reformulated in clauses with the copula *to be*, i.e. predicatively, with the same meaning as the original phrase:

   5a. *The expert is meteorological.
   6a. *The novelists are romantic.
   7a. The wine is French.
   8a. The student is reliable.

There are two kinds of ascription, **adjectival** and **class-inclusion**. (3) and (4) are adjectival, while (9) and (10) are class-inclusion ascriptions, because the modifier is a noun rather than an adjective:

   9. The politician John
   10. John is a politician

These distinctions can be summed up in Figure 3.1.

Activity 3.1

Explain the ambiguity on which the following joke depends, using the terms *associative, ascriptive, adjectival* and *class-inclusion* and applying the tests for association and ascription. Identify the connector and disjunctor.

Some nuns are renovating a church and getting very hot. The Mother Superior suggests they take off their clothes and work naked. The nuns agree, but bolt the church door as a precaution. They've all stripped down when there's a knock at the door. "Who is it?" says the Mother Superior.

> A voice replies "It's the blind man!"
> The Mother Superior opens the door and the man says, "Nice tits, Sister. Where
> do you want these blinds?" (Carr and Greeves 2006: 276)

Comment

The nuns interpret *blind* in "the blind man" as an ascriptive premodifier believing 'the man is blind', so they open the door. According to this meaning, *blind* functions as an adjectival ascription. However, it transpires that the man meant *blind* as an associative premodifier, a meaning which cannot be reformulated *"The man is blind'. "(Nice tits sister!) Where do you want the blinds?" is the punchline or disjunctor. The connector is obviously the ambiguous premodifier "blind".

The making explicit, through predication, of a relation between an entity and another entity, or an entity and a property is called **assignment**. Table 3.1 compares the non-assigned, or less explicit, with the explicitly assigned.

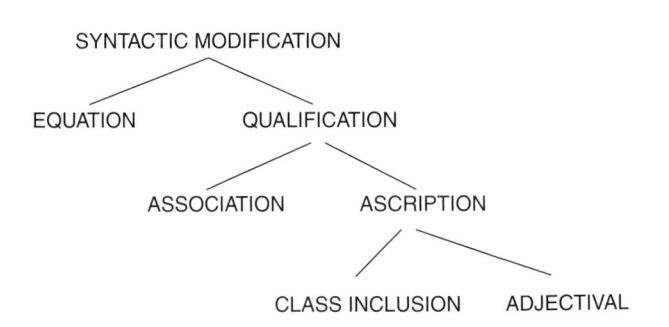

Figure 3.1. Sub-classes of syntactic modification

Table 3.1. *Entities, properties and assignment*

NO ASSIGNMENT	ASSIGNMENT
1. The Prime Minister, David Cameron	2. David Cameron is the Prime Minister.
1a. David Cameron, the Prime Minister	2a. The Prime Minister is David Cameron.
3. The green bottles	4. The bottles are green.
7. French wine	7a. The wine is French.
8. A reliable student	8a. The student is reliable.
9. The politician David Cameron	10. David Cameron is a politician.

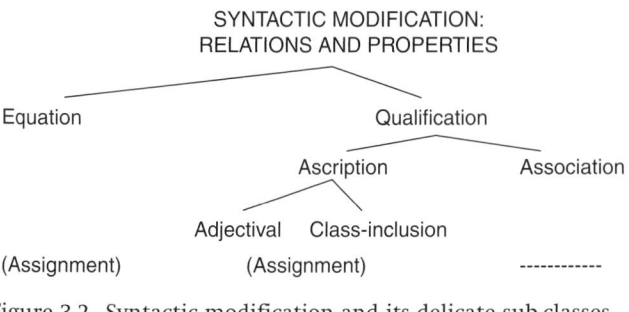

Figure 3.2. Syntactic modification and its delicate sub-classes

Assignment is only possible in the case of equatives and ascriptive qualifications, not associative qualifications ((5a), (6a)).

The full scheme for different kinds of modification is given in Figure 3.2.

3.2. EPITHETS AND CLASSIFIERS

Cutting across the ascriptive/associative classification is the distinction between epithets and classifiers. **Epithets** are always ascriptive. They indicate some quality of the set of objects referred to by the noun phrase and are either attitudinal (subjective) or descriptive (objective), e.g. "ugly (attitudinal) black (descriptive) buildings". **Classifiers** specify a particular subclass of the object in question and may be ascriptive or associative. One way to distinguish them from epithets is that they cannot take the comparative with *more* or *-er*, e.g. *wooden, metallic, electric, stone*, though the converse is not the case: not all epithets take comparatives (namely, complementaries (4.4.1)).

These distinctions help us to discover a principle of ordering within the noun phrase as in Table 3.2 (where ^ means 'is followed by').

Table 3.2. *Epithets and classifiers*

EPITHET			^	CLASSIFIER		
Attitudinal	^	Descriptive		Ascriptive	^	Associative	
Horrible		*old*		*non-aircon*		*Singapore*	*buses*

Activity 3.2

Returning to the blind man joke in the previous activity, analyse the ascriptive and associative meanings of "blind" according to the epithet/classifier and attitudinal/descriptive and ascriptive/associative distinctions, and demonstrate your analysis with the appropriate tests.

Comment

The meaning intended by the male visitor was an associative one, so in this meaning "blind" is an associative classifier. With this meaning it cannot take comparison "the more/very blind man". In the wrong meaning, which the nuns took, "blind" looks like a descriptive epithet. It might just about be used with the comparative or with *very*: "after his unsuccessful eye operation he was even blinder than before" or "I am a bit blind in this eye and very blind in the other eye", though generally it is part of the complementary pair 'blind'–'sighted'.

We discuss metaphor at some length in Chapter 7, but note how metaphor blurs the associative/ascriptive distinction. For example, if "chestnut" and "orange" are literal, as in "chestnut tree" and "orange tree", they are associative classifiers, disallowing assignment. But when used metaphorically for colour they allow assignment: "the light is orange", "her curls are chestnut".

Activity 3.3

My mum's a lollipop lady. By which I mean she has a very long thin body and a big round red sticky head. (Harry Hill, Carr and Greeves 2006: 78)

Comment on the ambiguity of the semantic functions of "lollipop" in the above joke.

Comment

In the normal phrasal compound *lollipop lady* "lollipop" is an associative classifier, where the lollipop is not assigned to the lady, but rather refers to a pole with a circular sign at the top which these ladies hold up to stop traffic while children cross the road. This is the meaning activated in the set-up. The metaphorical meaning forced by the disjunctor, however, is ascriptive: it could be rephrased "My mother/the lady is a lollipop", meaning 'My mother/the lady is, metaphorically speaking, a lollipop, resembling a lollipop by having a long thin body like the stick, and a red round sticky head like the lollipop sweet'. Here various features of lollipops are metaphorically ascribed to the speaker's mother.

3.3. *THE* OF-*GENITIVE*

One interesting kind of modification concerns the *of*-genitive, a structure used, sometimes as a pre-modifier, sometimes as a post-modifier (Table 3.3). How does modification by genitive fit into our scheme? With the appositive genitive, the paraphrase is ascriptive or equational. The analogic, like the metaphors analysed above, hovers between ascription and association. Origin looks like an associative meaning. Partitive (possessive), subjective and objective seem equivalent to associative classifiers: cf. *the house wall, a baboon call, environment(al) destruction*. Partitives of shape/measure are tricky to categorise; they are more likely quantifiers, not discussed here.

The last four of the categories in Table 3.3 allow the -'s-genitive. The partitive cannot, though the possessive almost always does. This may lead to ambiguity such as in "I've got Parkinson's disease, and he's got mine". The normal collocation would give us an associative/origin meaning 'the disease discovered by Parkinson', but the second clause suggests a possessive genitive.

It is an interesting question, especially with the appositional and partitive of shape/measure genitives, which of the nouns is the head of

Table 3.3. *The semantics of the* of-*genitive*

TYPE	SEMANTICS	EXAMPLE	TRANSFORM
APPOSITIVE	NP 2 is NP 1	the state of Singapore	Singapore is a state
(PARTITIVE OF) SHAPE/ MEASURE	NP 2 the shape/ size/ quantity of NP 1	a circle of trees a pint of water	trees the shape of a circle water the quantity of a pint
PARTITIVE (POSSESSIVE)	NP 1 is part of or belongs to NP 2	the wall of the house	the wall is part of the house
ANALOGIC	NP 1: Y :: X : NP 2	the rags of my self-respect	rags : [clothes] :: X : self-respect
SUBJECTIVE	NP 2 does NP1	the call of the baboon	the baboon called
OBJECTIVE	NP 1 is done to NP 2	the destruction of the environment	the environment is destroyed
ORIGIN/ ASSOCIATIVE	NP causes, produces or accompanies NP	the pain of a broken limb the madness of love	pain accompanies a broken limb love causes madness

the noun phrase and which is the modifier. Since "Singapore" and "the state" are appositional, referring to the same entity, the head/modifier distinction seems to disappear, as though it is an appositional compound. With shape/measure nouns, like *group*, perhaps the second noun functions as the head: "a group of boys was walking down the hill" or "a group of boys were walking down the hill"? Ambiguity about what is the head seems to underlie the following joke.

> A man on his first plane journey was told by the friend travelling with him that chewing gum would stop his ears popping. As they landed, the man turned to his friend and said, "The chewing gum works fine, but how do I get it out of my ears?" (Tibballs 2006: 48)

Activity 3.4

Using the terminology introduced in this section for analysing qualifiers, explain what kind of qualification the man gives to *chewing* at the end of this joke.

Comment

Presumably for the man who put the gum in his ears "chewing" was an associative classifier as it cannot take assignment. For him it resembled an associative/origin genitive, with "gum" as head, but for his friend resembled an objective genitive with "chewing" as head, cf. "the chewing of gum".

In fact, the genitive of origin in Table 3.3 seems to be a rag-bag of all the associative meanings not covered by more specific kinds of genitive and quite unpredictable in its meaning. This is a tendency with all associative qualifications, and may be a rich source of misunderstanding and ambiguity:

> A boy wandered into a pet store and asked for a quarter's worth of bird seed. The store assistant smiled at this odd request and asked, "How many birds do you have?" "None, yet," said the boy, "but I'm hoping to grow some." (Tibballs 2006: 65)

Activity 3.5

1. Say whether the underlined parts of the following noun phrases are associative or ascriptive qualifiers. And if they are ascriptive are they attitudinal epithets or descriptive epithets or classifiers.
   a. He made a <u>diplomatic</u> reply
   b. He was sent on a <u>diplomatic</u> mission
   c. The lecturer gave an unnecessarily <u>long logical</u> explanation
   d. She gave an <u>awful wooden</u> performance
   e. We had to sit on that <u>nasty hard narrow wooden</u> bench for three hours
2. Can you make up any jokes based on the potential ambiguities of these kinds of examples? You might try the words *civil, platonic, romantic* or *philosophical.*

Comment

1. a. diplomatic: ascriptive attitudinal epithet
   b. diplomatic: associative qualifier
   c. long: ascriptive descriptive epithet; logical: ambiguous – either ascriptive descriptive epithet or associative qualifier
   d. awful: ascriptive attitudinal epithet; wooden: ascriptive attitu-dinal/descriptive? epithet (normally an ascriptive classifier, but here a metaphor)
   e. nasty: ascriptive attitudinal epithet; hard: ascriptive descriptive (attitudinal) epithet; narrow: ascriptive descriptive epithet; wooden: ascriptive classifier
2. e.g. My aunt and uncle had no children. He was a not very civil civil engineer, and she was a not very romantic romantic novelist.

Note that genres that put a premium on conciseness, either to catch attention or because space is expensive, such as news headlines and ads, often pile up premodifiers, leading to potential ambiguities in word-class, e.g. SQUAD HELPS DOG BITE VICTIM (Bucaria 2004: 292).

3.4. THE SCOPE AND ORIENTATION OF MODIFICATION

A number of ambiguities arise from the scope of modification. In the following example the humour lies in being unsure whether "thumb" is an associative classifier of "print" or a separate noun phrase.

> Your thumb or fingerprint will be taken. (California driver handbook, Tibballs 2006: 492)

One might notate the two meanings thus:

> (your thumb or finger) print v. (your thumb) or (finger print)

Consider

> The club's celebration will also include a DJ and balloons falling from the ceiling at midnight. (US paper, Tibballs 2006: 490)

Here it is unclear whether the post-modifying clause "falling from the ceiling at midnight" includes within its scope the DJ or only the balloons.

Prepositional phrases can either function as adverbials oriented towards the rest of the clause or parts of the rest of the clause, or they can function as post-modifiers of the immediately preceding noun head. This allows for humorous ambiguity:

> I once shot an elephant in my pyjamas. How he got into my pyjamas I'll never know. (Groucho Marx in *Animal Crackers*)

Apparently the disjunctor makes clear that "in my pyjamas" postmodifies "elephant". This ambiguity type might even be preserved when the modified and the modifier are discontinuous, as in "Throwing acid is wrong in some people's eyes" (Carr and Greeves 2006: 44) meaning either 'It is wrong to throw acid into the eyes of some people' or 'In the eyes (opinion) of some people throwing acid is wrong'.

3.5.   A SEMANTIC APPROACH TO SYNTAX: HALLIDAY AND TRANSITIVITY

Having discussed various ways in which noun phrases can be modified and the semantic classes of modification, we now turn to the larger question of the conceptual meanings of clauses. Hallidayan Systemic Functional Grammar (Halliday 1985/1994) emphasises the semantic functions in clauses, making it suitable for exploring the semantics–grammar interface. Moreover it has developed a rich literature on the dimensions of social context, which we explore when discussing genre (6.4).

Halliday suggests that the clause represents the world through a transitivity choice among five process types:

- **Existential**: representing what exists in the world.
- **Relational**: representing what is the state of the things which exist and what relations they have to each other.
- **Material**: representing what is happening in the world, what actions and events are going on.
- **Mental**: representing how people are thinking, feeling and perceiving.
- **Verbal**: representing how people are communicating or expressing their perceptions, feelings and thoughts.

Processes are referred to by the main verb, and their subjects and objects/complements attract different participants according to the choice of process type (Figure 3.3). Note that some noun phrases do not refer to participants, but are part of prepositional phrases functioning as adverbials. In Hallidayan transitivity analysis, adverbials represent Circumstances.

PROCESS TYPE	PARTICIPANT	PROCESS	PARTICIPANT		
Existential:			**Existent**		
	There	*are*	*so many hotels called 'The White Swan'*		
Relational:	**Token** (Identified)		**Value** (Identifier)		
	Prof. Jones (Carrier)	*is*	*the President of the University* (Attribute)		
	Californians (Possessor)	*are*	*very smart creatures* (Possession)		
	Californians	*have*	*charm and intelligence*		
Material:	**Actor**		**(Beneficiary)**		**Goal**
	My partner	*cooks*			*breakfast*
	My behaviour	*gave*	*my mother*		*sleepless nights*
Mental	**Sensor**		**Phenomenon**		
		(Cognition)			
	I	*believe*	*that women should be educated*		
		(Affect)			
	I	*don't want*	*to look humiliated*		
		(Perception)			
	We	*saw*	*a subspecies of frog*		
Verbal	**Sayer**		**Target**	**Receiver**	**Verbiage**
	Berlusconi	*reminds*	*Italians*		*to have more children*
	John	*criticised*	*Mary*	*to her parents*	

Figure 3.3. Process and participant types in Hallidayan transitivity

Activity 3.6

Identify the types of process and participants in the following, just the underlined clauses in (5) and (6). (4) to (7) are jokes: explain the ambiguity of their process types and participants, by giving alternative analyses.

1. Iraq denounces world population conference to the UN.
2. I was given a present by John.
3. The present delighted me.
4. British left waffles on Falkland Islands (*Guardian*) (Tibballs 2006: 5006).
5. *Earl of Sandwich*: I do not know whether you will die on the gallows or of the pox. *John Wilkes*: That depends on whether I embrace your principles or your mistress. (Tibballs 2006: 647)
6. A small boy got lost at a baseball game. He went up to a police officer and said, "I've lost my dad." "What's he like?" asked the office sympathetically. "Beer and women," replied the boy. (Tibballs 2006: 61)
7. Time flies like an arrow. Fruit flies like a banana.

Comments

1.

Iran	denounces	world population conference	to the UN
Sayer	*Verbal Process*	*Target*	*Receiver*

2.

I	was given	a present	by John
Beneficiary	*Material Process*	*Goal*	*Actor*

3.

The present	delighted	me
Phenomenon	*Mental Process*	*Sensor*

4.

British left	waffles	on Falkland Islands	
Sayer	*Verbal Process*	*Target*	
British	left	waffles	on Falkland Islands
Actor	*Material Process*	*Goal*	*Circumstance*

5.

I	embrace	your principles
Sensor	*Mental Process*	*Phenomenon*
I	embrace	your mistress
Actor	*Material Process*	*Goal*

6.

What	is	he	like
Value …	*Relational Process*	*Token*	*… Value*
What	does	he	like
Phenomenon		*Sensor*	*Mental Process*

7.

Fruit	flies	like a banana
Actor	*Material Process*	*Circumstance*
Fruit flies	like	a banana
Sensor	*Mental Process*	*Phenomenon*

When performing this kind of transitivity analysis note that passivisation does not change participant roles, so that "The world population conference was denounced by Iraq" preserves the participant roles of the active equivalent in (1). And in (3), as with many mental process verbs like *please, annoy* etc., the subject can represent the phenomenon rather than the sensor. So the subjects of material, verbal and mental process clauses are not always the actors, sayers or sensors.

Note too that some quite common lexical verbs have a foot in more than one process. For example, *look* involves mental perception, but it is also a deliberate act, unlike *see* or *notice*, and hence somewhat material. *Surround* is partly relational as in "the moat surrounds the castle" ('is around') but in another meaning as in "the troops surrounded the city" ('moved into a position so that they were around') can be partly material too (Martin and Matthiessen 1991). In the analysis below (3.6) we note some uses of mental-material and verbal-material processes.

Activity 3.7

Our office policy is that we will do our utmost to see patients in discomfort as soon as possible. (California Dental Newsletter, Tibballs 2006: 491)

What processes does *see* refer to in the above extract, in both of its ambiguous meanings?

Comment

One unintended meaning seems to be 'we will do our utmost to make sure our patients are in discomfort as soon as possible', with the meaning of "see" 'make sure X is'; since this ensuring involves some action it is presumably part material, part relational. The other meaning is 'attend to', which is material.

3.6. AN EXAMPLE OF ANALYSIS

One discipline in which this semantic approach to grammar has proved useful is Critical Linguistics, an enterprise designed to show the power relations expressed in a text. Table 3.4 suggests a hierarchy of power for the various participants in processes.

By way of illustration, I perform a Hallidayan transitivity analysis to the following report from the Hong Kong newspaper *The South China Morning Post*, using this power hierarchy to identify the most powerful participants as constructed by the text.

Table 3.4. *The power hierarchy of participants in descending order (after Duan Jie 2007)*

Participants	Explanations	Examples
Actor in transitive material processes	An active participant powerful enough to affect other things/ people	Snow blocked the road
Actor in intransitive material process	An active participant but not affecting others	John went into the room
Sayer in verbal process	Participant who sends a message and affects the consciousness of the receiver	Peter told her the time of the bus
Possessor in possessive relational processes	Owner, to whom the possession belongs	Mary has a Mercedes
Phenomenon in perception mental process	Participant capable of impinging on the consciousness of the sensor	John noticed the bird
Sensor in cognitive/ affective mental processes	Participant with an active mental/ emotional life	James really enjoys Wagner
Existent, Phenomenon in mental process of cognition and affection, or Token or Value in attributive or identifying processes	Neutral	There are five chickens in the yard I knew he was mad
Sensor in perception mental process	Sentient and responsive to outside stimuli but affected by them	John noticed the bird
Receiver in verbal process	Receiver of information, affected by it	I told Frieda about the auction
Possession in possessive relational process	A possession under the power of the possessor	I have three cars
Goal in material process	A participant who is passive and affected by other participants exerting power over it	John was killed by a bus

South China Morning Post (Hong Kong)
April 29, 2001

Yorkshire and China so easy to confuse

JO BOWMAN

An American woman who confused two hotel web sites arrived at the White Swan Hotel in Guangzhou to find she had mistakenly booked a room at a bed-and-breakfast in the north of England.

New Yorker Claudia Niera tried to check in on April 9 but the White Swan was full and had no record of her reservation. When she checked her booking confirmation slip, she realised it was for the White Swan bed-and-breakfast in Yorkshire.

"It's never happened before," said Tristan Teters, guest relations manager at the Guangzhou White Swan Hotel. "If it had happened any other time of the year we could've just had a laugh and got her checked in, but we were absolutely full and had no option but to arrange alternative accommodation for her."

Most hotels in Guangzhou – population 6.7 million – were close to full at the time, because the Canton Commodities Fair was on.

Victor Buchanan, owner of the White Swan in Pickering, Yorkshire – population 6,000 – said Ms Niera had booked an eight-night stay via the Internet but did not turn up. The hotel soon received a desperate message from her – sent from the White Swan in Guangzhou – asking for help.

"We got an e-mail via the White Swan in Canton from her saying please, please, please could we not charge her credit card because she'd booked the wrong hotel," he said. "It's an easy mistake to make – to confuse Yorkshire with southern China. The Web addresses are quite similar, but even so. . ."

The Guangzhou hotel's Web site describes a setting on historical Shamian Island overlooking the Pearl River.

Recommendations from the chef include sweetened bird's nest with almond sauce, and double-boiled tortoise with snake and chicken soup.

In contrast, the British White Swan's Web site shows photos of the rambling Yorkshire countryside, a map of Britain and describes Pickering as a "bustling market town" with attractions such as Pickering Castle, "a well-preserved English Heritage site".

The hotel's menu includes a full Yorkshire breakfast with eggs Benedict, grilled Scottish kippers, porridge, black pudding and Yorkshire tea.

"It's pretty obvious from the start that it's not the White Swan in Guangzhou," Mr Teters said. "It's quite a surprising mistake to make to be honest, because the Web site says things like how to get there from places like London, which may suggest to some people that it's not actually in Guangzhou."

Guangzhou and Pickering are not the only places to boast a White Swan. A search on the Internet shows there is a 17th-century farmhouse in Plymouth, Massachusetts, called the White Swan Bed and Breakfast. The White Swan Inn in San Francisco is a "stunning tribute to the luxury hotels of London", and the White Swan Hotel in Stratford-upon-Avon – the birthplace of William Shakespeare – is a 400-year-old timber-framed establishment which promotes "real ale" and a Sunday night jazz session.

Mr Buchanan said he had waived Ms Niera's bill, and invited her to visit the White Swan's Web site again.

"It would be nice to think that one day she might book again and actually turn up here."

The material process clauses featuring Ms Niera as actor show how ineffectual she is – either her actions are negatived, or only possible but not real (technically *irrealis*), or intransitive, or amount to cries for help and futile attempts:

- [Ms Niera] did not **turn up**.
- [one day she might] actually **turn up** here.
- An American woman … **arrived** at the White Swan Hotel in Guangzhou.
- a desperate message from her – **sent** from the White Swan in Guangzhou –
- New Yorker Claudia Niera tried **to check in** on April 9.

Material-verbal clause analysis reveals the one decisive action performed by the female protagonist – the wrong booking, mistakenly made:

- because she'd **booked** the wrong hotel.
- Ms Niera had **booked** an eight-night stay via the Internet.
- one day she might **book** again.
- she had mistakenly **booked** a room at a bed-and-breakfast in the north of England.

Ms Niera seems more of a sensor in mental processes of cognition, rather than an actor, and therefore relatively low in the hierarchy of power (Table 3.4). The following are mental-material clauses, where she is partly sensor and partly actor:

- [An American woman] **to find** she had mistakenly booked a room at a bed-and-breakfast in the north of England.
- When she **checked** her booking confirmation slip …

Mental clauses with her as sensor are also quite frequent:

- "It's an easy mistake to make – **to confuse** Yorkshire with southern China …"
- An American woman who **confused** two hotel websites
- she **realised** it was for the White Swan bed-and-breakfast in Yorkshire.

If she is not a particularly powerful actor, she is not a powerful sayer either. Niera is never interviewed, denied (!) a voice. Claiming for themselves the managerial role, it is the white males who speak:

- "It's never happened before," **said** Tristan Teters, guest relations manager at the Guangzhou White Swan Hotel.
- Victor Buchanan, owner of the White Swan in Pickering, Yorkshire – population 6,000 – **said** Ms Niera had booked an eight-night stay via the Internet but did not turn up.
- Mr Buchanan **said** he had waived Ms Niera's bill, and **invited** her to visit the White Swan's website again.
- "It's pretty obvious from the start that it's not the White Swan in Guangzhou," Mr Teters **said**.

By contrast, Niera's is the voice of female helplessness:

- [a desperate message from her] **asking for** help.
- [an e-mail] "**saying** please, please, please could we not charge her credit card because she'd booked the wrong hotel".

And we notice here that it is not so much the woman who speaks as her e-mail message.

This is one of many cases where texts themselves become sayers, by-passing humans:

- [the British White Swan's website] **describes** Pickering as a "bustling market town" with attractions such as Pickering Castle, "a well-preserved English Heritage site".
- In contrast, the British White Swan's website **shows** photos of the rambling Yorkshire countryside, a map of Britain
- The Guangzhou hotel's website **describes** a setting on historical Shamian Island overlooking the Pearl River.
- because the website **says** things like . . .

The booking confirmation slip becomes a powerful sayer in its own right. The moral of this story might be that texts are overcoming the world, especially in the form of websites (swans' or not) that can be confused with each other.

But places too become sayers:

- Guangzhou and Pickering are not the only places **to boast** a White Swan.
- [the WSH in Stratford] **promotes** "real ale" and a Sunday night jazz session.

And also actors:

- the **rambling** Yorkshire countryside . . .
- and describes Pickering as a "**bustling** market town";
- Shamian Island **overlooking** the Pearl River.

There is an irony in giving such power to places – since ultimately globalisation ensures that they lose their distinctiveness, their "difference", and are thereby rendered impotent. The White Swan and the White Swan become indistinguishable, with the uniqueness of names (reference only) swallowed up in the non-difference of sense. Confusion arises because names here do not have their ideal one-to-one relationship with referents.

To sum up: Ms Niera is represented as powerless, because she tends to be ineffectual or mistaken as an actor in material process clauses, and is more often a sensor in mental process clauses, in a relatively low position on the power hierarchy. Moreover she is never given a voice to impinge on the reader or other characters in the article, apart from a desperate plea for help. By contrast, male managers are often sayers, as are places and documents/websites, which makes them relatively powerful, and hints at the power of technology to confuse and annihilate space.

3.7. TRANSFORMATIONS: PASSIVISATION AND NOMINALISATION

I have demonstrated the Critical Linguistic approach to which basic Halliday transitivity analysis can contribute. There are, however, two common transformations of this basic semantic grammar, **passivisation** and **nominalisation**. Passivisation allows the omission of actors, sayers and sensors, though they can optionally occur in a prepositional *by-*phrase.

> The comet was observed last night (by several thousand people in Swindon) (this is not a joke, by the way!).

Nominalisation of verbs and adjectives allows the optional omission of all participants.

> "The report was commissioned by the   Who reported what?
> Arts Council."
> "Such sights are rather distressing."   Who saw what?

Such uncertainty over participants produces ambiguity, especially when the participant mentioned in the text is not the actual participant involved in the nominalised process: MINERS REFUSE TO WORK AFTER DEATH (US paper, Tibballs 2006: 507).

In the following joke there are a few passive clauses which omit the actor in order to make sure the illusion is shared by actress and reader until the punchline.

> An agent found out that an actress he represented was selling her body at night for 100 dollars a time. Seeing her in a new light, he asked whether he too could have sex with her, but she told him he'd have to pay like the others. She wouldn't even allow him his ten per cent agent's fee as a discount. He wasn't happy about the arrangement, but the following night he went to her apartment, turned out the lights and had sex with her. *She fell asleep afterwards but an hour later she was woken and made love to again. Then half an hour after that she was made love to once more, and every thirty minutes for the next three hours.* Impressed with his virility, she purred: "I'm so lucky to have you as my agent." "I'm not your agent, lady," a strange voice answered, "He's at the door selling tickets." (Tibballs 2006: 12)

I wonder whether the joke would be more successful if nominalisation were employed instead of the italicised passives:

> She fell asleep afterwards but an hour later she woke up as the love-making was repeated. Then half an hour after that it occurred again, and every thirty minutes for the next three hours.

The problem with the original is that the rather awkward passive may alert us to an alternative script/schema before the punchline disjunctor in the last sentence.

Moreover, because nominalisation converts a clause into a noun phrase, it omits a finite verb which would anchor the process in time. In "The dissatisfaction with the government policy on new golf courses will cause a loss of popularity" we neither know who is dissatisfied, nor when they were dissatisfied or if they still are. To put the same point slightly differently, nominalisation leads to existential presuppositions, whereby referring to an entity with a definite noun phrase assumes its existence: >> There is/was/will be dissatisfaction with the government's policy on new golf courses.

Definite noun phrase nominalisations smuggle in a proposition by not overtly stating it. This might make it easier to accept than the equivalent clause: "The need for wage restraint in a globalised economy is increasing" might be easier to accept than "Workers (?) need to restrain their wages in a globalised economy..."

Some jokes depend upon an ambiguity in whether there is a nominalisation or not.

POLICE CAN'T STOP GAMBLING (Tibballs 2006: 507)

If "can't stop gambling" is a verb phrase, and "gamble" the main verb, the police lack the self-control to kick the habit. Alternatively, if *stop* is a main verb, and "gambling" a nominalisation, some unspecified actor is gambling, not the police.

Table 3.5. *Patterns of ergative verbs*

MEDIUM	PROCESS		INSTIGATOR	PROCESS	MEDIUM
The boat	sailed	v.	Mary	sailed	the boat
The cloth	tore	v.	The nail	tore	the cloth
The rice	cooked	v.	Pat	cooked	the rice
MIDDLE		v.	*EFFECTIVE*		

3.8. ERGATIVE MEANINGS

The label **ergative** was originally applied to a language type with distinctive kinds of case inflection.[1] In these languages the subject of transitive clauses is specially marked (with ergative case), while intransitive subject and transitive object have the same (generally zero-marked) form. Halliday uses this label for verbs in English where the participant designated by the intransitive (or middle) subject is identical to the participant designated by the transitive (or effective) object, e.g. *open* and *move*. The intimation here is that what seems to be the actor in an intransitive clause becomes the goal in a transitive clause.

The ergative paradigm centres on pairs of clauses like those in Table 3.5 from Halliday (1985: 146), where he substitutes the terms actor and goal with **instigator** and **medium**, and replaces the terms transitive and intransitive with **effective** and **middle**.

Ergative verbs, e.g. *sail*, *tear* and *cook*, contrast with verbs of the non-ergative type, such as *eat*, *swallow*. The difference is that when the middle version is transformed into the effective version by adding another participant, the added participant becomes the subject of the effective version. By contrast, when the intransitive transforms into the transitive by the addition of another participant, the added participant becomes object of the transitive version, as in Table 3.6.

Activity 3.8

Consider the ambiguities in the following texts. Explain whether the verbs *worry, kick* and *scatter* are ergative or not. How do ambiguities in these examples depend upon the intransitive-transitive or middle-effective contrasts?

1. On a farmer's gate: Please shut gate to stop sheep worrying. (Tibballs 2006: 499)
2. KICKING BABY CONSIDERED TO BE HEALTHY (Tibballs 2006: 506)
3. The new Head of Department scattered fear and gloom.

Comment

"Worrying" might be ergative, where "sheep worry" (middle) → "X worries sheep" (effective), though the effective meaning tends to be more specific than 'cause to worry'. As with "Police Can't Stop Gambling" above, we are not sure whether "stop" is a main verb. If so, "sheep worrying" is a nominalisation of an underlying effective clause, with an unspecified instigator; if not, "sheep worrying" is a nominalisation of an underlying middle clause in which the sheep are medium. In (2) "kicking" is, however, either an intransitive verb "the baby kicks" or transitive "X kicks the baby", since the latter does not mean 'X causes the baby to kick'. (3) depends on the ambiguity of the verb *scatter*: 'throw things so they are spread over an area' (non-ergative, transitive) or 'cause to suddenly move away in different directions' (ergative, effective). At least the second meaning is more obviously ergative than the first. The second has a middle equivalent 'suddenly move away in different directions', but a middle meaning for the first 'spread over an area' seems rare.

Table 3.6. *Patterns of non-ergative verbs*

ACTOR	PROCESS		ACTOR	PROCESS	GOAL
John	ate	v.	John	ate	a grape
John	swallowed	v.	John	swallowed	a coin
INTRANSITIVE		v.	*TRANSITIVE*		

3.9. RECIPROCAL VERBS

Reciprocal verbs, such as *meet, touch, interact, collide, fight, clash* and *marry*, emphasise the mutuality of cause and effect. The plural or joint subjects of such verbs are simultaneously actors and goals. With most verbs, to convey a similar meaning we have the rather clumsy option of adding *each other* to achieve a kind of reflexivity, but the event is then construed as two separate processes. Compare

| John and the car hit each other | | John and the car collided |
| The two men hit each other | | The two men fought |

Activity 3.9

Explain the ambiguity behind this joke, using the term *reciprocal verb*.

Boxers don't have sex before a fight. Do you know why that is? They don't fancy each other. (Jimmy Carr, Carr and Greeves 2006: 174)

Comment

Apparently *have sex* is ambiguous between a reciprocal and non-reciprocal meaning. So the ambiguity here is between the reciprocal meaning 'have sex with each other' and 'have sex with anyone'. Our schema for boxers suggests some hostility to each other before a fight, as well as in it. This schema rules out the reciprocal meaning. However, the "punch"-line suggests the possibility, denied, of a reciprocal meaning.

3.10. SUMMARY

In the first part of this chapter we looked into the semantic relationships of modification of noun phrases, considering equation, ascription, association, and using lack of assignment as a criterion for distinguishing association. We also investigated the semantic ordering of the noun phrase: attitudinal epithet ^ descriptive epithet ^ ascriptive classifier ^ associative classifier, pointing out that metaphor blurs the latter distinction, and aligning these with different semantic classes of *of*-genitives.

In the second part of the chapter we considered the various process types and participants for clauses: existential, relational, material, verbal and mental, and the overlaps between these categories. I showed how the participants in these different processes might be placed on a power hierarchy and analysed a news article to demonstrate how such a framework can be a tool of Critical Linguistics. We also considered passives and nominalisations as variations on these clause types, and the clausal meanings associated with ergative and reciprocal verbs. I illustrated with many examples how ambiguities in syntactic categories of premodifier, in scope of modification, and in semantic parsing of processes and participants give opportunities for humour.

Discussion

How convincing do you find the kind of analysis applied to the 'Yorkshire and Guangzhou so easy to confuse' news report? Did the analysis reveal patterns that you were not already aware of? Or were they just stating the obvious? What problems might arise in applying an analysis to texts with multiple levels of discourse or heavily ironic texts? Was there, in fact, any example of irony in this text? Should we distinguish between the representations provided by the reporter's voice and those provided by the characters quoted? Do these give us different representations?

Suggested Readings

- Ferris (1993) as the source of the first section of this chapter is an obvious candidate for following up on the meanings of modification and adjectives.
- Similarly Halliday and Matthiessen (2004: chapter 5) gives a detailed account of the ideational or conceptual meaning of grammar, both of transitivity and ergativity. For a simpler account, see Downing and Locke (1992: chapter 4).
- For further examples of the application of Critical Linguistics through the analysis of transitivity, nominalisation and passivisation, consider reading Goatly (2000: chapter 2) or Goatly (2008: chapters 2 and 3).
- Blake (2007: chapter 6) has an interesting enough chapter on grammatical ambiguity and humour, though his classifications are sometimes a little problematic.

4 Semantics and the conceptual meaning of lexis

Chapter 3 concentrated on the conceptual or ideational meaning of noun phrases and the clause. This chapter shifts to the more traditional concern of semantics, the conceptual meaning of lexis.

This concern with the logical meanings of vocabulary was an attempt to establish semantics as a "science". We can exemplify the logical approach by noting, for example, that the meanings for 'man', 'woman', 'girl', 'boy', 'child' and 'adult' involve systematic contrasts of the following kind.

Table 4.1. *Logical contrasts of lexical meaning*

	ADULT	MALE
'man'	+	+
'woman'	+	—
'boy'	—	+
'girl'	—	—
'child'	—	+/—
'adult'	+	+/—

Following this logical approach, this chapter considers relationships among senses and statements, namely, synonymy, entailment, inconsistency, tautology, contradiction, ambiguity, presupposition, hyponymy and meronymy. It also introduces several meaning oppositions: complementarity, multiple incompatibility, gradable or polar oppositions, converses, symmetry and transitivity (though with a different meaning from the previous chapter). The final section suggests some of the inadequacies of this logical approach to meaning in naturally occurring communication, and the need for less rigid approaches which acknowledge the fuzziness of concepts, such as prototype theory, radial categories and "family resemblances".

4.1. SENSE RELATIONS

The logical nature of sense or conceptual meaning is apparent in relationships like synonymy, entailment, inconsistency, tautology and contradiction:

'female fox'	is synonymous with	'vixen'
'this is a fox'	entails	'this is a mammal'
'this is a fox'	is inconsistent with	'this is a mobile phone'
'this fox is a mammal'	is tautologous	
'this fox is not a mammal'	is a contradiction	

Let's explore these sense relations in more detail, by considering what semanticists have called **basic statements**, of the form "X is synonymous with/entails/is inconsistent with/presupposes Y" or "X is tautologous/contradictory/ambiguous".

4.1.1. Synonymy

"X is **synonymous** with y" means "if x is true, then y is necessarily true, and if y is true, then x is necessarily true" and "if x is false, then y is necessarily false, and if y is false, then x is necessarily false". For example let's test whether "This person has many relatives" and "This person has many relations" are synonymous statements. If "This person has many relatives" is true, then "This person has many relations" is necessarily true, and vice versa. If "This person has many relatives" is false, then "This person has many relations" is necessarily false, and vice versa. If you agree with these last two sentences, then "This person has many relatives" and "This person has many relations" are synonymous. "Unlawful" might be synonymous with "illegal", except in the following joke: "What's the difference between unlawful and illegal?" "Unlawful means 'against the law' and illegal is 'a sick bird'" (Alexander 1997: 54).

Roget's *Thesaurus* is, of course, famous for its attempt to find (near) synonyms, which explains the following joke: "Roget's Thesaurus rules, dominates, regulates, OK, all right, adequately".

4.1.2. Entailment

"X **entails** y" means "if x is true, y is necessarily true, and if y is false, x is necessarily false, but not vice versa". For instance, let's test whether "This person has a brother" entails "This person has a sibling". If "This person has a brother" is true, then "This person has a sibling" is necessarily true, BUT NOT VICE VERSA. If "This person has a sibling" is false, then "This person has a brother" is necessarily false, BUT NOT VICE VERSA. Clearly the vice-versa condition does not apply because if "This person has a sibling" is true, it is not necessarily true that "This person has a brother". The person in question may have a sister.

4.1.3. Inconsistency

"X is **inconsistent** with y" means 'if x is true, y is necessarily false; if y is true, x is necessarily false'. So, let's test whether "The teacher has a sister" and "The teacher is an only child" are inconsistent. If "The teacher has a sister" is true, then "The teacher is an only child" is necessarily false. If "The teacher is an only child" is true, then "The teacher has a sister" is necessarily false.

Note that in everyday speech we call these two inconsistent statements "contradiction". But, technically, in semantics, contradiction is internal to a statement. The term we use for two incompatible statements is inconsistency. Attardo (1994: 189) suggests that humour might necessarily involve logical "contradiction", though using our terminology this probably means 'inconsistency', since the clashing schemas are inconsistent with each other.

Activity 4.1

Give labels to the logical relations between the following statements, if any.

1. Outside a dance hall: "Our Saturday night dance is very exclusive. Everybody is welcome."
2. "John is a cannibal" and "John is human".
3. In a barber's shop: "Haircuts [are] half-price today. [You can have] only one per customer."
4. "The Prime Minister of England is Prof James's grandad" and "The Prime Minister of England is Prof James's grandfather".

Comment

1. These statements are inconsistent. If "Our Saturday night dance is very exclusive" is true, "Everybody is welcome" is false. And if "Everybody is welcome" is true, then "Our Saturday night dance is very exclusive" is false.
2. The second statement is an entailment of the first. If "John is a cannibal" is true, then "John is human" is necessarily true. And if "John is human" is false, then "John is a cannibal" is false. But not vice-versa, in either case.
3. None of the sense relations apply in this case, which is anomalous because of our knowledge of the state of the world (connotative meaning, see 5.2) rather than sense or logic.

4. These are synonymous statements. If "The Prime Minister of England is James's grandad" is true, then "The Prime Minister of England is James' grandfather" is necessarily true, and vice versa. And if the first statement is false, the second must be false, and vice versa.

Synonymy, entailment, and inconsistency are relationships between the meanings of *two* clauses or statements. The next kinds of logical relations – tautology, contradiction and presupposition – concern logical relationships within *one* statement.

4.1.4. Tautology

"X is a **tautology**" means 'x is necessarily true'. For instance "An ant is an insect", "The butter was made from milk" and "War is war" are necessarily true. There is something hopelessly tautologous about this Bushism: "The thing that's important for me is to remember what is the most important thing" (George W. Bush, Tibballs 2006: 509).

In the following conversational example (Norrick 1993: 93) Jim's laughter prompts Teddy to recognise the tautology:

> TEDDY: And I said to her, Sara if you could read now, for yourself, *you* could read.
> JIM: Uh ha ha *ha* ha ha ha. Ha*ha*ha.
> TEDDY: Uh huh. Which I suppose is almost too obvious even to tell a five-year-old.

4.1.5. Contradiction

"X is a **contradiction**" means 'x is necessarily false', for example, "The bachelor has a wife" and "With our airmiles system you save what you spend". Contradiction, sometimes referred to as paradox, can also be abbreviated into an oxymoron, which lacks the "assignment" necessary for a contradiction (see 3.1): "death is living" → "a living death". In the following dialogue, two brothers, Brandon and Ned, are commenting on their mother Lydia's advice to Brandon's daughter, which they overhear from an adjoining room:

> LYDIA: We had such a nice day today, so you hurry and get rested. Because you're going to have a big nice day tomorrow.
> BRANDON: Hurry and get rested.
> NED: Uhhuhhuhhuhhuhhuh hehe.
> BRANDON: That's oxymoronic.
> NED: Uhhuhhuhhuh. Yeah. Can you imagine the ox? Hehehe.
> BRANDON: No. But I've spotted the moron.
> NED: I see. Huhhuhhuh. You'd think as dumb as oxes are, to call one a moron would be tautological. Huhhahaheh. (Norrick 1993)

It's not clear what kind of logical flaw is involved in "you hurry and get rested". It's more likely a contradiction, rather than the oxymoron that Brandon identifies, because it is necessarily false. Or it could be considered an inconsistency: "to hurry" is inconsistent with "to get rested".

Activity 4.2

Explain what kinds of logical relations give rise to the oddity of the following, using the diagnostic formulae introduced above:

   a. WAR DIMS HOPE FOR PEACE (US paper) (Tibballs 2006: 508)
   b. When you smell an odourless gas it is probably carbon monoxide. (exam howler, Tibballs 2006: 665)
   c. We didn't underestimate them. They were just better than we thought. (Bobby Robson, Tibballs 2006: 513)
   d.i. A poodle has eaten the lamb chops.
   d.ii. A dog has eaten the lamb chops.
   e.i. The world is experiencing global warming.
   e.ii. The earth is experiencing global warming.
   f. You can get anywhere in 10 minutes if you go fast enough. (Morreall 1983: 76)

Comment

a.   This looks like a tautology, as though it is necessarily true. It would be hard to negate this in any meaningful way "War does not dim hopes for peace", as that would be a contradiction.

b.   The first clause here is a contradiction. "You smell an odourless gas" is necessarily false.

c.   This demonstrates inconsistency. If "we didn't underestimate them" is true, then "they were just better than we thought" is false, and vice versa.

d.   i entails ii.[1]

e.   i and ii would appear to be synonymous, if one is true/false the other is true/false.

f.   This looks something like a tautology. But is it?

4.2. LEXICAL AMBIGUITY

By using basic statements we can also account for the meaning relation of **ambiguity**, by exploiting the definition of synonymy. For example

   a. "The meal was very hot"
might mean

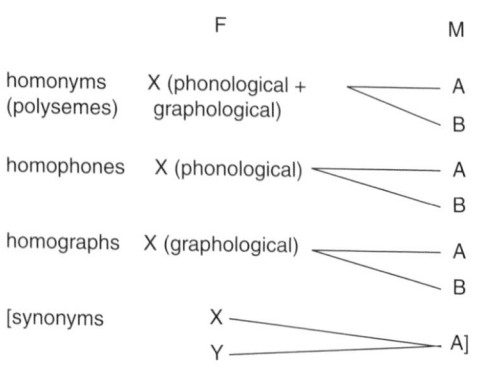

Figure 4.1. Form, meaning, ambiguity and synonymy

b. 'The meal was very high in temperature'
or
c. 'The meal was very spicy'.

(b) and (c) are not synonymous with each other: it is not the case that if "the meal was very high in temperature" is true, then "the meal was very spicy" is necessarily true, nor vice versa. However, one meaning of (a) is synonymous with (b) and the other meaning of (a) is synonymous with (c).

Figure 4.1 can help us distinguish the three main kinds of ambiguity – homophony, homography and homonymy. As it indicates, **homonyms** have the same graphological and phonological form but different meanings, e.g. *rock* meaning 'large stone', and *rock* meaning 'kind of pop music'. **Homophones** have the same phonological form but different graphological form and meanings, e.g. *hair* and *hare*. They are very common in English[2] because its spelling system is only partially phonetic – i.e. there is no one-to-one relationship between spelling and sound or vice versa, unlike languages such as Russian or Korean. And **homographs** have the same graphological form but different phonological form and meanings, e.g. *read* /riːd/ 'present tense', and *read* /red/ 'past tense'.

Notice that identity of both graphological and phonological form paired with different meanings gives rise to either homonymy or polysemy. Homonymy occurs when the two meanings are not perceived as related; coincidence of form seems accidental, e.g. *pool* 'the game like snooker', *pool* 'a small pond'. **Polysemy** occurs when the two meanings are perceived as related; coincidence of form seems motivated, e.g. the meanings of *crane* 'the wading bird with long legs and a long neck' and 'the hoisting machine used in building construction' can be related by metaphor.

Homonymy and polysemy can lead to both lexical and syntactic ambiguity. In "he grabbed the mouse" does "mouse" represent the lexical item meaning *mouse* 'a rodent like a small rat' or 'a computer attachment'? Or, in the following joke, "how long" is not the adverbial we would expect.

> Tourist: Can you tell me how long cows should be milked?
> Farmer: The same as short ones, of course. (Alexander 1997: 43)

Attardo *et al.* (1994) point out that in deliberate humour syntactic ambiguity is much less common than lexical ambiguity, because it is more difficult to process.

Activity 4.3

Decide whether the following jokes depend upon the ambiguity of homophony, homography, homonymy or polysemy.

1. Why did the Marxist only drink herbal tea?
   Because all proper tea is theft.
2. Men are like carpet tiles. Lay them right and you can walk over them for the next 30 years. (Carr and Greeves 2006: 91)
3. "Why are politicians like golfers?"
   "They get caught in one bad lie after another."
4. How did the 18-year-old feel when he was finally allowed into the pub?
   Entranced.

Comment

1. involves homophony since *tea* and *-ty* sound more or less the same but are spelt differently. But the *proper* part considered alone would be a homonym.

2. We might see a relation between the two meanings of *lay* and *walk over*.
   LAY₁ 'place flat upon a surface' could be metonymically related to LAY₂ 'have sexual intercourse with' since, prototypically, people are flat upon a surface (bed) during sex. WALK OVER, meaning 'dominate, oppress', depends upon a metaphor theme POWER IS HIGH/ABOVE (Chapter 7). If the reader perceives these meaning relations the joke depends upon polysemic ambiguity.

3. The two meanings of *caught* are metaphorically linked and thus polysemous. *Lie*, however, is simply a homonym, the deceit and positional meanings having no obvious connection.

4. This involves a homograph, with different pronunciations: /en 'trɑːnst/; and the nonce form /'en trɒnst/.

We noted earlier that ambiguity is essential to jokes, as a device for connecting two opposed schemas. An important question is whether we preserve the two opposed schemas or not, or resolve the ambiguity in one direction. Attardo (1994: 215) suggests that jokes are better if both schemas and ambiguous meanings can be maintained. For example, he claims "Why did the cookie cry – because his mother had been away for [a wafer] so long" seems a rather gratuitous pun. But when a prisoner in his cell is asked "Why are you flipping through the pages of that book" and replies "I am looking for a passage" both the reading and escape schemas can be preserved in the ambiguity of "passage", making a better joke.

Oaks (1994, 2010) catalogues the linguistic enabling devices which can be exploited to create humour through ambiguous word-class. He emphasises that much homophony, including that exploiting re-analysis (2.4), involves syntactic ambiguity. "Be alert." "Who needs lerts?" "Buddhist advice to avoid pain-killing injections at the dentist's: 'transcend dental medication'".

4.2.1. Homonymy

Jokes dependent upon homonymy-based ambiguity range over various word-classes and phrasal compounds. Although nouns are the most lexical of lexical words (1.5), and therefore might not display ambiguity/vagueness to the same extent as verbs, let alone prepositions, there are more of them in English and therefore more opportunities for homonymy, e.g. "Two fish are in a tank. One turns to the other and asks 'Do you know how to drive one of these things?'" (Carr and Greeves 2006: 11).

Verb homonymy might be proportionally even more frequent, though, as in: "He played the King as though somebody else might be about to play the ace" (Eugene Field on an actor playing King Lear, Tibballs 2006: 658). And "How does Michael Jackson pick his nose?" "Through a catalogue" (Tibballs 2006: 64).

The very frequent, grammatical and therefore very ambiguous prepositions, such as *for* and *through* also show enough homonymy to be humorously exploited or misused: "However much you give a homeless person for a cup of tea, you never get that tea" (Jimmy Carr, Carr and Greeves 2006: 105). And "A house-owner in Golders Green was forced to leave his house through dangerous cracks in the wall" (Alexander 1997: 49).

Phrasal compounds or idioms can also be homonymous, e.g. *have X for dinner*, or *go into*: "Mummy, mummy, when are we going to have aunt Mary for dinner?" "Shut up – we haven't finished your grandma yet" (Tibballs 2006: 553). And

> Out of the blue an accountant decided to leave his wife. He left her a
> note saying: "Dear Diane, I am 54 years old and have never done
> anything wild in my life. But now I am leaving you for a stunning
> 18-year-old model. We'll be staying at the Savoy."
>   When he arrived at the hotel, there was a message waiting
> from his wife. It read: "Dear Clive, I too am 54 years old. I have
> followed your example and am staying at the Royal with an
> 18-year-old Italian hunk. And I'm sure that you, as an accountant,
> will appreciate that 18 goes into 54 many more times than 54 goes
> into 18." (Tibballs 2006: 11)

But besides working at the level of the lexical item, homonymy may
operate at the level of the bound morpheme. For instance the
ambiguity of the form -*s* as representing the plural or first person
singular morpheme contributes to the ambiguity in the headline:
BRITISH LEFT WAFFLES ON FALKLAND ISLANDS.

4.2.2. Homophony

Other jokes or puns depend upon homophony: "What do you get if you
divide the circumference of a pumpkin by its diameter?" "Pumpkin pi"
(Tibballs 2006: 598); "She was only the miller's daughter, though bred
for a nobler role".

Activity 4.4

Explain the following joke using the terminology and correct notation for analysing
forms, sounds and meanings.

> A philosophy professor and a sociologist are holidaying at a nudist camp. The
> philosopher turns to his colleague and asks, "I assume you've read Marx." "Yes,"
> replies the sociologist, "I think it's these wicker chairs." (Carr and Greeves
> 2006: 121)

Comment

The phonemic sequence /red mɑːks/ is ambiguous because it can be
represented in written form as either *red marks* or *read Marx*. This is a
case of homophony – only the phonetic forms are the same, not the
written form. This joke presumably works better in speech than in
writing.

Many puns depend on near homophony, or **paronymy**, as in "Every
pun is its own reword" (Tibballs 2006: 282). In fact the less the
coincidence of form the more outrageous and, perhaps, inventive,
the pun seems, though paronymy does have its limits (Attardo
1994: 122).

The following three jokes seem progressively to stretch the phonetic identity on which the pun depends:

> Cheese-makers do it Caerphilly. (Tibballs 2006: 539);

> A Swedish explorer returned from his voyage to the New World, only to find that his name had been removed from his home town register. He complained bitterly to the leader of the town council. After investigating the oversight the council leader apologised, admitting he must have taken Leif off his census. (Tibballs 2006: 596) (cf. *taken leave of his senses*)

> Advice on where to invest your money in troubled times: Bradford and Bingoley; Dalliance and Leicester Gain Fund; Conning, Stinger and Freeloader (the Icelandic bank); Lemon Brothers; Goldman Sucks; Citicorpse.[3]

4.2.3. Homography

We might expect joke books to feature homograph-based jokes more than homophone-based ones, but in those sourced for this textbook this was not the case (cf. Ritchie 2004: 138). The scarcity of homograph-based puns indicates that jokes are basically an oral genre, and only read wholesale in print to be retailed later to friends in conversation. Nevertheless, here is one: "Why are disabled parking spaces always empty?" "Because their users have invalid parking permits."

Some jokes depend upon homographs that are near homonyms. "How different professions lose their jobs: Cashiers get distilled; Dry-cleaners get depressed." In the first case phonetic difference lies in the syllable boundary: /dɪ-ˈstɪld/ versus /dɪs-ˈtɪld/. In the second case the difference depends upon stress, so that there is a full form, a stressed /diː/ in the nonce form, rather than the reduced form of the familiar lexeme /dɪ/, an alternation commonly used in puns: "When the electricity at a school went off during a storm the students were delighted."

The notion of homography as a basis for jokes can also be extended to almost overlap with homonymy through different stress placements, as of "from" in the following: "An Essex girl is involved in a bad traffic accident. A paramedic rushes to her aid. 'Whereabouts are you bleeding from?' he asks. 'Well, since you ask,' the girl replies, 'from bleeding Romford'" (Carr and Greeves 2006: 219).

Another kind of near homography (paragraphy?) occurs in jokes like "the pen is mightier than the penis", where the form is identical, apart from the white space between "pen" and "is". We already identified these as a kind of deliberately false folk-etymology.

Despite the paucity of homograph-based jokes, graphological form might be used for humorous purposes, to give an added motivation (iconicity, 8.2) to the text (Alexander 1997: 21–2), e.g. Lewis Carroll's 'A Mouse's Tale' in *Alice in Wonderland*, or

TOO MUCH SEX   Yo-yos
Makes you   rule
Short-sighted   O

           –

           –
           K

4.3. PRESUPPOSITION

"X **presupposes** y" means 'if x is true, y is assumed to be true, and if the negation of x is true, y is still assumed to be true'. So if "My brother is at home" is true, then "I have a brother" is assumed to be true, and if "My brother is *not* at home" is true, then "I have a brother" is still assumed to be true. Moreover, one can apply the interrogative test: if I ask "Is my brother at home?" then "I have a brother" is assumed to be true. In other words, presuppositions are "the statements that must be true in order for the sentence to be true or false" (Attardo 1994: 185).

The difference between presuppositions and entailments, as predicted from the above test, is that presuppositions remain constant under negation (and in interrogative form), while entailments do not. So "John's dog was killed" entails "John's dog died" and presupposes "John has a dog", whereas "John's dog was not killed" does not entail "John's dog died" but still presupposes "John has a dog".

> **Activity 4.5**
>
> One of the sentences (b) and (c) is entailed by (a). The other one is presupposed by (a). Which is which?
>
>   a. I always manage to wake up at the crack of ice.
>   b. I always wake up at the crack of ice.
>   c. I always try to wake up at the crack of ice.

Comment

If we negate (a) we get "I don't always manage to wake up at the crack of ice". If that is true, then (b) cannot be true, so (b) is an entailment of (a). But if "I don't always manage to wake up at the crack of ice" is true, (c) is still assumed to be true, so that (c) must be a presupposition of (a).

We look at ten kinds of presupposition, as defined by the grammatical structures and lexical semantics that trigger them (Levinson 1983). First we have existential presupposition, presupposing that something/someone exists/will exist/did exist, which is triggered by definite noun phrases:

> John can see the child with twelve toes >> There is a child with twelve toes
> (the symbol >> means 'presupposes').

Existential presuppositions can have very strong manipulative force, especially when used in conjunction with nominalisation (3.7):

a. The intense competition among newly industrialising economies has put downward pressure on wages.
b. >> There is intense competition among newly industrialising economies.
c. >> Newly industrialising economies are competing intensely.

The presupposed proposition in (a) is, by definition, difficult for a hearer to negate or to question, compared with (b) or the denominalised (c).

Secondly, and perhaps as a subclass of the existential, we have possessive presuppositions. They arise when we use 's (or *of*) to indicate possession, or the pronominal "adjectives" *hers/his, their, my, our, your*. For instance "Don't accept your dog's admiration as conclusive evidence of your wonderful character" presupposes >> "You have a dog" and "Your dog has admiration [for X]", "You have a wonderful character".

Activity 4.6

What are the existential and possessive presuppositions in the following sentence?

The weirdest thing on the show was the guy that married his horse, and the horse wasn't even that attractive. (Jerry Springer, Tibballs 2006: 457)

Comment
>> "there is/was/will be a show"
>> "there is/was/will be a weirdest thing on the show"
>> "there was a guy that married his horse"
>> "there is/was/will be a guy"
>> "the guy has/had/will have a horse"

Clearly existential/possessive presuppositions are an economical way of establishing a schema/frame, as in "the show" and "his horse", and in this case bringing together two incongruous schemas for marriage and horse. This is before the real incongruity is achieved in the last clause, where the speaker chooses to ignore the first incongruity. There is an additional presuppositional incongruity in the fact that the most surprising clash of schemas (marriage and horses) is assumed and not stated.

Thirdly, change of state verbs. Any verb which indicates a change of activity, state or location carries with it a presupposition:

A stopped/finished/continued doing X >> A had been doing X
A started/began doing X >> A had not been doing X
A left Y >> A was at/with Y
A arrived at Y >> A was not at Y

For example in Reagan's "I have orders to be awakened at any time in the case of a national emergency, even if I'm in a cabinet meeting", the verb "awaken" carries the change of state presupposition "was asleep"! Or in "Television has brought murder back into the home, where it belongs" (Alfred Hitchcock, Tibballs 2006: 456), "brought back" involves two change-of-state presuppositions: "murder was not in the home" and "murder had been in the home".

The fourth kind of presupposition is triggered by factive verbs. These presuppose that the statement made in the clause they introduce is true or a fact, e.g. *regret, be aware, realise, be odd that, know, be sorry that, be proud that, be glad that, be amazed that.* For instance, "They say such nice things about people at their funerals that it makes me sad that I'm going to miss mine by just a few days" (Garrison Keillor, Tibballs 2006: 446) >> "I'm going to miss my funeral by a few days".

Fifthly, and in contrast with these, are counterfactual conditionals, using the past perfective tense, which presuppose the falsity of the clause. "If A had done X, Y wouldn't have happened" >> "A did not do X". And "If A hadn't done X, Y wouldn't have happened" >> "A did do X". For example, "If I had stood unopposed at the last election, I would still have come second" (John Major, Tibballs 2006: 455) presupposes "He [John Major] did not stand unopposed at the last election". Such a statement also seems to presuppose "I came second", though, strictly speaking, it does not pass the negation test. Note that the tense/aspect is crucial in triggering this kind of presupposition. "If I stood unopposed in the last election ..." is non-factive, presupposing "I may or may not have stood unopposed in the last election".

Sixthly, there are implicative verbs, e.g. *manage* >> *try, forgot to* >> *ought to have/intended to, X happened to A* >> *A didn't intend or plan X,* e.g. "First you forget names. Then you forget faces. Next you forget to pull your zipper up, and finally you forget to pull it down" (George Burns, Tibballs 2006: 3) >> "You ought to pull your zipper up, you ought to pull your zipper down".

Seventhly, there are temporal clauses introduced by subordinating conjunctions: *before/since/when Z* >> *Z happened/happens; while Z* >> *Z was/is happening; whenever Z* >> *Z happens regularly,* e.g. "Sign of old age: whenever you fall asleep people think you are dead" >> "you regularly fall asleep".

The eighth kind of trigger is the cleft construction. Instead of using one clause *A didn't do Z, A isn't/wasn't Z*, we can add a cleft clause construction or thematic equative to make it two clauses: *It wasn't A that did Z* or *It isn't A that is Z*. This presupposes *someone/something (else) did/is Z*. For instance, "It isn't the streets in Philadelphia that are dangerous …" >> "something else is dangerous". Even with the non-cleft equivalent it is possible in speech to convey this presupposition by putting contrastive nuclear tone on the subject of the sentence:

Old A̬GE isn't so bad [when you consider the alternative].

Discussion

Does this kind of presupposition pass the negation/interrogative test? Is it therefore a presupposition?

Related to this contrastive presupposition is the ninth kind of trigger, involving comparison and contrast constructions: *A is a better C than B is* >> *A is a C and B is a C*: "Federer is a better tennis player than Murray" >> "Federer and Murray are tennis players". Or *A does/has more X* >> *A already did/had some X*: "John didn't eat any more food" >> "John already ate some food". In *As You Like It* a starving Orlando interrupts the Duke's meal in the forest of Arden with the hostile injunction: "Forbear and eat no more!" to which Jacques replies, deflating his bravado, "Why I have ate none yet". Other words implying comparison or contrast, such as *other, also, another, not … either* would appear to generate similar presuppositions. Superlative forms of adjectives do so too: "'You will have the tallest darkest leading man in Hollywood.' Those are the first words I heard about King Kong" (Fay Wray, Tibballs 2006: 451) >> "There are other tall, dark, leading men in Hollywood".

Activity 4.7

What comparative presuppositions can you detect in the following humorous utterances? Do they also help to generate inferences?

1. The hotel has bowling alleys, tennis courts, comfortable beds and other athletic facilities. (Tibballs 2006: 493)
2. He had his eyebrows plucked, so now he's got nothing in front of his eyes either. (Jack Dee on David Beckham, Tibballs 2006: 650)
3. A sign of getting old: your ears are hairier than your head.
4. Do you realise that man is the only animal that chews the ice in its drinks? (Morreall 1983: 78)

Comment

In (1) "beds" are presupposed to be one kind of athletic facility. This might imply a very active sex life for those "sleeping" in them. (2), with a contrastive nuclear tone on "FRONT" in conjunction with "either", presupposes "he has nothing behind his eyes", i.e. no brain. (3) presupposes "your ears are hairy and your head is hairy". (4) seems to presuppose that "other animals have ice in their drinks".

Tenth, and last, we have non-restrictive (non-defining) relative clauses: "Television has brought murder back into the home, where it belongs" (Alfred Hitchcock, Tibballs 2006: 456) presupposes "murder belongs in the home".

4.4. *MEANING OPPOSITIONS*

Central to the enterprise of formal semantics, the attempt to apply logic to meaning illustrated above, was the notion of systems of oppositions. The idea, inherited from Saussure, the founder of modern linguistics, was that lexis and grammar do not achieve their meanings in isolation but by forming sets or systems of mutually exclusive options. The intimation here is that in a system, for example the system of starring hotels, 2-star, 3-star, 4-star and 5-star (6-star and 7-star in China and Dubai?), the meaning of the terms is not so much a positive one as negative: 'not the meanings of the other terms in the system'. For instance 3* means 'not 2* not 4* not 5* (not 6* not 7*)'.

In terms of grammatical meaning systems we might, for example, recall the transitivity system of process types from the last chapter (Figure 4.2). In terms of the meanings of lexical items within lexical sets, we might, for instance, say that 'single', 'married', 'separated', 'divorced', 'widowed' form a system of oppositions, so that *single* means

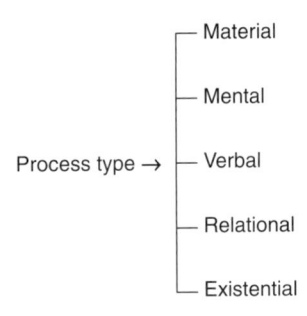

Figure 4.2. The process-type system

'not married, not separated, not divorced, not widowed'. While this idea is attractive, semantic fields or lexical sets do not incorporate such quite neat systems as hotel-starring systems. Lexical sets are less finite and are made less stable by new lexis. For instance, someone might invent a new term 'widowered' to apply to men who have lost their wives. And would the addition of any one new lexical item to a lexical set really cause a change in the meanings of all the other items in the lexical set?

Nevertheless, the idea of oppositions within a system was an important starting point for semantics. And below I shall discuss the traditional kinds of meaning opposition: binary oppositions and complementarity, multiple taxonomies and incompatibility, gradable opposites or polar oppositions, and converses, before exploring the rather abstract systems of meaning relations – transitive/non-transitive/intransitive and symmetrical/non-symmetrical/asymmetrical.

An initial point is that it is generally quite difficult to find antonyms or opposites (in the non-technical sense) for the meanings of nouns. This is because nouns represent bundles of properties/features rather than single properties, so the "opposite" might be the opposite in terms of any one of these properties. For example, using the features of [MALE] and [ADULT] to define meaning (see Figure 4.1), is the opposite of 'man' 'boy' or 'woman'? Is the opposite of 'girl' 'boy' or 'woman'? etc. etc. Paradoxically "opposites" have to be "close" in meaning. Otherwise 'girl' could be a better antonym for 'man' than 'boy' or 'woman' because it contrasts on two features not just one.

It has been suggested that, because of this paradoxical closeness in meaning of opposites (cf. Alm-Arvius 2009), punning with opposites achieves a kind of economy of mental expenditure close to repetition (Fonagy 1982: 51). Peter, a young boy whom his parents were encouraging to cook, tried cooking burgers, but his parents didn't enjoy them. When offered a second burger, his father said "Could you spare me another one?" meaning either 'give me one more' or 'allow me to avoid another one'. "Ends" in 20-YEAR FRIENDSHIP ENDS AT ALTAR can either mean 'reaches its natural conclusion' or 'ceases completely'. In addition to *end* and *spare*, the English word-forms *scatter* and *sanction* are antonymically ambiguous in this way. For *scatter*, "The new Head of the Department scattered fear and gloom", can mean either 'spread around' or 'dispel'. For *sanction*, "Imports to North Korea have now been sanctioned" can mean 'allowed' or 'prohibited'. The traditional label for this phenomenon is the Latin phrase: *lucus a non lucendo*, meaning 'A [dark] grove, by not shining'. It claims to exemplify what it labels, though it is, in fact, a false etymology.

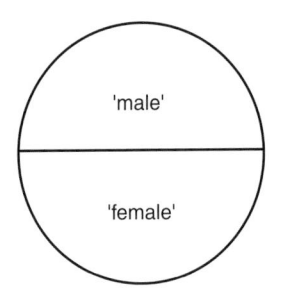

Figure 4.3. A semantic field of binary opposition

There are also pairs of nouns which are both ambiguous, such that they appear to be opposite in one meaning, but are not in another: "Buy old masters. They fetch a better price than old mistresses" (Lord Beaverbrook, Tibballs 2006: 443).

4.4.1. Binary oppositions and complementarity

We can find opposites more easily when there are only two mutually exclusive possibilities of properties for describing things in the world: the meanings 'dead' and 'alive', 'male' and 'female' are generally used in this way. If a thing or person is one, they cannot be the other. In other words, "Jean is male" and "Jean is female" are inconsistent statements. But more than this, if a thing or person is not one, they must be the other: if you're not alive you must be dead, if not male you must be female.

We can diagram this by suggesting that there is a semantic field – let's call it 'sex' or 'state of physical animation' – represented by a circle. And this is divided into only two categories with no overlap. So the semantic field of sex could be portrayed as in Figure 4.3.

This meaning relation is called **complementarity**; 'male' and 'female' are **complementaries**, or they are examples of **binary opposition** (Leech 1981: 99).

Activity 4.8

When Dan Quayle said "If we don't succeed we run the risk of failure" (Tibballs 2006: 510) why was this seen as a humorously obtuse statement?

Comment

Presumably it seemed stupid because 'failure' and 'success' are complementaries, where not succeeding must mean failing. So that "run the risk" looks like an understatement.

Consider the following extract from the 2007 film *The Duchess*.

FOX: We would like to see the vote extended ...
GEORGIANA: To *all* men ...?
FOX: Heavens no. But certainly to *more* men. Freedom in
                        moderation.
GEORGIANA: "Freedom in moderation".
FOX (*pleased with himself*):   Precisely.

GEORGIANA nods, then smiles faintly, but mischievously

GEORGIANA: I am sure you are full of the best intentions, Mr Fox, but I dare
                        say I would not spend my vote – assuming I had it – on so
                        vague a statement. Either one is free or one is not. The concept
                        of freedom is absolute. After all one cannot be moderately
                        dead, moderately loved, or moderately free. It must always
                        remain a matter of either or.

The Duchess tries to extend complementarity from the obvious binary
opposition 'alive'/'dead' to 'loved'/'unloved' and 'free'/'not free'. In fact
there may be three or more terms in these latter oppositions rather
than two.

4.4.2. Multiple taxonomies and incompatibility

Indeed, binary opposition is not the only kind of opposition. Sometimes a semantic field divides into more than two meanings, giving
multiple oppositions or taxonomies. Consider the meanings of fruits:
'orange', 'apple', 'banana', 'strawberry', 'peach', 'pear' etc. etc. As with
complementaries, these meanings are mutually exclusive: if X is an
orange, X cannot be a pear; in other words: "X is an orange" and "X is a
pear" are incompatible, inconsistent statements. But because there are
more than two terms in the system we cannot say "If X is not an
orange, X must be a pear". These oppositions or taxonomies involve a
relation of **multiple incompatibility** (Leech 1981: 100). Or they are
examples of a **multiple taxonomy**, which could be diagrammed as:

'orange'	'apple'	'banana'	'strawberry'	'peach'	'pear'	'mango'	etc.

Activity 4.9

Analyse this famous utterance of Donald Rumsfeld in terms of complementarity and
incompatibility, i.e. the use of binary or multiple oppositions. "Osama bin Laden
is either alive and well, or alive and not too well, or not alive" (Donald Rumsfeld,
Tibballs 2006: 509).

Comment

At least on the surface Rumsfeld seems to combine two binary oppositions:

(1) Well/not too well and (2) alive/not alive

However, one might somehow amalgamate these into a kind of multiple (3-way) opposition at two levels (Figure 4.4.):

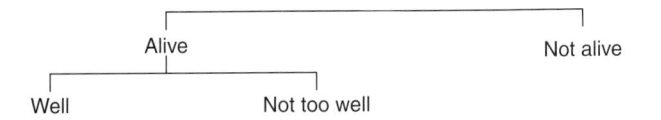

Figure 4.4. Rumsfeld's anomalous meaning oppositions

Discussion

As of December 2009, eunuchs in India are allowed to put "other" rather than "male" or "female" on their identity cards. Does this development provide evidence for the permeability of the line dividing World from Meaning in Figure 1.2? How?

4.4.3. Gradable opposites or polar oppositions

With adjectives in particular we sense that the oppositeness involves points on or near the end of a scale. 'Hot' and 'cold', for example, are not binary oppositions, as there are intermediate positions on the scale, involving finer gradations.

| Scalding | Hot | Warm | Lukewarm | Cool | Cold | Freezing |
| Scorching | | | Tepid | | | |

And Rumsfeld's Osama bin Laden comment 'not too well' represents a mid-point between 'well' and 'unwell', even though Rumsfeld constructs this as a binary opposition. (An alternative interpretation might be that he is using "not too well" as an understatement for 'unwell'.)

One test for **gradable antonymy** is whether adverbial modifiers like *extremely, somewhat* can be used, e.g. *extremely unwell*. Another test is whether you can use comparatives, e.g. *hotter, very hot*. Note that once one reaches the adjectives at the more distant ends of the scale, it is impossible to use these modifiers and comparatives: *very/more scalding, *very/more freezing. Even so, a financial pundit on

Hong Kong's RTHK radio 3 proclaimed, in response to the run on the Bank of East Asia: "Hong Kong has a very perfect banking system" (24 September 2008). That sounds as distinctly anomalous as the headline LEGISLATOR WANTS TOUGHER DEATH PENALTY (US paper, Tibballs 2006: 505): the death penalty would already seem the most extreme point of toughness. (However, some death penalties cause more suffering than others: humane means of killing, like nitrous oxide (laughing gas) combined with other lethal gas, have been rejected by neo-cons as too pleasurable.)

Three aspects of gradable adjectives have been noted in the literature. First, there is generally a **marked** and **unmarked** member of the pair. The unmarked, that is the more normal, salient or frequent word will be used in questions, e.g. "How tall is he?" not "How short is he?" and "Is it big?" not "Is it small?"

Second, their meanings are rather **vague**, that is the boundaries of the concepts are unclear. What exact temperature corresponds to the meaning 'warm'? Linked to this vagueness is the third feature: **semantic relativity**. This means the range which they cover is not absolute but relative to the norm for the entity referred to by the noun they modify. 'Cold' means something different in relation to drinking water, perhaps 4 °C, from what it means in relation to food, perhaps 20 °C. Similarly a big dog is smaller than a small elephant (Leech 1981: 101–2).[4]

Activity 4.10

Explain how gradability and complementarity contribute to the oddness of this examination howler and the pigs' well-known slogan in Orwell's *Animal Farm*:

   a. A fossil is an extinct animal. The older it is the more extinct it is. (Tibballs 2006: 666)
   b. All animals are equal; but some are more equal than others.

Comment

   a. 'Old' is a scalar concept, whereas 'extinct' is non-gradable, part of a binary opposition with its complementary, something like 'living' 'existing' or 'extant'. This examinee superimposes the scalar on the binary opposition, to make 'extinct' gradable.
   b. 'Equal' is not a gradable concept, but rather forms a complementary with 'unequal' (cf. 'odd' and 'even'). To pretend otherwise is to attempt to change the meaning of EQUAL to fit the unequal relations between the pigs and other animals, while maintaining that this represents equality.

4.4.4. Converses

Converseness is a meaning opposition involving the relationship between two entities, so that it is often associated with verbs or prepositional/adjectival constructions. Using X and Y to represent semantic relations, it can be formulated thus: if it is the case that when A X B is true then B Y A must be true, and vice versa, then X and Y are converses. For example, if "The cup contains coffee" is true, then "Coffee is in the cup" is true, and vice versa. Therefore 'to contain' and 'to be in' are converses (Leech 1981: 103).

Sometimes converses involve three entities (things/people), e.g.

John	bought the monkey from	Elaine
Elaine	sold the monkey to	John

Since the third entity, the monkey, is irrelevant to this reversal we can still say that 'buy' and 'sell' are converses.

> **Activity 4.11**
>
> Does the intended meaning of the headline VACCINE MAY CONTAIN RABIES involve one member of a converse pair?

Comment

The intended meaning of "contain" is clearly not the converse of "be in", i.e. the intended meaning cannot be paraphrased "rabies is in the vaccine". Rather the meaning intended is 'a vaccine may restrict the spread of rabies'.

4.4.5. Symmetry and transitivity

Having discussed relational opposites or converses, it is appropriate to introduce the meaning relations of symmetry and transitivity (Leech 1981: 104–5). Unlike converses, these concern the meaning of single expressions rather than pairs of expressions. Regarding symmetry, the question to ask is: if "A X B" is true, is it necessarily true that "B X A"? For instance, if A is next to B, it is necessarily true that B is next to A. This illustrates the relation of **symmetry**. Suppose another case: if "A X B" is true, "B X A" cannot be true, for example, if A is behind B, it cannot be true that B is behind A. Here X expresses the relation of **asymmetry**. In a third case, if "A X B" is true, it may or may not be the case that "B X A", so that if A is the sister of B, then B may be the sister of A, but perhaps not: maybe B is the brother of A. In this case X expresses the relation of **non-symmetry**.

One can interpret the slogan "all animals are equal, but some are more equal than others" as an attempt to force asymmetry on what is conceptually a symmetric relationship. If A is equal to B, then B is equal to A, which is symmetrical. But if X is more Y than Z, then Z cannot be more Y than X, which makes Y an asymmetrical relation (cf. Fonagy 1982: 46).

Activity 4.12

In the following dialogue (from Norrick 1993: 89) Patricia seems to have a different meaning for the word *belong* from her children Amy, Mary and Ralph. Explain the two different meanings in terms of converseness and symmetry. You might consider the meaning of *own*.

PATRICIA:	There's a red pen on the couch. Who belongs to it?
AMY, MARY, RALPH:	{all giggle}
MARY:	Who belongs to the red pen, Mom.
PATRICIA:	The kitten's playing with it. She's shoving it all over.
AMY:	And it's open.
MARY:	Well, I guess the kitten be*longs* to the red pen. Huh huh hehehe.

Comment

Patricia uses the word *belong to* as though it expresses a symmetrical relation. So if "The pen belongs to me" is true then "I belong to the pen" is true. However, the more normal usage, familiar to the three children, has 'belong to', in the sense 'is the property of', as a converse of 'own'. If the kitten owns the pen, the pen belongs to the kitten.

A second logical relation between entities is called **transitivity**, not to be confused with the grammatical notion of transitivity (3.5–6). With a predicate expressing a **transitive** relation X, if "A X B" is true, and "B X C" is true, then "A X C" must be true. Thus, if Paul is taller than John, and John is taller than Daniel, then Paul must be taller than Daniel. Here is another example: "A stale pretzel is better than nothing. Nothing is better than God. Therefore, a stale pretzel is better than God" (Morreall 1983: 74).

In a second case, if "A X B" is true, and "B X C" is true, then "A X C" cannot be true. For example, if Mary is the mother of Amanda, and Amanda is the mother of Louise, then Mary cannot be the mother of Louise. Here X expresses an **intransitive** relation. In the third case if "A X B" is true, and "B X C" is true, then "A X C" may or may not be true. So that if Paul hates Mary and Mary hates Bill, Paul may or may not hate Bill. Here X expresses a **non-transitive** relation.

So far we have considered "horizontal" meaning oppositions, complementarity, multiple incompatibility and converseness. We now explore conceptual meanings' "vertical" or general–specific structuring.

4.5. HYPONYMY

The inclusion of one specific meaning within a more general meaning is the sense relation of **hyponymy**. The more specific meaning is called the **hyponym**, the more general meaning the **superordinate** (or hyperonym). For example, 'apple' is the hyponym of 'fruit', and 'fruit' is the superordinate of 'apple', as in Figure 4.5.

Mathematically, in this figure the set of objects conventionally referred to through the meaning of the word *apple* is a subset of the set of objects conventionally referred to through the meaning of the word *fruit*. (This is not strictly correct, because hyponymy is a relationship between meanings not objects, a matter of sense not reference.)

'Fruit' will have other hyponyms besides 'apple', e.g. 'pear', 'strawberry', 'orange'. 'Pear', 'strawberry', 'orange' are therefore **co-hyponyms** of 'fruit', as in Figure 4.6.

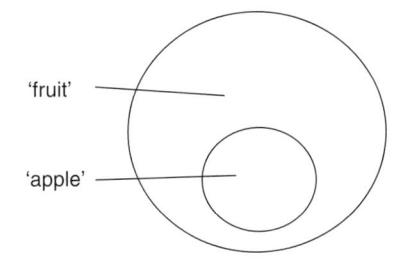

'fruit'

'apple'

Figure 4.5. A diagram of hyponymy

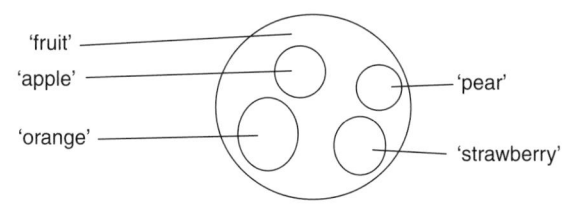

Figure 4.6. A diagram of co-hyponymy

Activity 4.13

How can the concept of hyponymy help us to explain the strangeness of the following extracts from a news report and ad?

1. Four people and Congressman Ryan were killed. (US newscaster, Tibballs 2006: 511)
2. I don't wear jeans. I wear Harley-Davidson jeans.

Comment

In both cases the normal hyponymic classification is dispensed with. In (1) apparently 'Congressman' is not a hyponym of person, suggesting sub-human (?superhuman) status. (2) seems to claim that 'Harley-Davidson jeans' is not a hyponym of 'jeans'; presumably they are so exceptionally better and distinctive that they are in a class of their own.

One way of testing for hyponymy is with the *kind-of* test. If X *is a kind of* Y, then the meaning of X is the hyponym of the meaning of Y, or more simply 'X' is the hyponym of 'Y'. However, a number of problems emerge with this test, because *kind of* can also be used to signal metaphor, as in "a glove is a kind of sock", and approximation, as in "turquoise is a kind of green". Despite such ambiguities the *kind-of* test is useful for detecting hyponymy if the phrase means 'X is one member of the class of Ys'.

Hyponymic chains, especially the meanings of nouns, can be quite long, even longer if technical terms are included in the hyponymic chain. The database WordNet (http://wordnetweb.princeton.edu/perl/webwn) demonstrates the complexity of such chains in the English lexicon. Here is an example: 'concrete'– 'animate'– 'animal'– 'mammal'– 'dog'– 'terrier'– 'Maltese terrier'.

Hyponymy has an important use in technical definitions. If successful, these indicate the superordinate class or classifier, and the distinguisher, which separates the meaning from the other members of that class, the co-hyponyms. For example, "A bicycle is a vehicle with two wheels which you ride by sitting on it and pushing two pedals with your feet" (Hudson

1995: 25). These criteria for a decent definition make the following totally inadequate: "A committee is an animal with four back legs". 'Animal' is not the superordinate for 'committee', nor is 'with four back legs' a useful distinguisher. Rather, it describes a committee metaphorically, as incapable of setting and reaching goals (lacking front legs, it cannot determine the direction in which the animal moves).[5]

Hyponymy is put to work in the meaning of proverbs, where the specific example is a colourful hyponymic instance of their meaning. "Don't count your chickens before they are hatched" is a hyponym of "Don't rely on a successful outcome before it has occurred".

Activity 4.14

Explain how the following joke depends upon a hyponymic relationship between what is said and what is meant.

A car dealer boasting about a new sports model to a prospective client:
"You get into this car at midnight and at 4 o'clock you are in Grimsby."
"What would I be doing in the middle of the night in Grimsby?" (Koestler, after Freud, quoted in Fonagy 1982: 43)

Comment

The trip to Grimsby is the car dealer's hypothetical example of how far the car can travel in four hours. The customer interprets it as a real suggestion. The dealer intends to convey a superordinate meaning by the example, whereas the customer interprets it in its literal hyponymic meaning.

Conversely, using superordinates instead of hyponyms can be a very effective technique of satire. Simpson (2003: 132–4) illustrates this with an extract from the satirical magazine *Private Eye*, targeting the tabloid press's revelations about Prince Harry's drug-taking and alcohol consumption:

World Exclusive to All Papers
Teenager Smoked Pot and had too Much to Drink
BY OUR ENTIRE STAFF

A 16-year-old boy went several times to a pub and smoked a joint in a shed outside *(Reuters)*

INSIDE

- That teenage boy story in full 2–6
- Hundreds of pics of teenage boy 7–8
- Blurred pics of boy's friends 9

The foregrounded choice of superordinates, rather than more specific hyponyms (or even more specific names) is incongruous in this particular discourse type, where identification by name and title is usually *de rigueur*. This attenuation, by giving less information than required, suggests that such behaviour is hardly newsworthy of boys in general, and therefore satirises the tabloid press's obsession with this particular boy's behaviour as both extreme and misplaced.

4.6.   MERONYMY AND SYNECDOCHE

Meronymy expresses a part–whole relation, e.g. 'wheel' is a meronym of 'bicycle' as are 'saddle', 'handlebars', 'pedals' etc., but involves relations in the real world (column 3 W of Figure 1.2) rather than sense relations (column 2 M). Meronymic relationships can operate at several levels (Figure 4.7). Dependent on meronymy is the figure of speech **synecdoche**: using a meronymic term to refer to the whole, e.g. "How much is this tour package per *head*?", meaning 'How much is this tour package per *person*?'

Sometimes hyponymy and meronymy are confused, possibly because the spatial metaphor of Venn diagrams, as in Figures 4.5 and 4.6, misleads us into thinking that the smaller circles are "part of" the meaning of the larger circles.

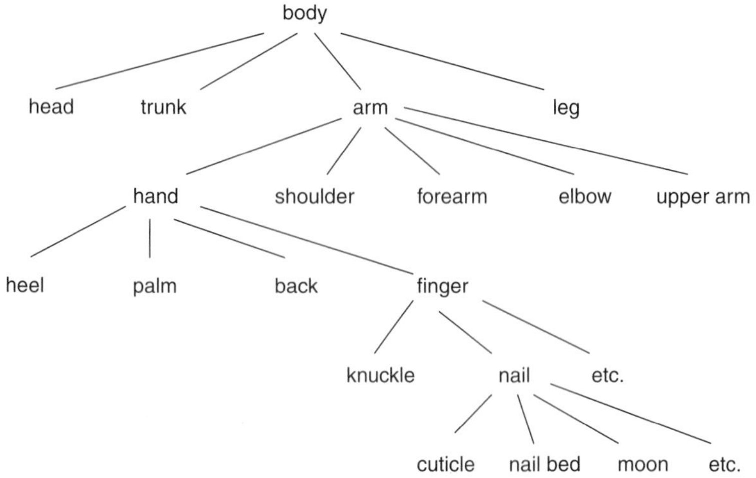

Figure 4.7. Multiple levels of meronymy

4.7. COMPONENTIAL ANALYSIS

A theory prevalent in the 1960s and 1970s held that the relationships between logical meanings, sense relations, can be usefully explored by **componential analysis**, that is, decomposing the meaning of words into smaller features or components of meaning as in Figure 4.1. The argument for componential analysis is that it shows the systematic analogies between meanings, for example: 'lamb', 'puppy', 'kitten', 'fawn', 'cygnet' versus 'sheep', 'dog', 'cat', 'deer', 'swan', the relevant contrast being [− ADULT] (Leech 1981). The same kind of analysis may be applied to the meanings of verbs using features like CAUSE: 'show' = [CAUSE ANOTHER TO SEE], 'find' = [CAUSE ONESELF TO SEE], 'kill' = [CAUSE TO DIE].

> **Activity 4.15**
>
> Could one use componential analysis to distinguish the meanings of 'chair', 'sofa', 'bench' and 'stool'? How many such features would be needed in order to successfully distinguish them? What is the superordinate of these co-hyponyms? And what might be the superordinate of that superordinate?

Comment

Three features seem to be sufficient to distinguish the four meanings (Table 4.2).
I suppose 'seat' is the superordinate of 'chair', 'stool', 'bench' etc. and 'furniture' is the superordinate of 'seat'.

Discussion

How sure are you of these features? And was there any disagreement on whether these features apply to the meaning, or about which features to use?

There are obvious problems in using a binary system to assign features to meanings. Typically stools are not upholstered, but bar stools and piano stools sometimes are, and some piano stools can accommodate two people playing pieces for four hands (and in some

Table 4.2. *Componential analysis of hyponyms of 'seat'*

	'sofa'	'bench'	'chair'	'stool'
# of sitters	[−1 SITTER]	[− 1 SITTER]	[+ 1 SITTER]	[+ (?) 1 SITTER]
upholstery	[+ UPHOLSTERY]	[− UPHOLSTERY]	[+/− UPHOLSTERY]	[+/− UPHOLSTERY]
back support	[+ BACK]	[+/− BACK]	[+ BACK]	[(+)− BACK]

dialects are called *piano benches*). If the "benches" in Parliament were not upholstered, how could MPs so routinely sleep on them? So these semantic features and the meanings they represent must be some kind of generalisation from our experience of referents, and the meanings we acquire in the Meaning column of Figure 1.2 depend upon repeated experience of the relationship between Form and World.

One model of language acquisition that chimes well with these observations is Putnam's theory of **ostensive reference** (Putnam 1975). He hypothesised that the referential scope of terms for natural objects and substances like *water* and *gold* are fixed ostensively, rather than through conventional definitions in a dictionary. That is, we are shown (ostension) a number of typical examples (exemplars, prototypes) and from these we form a concept applicable to other phenomena. For instance, once we have seen examples of tennis, football and chess, and heard *game* refer to them, when we see people playing darts, we can recognise and refer to it as a game. The boundaries of these ostensively acquired concepts are established through competition with adjacent concepts, so 'game', for example, will be established in distinction to 'fight', 'sport', etc. (Goatly 2011: 28).

4.7.1. Selection restrictions and componential analysis

Componential analysis, besides defining meaning relationships between individual lexical items, can be used to explain semantic anomalies. For traditional semantics, in the lexical component of the grammar, every verb (predicate) has, of course, its own componential feature specification. But, in addition, the lexical entry specifies what kinds of componential features the subject and object of the verb must possess for a clause to be semantically well formed. These are called its **selection restrictions**. So 'kill' has its own semantic specification [CAUSE [−ALIVE]] but, in addition stipulates its subject or actor is concrete and its object or goal animate [Subject, +CONCRETE; Object, +ANIMATE]. This rules out semantically ill-formed clauses (asterisked), e.g. *"Mysticism killed the sheep", *"John killed the stone", with their abstract subject and inanimate object, respectively. Compare this with the verb 'murder' [+KILL +DELIBERATE + UNLAWFUL]. Here the selection restrictions on the verb are [Subject +HUMAN; Object +HUMAN], ruling out *"The snake murdered Paul" and *"John murdered the horse".

Activity 4.16

"In Pierre Elliott Trudeau, Canada has at last produced a political leader worthy of assassination" (Irving Layton, Tibballs 2006: 648).

How might the above joke point to the selection restrictions for the verb *assassinate*?

Comment
> The selection restrictions for 'assassinate' are stricter than those for 'murder'– the victim of assassination, the object or goal of the verb *assassinate*, should be [+FAMOUS].

The concepts of hyponymy and componential analysis relate systematically to the basic logical relations between statements – entailment, inconsistency (incompatibility), contradiction and tautology. Entailment relates to hyponymy: "This piece of furniture is a chair" entails "This piece of furniture is a seat". It also relates to semantic components: "This piece of furniture is a chair" entails "This piece of furniture has a back". Inconsistency relates to incompatibility or co-hyponymy: "This piece of furniture is a chair" is inconsistent with "This piece of furniture is a sofa". Contradiction relates to semantic components and selection restrictions: "Chairs have no backs" and "The chair coughed" are contradictions; and to hyponymy: "Chairs are not seats" is a contradiction. Tautology relates to semantic components: "Chairs have backs" is a tautology; and to hyponymy: "Chairs are seats" is a tautology.

4.7.2. Selection restrictions and coherence of a text?

Attardo (1994: 68–9, 76) has suggested that we make a text by establishing an **isotopy**, a coherent schema or script that accounts for the meanings of a text. In non-humorous texts isotopy is a way of eliminating ambiguity, and selection restrictions have an important role to play because they are one kind of redundant or repeated semantic feature. But selection restrictions, like other aspects of meaning, are not as solid and invariant in real texts as in the abstract lexicon. Consider Tabossi's comments on the following sentences:

> 1. She sat on a tomato. 2. She likes tomatoes. 3. Her face was like a tomato.

"Most people would agree that different aspects of what one knows about tomatoes come to mind in the three sentences, namely tomatoes are squashy in sentence 1, they are food in sentence 2, and they are red in sentence 3 ... the saliency of the different aspects of an unambiguous word is affected by the sentence in which it occurs" (Tabossi 1989: 26).

Whatever the interplay between the abstract selection restrictions and co-text, they certainly have a role in establishing a coherent schema (isotopy). The distinctive feature of jokes is that they oppose one salient isotopical schema against another less salient one.

4.8.   SENSE RELATIONS IN THE DICTIONARY AND IN A TEXT

Activity 4.17

1. Look at this sensational report from the Singapore tabloid the *New Paper* (Monday 22 January 1996, p. 3) and identify superordinates and hyponyms which are found (created?) in the text. It has been suggested that word meanings can belong to a number of different superordinate classes according to context. Could any of these hyponyms be assigned to different superordinates in a different context?

2. Consider the other kinds of sense-relation/meaning opposition, besides hyponymy, the text displays, i.e. meronymy, complementarity (binary opposition), multiple incompatibility (multiple taxonomy), gradable antonymy (and perhaps converseness). Consider the semantic fields of Litter/Rubbish, Time, People, and any others you think significant.

She picks up your RUBBISH

(1) Madam Lim Quee Tin, 45, gets mad when she sees people littering. (2) The reason? (3) She is a cleaner with the Singapore Bus Service (SBS). (4) And she has to pick up litter everyday. (5) She works the "graveyard" shift – from 9 p.m. to around 3 a.m. – at the SBS Ang Mo Kio Depot, even on public holidays. (6) A New Paper team went with Madam Lim one night recently on her rounds. (7) On that Friday night, Madam Lim and her 10 male colleagues collected 16 bags of rubbish from buses that were parked at the depot.

SOILED NAPPIES

(8) The rubbish included chicken bones covered with ants, soiled nappies, melted ice-cream and fast food packaging. (9) One dirty double-decker bus also had bus tickets, bits of tissue and foam sticking out of a rear seat on the upper deck. (10) Madam Lim, a mother of two, is paid about $500 a month. (11) Her husband, Mr Lim Soon Tin, 46, an SBS bus driver, said: (12) "Some of my colleagues tell the litterbugs to pick up their litter" (13) But there is always litter said Madam

Lim. (14) "On rainy days, we find wet, mushy cardboard boxes and egg cartons," she added. (15) On weekdays, racing guides and lottery tickets top the litter list, alongside soft drinks cans and sweet wrappers. (16) Seeing the bags of rubbish made this writer wonder how much more litter would be left behind if there had been no stiff $1000 dollar fine or the corrective work order. (17) For the first time I actually felt angry that people could be so inconsiderate and selfish. (18) They leave litter for others like Madam Lim and her colleagues to patiently pick up.

MAMMOTH CLEANING

(19) Madam Lim said that on weekdays and Sundays, she and her team clean up to 488 buses. (20) On Saturdays they clean out more than 500 buses. (21) She said it takes about 15 minutes to clean each bus. (22) The litter-buster has this message for readers: "The next time you feel like throwing away that sweet wrapper or cigarette butt, spare a thought for us".

Comment

1.   Some hyponyms and hyponymic chains in Table 4.3 are relatively unproblematic and reflect de-contextualised dictionary meanings (those in parentheses are problematic). However, the most

      obvious hyponymic relationship created by the text is the list
      of items included in the class of rubbish-litter. Clearly in different
      contexts, or in the dictionary, many of these meanings belong to
      different super-ordinate categories: 'container' – 'can'; 'container' –
      'packaging' – 'box'/'carton'/'wrapper'; 'food' – 'chicken'/'ice-cream'.

2. The most obvious meronyms are 'double-decker bus' – 'rear seat';
      'double-decker bus' – 'upper deck'. But, metaphorically, time is a
      space which can be divided up into parts. This suggests a long
      meronymic chain for time (with the hyponymic chain for kinds of
      day included within it). Note that the meaning of 'day' is here
      'period of 24 hours' rather than its meronym 'hours of daylight':

      'time' – 'month' – 'day' | 'weekday' | 'Friday' | 'Sunday' | 'Saturday' |
      'public holiday' – 'night' – 'graveyard shift'; 'day' – 'minute'

      The text creates a complementary relationship: 'be inconsiderate'/
      'spare a thought'. You either spare a thought for M Lin or you are
      inconsiderate towards her. Other meanings are members of a system
      of multiple incompatibles: 'patient(ly)', 'angry', (synonymous with)
      'mad', etc.; 'pick up', 'throw away', 'leave' etc.; 'weekdays' | 'Sundays' |
      'Saturdays'.

What should emerge from this analysis is that texts often create their
own sense relations at odds with their strict dictionary definitions. This
text, notably, creates various hyponyms for rubbish. And humour can
often extend such tendencies to create anomalous superordinate–
hyponym relations. "What's the odd one out among AIDS, syphilis, herpes,
a Skoda and a Barratts[6] house?" "You can get rid of syphilis" (see also 6.5).

4.9. VAGUE AND FUZZY CONCEPTS

Concepts are inherently vague, since their boundaries are somewhat
ill-defined and variable, or **fuzzy**. There are several reasons for this
fuzziness. Semantic classes in column 2 of our model do not necessarily map clearly onto our experience of phenomena in the world of
column 3 (Figure 1.2). Indeed we often find ourselves searching for an
exact but perhaps non-existent word:

      And she saw that what they missed out of their experiments in magic
      which gave them little or no result, was just the stinky-poo bit, the
      breaking of rules, the using of people, the well-deep wish, the
      piercingness, the – what? (William Golding, *Darkness Visible*, p. 187)

Secondly there may be a problem of overlaps. A quince is part apple, part
pear. A minibus is something intermediate between a car and a bus, or an
SUV something between a minibus and a car (see Figure 4.8). Thirdly, objects
may possess some criteria for membership of classes but lack others. And

Table 4.3. Hyponyms and hyponymic chains in 'She picks up your litter'

People	Time	Rubbish	Work	Bus	Throwing away
people – cleaner – (? litter-buster)	day – weekday – Friday	rubbish – litter – chicken bones, soiled nappies, melted ice-cream, fast food packaging, bus tickets, bits of tissue, cardboard boxes, egg cartons, racing guides, lottery tickets, soft drinks cans, sweet wrappers, cigarette butt (New Paper?!)	work – clean – clean out – (? pick up rubbish)	bus – double-decker bus	throw away – littering
people – colleagues – male colleagues	day – weekday – public holiday				
people – team	day – Sunday				
people – mother	day – Saturday				
people – husband					
people – bus driver					
people – writer					
people – reader					
people – litterbug					

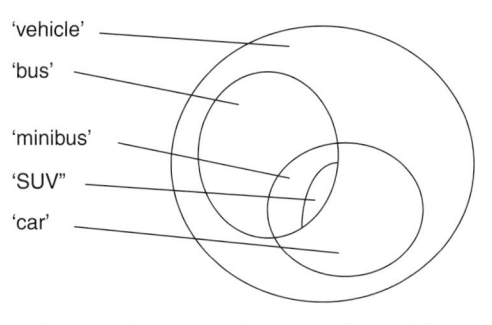

Figure 4.8. Overlapping semantic classes for vehicles

fourthly, speakers may be uncertain, or lack unanimity, about the exact features necessary for an object to qualify as a member of a class and so for that reference to be literal. We noted a symptom of this: the ambiguity of *a kind of* and *a sort of* as marking superordinacy, approximation or metaphor.

Activity 4.18

What features must an object possess in order to literally be called a bottle? What material must it consist of? What shape should it be? What function should it serve? What is it designed to contain? What size can it be? Consider how it is different from a box, a cup, a flask, a jug, a carafe, a phial.

Comment

Suggestions are [+CONTAINER +FOR STORING LIQUIDS +PORTABLE +GLASS/ PLASTIC +NECK +LID/TOP]. However, speakers of English may not agree on which of these features are necessary.

Adrienne Lehrer investigated speakers' concepts for various man-made containers, trying to discover whether they had a clear concept of 'bottle'. The problem was that if all optional components (those considered unnecessary by more than 90 per cent of the informants) were disregarded, there were not enough semantic features left to distinguish the different meanings, e.g. for distinguishing 'bottle' from 'flask'. However, if all optional features, e.g. [+MADE OF GLASS], were made obligatory then a sentence "Some bottles are not made of glass" would be contradictory (Goatly 2011: 20, quoting Lehrer 1974: 85–6).

Discussion

Does this raise the question of what are semantic features of the conceptual meaning and what are acquired through experience of referents (or connotative meaning, see 5.2)? Explain.

4.9.1. Prototypes

One way out of Lehrer's problem was suggested by Eleanor Rosch with her theory of **prototypes**. Psychologically, some members of conceptual classes are more central than others, or some referents of a noun phrase more typical than others. It has been shown, for example, that balls and dolls are more prototypically toys than are swings and skates; basketball is more prototypically a sport than fishing (Rosch 1975; Lakoff 1972: 184). Swings and fishing are marginal members of 'toy' and 'sport'.

Prototype theory suggests, like Putnam, that our concepts of objects result from our history of experience with word-forms and their referents. Speakers of Ghanaian or Singaporean English, with no experience of hot-water bottles, are unlikely to allow [+RUBBER] as a possible feature of bottles.

Schopenhauer saw non-prototypicality as a fundamental technique of humour. When an actor, who had been forbidden to improvise, found the horse he was riding defecating on stage he scolded the horse, "Don't you know we've been forbidden to improvise": defecation by a horse on stage becomes a non-prototypical member of the class of improvisations (Chafe 2007: 145–6).

4.9.2. Radial categories

Lakoff (1987) suggested a categorisation system developing from prototype theory, which he called **radial structure**, "one where there is a central case and conventionalised variations on it which cannot be predicted by general rules" (Lakoff 1987: 84). Because they are conventionalised, and reflect the (changing) state of the world or society, they have to be learned. And they differ from superordinate–hyponymic relationships, where the central case, e.g. DOG$_1$ 'canine', is only distinguished from the less central case DOG$_2$ 'male canine', by having one less property. For a radial structure the central case has to have a property not shared by the non-central case.

Lakoff 's example of a radial structure is the category 'mother'.

> MOTHER (CENTRAL CASE):
> Mother who is and has always been female, who gave birth to the child, supplied her half of the child's genes, nurtured the child, is married to the father, is one generation older than the child, and is the child's legal guardian.

> STEPMOTHER:
> Mother who didn't give birth or supply the genes, but is currently married to the father.

ADOPTIVE MOTHER:
Mother who didn't give birth or supply the genes, but is the legal guardian and has the obligation to provide nurturance.

BIRTH MOTHER/NATURAL MOTHER:
A mother defined in opposition to 'adoptive mother'; given an adoption schema, the mother who gives birth and puts the child up for adoption is the birth mother or natural mother.

FOSTER MOTHER:
Mother who did not give birth to the child, but is being paid by the state to provide nurturance.

BIOLOGICAL MOTHER:
A mother who gave birth to the child, but is not raising it, while there is someone else who is, and who qualifies to be called a mother of some sort.

SURROGATE MOTHER:
A mother who has contracted to give birth, and not perform any other role as mother. She may or may not have provided the genes, and she is not married to the father and is not obligated to provide nurturance. And she has contractually given up the right to be legal guardian.

UNWED MOTHER:
Mother who is not married at the time she gives birth.
(after Lakoff 1987: 83)

Lakoff points out that these are not predictable variations on the central case, but are conventional. For example, there is no conventional category yet established for transsexuals who have had a sex change since the birth of the child, because this is not yet a sufficiently common schema to warrant a new category.[7]

4.9.3. Family resemblances

The non-central categories in radial structures will have at least one property not shared with the central category. This means that non-central members of the category may share no properties with other non-central members. For example, an adoptive mother will share no property with a birth mother. Nevertheless, they are both mothers of some kind.

A similar approach is the suggestion that the overarching category is a matter of **family resemblances**. Wittgenstein (1953: 1: 66–71) showed that a category like 'game' neither has clear boundaries, nor can it be defined by a set of common properties. Some games are just fun, like ring-a-ring-a-roses, others involve luck, like board games when you throw a dice, others skill, like chess, others, like card games, usually a combination of skill and luck. For Wittgenstein, they could, however, still belong to the same overarching category, just as family members belong to the same family. All that is required for family resemblance is that you should share a few features with some members of the family, even if other members of the family share no features with you. For example, you may share the shape of your nose with your father, your maternal grandmother and your maternal uncle, and your hair colour with your mother and your sister. But you may share neither of these, or any other distinctive features, with your paternal uncle. Your paternal uncle may, however, share eye-colour with your father and your sister.

> Discussion

> "Swimming isn't a sport. It's just a way to keep from drowning." (George Carlin, Tibballs 2006: 456).

> Consider the rival categorisations of swimming in this humorous quote. Are they classical categories with a clear superordinate and hyponym, or radial, or do they depend upon prototypes of family resemblances? How would this compare with "Walking isn't a sport. It's just a way of moving around"?

4.10.   SUMMARY AND AFTERTHOUGHT

This chapter delineated logical relationships among senses such as synonymy, entailment, inconsistency, tautology, contradiction, presupposition, ambiguity, hyponymy, meronymy and ambiguity, using the basic statement approach. We explored the different kinds of ambiguity exploited in humour: homonymy, homophony and, to a lesser extent, homography. We then considered the meaning oppositions of complementarity, multiple incompatibility, gradable or polar oppositions, converses, symmetry and logical (not grammatical) transitivity.

How psychologically valid is this strictly logical approach? Aitchison (2002) gives plenty of evidence that co-hyponyms (what she calls co-ordinates), synonyms and antonyms have very strong psychological bonds. She also suggests that some links between hyponyms and superordinates are firmly established in the mind. Indeed, in order to remember a meaning it would seem efficient to automatically compute that the hyponyms contain the componential features of their superordinates, as well as some distinguishers or markers to differentiate them from their co-hyponyms (co-ordinates).

However, others meaning relations are worked out on the spot. So, in activity 4.17 we went on to explore how meaning relations are constructed in a real text, showing that the idea of fixed de-contextualised sense relations is sometimes a figment of the imagination. The final section of the chapter suggested further inadequacies of this logical approach to meaning in naturally occurring communication, and the need for less rigid approaches which acknowledge the fuzziness of concepts, such as prototype theory, radial categories and "family resemblances".

Discussion

Discuss the relative merits of the traditional (classical) approach to semantics spelt out in Sections 4.1 to 4.7 above, as opposed to a semantics that allows for fuzzy categories, prototypes, family resemblances etc. How might the text "She picks up your rubbish", or any other short text you can find, give evidence for the strengths or weaknesses of the traditional classical model?

Suggested Readings

- Leech (1981), whose taxonomy of meaning gives a framework for this book, and Saeed (2003) both give excellent introductions to traditional lexical semantics.
- Lakoff (1987: chapter 6) is the source for the brief introduction to radial categories, and is worth following up.
- For an accessible introduction to prototype and family resemblance theory, discussion of componential analysis and semantic networks, read Aitchison (2002: chapters 4–8).
- Oring (2003: 1–12) includes a critique of family resemblance theory, especially as applied to classification of humour. The book also has interesting observations about the differences between humour and metaphor, relevant to Chapter 7. Moreover, it challenges the notion of incongruity resolution, which forms part of the Raskin–Attardo theory assumed as a background to this book.
- Redfern (1984) is the classic text on puns (see homonymy, homophony etc. above), but a shorter more accessible treatment can be found in Blake (2007: chapter 5).

5 Personal, social and affective meanings

Chapters 3 and 4 discussed ideational or conceptual meanings of grammar and lexis, respectively. The other categories of meaning in Leech's taxonomy are collocative and thematic, which are textual and discussed in Chapter 6, and reflected, connotative, affective and social which are (inter-)personal and the topic of this chapter. The latter, social meaning, will be elaborated by reference to Crystal and Davy (1969), who point out that utterances might tell you who the speaker writer is (idiosyncrasy), their age or when they were speaking (age), where they come from (dialect) and their relationship with the hearer/reader (status /intimacy).[1]

In the lowest row of Figure 4.1 (p. 78) I suggested the existence of **synonyms**: lexical items with identical meanings represented by two different forms. It is probably the case that synonyms only exist if one confines oneself to conceptual meaning. Lexical items are seldom synonymous on all dimensions of meaning. For instance, 'grandfather' and 'grandad' obviously differ on the interpersonal dimension of formality.

5.1. REFLECTED MEANING

Reflected meaning can be detected when a word's meaning is affected by lexical items with the same form but different meaning, e.g. *intercourse* meaning 'two-way communication' disappeared from English to be replaced by *discourse*, because of the unwanted meaning 'sexual intercourse'. Or *titbit* changes its form to *tidbit* in US English to avoid the reflection from *tit*, slang for 'nipple'. Historically in the US, a sextet has been misleadingly called a quintet (Blake 2007: 43). And Chinese often avoid the word-form /seɪ/, meaning 'four', since it is a homophone for 'death'. So, if you live on the "fiftieth" floor of a condominium in Hong Kong you may well actually live on the thirty-sixth floor. Reflected meaning, as in these examples, drives the use of euphemism, which can even work cross-linguistically with less than competent translations. Chiaro (1992: 23) gives this example from a butcher's shop window, probably owned by an Italian: "Sausages made without conservatives". The correct word would be *preservatives*, but the equivalent Italian word-form *preservative* means 'contraceptive'. (Any avoidance of the similarity between a condom and sausage skin may be accidental.) The converse tendency is comedians' stock recourse to puns involving sexual innuendo.

Indeed, all the humorous examples and puns depending on identity of form (4.2) – homonymy (polysemy), homography, homophony – exploit the ambiguities caused by reflected meaning. It is very powerful in distinguishing near synonyms, so in the pun "in his candidature nepotism gave him a relative advantage" one cannot substitute *relation*: "*in his candidature nepotism gave him a relation advantage". Reflected meaning also makes possible this pun: "Success is a relative term – It brings so many relatives!"

5.2. CONNOTATIVE MEANINGS

I already introduced the distinction between sense and reference (1.4). **Connotative meaning** is the association which words acquire from what they refer to in the real world. This experience of referential use is basically a social or personal one, which justifies its inclusion in this chapter. From experience of the creatures referred to by the word *dog* we might build up the following expectations or connotations: 'has a tail', 'barks', 'has fur', 'has four legs'. These meanings are not intrinsic to the conceptual meaning because the following are not logical contradictions:

> the dog cannot bark
> the dog has no tail
> the dog is hairless
> the dog has three legs

Whereas the following are clearly contradictory:

> *the dog is not an animal
> *the dog is not a mammal
> *the dog is not a canine (negation of a tautology)

Connotative meanings tend to be less stable than conceptual meanings, because they refer to entities in the world, and the world is always changing. I dare say the connotation of 'banker', as well as its affective associations (rhyming slang apart), has changed considerably between the 1950s and 2011, largely due to the recent financial crisis.

Activity 5.1

What are the connotations of the meanings of the following words? How might these have changed since the beginning of the twentieth century and in different societies? *Priest, prime minister, wedding.*

Comment

Priest might have connoted 'male' in the US until the last quarter of the twentieth century, at which point women priests began to be ordained in the Anglican or Episcopalian Church. It was only recently that the strong connotation 'heterosexual' became weakened with the "advent" of gay priests. In Roman Catholic communities *priest* will connote not only 'male' but also 'celibate', though there has been a weak but growing connotation of 'paedophile' lately. In other religions like Hinduism and Buddhism, the word would maintain the 'male' and, I think, 'celibate' connotation. ("Catholic priests try to escape penal servitude"!)

Similarly *prime minister* might have connoted 'male' in the first half of the twentieth century, before the world was blessed with Golda Meir, Mrs Bandaranaike, Indira Gandhi, Margaret Thatcher, Mary Robinson and others.

At the beginning of the twentieth century in England most weddings were held in church, but now this is only true of 30 per cent.

Not only do connotations change over time, they may be highly personal. Trying to find componential features to define the conceptual meaning 'bottle' (4.9) is problematic because these features depend upon the generalisation of connotations. If you live in the tropics and have never encountered a hot water bottle, made of rubber, then you will be happier to accept [+PLASTIC/GLASS] as necessary componential features.

Two tests have been suggested for connotations, involving the conjunctions *so* and *but*. For the first, link two clauses with the same referent by *so*. If the resulting sentences seem acceptable then the second clause expresses a connotation. For example, "It was a book, so it was made of paper". For the second, link the two clauses, the second in the negative, with *but*. If the resulting sentence seems acceptable, then the positive equivalent of the second clause is a connotation; e.g., if "It was a book, but it wasn't made of paper" seems normal, then a connotation of *book* is 'is made of paper'.

This famous feminist riddle/joke depends upon connotation:

> A father and son were travelling home late at night and were involved
> in a high-speed car crash. The father was killed outright, and the son
> was rushed to hospital to undergo surgery to save his life. But the
> surgeon said to the hospital administrators – "Ethically I am unable to
> operate on this patient: he is my son."

Such is the strength of the connotation [+MALE] for 'surgeon', that it
might take the reader a while to work out that the surgeon was the
boy's mother.

> Discussion

> How watertight is this traditional distinction between sense
> and connotation? For example, if a dog can have three legs and
> still be a dog, since the possession of four legs is only a connotation,
> how much of a dog can be missing before it is no longer logically
> a dog? Is having a head a connotation or part of the sense?
> "The headless dog" seems acceptable. What quorum of limbs
> and members is logically necessary? Consider other cases of
> your own.

5.3.   AFFECTIVE MEANING

Affective meaning conveys attitudes, evaluations and emotions. Leech
describes such meaning as "how language reflects the personal feelings of the speaker, including his attitude to the listener, or his
attitude to something he is talking about" (Leech 1981: 15).

5.3.1.   Affective lexis

There are various means of expressing affective meanings through
lexis. Firstly we can use words which have no conceptual content and
only convey subjective attitudes, e.g. *nice* and *nasty*, *horrible* and
tremendous, *vile* and *beautiful*. Food that is nasty for one person (tripe,
durian, fish stomach) might be really nice for somebody else. This
lexis is subjective and cannot be verified or challenged, hence
its frequent use in ads. Other examples are the negative *terrible*,
awful, *disgusting*, *pathetic*, or the positive *fine*, *good*, *great*, *wonderful*,
fabulous, *cool*, *smashing*. Sometimes subjective lexis takes the form
of adverbial intensifiers: **terribly** *misguided*; **dreadfully** *hot*; **awfully**
exciting.

> The Bullingdon Club had a smashing party. There was hardly one window or chair left unbroken by the time they had finished their celebrations. But gentlemen will be gentlemen.

> Those hot pants of yours are really cool.

As these examples show, some of these purely emotive words share a word-form with lexemes which do have a conceptual meaning. But in their emotive meaning the concept has been drained away. This is especially obvious with swear words. If you tell someone to "piss off" you do not direct them to the toilet, and if something is "a bloody mess" you do not expect there to be blood around.

Secondly we can conceptualise affect. In the sentence "My sister's postnatal depression was intensified by her anxiety over whether she could cope with the new baby", "depression" and "anxiety" convey concepts of emotions. Presumably conceptualising them makes them more objective, at least in the sense that a clinical psychologist might attempt to measure their intensity.

Thirdly, emotion can be conveyed by choosing words with a positive or negative evaluation, a spin, along with their conceptual meanings. Sometimes English furnishes us with word triads which share conceptual meaning, but differ in affective polarity. Examples are 'skinny' (negative), 'slim' (positive) and 'thin' (neutral), and 'pig-headedness' (negative), 'perseverance' (positive) and 'determination' (neutral). Compare this with the epigram: "I'm easy-going, you are lazy, and he's slovenly" (Alexander 1997: 58).

Activity 5.2

Analyse the affective meaning in the following extract from the radio programme *In the Psychiatrist's Chair*. When looking for words with positive and negative spin try to suggest words that are neutral equivalents or with opposite spin. I chose this extract because Antony Clare is questioning Ken Russell about his religious beliefs, a topic which tends to provoke strong feelings.

> Key: stressed or nuclear syllables (see 6.2) in capitals. Numbers in parentheses indicate seconds pause, and (.) a shorter pause.

Introduction

Ken Russell was born in Southampton in July 1927. His father ran a boot and shoe business in that city. Ken went to primary school there and then to Pangbourne Nautical College. On leaving school he spent some time in the Merchant Navy and the RAF and was a member of a number of ballet companies and was an actor before working as a stills photographer. He went to art school   5 where he met his first wife and then began to make films. In 1962, a film on Elgar made for the BBC met widespread acclaim and was followed quickly by films on composers such as Debussy and Delius. Since that time he's become a world renowned film director with films which include The Music Lovers, Women in Love, The Devils, The Boyfriend, Valentino, Savage Messiah, and Gothic.   10

Ken Russell provokes widely divergent views amongst his critics. He has, for example, been dismissed as "a psychologist of the uglier emotions who treads all the foul ditches and sewers of human despair" or regarded quite simply as one of the greatest directors in the world.

K. I am as you said at the beginning of the programme considered to be   15
    a monster of depravity. Well, they've got that idea, I suppose, from
    the images in my films.

A. Why did you become a CATHolic?

K. I met someone who convinced me it was (.) the only thing to BE

A. AND IS it?   20

K. I I was converted to the faith when I was twenty eight (h) up until then
    I was a DRIFTer I I met this m er civil servant. called Norman Dewhurst
    who was in the same BOARDing house as myself (h) and he m sort of
    explained the CATHolic version of the New TESTament (1.0) t in such
    terms that to me it was like Science FICtion but it was er more you   25
    know I er I I it seemed to me almost (h) TOTally credible TOTally REAL
    TOTally meaningful and when he mentioned about the m the ability of
    the priest to turn the bread and wine into the body and blood of Jesus
    CHRIST I mean to me it was aMAZing and the reason I left it was
    I couldn't live UP to it I mean you're supposed to be (sniff) in a state of   30
    GRACE when you take comMUNion (1.0) well and obviously you go to
    confession just before you TAKE comMUNion but I'D step out of the
    conFESSional and have a dirty THOUGHT so I was in a state of mortal
    SIN so how could I (h). in a state of mortal sin TAKE ww parTAKE er erv v
    this BANquet of the body and blood of CHRIST I mean it was it was I I   35
    I COULDn't (1.0) I couldn't live UP to it I I I COULDn't so I LEFT.

Comment

Several words here have a core of conceptual meaning accompanied by affective "spin". Table 5.1 lists these words, with line references, and contrasts them with words of equivalent conceptual meaning but which are neutral or express opposite evaluation, though exact equivalents can be elusive.

Table 5.1 *Affective spin in 'In the Psychiatrist's Chair'*

POSITIVE	NEUTRAL	NEGATIVE
acclaim (l. 7)	notice	notoriety
renowned (l. 8)	well-known	infamous
laid-back	without purpose	a drifter (l. 22)
banquet (l. 35)	meal	
acclaimed/ hailed	regarded (l. 13)	dismissed (l. 12)

We also find subjective words with little, if any, conceptual meaning, simply used to express disapproval or negative feelings.

  uglier (l. 12)
  greatest (l. 14)
  foul (l. 13)
  dirty (l. 33)
  monster (l. 16)
  depravity (l. 16)
  meaningful (l. 27)

Perhaps as we go down the list conceptual meaning begins creeping back in. "Uglier" and "greatest" are most obviously conceptually empty. With "foul", "dirty" and "monster" an original conceptual meaning has been lost through metaphorical use. "Depravity" and "meaningful" seem to have been drained of their conceptual meaning by over-use. *Meaningful* is conceptually meaningless, if that's not a contradiction.

There does not seem to be much conceptualisation of affect in this extract, except perhaps "despair" (l. 13) and "amazing" (l. 29).

The linguistic theory of affective meanings has been quite neglected. But lately Jim Martin and Peter White (2005) have developed a theoretical framework for affective and evaluative meanings called **appraisal**. Martin (2000: 145ff.) suggested the system diagram in Figure 5.1, though he prefers to see the classification as gradable

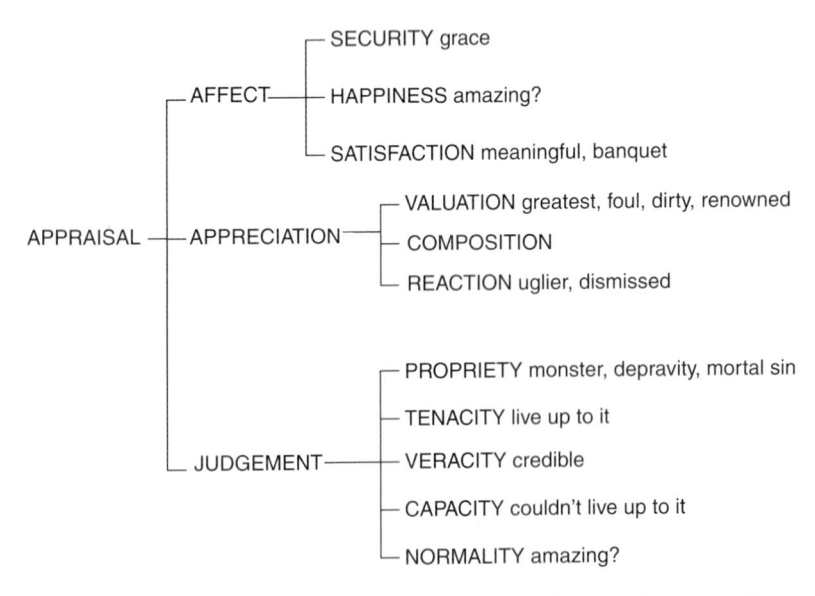

Figure 5.1. Appraisal systems with examples from the Ken Russell interview (Activity 5.1)

(or topological/analog) rather than discrete (typological/digital). In his system affect is the expression of inner emotion, **appreciation** the evaluation of a text, artefact or natural object, and **judgment** evaluation of the behaviour of others. In Figure 5.1 I have tried to give examples from the Russell interview to illustrate each branch of the system diagram, but the linguistic expressions overlap in some cases (are we judging Russell, i.e. judgment, or his films, i.e. appreciation?), and there is no appreciation of the compositional qualities of his films.

An obvious and acknowledged problem in appraisal theory is that words which in their semantic dictionary meaning appear positive easily switch their polarity to negative in texts. For instance, *help* in its general dictionary meaning appears positive in its judgment. However, in the sentence "The CIA helped Pol Pot" it clearly becomes negative. As Thompson and Hunston (2000: 14) suggest, it is probably better not to reduce appraisal or evaluation to semantics, but to think of it in terms of goal-directed behaviour and to factor in the co-textual and contextual meanings. This would require a pragmatic approach to appraisal.

Moreover, some emotional responses to words are not really part of the semantics of language. Lexical semantics should, technically, only investigate meanings which are part of the language code, shared by a large section of the language community. So, although a word or phrase may provoke idiosyncratic emotional responses, these do not count as affective semantic meaning. For instance, the phrase "a white bull-terrier" may produce a negative emotional response, because I was mauled by such a dog when I was five years old. But this affective response cannot be counted as part of its meaning.

However, it is difficult to ignore individual or sub-cultural emotional responses to words, which are rather like emotive connotations. "Boarding house" (l. 23) has rather seedy connotations for me, "science fiction" (l. 25) has positive connotations for Russell, and "mortal sin" (l. 33) and "grace" (l. 30) will only have negative and positive overtones within a Christian-Catholic sub-culture.

The extent to which negative affective connotations depend upon sub-cultural values is apparent in the increasing number of **contested terms**. For radical environmentalists "growth" has negative affective spin. For development workers, "Third World" might be offensive, because it suggests less importance or value (cf. *third-rate*). There is a tendency to challenge such terms (e.g. *property is theft* is a socialist/anarchist slogan), or to replace them with more sub-culturally acceptable terms (e.g. *developing nations* → *the South* → *the majority world*). On the other hand some sub-cultures or individuals might find these too euphemistic and prefer the direct *poor countries*. Or users of the more euphemistic terms might be pejoratively labelled *politically correct*, a term which itself differs in its affective value according to cultural beliefs. In a sense the affective meanings provoked by contested terms are directed towards the speakers using them, as much as against the concepts they convey.

Euphemisms, i.e. words used to avoid a direct reference to something considered impolite, are ways of disguising or removing affective connotations; for instance, *comfort woman* sounds less negative than *prostitute* or *sex slave*, *motion* than *faeces/shit*. Sex, urination/excretion, and death are the commonest topics for euphemism: *sleep together* is a euphemism for sex (those involved certainly do not sleep), and my favourite, humorously misfiring, euphemism for a funeral wake is *cold meat party* ("cold meat" has double reference: the hosts attending the funeral have no time to cook hot food, and the corpse is cold meat). Euphemisms, because they acquire a connotative affective meaning, are notoriously short-lived, since what they refer to remains the same: *shit-hole* → *toilet* → *washroom* → *restroom* → *comfort station*. A number of politically correct jokes play with euphemism. For instance "A man does not fart and belch – he is gastro-intestinally expressive" or "A man does not sleep around – he is monogamously challenged", the last illustrating replacement of one euphemism with another.

Consider the following extract from a comedy routine entitled "Record Choice" by Dawn French and Jennifer Saunders, where polite euphemisms are finally abandoned:

> Jennifer: Before we go for your record choice, let's see if we can paint a picture of the young Eleanor Wood, and maybe recall a few childhood memories for you. You excelled in school academically and at sport. I love to imagine this picture of you, this Cornish dumpling, probably goalie in the hockey team, cheerfully bouncing around in goal, lifting everyone's spirits. You were, I should imagine, a happy, jolly, sturdy person.
>
> Dawn: I suppose so.
>
> Jennifer: The class clown, perhaps? So many people with physical disadvantages like yourself often end up compensating. Was it, dare I say, your chunkiness, the fact that you were and are a fuller-figured person that made you more determined to succeed?...
>
> Dawn: Oh all right, you can describe me as chunky, ample, bubbly, huggable and so on, as long as I can describe you as slow-witted, uninteresting, obtuse, dull, tedious, mentally stagnant... Because what you're really wanting to say about me is "fat" and what I'm skirting around about you is "stupid".
> (quoted in Ross 1998: 54)

> **Activity 5.3**
>
> How does euphemism work, or not work, in the following humorous epigram?
>
> Trouble with life in the fast lane is that you get to the other end in an awful hurry.

5.3.2. Intonation, rhythm and syntax to express affect

Other ways of expressing emotion and evaluation are apparent in the Ken Russell extract (Activity 5.2), for example stress, intonation, syntactic parallelism and rhythm. The multiple hesitations and stutterings in the concluding passage betray a considerable mental tension, perhaps due to suppressed guilt:

> how could I (h). in a state of mortal sin TAKE ww parTAKE er erv v
> this BANquet of the body and blood of CHRIST I mean it was it was
> I I I COULDn't (1.0) I couldn't live UP to it I I I COULDn't so I LEFT.

By contrast, consider the following passage:

> it seemed to me almost (h) TOTally credible TOTally REAL TOTally
> meaningful and when he mentioned about the m the ability of the
> priest to turn the bread and wine into the body and blood of Jesus
> CHRIST I mean to me it was aMAZing

Notice the emphatic repetition of words, structure and intonation with multiple stresses in "it ... meaningful" and then the very quick un-emphatic stretch up to the stresses on "Christ" and "amazing", conveying high excitement.

Martin (1992: 533) identifies such repetitive structures as **amplification** of affect. They can be syntactic or rhythmical or both simultaneously. For example, syntactic repetition can be seen in "The change to a modular system was the most ill-considered, most hastily-implemented and most blatantly anti-educational initiative of the 1990s":

Superlative	Adverb	Adjective/Past participle
most	ill-	considered
most	hastily	implemented
most	blatantly	anti-educational

Rhythm, to put it crudely, is a regular pattern of stressed syllables (louder, and marked /) and unstressed syllables (softer, and marked x). In words of two syllables (or more) one syllable will be stressed and the other unstressed e.g. *Never* (/ x), *remain* (x /), *allow* (x /), *allergy* (/ x x).

Monosyllabic lexical words (1.5) will likely be stressed, i.e. nouns, main (not auxiliary) verbs, adjectives and adverbs.

Rhythm is often used to express emotion in advertising jingles:

```
x  /  x x   /      x     / x  /      x  /  x x   / x       / x    /
a million housewives every day    a million  students every day
 /   x  x  /  x   /   x    /       /   x    x  /    x    /  x    /
pick up a can of beans and say    Put down a spray-paint can and say
   /      /      /                     /      /      /
"Beans Meanz Heinz"               "Deanz Meanz Finez"
```

English is a **stress -timed language**, that is, the time it takes to utter a sentence depends on the number of stressed syllables in it. Consequently, the higher the proportion of stressed syllables the slower we read and the more emphatic the effect, while the higher the proportion of unstressed syllables the faster the words flit by, and the more exciting or light-hearted it feels. This second kind of faster rhythm is more suitable for humorous verse, as in this anonymous poem:

```
 x  / x x  /    x  x / x
The sexual urge of the camel
x  /   x   x   / x x   /
Is greater than anyone thinks
 x   x  /  x x / x  x  / x
And can only be satisfied fully
x / x  x /   x    x   /
By going to bed with The Sphinx
x   x  /     x x  / x x / x x
Now the Sphinx has an external orifice
 x   x  /    x   x  /   x  x  /
Which is choked with the sands of the Nile
 x   x  /    x  x  /   x   x  / x
Which accounts for the hump on the camel
 x   x  /   x x  / x x  /
And the Sphinx's inscrutable smile.
```

5.4. SOCIAL MEANING

Besides reflected, connotational and affective meanings, there are various kinds of social meaning: that indicating the geographical provenance or dialect of the speaker (writer); that expressing the age of the speaker (writer)/hearer or the archaism of the text; that indicating the status of the reader or speaker vis-à-vis the hearer, or their level of intimacy.

5.4.1. Dialect

Besides the conceptual meaning it conveys, does an expression tell us where the speaker is from? *Hawker centre*, for instance, is a peculiarly Singaporean and Malaysian English expression for an open-air food court. And the spelling *color* indicates we have a North American writer.

    Some jokes work better or differently in one dialect rather than another.

Activity 5.4

Which of the following work better in different dialects: Scandinavian English, British English, American English or a particular dialect of American/British English? Can you relate this to different patterns of homophony/homonymy in the different dialects ?

    a. He wears glasses during maths because it helps with division.
    b. – What's a zebra? – 25 sizes larger than an A-bra.
    c. Scandinavian vacuum-cleaner manufacturer Electrolux ran a US campaign with the slogan: "Nothing sucks like an Electrolux".

Comment

a. Might work better in US black dialect or West Indian UK dialects where /dɪ/ replaces /ðə/.
b. Only works in US English where *Z-bra* is homophonous with *zebra*. In the UK the first would be pronounced /zedbrɑ:/.
c. Is presumably not funny at all in Scandinavian English, in fact it's a rather snappy slogan with its carefully constructed rhyme and rhythm. Unfortunately in most US dialects it means 'nothing is as bad as an Electrolux'.

Some jokes target the dialects of other speakers. Welsh, with its tendency to "drop" /h/, reduce /e/ to /ɪ/ and make less of a difference between stressed and unstressed syllables than other British dialects, is one butt of the following joke:

> Gwendolyn, a young Welsh woman returned from her honeymoon, and her mother asked how it went. "Oh mother, what a penis!"
> "No Gwendolyn, you mean 'What happiness!'"

George Bernard Shaw in *Pygmalion* exploits the fact that dialect involves variations in accent, lexis and grammar. When Eliza Doolittle is first introduced into society Henry Higgins has already managed to alter her Cockney accent to an upper middle-class one, but has not amended her lexis and grammar. Her utterances include "Somebody pinched it, and what I say is, them as pinched it done her in." [cf. "those who stole it killed her"] "If I was doing it proper what was you laughing at" [cf. "properly what were you ..."] (Blake 2007: 10). The incompatible accent and lexico-grammar create conflicting social dialectal meanings.

Dialect represents a centrifugal force in language: the tendency for language to vary so much that it prevents communication as much as enabling it. Taken to the extreme it becomes what Halliday (1978) calls "anti-language", a dialect so restricted it is only comprehensible to the members of a small sub-culture. I imagine some text messages are instances of anti-language with abbreviations like *iohis4u* ('I only have eyes for you') or *:-@ iydkidkwd?* (= screaming 'if you don't know I don't know, who does?') (Crystal 2008: 54).

5.4.2. Age/archaism

Besides the conceptual meaning or information it conveys, the choice of lexis may tell us something about the age of the speaker/writer/ hearer. My grandmother, who died in 1966, would refer to someone's boyfriend as someone's *young man*, and boyfriend/girlfriend as *sweetheart*. This indicated her age even at the time, and is even more archaic now. In Shakespeare's time one of the meanings of *baby* was 'doll', as in "the baby of a girl". There has been a tendency for poetry (partly because it is less ephemeral than other genres) to be associated with **archaism**. *Steed* for *horse*, *swound/swoon* for *faint*, *ere* for *before*, *e'er* for *ever*.

When addressing young children we tend to use diminutive, onomatopoeic and reduplicative forms such as *choo-choo* for *train*, *pussy* for *cat*, *beddy-byes* for *time for bed*, *tummy* for *stomach*. Presumably toddlers tend to use these forms themselves, too, especially those easier to pronounce.

5.4.3. Social status, familiarity and formality[2]

Besides the conceptual meaning it conveys, an expression may indicate the class or relative status of the speaker/hearer and/or their degree of intimacy. Compare, for example, the terms of address "Professor Robinson" versus "Doug", or this formal request with its working-class informal (Australian dialectal) equivalent:

"Could you pass me a sandwich, please?" "Chuck us a sanger, mate."

Social relations can be diagrammed along two dimensions: **power**, the vertical dimension, and **solidarity** the horizontal dimension.

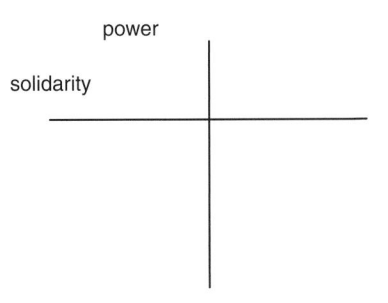

Figure 5.2. Two dimensions of interpersonality

On the vertical dimension, power or domination may be exerted through force, institutional authority, expertise or status. On the horizontal dimension, solidarity, closeness and affection reflect the degree of contact, whether it is frequent or intermittent, and whether it extends over a long period of time or not (Poynton 1989).

These dimensions vary independently. Parents have power over young children, but this does not prevent them from being intimate. Lecturers, who through expertise are above a student on the vertical dimension, may be friendly to varying degrees. These dimensions are reflected in the choice of vocabulary.

The vocabulary of modern English consists of three main strata, which are progressively more formal.

1. Basic **Old English** words which occur across the whole range of genres and are generally quite short, e.g. *help, give a hand to.*
2. A thick layer of **French** words, which flooded into English in the fourteenth century, e.g. *aid.*
3. **Greek** and **Latin** words/roots which were borrowed widely into the language from the sixteenth to eighteenth centuries, e.g. *assist, intervene.* Technical words are still being coined from Latin and Greek today.

Words of French origin, and even more those from Latin and Greek, express distance or minimal contact on the horizontal dimension. Formality also correlates with suffixes, that is to say, words of different origin select different derivational suffix-types (Table 5.2).

I once revisited the National University Hospital in Singapore and was surprised to find it more than usually busy, with crowds milling around in different directions. It transpired that the hospital administrators, in an attempt to enhance professional image or status, had replaced all the relatively common core signage with technical

Table 5.2. *Old English and other affixes*

Origin	Old English tendency	French/Latin/Greek tendency
Prefixes	*fore-, after-*	*in-, pre-, post-, anti-, de-*
Suffixes	*-ish, -dom, -hood*	*-ine, -ous, -al/-ial-/ual, -ian/ -ic-/iac*
Nominalisation of verbs of adjectives	*-ing (or no suffix) -ness*	*-ion/-tion/-ation -ity*

medical terminology. "Blood test" had become "venepuncture", and "ear nose and throat" "otorhinolaryngology". I suppose the extra kudos was worth the lost patients and wasted paint.

Old English words are shorter than those of French or classical origin, e.g. *blood test* is shorter than *venepuncture*, and *ear, nose and throat* individually shorter than *otorhinolaryngology*. Shorter still is *ENT*, an abbreviation, but this, like the technical Greek term, assumes a degree of professional contact. Informal equivalents resort to word compounds or phrasal compounds rather than single words, *take to pieces* for *disassemble, hand in* for *submit*.

Much humour depends upon a deliberate mixing of formal and informal styles. Queen Elizabeth had several family problems in 1992, and her palace at Windsor burnt down. She referred to this in a speech as her "annus horribilis", using the extremely formal Latin phrase. A British tabloid reported the speech with the headline "One's bum year" (Blake 2007: 79). Not only does this exploit the paronym *annus/anus*, but juxtaposes the extreme formality of *one* as a personal pronoun, with the slang *bum* 'terrible'. Or consider this mixture of common core and academically sophisticated vocabulary:

> Woman: Do you think it's alright to wear erotic underwear? Or do you think it's just pandering to patriarchal fantasies to the point where we've internalised male values so profoundly that we even take a narcissistic pleasure in the objectification of our own bodies?
>
> Friend: You're in a funny mood.
> (Jackie Fleming cartoon quoted in Ross 1998: 61)

Chiaro (1992: 119–20) points out the necessity for relative informality in narratives designed to be humorous. There is also an interesting relationship between formality and irony (Kotthoff 2009: 59–60). Most theories of irony suggest a contrast in ideational or conceptual meanings (7.6, 10.6), but the following example shows the importance of formality and affective spin. It is taken from a letter in Hong Kong's *South China Morning Post*, which deplored the misleading way in which the floor area of flats is calculated. The government (represented by Mr Fung, the Assistant Secretary for Housing) has changed the way of calculating floor area for new flats, but the writer would prefer the same calculation method for all properties, including old flats.

> Finally, Mr Fung says that it could have made the situation more complicated if the new rules were applied to sales of all properties (1). How so, Mr Fung? (2). Would you care to enlighten us on what this confusion would entail? (3). I, for one, cannot see a problem by using the same standard for all sales (4).

Notice the shift from the informality of sentence 2 to the formality of sentence 3, with its "enlighten" and "entail". This shift emphasises the irony, perhaps by suggesting a veneer of politeness which contrasts with the aggression in the rather rude sentence 2. But it also involves interesting modifications to affective spin. *Enlighten* contrasts with the core word *tell* or the slightly more formal *inform*, by stressing the positive effects on the mind of the listener of the knowledge imparted. The implication of the irony is that there will be no such positive effects since, indeed, there is nothing to tell, as sentence 4 plainly states.

5.4.4. Summary of social meaning

The dimensions of meaning discussed so far might be summarised with the help of Table 5.3. If you speak a different dialect and can add more items to the table, so much the better.

Clearly much humour derives not simply from clashes of conceptual aspects of schemas but also clashes between degrees of formality and technicality, or other of these dimensions of social and affective meaning (Attardo 1994: 234). These tend to reflect a clash of register (6.4).

Activity 5.5

Can you explain how the Les Dawson monologue below achieves its humour by exploiting the non-conceptual dimensions of meaning discussed in this chapter?

> I sat at the bottom of the garden a week ago, smoking a reflective cheroot, thinking about this and that – mostly that – and I just happened to glance up at the night sky. And I marvelled at the millions of stars, glistening like quicksilver thrown carelessly on to black velvet. In awe I watched the waxen [sic] moon ride across the zenith of the heavens like an amber chariot, toward the void of infinite space within which the tethered bolts of Jupiter and Mars hang forever in their orbital majesty, and as I looked at this, I thought, "I must put a roof on this lavatory". (Les Dawson)

Table 5.3. Dimensions of interpersonal or social meaning

Core	Positive Affective	Negative Affective	Technical/Formal	Informal	Dialectal	Age/Archaic
dog	man's best friend	cur	canine	doggy	pooch	bow-wow
cat		cunning	feline	pussy, mog	dug	pussy
clever	brilliant	cunning	gifted	brainy	canny	apt
determination	perseverance	obstinacy, pigheadedness	motivation	will-power, pigheadedness	obstinacy	
help	help	interfere	intervene, assist	give a hand to	muck in	
throw			project	chuck, sling	hoy	cast
??		shit	excrement, faeces	shit, pooh	crap, clarts	business, poo-poo
??		piss	urine	pee, piss	piddle	wee-wee
house	home	hovel	residence, domicile	place, pen, pad	hoose	pad

5.5. GRAMMAR AND INTERPERSONAL MEANINGS

Just as it communicates conceptual meaning or sense, grammar can convey interpersonal or social meaning. The main grammatical resources for establishing social positions are the systems of **mood** and **modality**.

5.5.1. Mood as interpersonal resource

The four moods conveyed by the clause in English – **declarative**, **imperative**, **interrogative** and **exclamative** – are defined by the order and presence of Subject, **Finite Verb** and *wh-* element (Table 5.4).

When Subject precedes Finite we have declarative mood (1), unless the Subject is a *Wh-* pronoun, which gives us one kind of interrogative (3), or unless a *Wh-* element is followed by a Subject and then a Finite, which marks exclamative mood (6, 7, 8). When Finite precedes Subject we always have interrogative (2, 4). When Verb occurs without a Subject we have imperative (5).

What are the interpersonal consequences of mood? The exclamative is a strong expression of emotion, suggesting little horizontal social distance. The imperative assumes the speaker is in the position to give orders to the hearer, higher on the vertical dimension. The interrogative, when used for asking questions, is ambiguous in relation to

Table 5.4. *Mood and the configuration of Subject, Finite and* wh- *element*

EXAMPLE	ORDER OF ELEMENTS	MOOD
1. He **went** to Lagos.	Subject ^ Finite	= Declarative
2. **Did** he go to Lagos?	Finite ^ Subject	= Interrogative
3. Who **went** to Lagos?	*Wh-*(Subject) ^ Finite	= Interrogative
4. How **did** he go to Lagos?	*Wh-* ^ Finite ^ Subject	= Interrogative
5. **Go** to Lagos.	Finite? Verb	= Imperative
6. How stupid he **was** to go to Lagos!	*Wh-* ^ Comp. ^ Subject ^ Finite	= Exclamative
7. What a trip we **had** to Lagos!	*Wh-* ^ Obj. ^ Subject ^ Finite	= Exclamative
8. How quickly he **went** to Lagos!	*Wh-* ^ Adv. ^ Subject ^ Finite	= Exclamative

(Key: Comp. = Complement; Obj. = Object; Adv. = Adverbial, *Wh-* = *who, what, when, why, how, which, where*)

vertical authority. The speaker presumes the right to ask questions, to trespass on someone's personal space, but a genuine question (rather than a rhetorical or an exam question) assumes that the hearer is superior in expertise, knows something the speaker doesn't. The declarative assumes the speaker knows something the hearer doesn't and is therefore an authority.

5.5.2. Modality

Modality is a grammatical resource for conveying degrees of **probability**, **ability**, **usuality**, **obligation** and **inclination**, expressed by verbs, adjectives and adverbs (Table 5.5). There are problems of ambiguity with modal verbs like *may*, *must/have to*, *can* and *will/would* but these can often be solved by reference to the adjective and adverb columns. Note, too, that permission is located at the low point on the obligation scale. The right-hand column attempts to link modality with declarative and imperative moods.

Activity 5.6

Are the modal verbs in sentences (a)–(s) being used to express probability, ability, usuality, obligation or inclination? (Substituting an adjective from column 3 of Table 5.5 might help.) Are any of these uses ambiguous as between different kinds of modality?

   a. You **may** smoke if you **must**.
   b. Living on Earth **may** be expensive, but it includes an annual free trip around the Sun.
   c. Poverty **must** have many satisfactions, otherwise there **would** not be so many poor people. (Don Herold, Tibballs 2006: 455).
   d. How many roads **must** a man travel down before he admits he is lost?
   e. You **must** not attempt to use this hairdryer under water.
   f. "Incontinence hotline – **can** you hold please?"
   g. If that phone was up your ass maybe you **could** drive better. (bumper sticker)
   h. I didn't believe in reincarnation in my last life, so why **should** I in this?
   i. Due to budget cuts the light at the end of the tunnel **will** be out.
   j. People **would** give their right arm to be ambidextrous.
   k. I **would**n't be caught dead with a necrophiliac.

Reasons Why it's Great to be a Woman (Tibballs 2006: 372)

   l. You **always** get to choose the movie.
   m. You **never have to** buy your own drinks.
   n. You don't **have to** understand the offside rule.
   o. You don't **have to** adjust your genitals constantly.
   p. If you forget to shave, no one **has to** know.

Table 5.5. Modals (and their link to mood)

Modality	Degree	Modal Verb	Modal Adjective	Modal Adverb	Mood Link
Possibility	High	must/have to/will be	bound to/certain	certainly/definitely/positively	Declarative
	Median	may/could be	likely/expected to	probably	
	Low		possible	possibly, perhaps	
			unlikely		
Ability	High	can/could	able to		Declarative
	Median		possibly able to		
	Low		probably unable to		
Usuality	High	must/has to be		always/usually	Declarative
	Median	will be/may be		sometimes	
	Low			rarely/seldom	
Obligation	High	must/have to	required	definitely/positively	Imperative
	Median	should/ought to/will do	supposed		
	Low	may/might/can do	expected		
			allowed		
Inclination	High	must/have to/need to	determined	gladly/willingly	Imperative (Let's)
	Median	shall do/would	keen		
	Low	may/might do	willing	reluctantly	

q. You **can** always get a taxi to stop for you.
r. You **can** wear no underwear and be considered wild and sexy; a man who does the same thing is merely thought of as disgusting.
s. You **can** get laid any time you want.

Comment

Many of these modals seem highly ambiguous, but these are my suggestions:

> (a) obligation, inclination; (b) probability. Note that in this formulaic clause sequence "may" has a much stronger degree of probability than normal, almost equivalent to "Living on earth is expensive"; (c) probability; (d) probability, ability, inclination?; (e) obligation; (f) inclination, ability; (g) ability; (h) obligation, probability?; (i) probability; (j) inclination; (k) inclination.
>
> (l) usuality; (m) usuality, obligation; (n) obligation; (o) inclination; (p) probability; (q) ability; (r) obligation; (s) probability.

One can think of the social meanings of modals in terms of the vertical interpersonal axis of power and knowledge. Status as expert is associated with high degrees of probability and usuality, i.e. certainty of assertions/predictions, e.g. (l), though note that complete certainty is expressed by total lack of modals. By contrast, low status is associated with low degrees of probability and usuality, i.e. tentativeness: "there might be other examples of affective meaning if I could find them". Power is exerted by high obligation modality directed towards the hearer, e.g. (e). Status dependent on power is reflected by modals of ability with *I* as subject, but with the power of the other with second and third person pronouns as subject. Repeated expression of inclination might be a symptom of powerlessness: you keep saying you want to do something, because you can't, like Chekhov's Three Sisters reiterating their desire to go to Moscow.

5.6.　HUMOUR AND SOCIAL OR INTERPERSONAL MEANINGS

Humour in general and jokes in particular appear primarily interpersonal in function. Poynton (1989), like Martin and White (2005), identifies the expression of affect as basically interpersonal, a third dimension besides those of power and contact (solidarity in Figure 5.2). And, commonsensically, humour provokes emotions leading to laughter, or is used as a psychological defence. Various theories, even in their names, emphasise these interpersonal functions, e.g. the superiority theory or the aggression theory (Norrick 1993: 8–9). Moreover, humour generates intimacy (Cohen 1999) or rapport (Lundberg 1969, quoted in Purdie 1993), and laughter tends to be socially contagious (Chafe 2007: 67). Humour also functions as a control mechanism for enforcing norms within a group, including language norms. For instance, in the following dialogue Sally and Leona mock people who use phrases like *top of the line*, *state of the art*, *cutting edge*, *all of the above* and, perhaps, even *nice*, *a beauty*.

LEONA:	It's a good tape-recorder. It's a *nice* one, huh?
SALLY:	It's a beauty.
LEONA:	Beauty. Yes. Top of the line. State of the art.
SALLY:	Huh huh [huh]
LEONA:	[And the] cutting edge.
SALLY:	*All* of the above.
LEONA:	*All* of the above. Oh, I *love* it. Can I *have* huh huh heh heh he he [he.]
SALLY:	[Huh] huhhuhhuh.
LEONA:	It's beautiful, oh my God. (Norrick 1993: 86)

On the other hand, Norrick discusses and exemplifies interpersonal facets of humour which contrast with its solidarity-building function. To be the master of humour raises one's profile or one's status in interaction, so, for instance, telling humorous anecdotes is an act of self-assertion or self-presentation (Norrick 1993: 44). Humour is often disruptive of the conversation. It can be mildly aggressive, and not only through mockery and banter. Because it achieves its intimacy (Cohen 1999) by excluding those who don't get the joke, or those who, while getting it, still choose not to laugh at it, it has a slightly hostile testing function (Norrick 1993: 105–6). Given that humour is a widely used resource for creating and reinforcing interpersonal relationships, or exerting power through control or aggression, it is somewhat surprising that it has been neglected in the Critical Linguistics or Critical Discourse Analysis tradition (Simpson and Mayr 2010: 25–6).

Since an ambiguity producing a clash of schemas is essential in the humour theory underpinning this book, it is worth mentioning that access to schemas may be more or less restricted. And the more restricted the schema on which the humour depends, the more intimacy it creates and the more it excludes those without access to the necessary schemas. If I hear news of the Pope (God's Rottweiler, the German Shepherd (2.4)) being knocked to the ground during a Christmas procession in St Peter's in 2009, and the immediate intense media speculation about possible injury, I might turn to my wife and draw a humorous comparison by saying "another case of Doodoo".

In Singapore my neighbour's dog, Doodoo, a Maltese terrier, was run over by a taxi which failed to stop. My neighbour pursued the taxi-driver wielding a hockey stick, and was later charged with grievous bodily harm – of which he was acquitted when the case came to court a year or so later. The dog was knocked unconscious but recovered quickly and was back to normal health the day after the accident. However, when the court case was reported, both newspapers sensationalised the accident – in the tabloid Doodoo had died, in the broadsheet he was still in veterinary hospital a year after being run over.

As Attardo (1994: 247) remarks, several scripts/schemas operate in my humorous comparison. There are linguistic scripts for newspapers, tabloids and the media, and general knowledge scripts about how sensational and lurid they can be. There may also be restricted knowledge scripts about the tendency for the media to fabricate. More restricted still is the nearly individual script, or dyadic tradition (Oring 2003: 79–80) concerning the accident to Doodoo, shared between myself, my wife and only a few other people. The humorous comparison between the Pope's accident and Doodoo's reinforces intimacy with my wife, one of the few people with access to this almost individual script. In addition, she might evoke the restricted script comparing the Pope to fierce dogs. Use of such restricted and individual scripts is equivalent in effect to those centrifugal language forces which produce dialects and anti-languages.

Satire, like many other kinds of humour, has important consequences for interpersonal relationships. Simpson has explored these, diagramming the discourse positions in operation (Figure 5.3.).

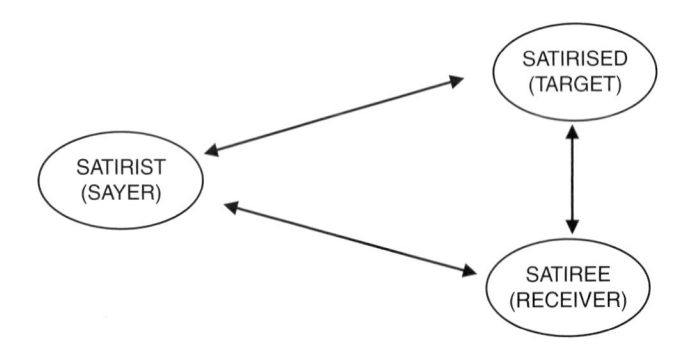

Figure 5.3. The satirical triad (after Simpson 2003: 86)

Humour/satire can create a closer relationship between satirist (Sayer) and satiree (Receiver), and, in prototypically aggressive satire, distance both satirist and satiree from the satirised (Target). But conversely, if there is little cultural or ideological gap between satirised and satiree, then the satire may fail, and the distance between satiree and satirist increase (Simpson 2003: 86–7, 154–7). For example, readers who are Catholic may not appreciate my jokes at the expense of His Holiness the Pope. Joke websites therefore become a way of declaring and promoting one's own identity (Oring 2003: chapter 10).

An added complication arises from the distinction between outsider and insider humour. Negative jokes with particular social groups as the satirised may be considered discriminatory if the satirist is not a member of the satirised social group, but be perfectly acceptable if they are. Black comedians can, with impunity, tell jokes that would be thought racist in a white person's mouth, especially if the satirees are also black (Simpson and Mayr 2010: 194).

5.7. SUMMARY

This chapter explored interpersonal meanings: reflected, where homonyms affect each other's meaning; connotative, which depend upon what the words refer to in the real world, rather than meanings "internal" to the language system; affective or emotional, as conveyed by the lexis of appraisal, intonation, rhythm and syntax; social – including aspects of the speaker such as dialect, age, status, familiarity and formality. It proceeded to consider how grammar encodes interpersonal meaning, namely through mood and modality. Finally it stressed the interpersonal functions of humour, in cementing relationships or excluding, targeting or controlling the behaviour of outsiders, introducing the satirist–satirised–satiree triangle as a framework for understanding humour's interpersonal dynamics. It noted how humour can exploit reflected taboo meanings, or unsuccessful attempts to avoid euphemism or unwanted reflected meanings. Humour was shown to be enhanced by rhythm, to be affected by dialect, and to depend upon clashes in degrees of formality and technicality as much as upon clashes of conceptual schemas.

Note that the interpersonal, social and affective meanings in this chapter, and the conceptual meanings in Chapters 3 and 4, are revisited in the context of genre in the next chapter. Specifically, Attardo's taxonomy of the social functions of humour, while relevant to Section 5.6, is reserved for discussion in Section 6.4.2.

Discussion

One notes in Table 5.3 the absence of core terms for bodily waste, and the same is probably true for sex (Attardo 1994: 266), with only slang/swear/obscene words or medical/technical terms available. Why should this be, and how does it relate to the fact that excretion and sex are often one of the schemas involved in humour? Is this absence apparent in other languages that you speak?

Suggested Readings

- The introduction of Barthes (1972) is a classic account of connotative meanings and how through second-order meaning they develop into symbols. Following this introduction Barthes presents case studies of cultural objects which have acquired symbolic value. ("Symbol" is not used by him in Peirce's technical sense (8.2) – icon might be more apt.)
- Martin and White (2005) is a standard exposition of appraisal theory, though Martin (2000) is a shorter introduction.
- Halliday and Matthiessen (2004: chapter 4) gives a detailed account of the systems of mood and modality and how they are instantiated in lexico-grammar. There is a simpler account in Downing and Locke (1992: chapters 5 and 9), which also has the advantage of relating mood to speech acts (see 8.5).
- McEnery (2006), especially chapter 2, is an interesting reading, since it not only deals with the expression of affective meaning, through swearing, but also demonstrates how other social variables, including sex and social class, correlate with different forms of bad language.
- Cohen (1999: chapters 2 and 3) emphasises and celebrates the fact that humour creates, maintains and reinforces interpersonal intimacy, providing it meets with the appropriate response and uptake.
- For a more academic discussion of how language and discourse create individual identity and group solidarity, see Le Page and Tabouret-Keller (1985).
- Oring (2003: 71–84) discusses the relation of Freud's theory of humour to Victorian sentimentality and sensibility. He concludes that in fact humour can be used to express these positive emotions, if in a disguised form. Besides affect, he also expands on the social solidarity aspects of humour, notably "the roast" as institutionalised banter. This reading is also relevant to the sections of Chapter 9 on politeness (especially 9.7).

6 Textual meaning and genre

Chapters 3 and 4 examined conceptual or ideational meanings, and Chapter 5 interpersonal, social and affective meanings. This chapter considers the meanings words and larger stretches of language acquire through their positioning and occurrence in texts. And it uses this as a springboard to discuss larger textual structures above the level of the sentence in various genres. By ending our survey of semantic meaning with genre we can appreciate how all these different kinds of meanings might coalesce under the umbrella of register, which spells out the relationship between social context and ideational (Chapters 3 and 4), interpersonal (Chapter 5) and textual (Chapter 6) meanings.

The chapter ends with a critique of the traditional approaches to semantics illustrated so far in this book, summarising some of the problems and objections that have already emerged. The elusiveness and instability of meanings is illustrated through a brief discussion of meaning change.

6.1. COLLOCATIVE MEANING

Part of the meaning of a word is the words and meanings which frequently occur in its textual environment, its normal **collocations**. "You may know a word by the company it keeps." Since collocations can now be computed by concordancing programs, this kind of meaning has received a great deal of attention recently, and Hoey's theory of lexical priming, discussed at length in my final chapter, exalts collocation to an overriding principle of lexical acquisition. As already noted, collocation is very important when storing words in the mind (Aitchison 2002).

Some words collocate very freely, with few restrictions, e.g. *take*. Others are very restricted, as this joke makes clear: "I hate to spread rumours: but what else can one do with them?" (Amanda Lear, Alexander 1997: 54). One of the few verbs which takes *rumour* as an object is *spread*. Degrees of collocability can be exemplified by the relative restrictedness of *rancid*, *addled* and *rotten* (Carter 1987: 52).

> *rancid milk/butter,*
> *addled eggs/brains/senses,*
> *rotten eggs/fruit/wood/apples/luck* etc. etc.

Words which, like *rancid*, pair up with only a few other words in a particular syntactic frame can be called **restricted** in their collocations, and those like *rotten*, slightly more promiscuous, participate in **semi-restricted collocations**. As another example, these are the restricted collocations for *key* in the Collins WordsOnline database.

premodifying noun *key* + noun: *role, issue(s), players, factor, areas, figure(s), element, part*

Some common collocations of colour words in English are *blood red*, *deep purple*, *jet black*, *yellow fever*, *blue moon*, *green fingers*.

Activity 6.1

Authors often exploit unusual collocations (violate selection restrictions) for stylistic purposes. What's unusual about the following?

"Her son was damaged in an accident."

Comment

It seems rather unusual to collocate the verb *damage* with an object or goal which refers to a person, probably preferring *injured*. It might suggest that her son was brain-damaged and lost his personhood, somehow, as a result of the accident.

Like many non-conceptual meanings, collocational meaning seems relatively fluid. Back in the 1970s *damaged a foot* was an unusual collocation in my dialect of English, as *damage* collocated with objects referring to inanimate things or internal organs rather than external body parts and limbs. However, this has changed over the last forty years, though it still seems unusual to collocate it with persons.

Sometimes jokes depend upon the overlapping of collocations that have petrified into fixed expressions. Two different collocational patterns activate incompatible schemas, the overlap between them represents a connector, and the second collocational pattern is a schema-switch trigger or disjunctor. For example in "cleanliness is next to impossible" the "next to" is an overlap between the dictum "cleanliness is next to godliness" and the common collocation *next to impossible*. But collocational surprises can operate at a more general level, creating humorous effects through incompatibility of social meaning in spite of conceptual compatibility. The following account lacks a consistent level of formality:

> Quite honestly, after the considerable exertions demanded by my employment this afternoon I couldn't be assed to ascend to your residence on the 5th floor.

The very formal *considerable exertions, ascend* and *residence* do not collocate very smoothly with the slang *couldn't be assed*.

6.2. THEMATIC MEANING AND INFORMATION FOCUS

One aspect of textual meaning concerns the distribution of information throughout a text. Thematic meaning captures the idea that (a) "My sister walked the dog" and (b) "The dog was walked by my sister", while synonymous in conceptual meaning, differ in terms of information distribution. In discussing thematic meaning, two kinds of distinction are important: first, using A to refer to the speaker/writer and B for the hearer/reader, the distinction between given information (AB information), and new information (A information); second, that between the starting point of the clause, the theme, and the remainder of the clause, the rheme. **Theme**, in English, is determined by the first element from among subject, verb, complement/object, adjunct to occur in a clause. The remainder of the clause is the **rheme** (Halliday and Matthiessen 2004: 64ff.). So in (a) above the theme is "My sister" and the rheme is "walked the dog". In (b), the passive version, "the dog" is theme, and "was walked by my sister" is rheme. Normally, especially in writing, AB (given) information is placed in theme position, and A information, which is new to B, near the end of the rheme. So in (a) "My sister" is presented as given and "walked the dog" as new, while in (b) "the dog" as given and "was walked by my sister" as new.

Attardo mentions that the punchlines of jokes occur towards their end, i.e. in the rheme, usually in final position (Attardo 1994: 100–1). This is not surprising since the disjunctor is unpredictable and therefore carries more information. The theme and end of the rheme are important as the places for given and new information respectively, creating the "bathtub effect" (Attardo 2001: 91), in jokes, as in discourse in general.

Spoken language is, however, more flexible than written in marking the position of new information, employing intonation to indicate

this focus. We need a short digression here to explain tone-unit structure, and the meaning of nuclear tones.

Speech can be divided into tone units consisting of the following
structure:

Pre-head | Head |
         | onset + NUCLEAR SYLLABLE + tail |

The *pre-head* consists of unstressed syllables. The *onset* syllable is the
first stressed syllable. Informationally, the most important syllable
in the tone unit is the **nuclear syllable** (in upper case), the location
of the most prominent pitch movement or **nuclear tone**. Generally
it (a) carries the focus of new information, and (b) falls on the
stressed syllable of the last lexical word in the tone unit. If it is
placed earlier in the unit for emphasis or contrast it is **contrastive**.
For example, a primary school teacher, recounting how she explains
the tooth fairy custom to immigrant children in her class, distinguishes these children from the English ones with contrastive
stress:

> |What I like to do with the children the INDian children| and the
> PakiSTANi children|... (Crystal and Davy 1975: 76)

Activity 6.2

The ambiguity in the following jokes depends upon placing the nuclear tone in
different places. Explain how.

1. Two fonts walked into a bar. The bartender said, "Sorry we don't want your
   type in here." (Tibballs 2006: 60)
2. Khrushchev is being driven in a limousine in a rural area of Czechoslovakia. Suddenly
   the car strikes and kills a pig which has wandered onto the road. Khrushchev
   says, "We'd better go up to the nearest farmhouse and pay some damages." So
   the chauffeur goes off to the farmhouse to offer the farmer some compensation.
   An hour passes, and the chauffeur does not return, so Khrushchev begins to
   wonder what has happened. Finally Khrushchev sees the chauffeur returning,
   staggering under the weight of all sorts of packages and gifts.
   "What happened?" asks Khrushchev. "I sent you to pay them."
   "I don't know," replies the chauffeur, "all I said to them was: I have Khrushchev
   in the car and I killed the pig." (Carr and Greeves 2006: 250)

Comment

1.   The nuclear tone can fall on different syllables: "Sorry we don't
      want YOUR type in here", where contrastive tonicity distinguishes
      the fonts from the other kinds of customers they welcome to the
      bar; or "Sorry we don't want your TYPE in here" which connects to
      the meaning of *font* 'typeface'. The former is the unmarked or

salient reading and therefore consistent with the script/schema of customers entering a bar and being made to feel unwelcome. But we are compelled to do a retake to make sense of the font schema to which the other meaning of "type" is relevant. Only in written form does the punchline really act as a connector.

2. "I have Khruschev in the car and I killed the pig" is more subtle. In one spoken version "I killed the PIG", 'pig' or 'killing the pig' is presented as new information, indicating the farmer's pig has been killed. With the alternative placing of the nuclear tone "I KILLed the pig", only 'killed' is presented as new. This implies a prior textual reference to the referent of "the pig", presumably by "Khruschev". So "the pig" must be a metaphor for Khruschev, and the unpopular president, not the literal pig, has been killed.

There are four main kinds of tone in English, falling \, rising /, rise-fall ∧ and fall-rise ∨.

Falling e.g. |Come to$\overset{\textstyle\backslash}{\text{MOR}}$row.|

Rising e.g. |Did he $\overset{\textstyle/}{\text{COME?}}$|

Rise-fall e.g. Of| $\overset{\textstyle\wedge}{\text{COURSE}}$ I'll come.|

Fall-rise e.g. (The | Wongs have bought a plasma t$\overset{\textstyle\backslash}{\text{V,}}$|) so they | $\overset{\textstyle\vee}{\text{TELL}}$ me.|

The phonetician David Brazil identified the four tones, fall-rise, falling, rising and rise-fall, and explained their significance in terms of information distribution (Coulthard 1985). The basic distinction is between fall-rise and falling: **fall-rise** is used to mention information which is given or AB information (shared between addresser A and addressee B) and is labelled *r* for **referring** tone; **falling** is used to introduce new (A) information, which expands upon the information shared between A and B, and is labelled *p* for **proclaiming** tone. One can, for example, vary the tones on the same sentence, to give different implications for what is new (A) and what is shared (AB).

(1) |When I've finished White $\overset{\textstyle\vee}{\text{TIG}}$er | I shall | read $\overset{\textstyle\backslash}{\text{FREE}}$dom |
                                    r   P

(2) |When I've finished White $\overset{\textstyle\backslash}{\text{TIG}}$er | I shall | read $\overset{\textstyle\vee}{\text{FREE}}$dom |
                                    p   r

In (1) the hearer is supposedly aware that the speaker is currently reading *White Tiger*, and the speaker's intention to read *Freedom* afterwards is presented as new information. In (2) the reverse is the case: the hearer is supposed to know of the speaker's intention to read *Freedom* but to be unaware that the speaker is currently reading *White Tiger*.

The function of the rising tone, labelled $r+$, is to remind, to reactivate information already in the hearer's long-term memory. Only dominant speakers have the right to issue reminders of common ground by using this tone. For instance a lecturer might say:

$$\qquad\qquad / \qquad\qquad\qquad\qquad\qquad\qquad \backslash$$
The | portfolio assignment I SET you | is | due in on FRIday |
$$\qquad\qquad\qquad r+ \qquad\qquad\qquad\qquad\qquad p$$

The rise-fall tone, $p+$, traditionally viewed as an expression of surprise or horror, signals that the information is not only new to the hearer but also to the speaker. It is commonly used when reading aloud interesting information, and in TV documentaries. In responses such as "REALly", which register new information, it means something like 'That alters my world view'.

A: The government plans to fully nationalise the high street banks.
$$\qquad \wedge$$
B: REALly?
$$\qquad p+$$

A final aspect of thematic meaning is the use of **marked theme**, when, in declarative mood clauses, an element other than subject takes initial position. In this opening stanza of an A. E. Housman poem, all themes are marked. The subject is underlined and the theme bolded.

> **On Wenlock Edge** the wood's in trouble
> **His forest fleece** the Wrekin heaves.
> **The gale**, it plies the saplings double
> And **thick** on Severn snow the leaves.
>
> (The Wrekin is a steep wooded hill in Shropshire, bordering the river Severn.)

Even in line 3, which may be unmarked, there is in fact a pre-posed theme, "the gale", before the subject "it".

Textual meanings are a particularly dynamic kind of meaning, generated in the reader's head during linear processing. Notice, for example, the effect of line 4, where the subject is delayed until the end of the rheme. As we read we might take "snow" as a noun and subject of the clause, until we reach "the leaves" and realise that "snow" must be a verb. In unmarked form the clause would be "The leaves snow thick on Severn", but in its actual marked form it mirrors the process of perception in which something is seen thickly falling onto the river, first surmised to be snow, and finally identified as leaves (Goatly 2008). It is such dynamism in text processing created by marked forms of language which creates the incongruous element necessary for humour.

6.3. COHESION

Another aspect of textual meaning concerns the meaning relations of a text across clauses. This is known as cohesion/coherence. Two important ways of stitching a text together are by sense relations and co-reference. We already saw (1.4) how co-reference operates in the opening of James' *A Portrait of a Lady*. But we can also identify the contribution of the sense relations we discussed in Chapter 4, such as **hyponymy** (a 'kind of' relationship), **meronymy** (a part–whole relation), **synonymy**, **antonymy**, as well as **repetition** (which is not necessarily co-reference) and metonymy (see Chapter 7). Metonymy, briefly, is a semantic association based on real-world association or contiguity in experience. A metonymic term can substitute for the concept to which it is metonymically linked, e.g. EVENT AS PLACE, "I've been watching *Wimbledon* all afternoon", CAUSE AS EFFECT, "Murray, you are my *happiness*", CONTENTS AS CONTAINER, "To celebrate I drank five *bottles* of champagne", INHABITANTS AS AREA, "*Britain* loved the victory" etc.

Activity 6.3

Look back at the Henry James passage (1.4, p. 14)

1. What examples do we have of hyponymy/superordinacy in sentences (1), (3) and (4)?
2. In sentences (1) and (2) what meronyms do we have for Ralph?
3. In sentence (3) what is a metonym for dog?
4. What are close to synonyms across sentences (3) and (4)?
5. What are the possible antonyms within sentence (3) and sentence (4)?

Comment

1. "terrier", "dog", "beast";
2. "hands", "heels", "face", "eyes";
3. "barks";
4. "welcome", "greeting";
5. "welcome", "defiance"?; "person", "beast"?

6.3.1. Cohesion and coherence

It is useful to distinguish **cohesion** – the explicit means by which a text is stitched together (like meronymy, metonymy, hyponymy, antonymy and synonymy) – from **coherence**, the schema consistency by which the meanings of the text are integrated psychologically. Sometimes coherence is achieved by cohesion, but not always – it may be achieved by inference. This attested dialogue "I buried a rabbit this morning", "At least it wasn't a cold night" (Peter Skehan, personal communication) lacks overt cohesive devices, apart from antonymy between "night" and "morning". But by supplying information that on frosty nights the earth freezes solid, we infer a cold night would make burying a rabbit difficult, and make a coherent text out of a non-cohesive one.

Coherence (achieved through cohesion or otherwise) has an important relation to humour. Firstly, some puns achieve an extra degree of coherence, reflecting humour's poetic function. For instance, "In a course on human sexuality there's a lot to cover" has an extra layer of coherence compared with "In a course in linguistics there's a lot to cover". Or the metonymy linking "sour" and "lemon" gives cohesion/coherence to the following pun: "This girl comes into my class looking real sour. I knew she was gonna be a lemon" (Sherzer 1978: 338, Attardo 1994: 314–16).

However, other theorists of linguistic humour claim that disjunctors in jokes create an initial incoherence: "In a forced re-interpretation joke, if the differing set-up interpretations are caused by linguistic ambiguity, then the punchline will cause discourse incoherence with the more obvious interpretation" (Ritchie 2004: 95). Norrick (1993: 161) and Chiaro (1992: 20), following Sherzer, contrast such conscious puns that disrupt coherence with unconscious ones that enhance it, e.g. the unconscious "Baloney! You don't eat meat." (Baloney is literally a kind of sausage.) We can reconcile such apparently opposing views by acknowledging that, although the initial disjunction in conscious jokes/puns creates incoherence, the eventual understanding through a connector linking two schemas may create an alternative, or even extra level of coherence.

At a more macro-level of discourse coherence, Chiaro (1992: 105ff.) gives evidence that one joke will often initiate a joke sequence. More specifically, jokes with the same subject matter (e.g. two jokes about cauliflowers) or different sub-genres of jokes (e.g. riddles) tend to follow each other and so cohere.

6.4. *GENRE*

Besides its conceptual meaning, does a sentence or text tell us what activity/occupation the speaker is involved in? If we hear "Game to Nadal. Nadal leads 5 games to 4. New balls please", we presumably identify the occupational activity as tennis (umpiring), not transplant surgery.

Genre is a highly developed and widely applied theoretical concept, especially in the systemic functional tradition. It subsumes the related concept of **register**, which deals with the co-variance of context and linguistic features at the sentence level and below. **Genre** is a wider concept as it also includes the co-variance of context and discourse structure at the level above the sentence. At least as I use the terms, Genre = Register + Structure. (These roughly correlate with LA (language) + NS (narrative structure), two of the KRs (knowledge resources) necessary for humour (Attardo 1994: 223); see Section 11.5.1.)

6.4.1. Register

So let's start with register. For Halliday, sentence grammar encodes three functions or types of meaning: the ideational (our conceptual), the inter-personal (our social/affective etc.), and the textual. As shown in Chapter 3, ideationally a sentence represents the world as things and processes, with the logical connections between them. Interpersonally, a sentence constructs or reflects relationships between hearers/speakers and readers/writers and their exchanges of goods/services or information. Chapter 5 explored the interpersonal role of mood and modality. The textual aspect of the sentence is the way in which it orders and manages information distribution and connects it with the other parts of the text (cohesion) and the world beyond the text (reference, coherence).

For Halliday, each function operates simultaneously in the clause, which represents the world, is an interpersonal exchange, and is a text. As an example of these three independent variables consider the following sentences:

1. The angel put the olive oil drops in Mary's ears.[1]
2. The olive oil drops were put in Mary's ears by the angel.
3. Did the angel put the olive oil drops in Mary's ears?

These sentences are ideationally the same. (1) differs from (2) in its textual meaning – with different theme and rheme. (1) and (2) differ from (3) in interpersonal meaning: (1) and (2) give information, while (3) demands it. These three kinds of meaning are essential to register analysis.

The concept of **register** allows us to develop a quite sophisticated notion of the social context of language.

> A register is a semantic concept ... a configuration of meanings that are typically associated with a particular situational configuration of Field, Mode and Tenor. It will, of course, include the expressions, the lexico-grammatical and phonological features, that typically accompany or realize these meanings. (Halliday and Hasan 1989: 38–9)

To clarify, we need to define field, tenor and mode (where possible linking them to Jakobson's functions (1.3)).

> **Field** is what is happening, the nature of the social action that is taking place; what it is that the participants are engaged in, in which the language figures as some essential component. Field links with or is expressed by ideational or conceptual meaning or Jakobson's referential function. (See Chapters 3 and 4.)
>
> **Tenor** is concerned with who is taking part, the nature of the participants, their statuses and roles: what kinds of role relationships obtain among the participants, both the types of speech role that they are taking on in the dialogue and the whole cluster of socially significant relationships in which they are involved. Tenor links to or is expressed by interpersonal or social meaning or Jakobson's expressive, conative and phatic functions. (See Chapter 5.)
>
> **Mode** involves what part the language is playing. Is it constitutive, that is essential to the field (e.g. a lecture), or ancillary to it, that is marginal to the field (e.g. a football match). It concerns what the participants are expecting the language to do for them in that situation: the symbolic organization of the text, the status that it has and the function in the context, including the channel (is it spoken or written or some combination of the two?) and also the rhetorical mode, what is being achieved by the text in terms of such categories as persuasive, expository, didactic and the like. Mode links to or is expressed partly by textual meaning or Jakobson's poetic and perhaps metalingual function. (See this chapter.) (after Halliday and Hasan 1989: 12)

To exemplify the concept of register, consider how we might contrast the contextual configuration of magazine advertising and conversation.

Magazine Advertising

Field: economic, buying and selling: description and recommendation of product as persuasion to buy, and information gathering and decision-making about purchases

Tenor: company/advertising agency to reader;
hierarchic: advertiser less powerful than potential buyers who are non-assured, perhaps reluctant addressees;

Mode: social distance maximum, but shows fake intimacy (synthetic personalisation)

Mode: language role: mainly constitutive, partially ancillary to selling;
channel: visual;
medium: print with heavy reliance on graphics/visuals (and in phonological patterning often reflective of spoken language);
mass;
read/looked at selectively;
rhetorically persuasive.

Conversation

Field: social interaction, conversation (a Field or end in itself – if subordinated to other purposes it ceases to be conversation)

Tenor: interlocutors; close to equal;
social distance: medium to intimate;
has largely phatic function (which overlaps with field)

Mode: language role: constitutive;
channel: phonic;
medium: spoken, with visual contact/feedback;
small group or dyadic;
rhetorically multifunctional (phatic?) (Goatly 2011: 315–16)

These descriptions define the social context (for both register and genre), but they correlate with linguistic register features at the sentence level and below. For example, because they are persuasive, and make offers that are supposedly of benefit to the reader, magazine advertisements frequently use imperatives.

My attempt to delineate the contextual variables for conversation underspecifies field, by comparison with ads, and indicates the dominance of the interpersonal function. As we shall see, this is one reason jokes are thought of as appropriately inserted in a conversational matrix.

6.4.2. The register of jokes

Jokes too seem to underplay ideational field (referential function) and highlight textual mode (poetic, metalingual) and interpersonal tenor (phatic, expressive). Norrick claims that humour and joking have little to do with the efficient exchange of information:

> The existence and especially the persistence of humour in conversation indicates that it must appeal to some principle higher than that which mandates relevance to the current information exchange. Punning and banter are not simply games conversationalists play in lieu of speaking topically: wordplay ... provides conversationalists with an opportunity to cooperate in

> creating a particular form of talk with conventions of its own for the
> ongoing interaction – and this too counts as metalingual activity in
> the broad sense. (Norrick 1993: 95)

Normally speaking, text is a tool for the interpersonal and the ideational discourse functions, a means to an end. By contrast, in humour,
jokes and other ludic genres like literature, the textual function takes
on a life of its own. If normal text is like footprints on the beach, the
traces (text) which are by-products of some other activity like walking
(field) with one's partner (tenor), then these ludic genres are more like
deliberately going down to the beach in order to make pretty patterns
in the sand or to build a sandcastle together. In Jakobson's terms, they
seem poetic and phatic, if not metalingual, rather than referential,
though Oring (2003) and Billig (2005) demonstrate their more serious
ideational potential.

The interpersonal function of jokes is highlighted by Attardo (1994).
His table (Attardo 1994: 322) lists the social functions of humour,
though I have modified it in order to show how the last three columns
shade into the ideational and textual (Table 6.1).

The importance of context to joking is discussed by Norrick (1993:
3–4), using the following example:

> A plane was loading passengers for a flight from New York to Chicago.
> Passengers were helping each other to stow luggage and find their
> seats when a man with a New York accent said "What's everybody
> being so nice for? We're still in New York." A second man laughed and
> replied: "Yeah. We'll be back in Chicago soon. Then it'll be OK again,"
> which evoked general laughter.

Norrick points out the importance of setting (field): a plane rather than
a bus, because humour can relieve the slight tension during a plane's
take-off; it must be from New York to Chicago rather than, say, to
Boston, because the cities have different stereotypes; and of the participants (tenor): joking in public with strangers is part of New Yorkers'
conversational style, and the joke, because it might imply criticism of
New Yorkers, the satirised, is better uttered by a satirist with a New
York accent rather than a Chicago accent (see Figure 5.2).

Not only are jokes a register or genre in their own right, but joking is
typically contextualised in other registers/genres (Norrick 1993). (Joke
books and comedy routines are a secondary parasitic form of the
original contextualised joke.) Certainly cultures are selective about
the genres where jokes are embedded. Ross points out, for instance,
that risqué double entendres appear on bumper stickers, notice boards
in workplaces and birthday cards, but not on condolence cards, new
baby congratulations or Easter cards (Ross 1998: 72).

Table 6.1. *The functions of jokes*

INTERPERSONAL					[IDEATIONAL]	[TEXTUAL]	
social control	*conveying norms*	*ingratiation*	*creating common ground*	*social play*	*cleverness*	*repair (decommitment)*	*discourse management*
Embarrassing, intimidating	Highlighting taboos	Attention and fostering liking	Attention, understanding, bonding, social cohesion	Camaraderie	Extra cognitive work	Defusing unpleasantness, retracting	Initiation, termination, passing a turn, topic shift, checking

Conversation is the matrix within which jokes and joking usually occur. But why? Our register description of conversation defined the field in terms of the tenor. That is, conversation is an end in itself with primarily interpersonal or phatic functions. Aspects of its tenor are the relatively symmetric positions for the participants in terms of rights and duties, and an emphasis on co-operation more than competition (Priego-Valverde 2009). This tenor emphasis means the genre is free in various ways – varieties of intonation, tenses, voice qualities, tempi, purposes and subject matter (Crystal and Davy 1969). One can "speak about everything and nothing, in a spontaneous way without a precise goal" (Priego-Valverde 2009: 170). Setting an agenda for a conversation turns it into a discussion or debate or meeting, and ulterior motives transform it – for instance, chat might become chatting up. Similarly jokes, as noted, often have a minimal field function, and the textual wordplay on which they depend can be an end in itself – interactional rather than instrumental. Table 6.1 makes most social functions of humour interpersonal, apart from discourse management and repair, partly textual, and creating extra cognitive work, perhaps ideational. Like literature and dreams, humour and conversation are a holiday from the ordinary instrumental purposes necessary for economic activity and physical survival.

In fact conversation's relative freedom has led some theorists (Swales 1990) to dub it a "pre-genre" rather than a genre proper, more casual than talk in institutionalised discourse. However, when jokes are incorporated or inserted into conversation they cease to be casual in this sense. "Non-casual language contains an additional layer of meaning, having to do with its specific function ... to cause laughter in the case of humour" (Attardo and Raskin 1991: 299). Accordingly, jokes do not count as conversation – they are distinct from it.

6.4.3. Defining genre

Having defined and exemplified register we return to our definition of genre as register + structure. A genre is a staged event with the stages reflected in the discourse structure, e.g. narrative, magazine ad, telephone directory. The generic structure of an entry in the latter might be

surname ^ initial ^ address ^ telephone number

The ordering is paramount in a genre. Hence the oddity of the opening of the following sales encounter in a chemist's shop:

Customer: Good morning. Do you have anything to treat a complete loss of voice?
Shopkeeper: Good morning, sir. And what can I do for you?
                     (Alexander 1997: 63)

Martin's definition and description of genre are to the point:

> Genres are how things get done, when language is used to accomplish them. They range from literary to far from literary forms: poems, narratives, expositions, lectures, seminars, recipes, manuals, appointment making, service encounters, news broadcasts and so on.

> Genre refers to "the staged purposeful social processes through which a culture is realised in language." (Martin, in Swales 1990: 40, 41)

Culture may even be defined as the sum of the genres that conventionally take place in a society (Martin 1992).

We now proceed to discuss genre in relation to humour. We begin with two genres typically associated with humour, next consider the ways in which genre-mixing constitutes a clash of schemas leading to humour, before proceeding to an exploration of the structure of joke genres and sub-genres.

6.4.4. Generic structures: ads and narratives

Generic structures can be defined in terms of their elements, obligatory and optional, and the ordering of these elements, which may involve the embedding of one element within another, or the recursive introduction of elements.

Generic structure of ads

Toolan (1988) suggested a simple generic structure for magazine ads, consisting of headline, body copy, signature line, logo, slogan and standing details, though not necessarily in that strict order, all surrounded by illustration. Most of these elements are self-explanatory. The signature line is usually the name of the company, and the standing details are the contact details.

In the Anglia ad (Illustration 1) the generic elements might be identified as follows:

headline:	"If buying a house ... try Anglia"
body copy:	"Buying a house can seem a terribly complicated business ... for more details call in at your local Anglia branch."
signature line:	"ANGLIA"
logo:	the pyramid, with "Homemaker"
slogan:	either "BUILDING SOCIETY" beneath the signature line "Anglia", or "The building society that cares about what you want."
standing details:	"Anglia Building Society, Moulton Park, Northampton NN3 1NL"
illustration:	the vicious circle at the top (with explanatory text), and the two pyramids

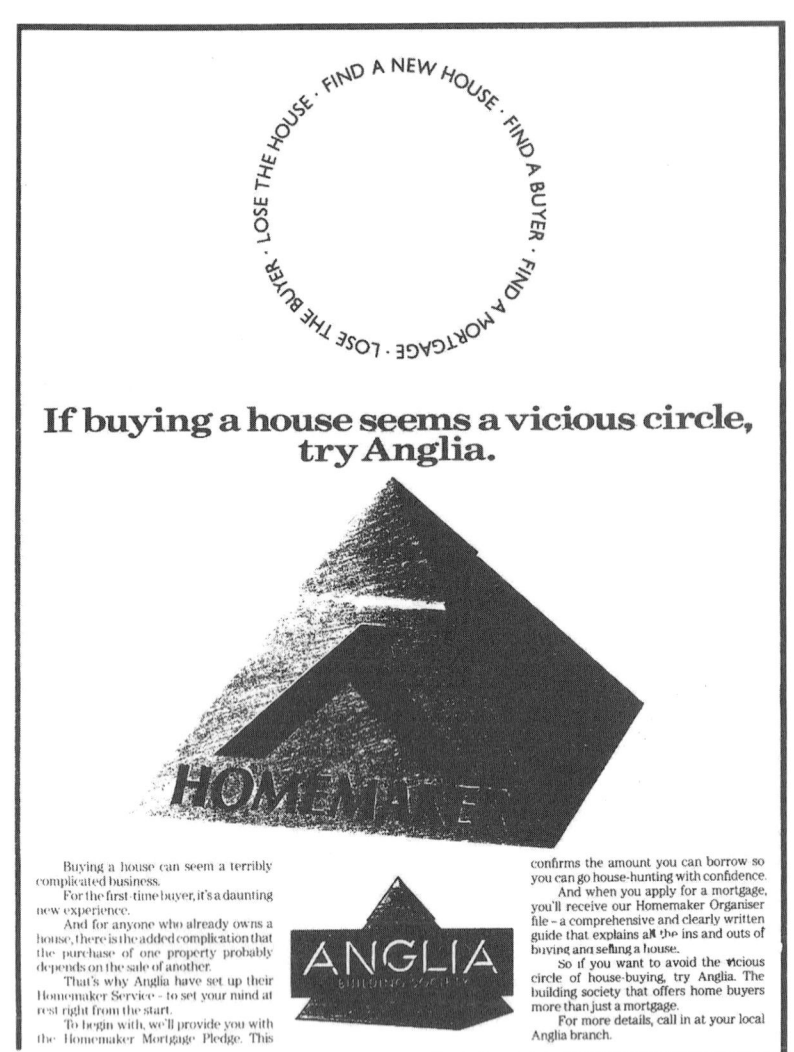

Illustration 1. Anglia Building Society ad. (Written credit details from Anglia Building Society, Moulton Park, Northampton NN3 1NL)

This ad also exemplifies aspects of the register, the comparatively frequent use of the following linguistic features:

imperative	"try Anglia" three times, "call in …" etc.
minor sentences	all the sentences forming the vicious circle, which lack a subject, "the building society that cares about what you want" without a main verb, etc.
premodifiers	"terribly complicated business", "first-time buyer", "daunting new experience" etc.
postmodifiers	"anyone who already owns a house", "the purchase of one property" etc.

These register variables partly reflect mode: the imperative is predictable given ads' persuasive rhetorical function, while the need to allow space for graphics as part of the symbolic organisation of the text mandates conciseness in the form of heavy modification. As for tenor, an informally conversational tone is realised through minor sentences; and the spurious intimacy of "synthetic personalisation" is realised by the not-so-obvious homonymic pun on "Building Society" (noun phrase or verb present participle + noun?), and the wicked paronymic pun "Try Anglia" (triangular, not circular). Such informality and pseudo-intimacy are precisely the point of humour when embedded in the advertising genre.

The generic structure of narrative[2]

From his investigation of oral narratives William Labov (1972) devised the following elements of **narrative structure**. While explaining the generic elements I will also point out the register features of the sentence/clause grammar typical or diagnostic of each element.

Abstract

This is a short introduction to the story provided before the narrative begins. It encapsulates the "point" of the story, or what it exemplifies. Though not compulsory, it signals that a narrative is imminent, and that the speaker wishes to hold the floor uninterrupted. Moreover, it is a bridge to make the narrative relevant to the preceding conversation. For example, if the conversation is about how frightening childhood experiences generate phobias, to make the transition to narrative you could say "There's this child I knew of who had a dreadful experience with bears, and it changed her behaviour for years afterwards". There is a similar tendency when telling jokes in the course of a conversation to justify the relation of the joke to the conversational context (Oring 2003).

Orientation

The orientation gives information about the time, place, persons and situation/activity type they are engaged in. Typically it employs adverbials of time and place, and relational process verbs for description. When reference is to an action which is ongoing when the narrative commences, it uses the **progressive** *-ing* forms of the verb. For example:

relational   relational
verb   verb
Her name was *Goldilocks and she* was *a very brave young girl.*

time adverbial   progressive   place adverbials
One July day she was walking   to town *along the outskirts of the wood.*

Strictly speaking this orientation element is not compulsory either, but is normal in written narratives.

Complicating Action

The complicating action and the resolution are the essential elements in a narrative. In fact, the minimum requirement for a narrative is two or more clauses describing a pair of linked events or actions, ordered chronologically, e.g. "Goldilocks slept in baby bear's bed. Baby bear frightened her away". Reversing the order of the clauses changes the interpretation of the events, resulting in a different narrative. Even in contemporary society "She had a baby and got married" is a rather different story from "She got married and had a baby". These clauses are in simple present or simple past tense, in contrast with the progressive forms of the orientation.

Resolution

The resolution is provided by the last of the narrative clauses which began with the complicating action, bringing the sequence of actions and events to an end, e.g. "Pumping adrenaline, Goldilocks sprinted away from the house of the three bears".

Coda

The coda completes the narrative and moves the listener out of the past back to the conversational present. It has the opposite purpose to the abstract, making a bridge out of the narrative, and signalling the speaker's relinquishing the floor. The transition back to the present is often signalled by changes of tenses and time adverbs. "So, she still refuses to eat porridge, sit in a rocking chair, and prefers to sleep on the carpet". Oring (2003: 86ff.) gives examples of whole jokes commenting on a theme or situation, and these glosses, equivalent to the morals in fables, may be spelt out in the coda (or the abstract).

Evaluation

Although these previous elements occur in a particular order, evaluation may occur at any point between the abstract and coda. It is realised by clauses which, outside the narrative action, delay its forward movement. These comprise:

- comments by narrator: "At that moment Goldilocks looked like a little angel"
- comment of character: "'Eating my porridge was a horrible thing to do'"
- comments of a third party: "'Mama bear told you it was naughty not to lock the door'"
- emotive devices – e.g.
  - exclamations: "What a soft bed it was!"
  - interjections/swear words: "'**Oh shit**, look at my chair!'"
  - emotionally laden vocabulary: "'You **greedy, lazy, vandal!**'"
- comparators:
  - *if* clauses: "**If** Goldilocks had wept,
  - comparisons: **more like** a typical female
  - modals (*can, shall, must, might* etc.) Baby Bear **might** have comforted her.
  - negatives But she did**n't**.
  - futures **Will** she ever go exploring the
  - questions woods again?"

Labov's model is summed up in the following formula, with optional elements in parentheses, and ^ meaning 'followed by'.

(ABSTRACT ^)(ORIENTATION ^) COMPLICATING ACTION ^ RESOLUTION
(^ CODA) + (EVALUATION).

This means that a minimum narrative consists of two linked clauses, the first belonging to the complicating action and the second constituting the resolution.

Here is an example of a narrative/joke with its generic structure features labelled (orientation = O, complicating action (speech act) = CA (SA), evaluation = E, resolution = R):

A motorcyclist was riding home on a winter's night [O], and stopped to pick up a hitch-hiker [CA]. After 10 minutes the hitch-hiker complained in the ear of the biker [CA (SA)] "I'm so bloody cold – and I have a weak chest. What can I do?" [E] So the motorcyclist stopped, turned to him [CA] and said [CA (SA)], "Why don't you put your coat on backwards? That'll keep your chest warm" [E]. So they stopped, he took off his coat, put it on backwards and the biker helped him button it up down the

back [CA]. This wasted a bit of time, and the biker wanted to get home
for dinner [E], so he drove faster [CA], despite the bumpy road [E]. After
a while he looked back and found his pillion passenger gone [CA]. So he
turned the bike round and rode back the way he'd come [CA]. He saw a
crowd gathered round a man lying on the ground and as he approached
he recognised him as the hitch-hiker [CA (E)]. A young woman was giving
him first aid [O/CA].
"Is he OK?" [E] he asked her.[CA (SA)]
"Well, he seemed OK," [CA (SA)[E]] she replied, "until we turned his
head around the right way."[E][R]

Obviously enough, shaggy dog stories are a kind of humorous narrative
that lacks an adequate resolution.

6.4.5. Jokes and genre mixing

Some kinds of humour depend upon a confusion of genres (Attardo 2001:
104–9), a generic schema clash. "A man loses his dog so he puts an ad in
the paper. And the ad says, 'Here, boy'" (Spike Milligan, Carr and Greeves
2006: 12). The language appropriate to the genre of dog training colon-
ises, as it were, the advertisement genre. Or, "I felt like a man trapped in
a woman's body. Then I was born" (Chris Bliss, Carr and Greeves 2006: 61).
Here the clash of genres is more subtle. We expect a trans-sexual autobiography, but it turns out to be a simple autobiography.

The Les Dawson joke (5.4.4) achieves humour by mixing perhaps
three genres: personal anecdote "I sat ... night sky"; poetic meditation
"And I marvelled ... the tethered bolts of Jupiter and Mars hang
forever in their orbital majesty"; self-reminder about jobs to be done
around the house "I thought ... 'I must put a roof on this lavatory'".

Activity 6.4

Explain the clash of genres underlying the following jokes.

1. Somewhere on this globe, every ten seconds, there is a woman giving birth to a
   child. She must be stopped. (Sam Levenson, Carr and Greeves 2006: 60)
2. – If you had 10p and you asked your Dad for another 10p what would you have?
   – 10p, sir.
   – You don't know your arithmetic, boy.
   – You don't know my dad, sir.

Comment

The first sentence of (1) looks like some kind of popular magazine
account of population growth. But the second sentence appears to
belong to the genre of alerting the public to criminal threats or of
"Wanted" posters.

(2) is intended by the teacher as a hypothetical scenario for testing mental arithmetic skills. But the pupil interprets it as a question about the real life character of his father.

6.4.6. Joke genres

Before investigating the generic structure of jokes and their sub-types, we should ask whether jokes do actually have a structure unique to themselves, or whether they are parasitic on other genres. An argument for the latter is that jokes can often change their generic form, for example, from a riddle/question-answer structure to a parody of a classified ad: "How many men does it take to change a light bulb?" "Five – one to hold the bulb and four to turn the table" might transform into "Need help changing a light bulb. Have bulb. Wanted: four strong men to turn the table" (Attardo and Raskin 1991: 300).

An alternative take on the generic structure of jokes might see them as the specific manifestation of a more general pattern. Chiaro (1992: 50–8) suggests a four-part structure: Situation – Problem – Response – Result/ Evaluation. This looks comparable to the generic structure of narrative: Situation-Problem (Orientation/Complicating Action) ^ Response (Complicating Action ctd.) ^ Result (Resolution) ^ Evaluation (Coda).

Indeed, both Attardo (1994, 2001) and Alexander (1997) mention the similarities in the generic structures of jokes and narratives. Attardo (1994: 89ff.) suggests three "functions" in joke structure: Function 1, the situation, which is sometimes implicit [cf. Orientation]; Function 2, the problem to be solved [cf. Complicating Action]; Function 3, conclusion of narration, which includes the disjunctor, the element causing the transition from script 1 to script 2 [cf. Resolution]. However, there are differences between narratives and jokes. First, the joke resolves the process in an unexpected way, inconsistent with the assumptions set up in F1 and F2. And second, the disjunctor or punchline achieves its effect implicitly rather than overtly (Chiaro 1992: 53). In fact, the problem and its resolution in jokes are mental in the reader's head, whereas the problem to be resolved in a narrative is material in the fictional world.

One important distinction in considering the genres of jokes/ humour is whether the jokes are conversational ones, witticisms, original spontaneous contributions to an ongoing conversation, or whether they are canned jokes, which have been learned and/or rehearsed, and are relatively detached from the context or co-text. Alexander (1997: 11) notes some of the differences in Table 6.2.

The structure in Table 6.3, based on conversational analysis (8.6) has been suggested for these two types of jokes (Attardo 1994: 300ff.),

Table 6.2. *Contrasts between witticisms and canned jokes*

Witticisms	Canned jokes
Spontaneous	Planned
Open-ended, ongoing, linear	Circumscribed, closed, complete
Temporally limited	Time-independent
Back and forth (multi-sourced)	Structured, unidirectional
Co-equal, dialogic	Dominant role, monologic
Preferred by women	Preferred by men

Table 6.3. *The structure of canned jokes*

Canned joke	Teller	Hearer
Introduction	Disclaimers, secure floor, introduce playfulness [cf. Abstract]	Accept or refuse joke, accept and set to playfulness
Text	Text performance [cf. (Orientation) Complicating Action, Evaluation, Resolution?]	Interrupt (or listen)
Reaction	Signal end [cf. Coda], incite laughter	– Registering understanding: comment – Negative reaction: silence, groan, mock laughter, polite laughter, negative evaluation, ironic "appreciations", verbal/physical attack on teller – Positive reaction: laughter,[3] positive evaluation, echoing teller's words – Humorous response/other joke

but I have modified it – especially the reactions – with further insights from Chiaro (1992), Hay (2001) and Bell (2009) plus comments on how it might reflect an underlying narrative structure.

The only difference between canned and conversational jokes is in the first part of the genre row 1 (Table 6.4). In a conversational joke there is no framing that signals the switch from non-casual to casual communication, from the relatively serious and co-operative exchange

Table 6.4. *The opening of conversational jokes (witticisms)*

Conversational joke	Teller	Hearer
Introduction	Pre-text, joke situation [cf. unmentioned Abstract]	N/A

of information to the playfulness (non bona-fide communication) of the ludic genre. In other words there are no "play frames" or "brackets" (Alexander 1997: 12), no equivalent of the abstract/coda.

It is worth remembering the more abstract psychological level of joke structure developed by Attardo (1994: 95, 2001), called the disjunction model. We begin with the set-up of the joke which develops a text that is coherent in terms of a first schema (script). But this coherence is disturbed by a disjunctor which triggers activation of a second schema. The ultimate coherence of the second schema (and perhaps the first too) is justified by the presence of a connector. Attardo believes that one crucial aspect of the generic structure of different joke genres is whether the connector and disjunctor merge in the same utterance unit or not. For instance, in humorous headlines, if these can be called jokes at all, there are cases where the disjunctor precedes the connector, LINGERIE SHIPMENT HIGH-JACKED – THIEF GIVES POLICE THE SLIP, or where an element functions as both connector and disjunctor DRUNK GETS NINE MONTHS IN VIOLIN CASE (Bucaria 2004: 280, 292).

6.4.7. Sub-genres of jokes

The ordering of the elements and information in jokes is crucial (Ritchie 2004: 17), because their effect depends on their linear structure. Nash (1985: 33ff.) suggested that short one-line jokes often conform to the following generic structure:

Table 6.5. *Generic structure of one-line jokes*

PRELOCATION	LOCATION		
Did you hear about	the Irish forward	who missed a penalty but	scored on the action replay
Signal	*Orientation*	*Context*	*Locus*

The *signal* indicates the intention to tell a joke. The *orientation* indicates the type of joke. The *context* provides information about the situational context in which the joke operates (cf. Attardo's set-up as orientation + context). And the *locus* is the word or phrase which clinches or discharges the joke (the disjunctor). According to Nash, signal and locus are obligatory but may vary in their position.

> *headed sequence* = signal ^ locus
> *spanning sequence* = signal–locus–signal
> *tailed sequence* = locus ^ signal

The Irish joke above is a headed sequence. "Come back, Guy Fawkes, all is forgiven" is a spanning sequence. "Guy Fawkes, where are you, now that we need you?" is a tailed sequence.

Certain formulae for opening jokes are so common that they combine orientation and signal, as the barman recognises in the following: "A priest, a rabbi and vicar walk into a bar. The barman says 'Is this some kind of joke?'" So there is the *X goes/walks into a bar*, or even the more general *There are X in a place/X is in a* place, e.g.

> Two muffins are in the grill. The first muffin says, "Boy, it's hot in here." The second muffin says, "I don't believe it, a talking muffin!"
> (Carr and Greeves 2006: 107)

Nash (1985), Chiaro (1992: 50–8) and Blake (2007) identify other subgenres of jokes, some defined by such specific formulae, which I have attempted to combine into Table 6.6.

These various joke types, especially the formulaic ones, prime us to expect certain patterns, and they become all too predictable in their unpredictability. So they are open to a subversion that overrides their priming (Ritchie 2004: 105) by twisting the formula (Chiaro 1992) to produce what have been called "parajokes" or "second-generation jokes" (Attardo 2001: 70). For instance the elephant riddle in Table 6.6 provides intertextual priming which is subverted by "How do you get two elephants in a mini?" "One in the front, one in the back", which in turn provides a false priming for "How do you get two whales [to Wales] in a mini?" "Across the Severn Bridge". The knock knock joke is subverted by "Who's there?" "The Avon lady – your bell's broken".

Inventive examples of intertextuality in jokes are found in the species of graffiti ending "rules OK". Originally written by football supporters in a form such as "Arsenal rules, OK", they then spawned jokes like "French dockers rule, au quai" (dependent on homophony), "Dyslexia lures, KO" (transposition or metathesis), "Saliva drools, OK" (rhyme/paronymy), "Amnesia rules, O ..." (deletion), "Royce Rolls, KO" (paronymy and metathesis) – the latter referring to a factory closure (Alexander 1997: 79). These subversions and inventions highlight the fact that genres are by no means fixed, and, perhaps especially the playful ones, are open to a modification which defeats old expectations.[4]

Table 6.6. *Sub-genres of jokes*

Utterance type	Sub-genre	Example
One utterance	Catchwords	She was only the miller's daughter, though bred for a nobler role.
	Wellerisms	"Philately will get you nowhere," as the geisha said to the amorous stamp-collector.
	Tom Swifties	"I need a pencil sharpener," said Tom bluntly.
	OK	Dyslexia lures: KO.
	Do-it	Accountants do it with double entry.
	I thought . . . *but then*	I thought youth in Asia was an indication of population increase, but then I realised it was a form of population reduction.
	Shop signs	"Remains to be seen" on an antique shop.
	Definitions	A committee is an animal with 4 back legs.
	Exhortations	Help stamp out philately!
	Comments	Picasso paints by numbers.
	Rejoinders	["See you later."] "Not if I see you first."
	Oxymora	Instant classic. Airline food.
Two-utterance monologue	Glossed statements	A woman is like a piano. If she's not upright she's grand.
Reported dialogue	*Mummy, mummy,*	"Mummy, mummy, I don't like grandma." "Then leave her on the side of your plate."
	Waiter,	"Waiter, what's this fly doing in my soup?" "Looks like breast-stroke, sir."
Optional dialogue with hearer	Question ^ answer	"What do you get when you pour boiling water down a rabbit hole?" "I don't know." "Hot cross bunnies."
	Riddles	"How does an elephant get down from a cherry tree?" "Sits on a leaf and waits till autumn."
Dialogic ritual	*Knock knock*	"Knock, knock." "Who's there?" "Noah." "Noah what?" "Know a fool when I see one."
Extended text	Limericks Clerihews Parodies	

6.4.8. Variability of processing in different genres

The degree of attention to the morphology of words and compounds/
idioms will vary according to genre. While we normally process compounds and idioms as a chunk, in specific genres or under pressure to be
creative these may be remotivated by drawing attention to their parts.
So *up the creek* becomes *up the creek without a paddle*, emphasising the word-
form *creek*. Or *fed up* intensifies to *fed up to the back teeth*. At one extreme,
in genres like poetry, puns and advertising copy, sub-morphemic patterns are identified to draw attention to meaning, as when poetic sound
repetitions suggest emergent morphemes, e.g. /fl/ 'intermittent light'
(*flicker, flame, flash, flare*) or /gr/ 'harsh friction' (*grate, grind, growl, grunt*).
The genre of word-play jokes often invents non-existent morphemes
analogous to folk-etymologies (see 2.4). And (pseudo-) re-motivating
devices are often taken over into punning ads: "Out standing garden
furniture", "If selling a house sounds like a vicious circle try Anglia". The
emphasis on form in ludic genres is a kind of pretence that the signifier–
signified relationship is not an accidental or unmotivated one (Attardo
1994: 149–51) (see 2.4, 8.2 and 11.8). At the other extreme we have news
reports and conversation, where time constraints on encoding are
severe and awareness of the literal meanings of the word-forms which
make up idiomatic metaphors is so low it leads to mixed metaphors:
e.g. "Sino-Indian thaw continues though still at a snail's pace".

6.5. A CRITIQUE OF TRADITIONAL DE-CONTEXTUALISED SEMANTICS, AND MEANING CHANGE

So far this book has introduced the topic of semantics by more or less
accepting the traditional paradigm common up until the 1970s which
culminated in Lyons' masterful two-volume survey, *Semantics* (1977).
However, I have, in passing, mentioned challenges to this "scientific"
and "logical" model, which are worth summarising here.

I touched on five main objections. This theory of semantics is an
objectivist one, indeed, most extremely it has been called "truth conditional semantics", suggesting that meanings simply reflect an existing
state of the world which can be objectively described. However, to varying
degrees in different fields, language creates the world, simultaneously
constructing and referring, we might say *conferring* a reality. We will see
this most clearly when discussing speech acts (declarations) (8.5.2). But
following Whorf (1.4) we might acknowledge that there are no given
categories in nature – different languages cut it up in different ways.

Second, because word meanings lack clear-cut boundaries and experiences do not always match our existing concepts, prototype, radial category and family resemblance theories have been developed. One symptom of this lack of "definition" would be the ambiguity in the meanings of *kind/sort/type of* as signalling approximation, class-inclusion or metaphor.

Third, as in the *Straits Times* anti-litter propaganda news article (4.8), sense relations are far more fluid and dynamic than a logical, de-contextualised approach allows. More generally, the force of collocational meanings has probably been underestimated, along with the possibility that every lexical item is somehow primed for its collocations, colligations, and likely position in grammatical structures (Hoey 2005, see Chapter 11).

Fourthly, conceptual or logical meaning, as so far discussed, is obviously an idealisation, involving de-contextualisation and generalisation, and thereby distortion. We noticed the impossibility of agreement among native speakers on the logical components of meanings like 'bottle', since the semantics we attach to words depends upon and differs in step with our experiences of their referents. This problematises the connotative–conceptual meaning distinction.

Consequently, fifthly, meanings are not as stable as a logician might wish. Their fluidity and variability can be illustrated by examining meaning changes, a topic to which I devote the remainder of this chapter. Changes take place over different time spans: (1) in the course of a text, (2) during language acquisition and (3) in the course of development of a language, that is changes in dictionary meanings.

(1) A text may use words somewhat idiosyncratically. In the extract below from *Wild Swans* (p. 378) near synonyms *torture* and *torment* are distinguished, the first presumably with a physical, the second with a psychological meaning.

> Up to the beginning of the cultural revolution **torture**, as distinct from **torment**, had been forbidden.

Conversely, a text might obliterate dictionary distinctions. Ken Russell, elsewhere in the interview quoted in Chapter 5, erases the differences between the meanings of *fantasy* and *vision*:

> One has a **vision** of someone and I suppose the **vision** often takes over the reality and er one shouldn't look at visions one should look at the **reality** and er keep looking at it. I suppose that was my my falling into my own **fantasy** trap I had a picture of my wife that wasn't the real picture and so there's no reason why it was in my my fault not her fault that the picture was a **fantasy**.

According to the dictionary *fantasy* means 'delusive imagination or hallucination', while *vision* is glossed 'supernatural or mystical insight, grasping what is real or possible but not present' (Goatly 2011: 24). Such changes in meaning are possible because, although schemas and concepts incorporate components with established degrees of saliency, their saliency may change according to context (Attardo 2001: 19). For instance, "He's not a thief; he's just a boy" creates a local antonymy: outside this co-text [+ADULT] is hardly a salient feature of thief.

The text of *She Picks up your Rubbish* (4.8) creates hyponyms for the concept of 'rubbish' not found in the dictionary: 'bus-ticket', 'racing guide', 'soft drinks can'. Writers often achieve humorous effects by listing obvious co-hyponyms and then inserting anomalous words as disjunctors, switching us away from the superordinate schema we had adduced (Fonagy 1982: 39). Gulliver, in Swift's *Gulliver's Travels* (book 4, chapter 10), recommends Houyhnhm society: "here were no gibers, censurers, backbiters, pickpockets, highwaymen, house-breakers, attorneys, bawds, buffoons, gamesters, politicians, wits, splenetics, tedious talkers, controvertists, ravishers, murderers, robbers, virtuosos" (see also Blake 2007: 16–17).

Activity 6.5

What is the effect of this spurious list?

Comment

It suggests that gibers, censurers, attorneys, buffoons, politicians, wits, tedious talkers, virtuosos etc. are somehow as harmful to society as criminals – pickpockets, highwaymen, house-breakers, bawds, ravishers, murderers and robbers. "Virtuosos" is particularly surprising after "ravishers, murderers and robbers".

Turning from nonce superordinate–hyponym relations, involving entailments, we can see how humorous texts might create nonce contradictions. The following list is presented as oxymoronic, inherently contradictory:

Tory party
Socialist worker
Military intelligence (Ross 1998: 32)

In such texts indeterminacy is "introduced" by changes of meaning. They seem to create rather than reflect a reality. Perhaps, once the text processing has finished, the meanings more or less revert to their conventional ones. This is very similar to what happens in jokes involving pseudo-morphs or false etymology, e.g. "wombat" 'bat for playing wom'.

(2) Word meanings clearly change during language acquisition. Children narrow down or modify their own hypothetical meanings until they approximate adult usage. My own daughter, Julia, had trouble using the words *gate* and *door* with their adult meanings, using *door* for the barrier used to stop toddlers climbing the stairs. By doing so she privileged the semantic component [+INDOORS] rather than the adult's [+SOLID SURFACE WITH NO GAPS]. Such gates generally have bars with large gaps between them. A lack of lexical resources might lead a child to use a word in ways different from the adult usage. Not having the word *crust* in her vocabulary Julia used the word *shell* instead, through the analogy x : bread :: shell : egg (Goatly 2011: 26–7).

(3) Lastly, at a more de-contextualised level, dictionary meanings change over time, narrowing, widening, splitting, transferring or shifting (Ullmann 1962; Waldron 1967). The etymology of the word *germ* illustrates **narrowing**. It used to cover the semantic area now covered by *seed* and *bacteria*. But the *seed* meaning disappeared except in the compound *wheatgerm*, and even there it narrowed to mean 'the embryo within the seed'. In its stand-alone form *germ* is now conceptually synonymous with *bacteria* (Waldron 1967: 173).

The opposite kind of change, **widening** or **merging**, is exemplified by the word *uncle*. The original Latin distinction between 'maternal brother' *avunculus* and 'paternal brother' *patruus* disappeared when *patruus* fell into disuse, and the meaning of *avunculus* widened to take over its meaning, later being abbreviated to *uncle* (Ullmann 1962: 228).

Splitting occurs where the unitary concept conveyed by the word divides, so that the word-form comes to represent two distinct meanings. *Current* used to mean 'flow of fluid' and this concept included electricity, in those days considered a fluid. However, as physics progressed, and no longer conceived electricity as a literal fluid, *current* split into two separate meanings one 'flow of fluid' the other 'movement of electrons' (Waldron 1967: 173).

If we are unaware of this etymology, we might simply think of the electricity meaning as a transfer metaphor from water to electricity. **Transfer** occurs when a new use of a word bridges two quite distinct semantic fields. So *mouse* originally 'the small rodent' within the semantic field of mammals, transferred to the semantic field of computing, meaning 'computer attachment used for moving the cursor'.

The final kind of meaning change is **shifting**. This can be exemplified with the etymology of the word *write*. In Old High German *rizan* meant 'to tear'. In Old English the component of meaning [+DIVIDE] was lost in favour of the component [+MAKE AN IMPRESSION], so that *writan* meant 'to score, to outline'. To reach the modern meaning of *write* 'to form letters' the [+MAKE AN IMPRESSION] was modified and replaced by [+MAKE A SHAPE] (Goatly 2011: 30–1).

If meanings were as stable as synchronic semantics assumes for purposes of logical analysis, then presumably they would resist the changes we have illustrated, in text, in acquisition and in the lexicon. One of the major instruments of semantic change is metaphor, the topic of the next chapter.

6.6. SUMMARY

The focus of this chapter has been textual meaning – how words connect to each other in text, form patterns according to register and genre, and change meaning in texts and in the history of their use. I began by introducing the concept of collocative meaning, where a word's meaning is affected by the words in its co-text. I proceeded to discuss thematic meaning, how the informational prominence of a word is affected by its positioning in a clause or the intonation given to it, touching on the varieties of intonation available in English and how they are related to given and new information. I illustrated how contrastive intonation can be humorously exploited. We next considered how semantic relationships between words create cohesion and coherence, and discussed the double coherence of jokes. Then we explored how social context (field, tenor and mode) is reflected both by the linguistic features of sentences (register) and larger discourse structures (genre). I discussed the register of jokes which, like the conversation in which they embed, emphasises the interpersonal functions of tenor, but also the metalingual functions of mode. I illustrated two genres/registers, magazine ads and narrative, as humour is often used in the former, and jokes very often appear as narratives, or resemble narrative structure. I identified genre mixing as a means of creating humorous incongruity. I went on to survey some of the literature on joke genres and sub-genres. As this is the last chapter of the book dealing specifically with semantics, I took an opportunity to critique the traditional approach of defining words in isolation, by showing different kinds of meaning change in texts, in the life of individuals, and the life of the language. Were meanings fixed, like a collector's dead butterflies, change would be impossible.

Discussion

One can cite in defence of de-contextualised semantics, that we would not be able to develop any kind of systematic treatment without such de-contextualisation and generalisation. The soundness of de-contextualised semantics can be demonstrated by its predictive power. What do you think are the pros and cons of de-contextualisation?

Suggested Readings

- As a follow-up to this discussion you might read Robinson (2006: chapter 2), which distinguishes constative linguistics (associated with traditional de-contextualised semantics) from performative linguistics (which allows for more context-based fluidity in meaning).
- It would be misleading to suggest that formal logical semantics has altogether ignored the problem of the dynamism of texts and the fluidity of meanings. For one of the more interesting theories of dynamic semantics, see Groenendijk and Stokhof (1991) or Kamp and Reyle (1993).
- Halliday and Matthiessen (2004: chapter 3) gives the standard account of the theme/rheme distinction and its relation to given and new information.
- Coulthard (1985) provides a useful introductory summary on Brazil's early work on the meaning of intonation, but Brazil (1997) is a more developed and recent exploration.
- Halliday and Hasan (1976) is the classic text on cohesion as an aspect of textual meaning.
- Labov (1972) first sketched the generic structure of narrative introduced above, as part of his investigations of black conversations in inner city New York.
- Cheong (2004) is of interest especially in terms of multimodal discourse. It elaborates an alternative generic structure for print advertisements to Toolan's, though with some overlaps.
- Chiaro (1992), Attardo (1994) and Alexander (1997) all discuss the genres of jokes, and I have attempted to summarise their findings in this chapter, but they are worth reading in their own right.

7   Metaphor and figures of speech

Traditionally literal language has been distinguished from tropes or figures of speech, including metaphor, metonymy, simile, understatement, overstatement or hyperbole, and irony. This chapter concentrates on metaphor, and only briefly discusses irony, which is given fuller treatment in 10.6–10.8 in relation to Relevance Theory.

All these figures of speech are utterances whose meanings fail to match the state of affairs in the world being described. In understatement and hyperbole the mismatch is a matter of scale, as in the headline "'PLANE TOO CLOSE TO GROUND' CRASH PROBE TOLD". Irony is even more extreme, at least the type where what is stated is the opposite of the case, e.g. "Sarah Palin was the best-educated vice-presidential candidate". Metaphor and metonymy involve using unconventional language, metaphor by substitution, metonymy by deletion. In metaphor a stretch of text has an unconventional referent, so *a mouse* conventionally refers to a small rodent, and only less conventionally to a computer attachment. Its interpretation depends on some perceived similarity or analogy, in this case shape or colour, wire as a tail, movement in sudden short spurts, etc. But **metonymy** could be considered a kind of shorthand, so that "I drank five bottles of wine" is a shorter form of "I drank the contents of five bottles of wine". Its interpretation depends upon contiguity in experience, since experientially we associate bottles with their contents.

One of the obvious features of metaphors and metonymies is that, more than irony and under-/overstatement, they tend to become conventionalised. *Bottle* now has two dictionary meanings: (1) 'a glass or plastic container for storing liquid etc.' and (2) 'the contents of (1)', as does *mouse*: (1) 'small rodent etc.' and (2) 'computer attachment used for moving the cursor on the screen etc.'

Metonymy/metaphor-based polysemy of this kind is an ambiguity which jokes or puns may exploit. Metaphor makes possible the following advertising pun:

> A beautiful new bathroom from Graham makes freshening up a positive pleasure. But with interest free credit as well it feels even better. Because that means you won't have to **splash out** too much. (*Good Housekeeping*, May 1987: 155)

One commonly conventionalised metonymy is PEOPLE AS PLACE, as in "Beijing is celebrating a very successful staging of the Olympic Games", where the place *Beijing* refers to the people (inhabitants or government) in Beijing. A metonymy like "the streets are unsafe in Philadelphia" is unpacked and made explicit in the following:

> The streets are safe in Philadelphia. It's only the people who make them unsafe. (Frank Rizzo, ex-police chief and mayor of Philadelphia, Tibballs 2006: 511)

Activity 7.1

Since metonymies involve deletion, one expects to find metonymic ambiguities in headlines, which, after all, employ deletions for conciseness and impact. Explain what might have been deleted in the following headlines to create the unintended humour:

1. NEVER WITHHOLD HERPES INFECTION FROM LOVED ONE (Tibballs 2006: 507)
2. 'NAGGING' WIFE CRITICAL AFTER HAMMER ATTACK (Tibballs 2006: 508)

Comment

Presumably the intended meanings are:

1. 'Never withhold *knowledge of your* herpes infection from a loved one.'
2. 'A "nagging" wife is *in* critical *condition* after a hammer attack.'

7.1. TERMINOLOGY FOR METAPHOR ANALYSIS

From a cognitive perspective **metaphor** can be briefly defined as thinking of one thing (A) as though it were another thing (B), with the linguistic result that an item of vocabulary or larger stretch of text is applied in an unusual or new way.[1] A is the **target** and B is the **source**. To distinguish metaphor from other figures of speech we must stipulate that metaphorical thinking of a target schema in terms of a source schema involves establishing some similarity or analogy linking A and B. This process is **mapping**, and the similarities or analogical relationships found are the **grounds**.

An example from *Private Eye* will make this clearer.

Product Recall

New Labour
Placed on market 1 May 1997

The manufacturers of the above product wish it to be known that a large number of faults have developed in the New Labour™. Under certain circumstances, the New Labour will bend, buckle and fall to bits, rendering it wholly useless. Customers are advised that the New Labour cannot in any circumstances be returned, and that no claims for compensation will be considered. (From *Private Eye* 969, February 1999: 22)

The target is "New Labour" and the source is "Recalled Product". Besides the grounds of both having "a large number of faults", and being "wholly useless", the mapping extends the source as an analogy for a faulty product – "bend, buckle and fall to bits" suggest that the Labour party has buckled and bent under pressure, and is no longer united. Note that non-grounds or contrasts are also spelt out: unlike with product recalls, "the New Labour cannot in any circumstances be returned", and "no claims for compensation will be considered" (notice the punning "returned": 'elected' and 'sent back') (Simpson 2003).

Activity 7.2

Explain how the metaphor works in the following joke, using the terminology target, source and grounds. Are the grounds given in the text? If not how are they worked out?

Two slugs were slithering along the pavement. Rounding the corner they found themselves behind two snails. "Oh, no!" groaned one of the slugs. "Caravans." (Tibballs 2006: 37)

Comment

The source is obviously 'caravans' (trailers in US English). From the preceding text we identify the target as 'snails'. The grounds are partially given by "found themselves behind", because we know from our schema of motoring that it is annoying to be stuck behind a caravan or trailer. We also know that the difference between a slug and a snail is that the latter takes its "living accommodation", its shell, with it, just as cars with caravans do. So

slug : snail :: car : car + caravan.

As in this example, some metaphors do not fully specify the ground and target. Conventional metaphors seldom do, especially those which fill a gap in our vocabulary, like *mouse* referring to the computer attachment. Sometimes even the source is not made explicit, but simply implied.

Activity 7.3

In this gag by Joan Rivers which parts of the metaphor are specified, if any?

> I love being a grandmother. It's great finally to be greeted by someone who's bald, drooling, and wearing a diaper, who's not my date. (Joan Rivers, Tibballs 2006: 53)

Comment

Here the grounds are stated: "bald, drooling and wearing a diaper"; the potential target is explicit: "my date"; but the source 'baby' has to be inferred.

Some stock "witticisms" depend upon the ironic specification of grounds, as in the cliché simile *as clear as mud* (Norrick 1986: 204). Here either the ground fails to match the source, or otherwise *clear*, like many gradable adjectives, is interpreted as referring to a scale of clarity, not just its positive end.

In our slugs example the phrases referring to target and source are noun phrases, but metaphorical sources commonly take the form of adjectives and verbs. With these word-classes the source may be only partially specified. When Matthew Arnold in the poem 'Dover Beach' refers to "the **naked** shingles of the world", we supply the usual collocate or semantic selection for *naked*, i.e. *body*, as a basis for exploring the grounds of comparison between a naked body and a shingle beach when the tide has gone out. Or, with more conventional metaphors, like *spending* or *investing* time, we easily infer that time is being compared with money, the usual object collocate of *spend* and *invest*.

Table 7.1 shows how selection restrictions (4.7.1) of increasing specificity evoke more and more specific Subject/Object (Head) collocates. The actual collocate, part of the target, to which the conventional collocate is to be compared, is underlined.

Activity 7.4

What kind of collocational metaphor is used in these humorous examples? At what level in the hierarchy of Table 7.1 does the selection restriction violation work?

> 1. If you've lost your virginity, can I have the box it came in? (Tibballs 2006: 518)
> 2. Losing one parent might be considered unfortunate. Losing two looks like carelessness. (Oscar Wilde, *The Importance of Being Earnest*)

Comment

In (1) the collocation "lost your virginity" reifies the abstract virginity as a concrete physical object. In its most prototypical meaning *lose* applies to possessions, generally inanimate, though it might apply to pets. When *lose* collocates with human objects it tends to be a euphemism for bereavement, and maybe we interpret it as such in the first sentence of (2). However, the prototypical meaning, with its prototypical collocation, seems likely in the second sentence of (2), especially with the co-text "looks like carelessness". This reduces humans to inanimate objects, in the same way as, in the play, baby Jack himself is, like an object, left in a handbag at the baggage office of Victoria Station.

Table 7.1. *Specificity of collocates (adapted from Goatly 2011: 88, Table 3.1) Examples from William Golding's novels: LF = Lord of the Flies, DV = Darkness Visible, TI = The Inheritors, TS = The Spire, FF = Free Fall*

Physical
The **rising** antagonism (LF130)
  Inanimates
    Liquid
  Their scent **spilled** out into the air (LF62)
    Blood
  The sun mixed and **clotted** ... among the thorns (DV61)
  Solid
  His voice **struck** them into silence (LF76)
    Pliable solids
  The walls of rock **folding** back (TI223)
    Powdered solids
  The trees **sifted** chilly sunlight over their naked bodies (TI15)
    Rigid solids
      Sharp instruments
      Goody with her red hair would **stab** his mind (TS112)
    Machine
    [They] **overhauled** their clothes (DV129)
      Clock/Watch
      Yet I was **wound up**. I **tick**. I exist (FF10)
  Animates
  Small flames **stirred** at the bole of a tree (LF48)
    Plants
  Great bulging towers that **sprouted** away over the island (LF152)
    Animals
  Then the sea **breathed** again (LF200)
    Mammals
  The new one **milked** her (TI44)
      Cat
      He **mewed** before he sucked (TI65)

7.2. ORIGINAL AND CONVENTIONAL METAPHORS

Although metaphors are unconventional uses of language, they can be located on a cline of unconventionality from the most conventional, dead and buried, through the sleeping and tired, to the original (Goatly 2011). Or, less delicately, one might simply distinguish the conventional inactive and the original or active metaphors (Table 7.2).

The further we descend the table from dead to active the more likely the expressions will be processed as metaphors, that is, the item will be recognised as a source term, and grounds will be actively mapped. Towards the bottom of the table the grounds will become less and less predictable.

RED HERRING$_2$ is a **dead** metaphor, a lexical phrasal compound which nowadays has no corresponding more literal meaning. In its literal use *red-herring* once referred to a highly spiced fish that escaping convicts scattered to confuse chasing bloodhounds. When first encountered to mean 'distraction', it would have been possible to trace a metaphorical connection between the two meanings. However, nowadays this is not normally possible, since the original source of the metaphor is no longer part of our experience – we no longer come across such a fish used as a decoy for hounds.

CRANE$_2$ is a **sleeping** metaphor with potential for metaphoric re-awakening, since the grounds mapped – the shape of the bird's neck and shape of the hoisting machine – are relatively salient. There is no clear dividing line on the continuum of inactivity between sleeping and **tired** metaphors. Nevertheless CUT$_2$ appears more capable than

Table 7.2. *Degrees of conventionality: tired, sleeping and dead metaphors (after Goatly 2011: 32, Figure 1.3)*

RED HERRING$_1$	a spiced fish		
RED HERRING$_2$	irrelevant matter, distraction	*DEAD*	
CRANE$_1$	species of marsh bird		
CRANE$_2$	machine for moving heavy weights	*SLEEPING*	*INACTIVE*
CUT$_1$	an incision		
CUT$_2$	budget reduction	*TIRED*	
[TRACTOR	vehicle for pulling loads or machinery		
ICICLES	hanging rod-like ice formation]	*ACTIVE*	

the previous examples of evoking the original source. Even in news-paper reports, a genre where sensitivity to metaphor is low, it seems that CUT_2 easily evokes CUT_1, e.g. "George Osborne's axe". "Axe" increases the likelihood that CUT_2 will evoke a double reference, and perhaps even provoke a search for grounds.

All these inactive or dead metaphors contrast with the original **active** metaphors in these lines form Charles Causley's 'Death of a Poet':

> His **tractor** of blood stopped thumping.
> He held five **icicles** in each hand.

In the first 'tractor', the source, refers to the heart, the target, and the grounds are that in the same way as a tractor pulls machinery around a farm, so the heart pulls blood around the body. 'Icicles', the source, refers to the fingers of a dead man's hand, the target, the grounds being coldness, tapering shape, stiffness etc. These meanings for *tractor* and *icicles* are not lexicalised, and are therefore absent from the dictionary.

Inactive metaphors have a second lexicalised meaning. So their word-forms represent two lexical items which are, as it were, wired "in parallel"; the conventionalised secondary meaning can be accessed without going through the source concept, the primary meaning. By contrast, active metaphors, lacking a second dictionary meaning, have to be interpreted via the source, as though wired "in series". Inactive metaphors might be processed as homonyms, but, unlike dead meta-phors, the metaphorical connecting wires are still there, and the first literal meaning of the source may be "lit up", in which case the user perceives the word-form as polysemous.

7.3. *CONCEPTUAL METAPHOR THEORY*[2]

For many years metaphor and metonymy were considered marginal phenomena, decorative or poetic. But since the 1980s Lakoff and John-son (1980, 1989), Lakoff (1987, 1993, 1996 etc.) and their followers within cognitive linguistics have alerted us to the importance of meta-phor in everyday language and thought. Cognitive metaphor theorists showed this importance by concentrating on the numerous inactive metaphorical expressions in the dictionary.

First, Lakoff and Johnson stressed the ubiquity of inactive or conven-tional metaphor. As speakers and thinkers we rely on it, especially when considering abstract targets. One might go so far as to claim that abstract thought is only possible through metaphor. Even mathematical thinking, for instance Boolean set theory, depends

Table 7.3. *Lexis for the conceptual metaphor theme* UNDERSTAND IS HOLD/GRASP *(Goatly 2011: 14, Table 1)*

LEXIS	MEANING	EXAMPLE
get hold of	understand	*she finds even the easy concepts difficult to get hold of*
get a grip on/to grips with	understand correctly, begin to solve	*new techniques should help us get a grip on the problem*
feel	natural understanding of or ability in	*he has more of a feel for mathematics than biology*
have your finger on the pulse	know or understand everything about something	*the commodities market fluctuates really quickly so it's important to keep your finger on its pulse*
catch on	understand after initial lack of understanding	*there was a pause until the audience caught on*
have at your fingertips	have a complete understanding of something	*he's been in the job for years and has all the political factors in the company at his fingertips*
get hold of the wrong end of the stick	misunderstand	*half the class got hold of the wrong end of the stick and put the metal in the acid*
grope	try with great difficulty to think, understand or act	*the police were groping for the motive of the murder*
grasp	understand something difficult	*I managed to grasp the main points of the lecture*

on the metaphor of containers or bounded spaces, with the boundary separating members inside from non-members outside (Lakoff 1987: chapter 20).

Another important insight of conceptual metaphor theory is that these concrete sources for abstract targets are not random, but fall into patterns, called variously conceptual metaphors or **metaphor themes**. These are conventionally referred to by the capitalised formula A (TARGET) IS B (SOURCE). For example, the conceptual metaphor theme UNDERSTAND IS HOLD/GRASP is elaborated in English as in Table 7.3.

According to Lakoff's theory, these metaphor themes derive from our experiences as infants. For instance, during the first two or three years of life we acquire increasing control over the objects we handle, initially grasping with all fingers in a palm grasp, and progressing until finally able to pick up small objects between thumb and index finger; this bodily childhood experience provides the source for UNDERSTAND IS

HOLD/GRASP, but also the motivation for CONTROL IS HANDLE. Early on we crawl towards desired objects giving us the basis for PURPOSE IS DIRECTION and DEVELOPMENT/SUCCESS IS MOVEMENT FORWARDS.

Many of the basic conceptual metaphor links originate in metonymies such as CAUSE AS EFFECT, or ACTIVITY AS PLACE. So, for example, numerous languages metaphorise anger as heat. This metaphorical pattern is based on cause and effect – anger often does make us feel hot, so heat and anger are associated contiguously in our experience. Similarly, many lexical items conceptualise activity as place: we talk of "filling a position", or "the office of the President" (different from "the President's office"), where an activity is associated with the place where it is practised. These metonymies, are, however, later developed metaphorically, so anger can be expressed in a "blazing" or "smouldering" temper, or we can talk about being on the "verge" of doing something or "quitting" an activity.

Conceptual metaphor theory was prompted by considering lexis, which provides evidence for the most common metaphor themes. Over many years I undertook lexicographical research in order to substantiate intuitions about which metaphor themes are most important in English, and presented the results on the website 'Metalude' (Metaphor At Lingnan University Department of English).[3] It has a useful map of metaphor themes as well as an interactive database.

7.4. COGNITIVE METAPHORS EXPLOITED IN HUMOUR

In this section I present a selection of the metaphor themes catalogued in Metalude with some of the lexis that instantiates them, and examples of humour which depend upon them.

The extent to which metaphors determine human cognition can be illustrated by metaphor themes for conceptualising change and its hyponyms and metonyms. At the most general is the Canonical Event Schema (Lakoff 1993; Lakoff and Johnson 1999; Kövecses 2005: 43–7). In this, metaphorically speaking STATE IS PLACE, SO CHANGE IS MOVEMENT and CAUSE IS FORCE, bringing about the change or movement from one place/ state to another (see Figure 7.1). European languages usually conceptualise events in terms of what Langacker calls "the billiard-ball model".

> We think of our world as being populated by discrete physical objects. These objects are capable of moving about through space and making contact with one another. Motion is driven by energy, which some objects draw from internal resources and others receive from the exterior. When motion results in forceful physical contact, energy is

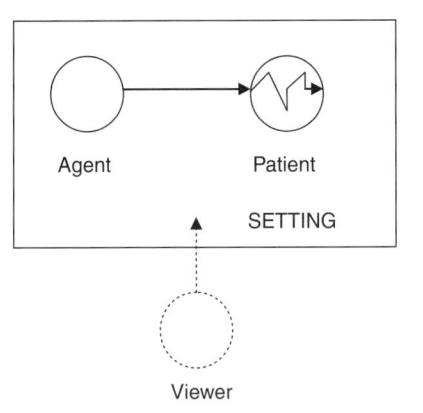

Figure 7.1. The canonical event model (after Goatly 2007: 285)

transmitted from the mover to the impacted object, which may thereby be set in motion to participate in further interactions. (Langacker 1991: 13–14)

One specific kind of event is human action, so ACTIVITY IS MOVEMENT (FORWARDS), in which schema PURPOSE IS DIRECTION (with many sub-themes), and DIFFICULTY/PREVENTION IS OBSTACLE (also with sub-themes). This proliferates into other themes such as DEVELOPING/SUCCEEDING IS MOVING FORWARD, INTENSE ACTIVITY IS SPEED, SUCCESS/EASE IS SPEED, and ACTIVITY/COMPETITION IS RACE.

Basically, processes or activities, even those not involving movement from one place to another, are conceptualised as motion. *Move* then means 'happen' ("now we have a new boss things are beginning to move faster"); 'to start working' is to *get moving* so that things are *in motion* 'happening or taking place'. In particular, activity/process is seen as going forwards as in *go* 'function' ("that clock isn't going"), *go on* 'happen' ("her parents didn't know what was going on"), *go forward* or *proceed* ("we need to proceed with stock-taking").

The converse of this metaphor theme is CEASE IS STOP: *stop*, 'finish doing something', *come to a standstill*, 'cease' ("entertainment in Hong Kong came to a standstill during SARS"), *halt*, 'stop something happening' ("the government halted IMF repayments"), *stop*, 'prevent from doing something' ("I stopped him spending so much time on snooker").

The resulting polysemy of *stop* facilitates the following joke:

> While working on a car, a mechanic accidentally swallowed some brake fluid. To his surprise he quite liked the taste. The next day he took another swig and enjoyed it so much that by the end of

the week he was hooked on the stuff. His friend said "You must
be mad drinking brake fluid. It's poisonous. You must give it up."
"Don't worry," said the mechanic. "I can stop any time."
(Tibballs 2006: 46)

This metaphor theme modifies and merges into DEVELOPING/
SUCCEEDING IS MOVING FORWARD. An 'improvement or successful development' is an *advance, progress* or a *leap*; if you 'succeed or
improve' you *go places, go far, go/come a long way, forge ahead*; if you
are 'likely to successfully complete' something you are *well on your
way to* it, or *making headway*. Conversely 'not developing' is *going
nowhere*.

The opposite is FAILURE/GIVING UP IS BACKWARDS: *back off* 'stop doing'
something ("he started arguing, then suddenly backed off"), *turn back*
'change your plans and abandon an action' ("I've invested so much
time in the business I can't turn back"), *pull back from* 'refrain from
doing what you were going to do' ("the headmaster pulled back from
expelling the boy"), *retreat from* 'give up a plan or way of life' ("he
retreated from his plan to open a bookshop"), *go into reverse* 'happen
in an opposite way from before' ("poverty reduction went into reverse
due to the financial crisis"), *reverse* 'defeat or failure' ("Waterloo was a
serious military reverse for Napoleon") and *U-turn* 'change of action to
its opposite' ("the government made a U-turn on public housing
policy"). So consider

> We are going to turn this team around 360 degrees. (Jason Kidd of
> Dallas Mavericks, Tibballs 2006: 516)

According to the metaphor theme this wish is absurd: if you turn
through 360 degrees you are facing in the same direction that you
started, and if the team is failing ("going backwards") it will continue
to do so.

Developing the theme further, the intensity or rate of an activity
or process becomes associated with *speed/pace*: *quick, fast, rapid, swift,
brisk* are such familiar metaphors they easily go unnoticed; *rush* and
hurry not only mean 'move fast' but 'do something/act quickly' ("he
rushed his meal so he could watch the football"); 'working with
extremes of intensity, energy and effort' one is in *top gear* or *at full
throttle* or performing at *breakneck speed*. *Rush* also means 'exhilaration'.
A life style that is intense, energetic, and glamorous is, thus, *life in the
fast lane*.

> Of Walter Mondale: "he has all the charisma of a speed bump".
> (Will Durst, Tibballs 2006: 645)

If speed bumps slow you down, according to this metaphor theme, they also make your life less intense and exciting, not very charismatic.

Activity 7.5

Explain the workings of metaphor themes in understanding the following joke:

Trouble with life in the fast lane is that you get to the other end in an awful hurry.

Comment

Notice that not all the aspects of a particular source schema are mapped onto the target. So this joke depends upon two probably incompatible themes: INTENSITY/EXCITEMENT IS SPEED and LIFE IS A JOURNEY/DEATH IS A DESTINATION.

These speed metaphors for intense activity often double up as metaphors for success. (Note that in Old English *spede* meant 'success' or 'prosperity' rather than 'velocity'.) Developing from SUCCESS IS SPEED, we observe the profusion of metaphors where (competitive) activity is metaphorically viewed as racing. *Race* can mean 'competition for power or control' ("Paul and Elsa are involved in a race for the CEO position"), *the rat race* 'ruthless competition for success'. To take part in competitive activities you *run* ("McCain ran in the last presidential election").

Equality of speed metaphorises equality in a competition, so if you *keep up with* you 'work as well as' other people, and if you *get behind* you may be able to *close the gap on* 'reduce the difference in success rates' or *catch up with* 'reach the same standard or level' as someone else ("he's much better than me at dancing, I' not sure I can catch up with him").

Getting behind in the race indicates failure: you may *trail* 'be less successful than' ("Cameron is trailing Miliband in opinion polls"), be *behind* or *lag behind* ("publishers who don't produce e-books are lagging behind technologically").

Leading in a race indicates present success: *streak ahead, pull ahead, get ahead* or *outdistance* 'be more successful than others' ("Chinese growth outdistanced Indian growth in 2008"). The ultimate success is winning the race. Sometimes the winner is in doubt and it's *down to the wire* 'uncertain until the very last moment or end of an activity/competition', where the leader may be overtaken at the last minute – *pipped at the post* 'beaten by a small margin' ("it was down to the wire – we thought Gore would win but Bush pipped him at the post").

> ### Activity 7.6
>
> How does this joke achieve its humour by exploiting metaphor themes?
>
> In the ongoing battle between objects made of aluminium going hundreds of miles per hour and the ground going zero miles per hour, the ground has yet to lose. (Tibballs 2006: 51)

Comment

According to the metaphor theme the fast airplane should be more successful in the battle or competition than the stationary ground, which is "going nowhere". However, the plane is destroyed by the stationary ground and the ground never loses the competition. Here the metonym cancels out the metaphor, so to speak.

One of the most productive sets of metaphor themes is subsumed under the umbrella of UNDERSTAND/KNOW IS SEE. Concentrating on visibility, the conceptual metaphor develops as OBVIOUS IS CLEAR, INCOMPREHENSIBLE IS NOT CLEAR, KNOWN IS UNCOVERED/OPEN, UNKNOWN IS INVISIBLE/COVERED, MAKE KNOWN IS UNCOVER/OPEN/DIG UP. They include aspects of the seeing schema: CONSIDER IS LOOK, KNOWLEDGE/UNDERSTANDING IS EYESIGHT, KNOWLEDGE/OPINION IS VIEW AND OPINION IS PERSPECTIVE/ORIENTATION. In the latter *position, point of view, viewpoint* can all mean 'opinion' ("what's your point of view on abortion?"). Alternatively *viewpoint*, along with *perspective/ angle* mean 'particular way of considering an issue or topic' ("from a birth control perspective homosexuality is useful"), while *standpoint* means 'beliefs or attitudes which affect opinions or decisions' ("from the standpoint of the Third World, heart transplantation is a waste of money"). Consider

> STARR AGHAST AT FIRST LADY SEX POSITION (Washington Times, Tibballs 2006: 505)

Presumably the metaphorical meaning was intended, 'opinion about sex', not a metonymically shortened literal meaning 'position of the body when having sex'.

Connected with the MAKE KNOWN IS DIG metaphor or UNDERSTAND IS PENETRATE, we have SERIOUSNESS/INSIGHT IS DEPTH. *Deep/profound* means 'needing or involving serious thought' ("Whitehead's philosophy is too deep for me"), so that *still waters run deep*, 'people who say little know a lot' ("he is taciturn, but perhaps in his case still waters run deep"). 'To understand or gain insight into' serious matters is therefore to *fathom* them ("he tried to fathom the mystery of the big bang"). Non-serious matters are *shallow* 'of little value or seriousness' ("arguments for euthanasia are morally shallow"). So

> You could walk through Ronald Reagan's deepest thoughts, and not
> get your ankles wet. (Tibballs 2006: 646)

Another conceptually important group of metaphor themes
comprise MORE IS HIGH, LESS IS LOW, INCREASE IS RISE, DECREASE IS FALL.
As lexical instantiations of the latter *drop, fall, go down* all mean
'decrease' ("oil prices have dropped/fallen/gone down and this should
help the economy") while *plunge, collapse, plummet, tumble, dive* mean to
'decrease suddenly'. To 'reduce prices or amounts' is, therefore, to
lower, bring down or *mark down*. Consider

> An 83-year-old man visited the doctor and said: "Doc my sex drive is
> too high. I want it lowered." The doctor couldn't believe his ears.
> "You're 83 and you want your sex drive lowered?" "That's right," said
> the man pointing to his head. "It's all up here. I want it lowered."
> (Tibballs 2006: 23)

Metonymically QUANTITY IS SIZE, QUANTITY IS LENGTH, NUMEROUS IS
BIG, FEW/LESS IS SMALL, because large piles or lengths of things indicate
larger quantities. Therefore DECREASE IS CUT. *Cut* means 'decrease'
("they cut my salary during the financial crisis"), *cut down/back on*
'decrease activity or consumption' ("I cut down on cigarettes from 20
to 5 a day"). The more savage the cutting the more drastic the reduction: *axe/slash* 'decrease drastically' ("Osborne axed/slashed the funds
for humanities subjects by 80%"), in contrast with 'reduce by a small
amount', *clip/shave/trim* ("he clipped/shaved two tenths of a second off
the 100 meters record"). Thus

> Two things should be cut: the second act and the child's throat. (Noël
> Coward reviewing a play featuring a child actor, Tibballs 2006: 658)

This bon mot exemplifies **zeugma**, where a single verb has to take on
two different meanings according to its object or subject collocate, in
this case a metaphorical followed by a literal meaning.

Less conceptually important, but nevertheless ideologically important, is SEX IS VIOLENCE. The number of English metaphors instantiating
it is disturbing. The male is usually constructed as the aggressor, so that
the penis is a *chopper, weapon* or a gun for him to *shoot his load* 'ejaculate
semen' or *fire blanks* 'produce semen without sperm'. The weapon might
be a sword as in *make a pass at*, literally 'attempt to stab with a rapier'
and metaphorically 'speak to or touch to show sexual attraction',
perhaps enclosed in a *sheath* 'condom'. Through such violence, men
achieve their *conquests* 'women they have had sexual intercourse with',
and are *lady-killers* 'seducers'.

Activity 7.7

Explain how this news report becomes unintentionally humorous.

> Dale Martin, an entertainer, has been ordered by a provincial court judge
> to avoid making anyone pregnant for the next three years. The order not to
> impregnate any girls came from Judge Leslie Bewley, who gave Martin a
> suspended sentence and three years probation for possession of an offensive
> weapon. (*Toronto Globe*, Tibballs 2006: 490)

Comment

Since weapons were not mentioned in the previous context, we are
inclined to see sex as the target and weapon as a source, in line with
the metaphor theme delineated above. But judges would be unlikely to
use such metaphorical slang in passing judgment. "Offensive" also has a
double meaning here, either literal, 'with potential use for attack' as part
of a legal phrasal compound, or the free phrase meaning 'disgusting'.

Koestler (1964) and Fonagy (1982), following Freud, suggest that
jokes (with their "punch" lines) are both aggressive and sexual. It is
then no accident that we talk of jokes "misfiring", since this links with
the idea that talking aggressively is fighting (ARGUING/CRITICISING IS
FIGHTING) or that sex is violence. Joking may also inflict a metaphorical
violence on language as in paronyms. Lecercle (1990) entitled his book
on linguistic creativity *The Violence of Language*.

7.5.   METAPHORS AND THEIR CO-TEXT

7.5.1.   Literalisation of metaphors

A deliberate confusion of metaphorical and literal levels is quite widespread. It is a frequently used technique in advertising copy, as in a
previous example: "A beautiful new bathroom from Graham makes
freshening up a positive pleasure. But with interest free credit as well
it feels even better. Because that means you won't have to **splash out**
too much" (*Good Housekeeping*, May 1987: 155). The same device figures
in several dialogic jokes: "'How's your plumbing business going?'
'We're flush'" (Oring 2003: 10). Using nautical metaphors when literal
sailors speak or are spoken of is a rather hackneyed humorous device,
as in the elegy for Tom Bowling:

> Yet shall poor Tom **find pleasant weather**,
>   When He, who all commands,
> Shall give, to call **life's crew** together,
>   The word to **pipe all hands**.

> Thus Death, who kinds and tars despatches,
>   In vain Tom's life has doff'd,
> For, though his body's **under hatches**
>   His soul has **gone aloft**.

Using a lexical item literally at one point in the text and at another point metphorically I call "**literalisation** of vehicles" (Goatly 2011: 290–8). It is much used for comic effects. Indeed most of the jokes above have a context which reminds us of the literal meaning, the source schema, e.g. "I can stop any time" in the context of brake fluid. Literalisation may impart a symbolic value to the literal referents. Prolific metaphor themes can be evidence of the symbolic value of a concrete object or action, as when, for example, tall buildings become symbolic of power, in step with the numerous metaphors in the dictionary in which POWER (target) is conceived of in terms of HEIGHT (source) (Goatly 2007).

In analysing metaphors in text we face the problem of how to treat references to representational artworks. These could be accorded metaphorical status: any picture, for example, resembles the shape or colour of what it represents, though it is not literal since it lacks, among other things, three dimensions. I called this **mimetic metaphor** (Goatly 2011). It can also apply to non-artistic imitative contexts:

> During camouflage training a private was disguised as a tree. But he made a sudden noise which was spotted by a visiting general. The general took him to task. "Don't you know that your yelling and jumping could have endangered the lives of the entire company?"
>   "I'm sorry, sir," replied the private. "But I can explain. You see, I stood still when pigeons used me for target practice. And I didn't move a muscle when a large dog peed on my trunk. But when two squirrels ran up the leg of my pants and the bigger one said 'Let's eat one now and save the other till winter' that did it".
> (Tibballs 2006: 38)

The punchline, indicating the squirrels have been deceived, shows that the miming of the tree was more successful than intended.

7.5.2. Extended metaphors

The previous example suggests an extended metaphor, especially since both meanings of *nuts* are implied. Extension is achieved when several sources belong to the same semantic field, and when the targets share a distinct semantic field too. Usually the sources in an extended metaphor are all connected to some consistent image or schema.

> I've got the **ship**. You've got the **harbour**. How about I **dock** for the night? (Tibballs 2006: 520)

Idioms can even be combined creatively to extend the metaphor:

> "What do you think of our recently appointed Vice-Chancellor?"
> "He's the new broom that sweeps the dirt under the carpet."

In some cases the extension is not merely lexical but also syntactic.[4] One could, for example, rewrite the first joke above as "I'd like to dock my ship in your harbour for the night", syntactically articulating the verb "dock" with the object "my ship" and with the adverbial "in your harbour".

> On leaving the army an old soldier got a white-collar job. One day he arrived at the office to find that he had been given a new young secretary. While taking dictation she noticed his fly was open. She hesitated to mention it, but in the end thought she had better say something. So she said discreetly, "Did you know your barracks door was open?" The old man looked mystified but later realised what she meant when he discovered his zipper was open. Overtaking her in the corridor, he said, grinning "By the way, Miss Perlman, when you saw my barracks door open this morning, did you notice a soldier standing to attention?" "No," she replied coolly, "all I saw was a disabled veteran sitting on two old duffel bags." (Tibballs 2006: 38)

This joke contains articulated extensions as there are syntactic relationships between two source-terms in "a soldier standing to attention" and "a disabled veteran sitting on two old duffel bags". In both the targets are not specified, only implied.

It has been suggested that extended analogy of this kind is one of the logical mechanisms used in the processing of jokes. For example

> George Bush has a short one. Gorbachev has a longer one. The Pope has one but does not use it. Madonna does not have one. What is it? A last name! (Attardo and Raskin 1991: 303)

7.5.3. Mixed metaphors

The term **mixed metaphor** is usually used to criticise a careless writer. In most cases one or more of the metaphors is inactive, and the writer has ignored their sources. But the reader has evoked them, and tried unsuccessfully to interpret them as an extended metaphor. The resulting incongruity is exaggerated when they are intimately connected syntactically.

> Sino-Indian **thaw** continues, though still at a **snail**'s pace ... Indonesia was "ideologically ready" to **reopen** economic **ties** with China ...
> One important **obstacle** to **forging closer ties** with China is Indonesia's relatively **warm ties** with Vietnam. (*Far Eastern Economic Review* 19 May 1988: 42) (quoted in Goatly 2011: 288)

The use of "tie" as a synonym for 'relationship' is ludicrously incongruous, if we activate the source image of a rope tying two objects
together: firstly because "reopen ties" would then suggest that the
relationship will fall apart, with the two partners no longer bound
together; secondly, because "warm ties" makes no sense on the literal
level, suggesting burning rope, and nor does "forging closer ties"
unless what is tied is a metal cable. If we mix in and stir the incongruous "thaw", "snail" and "obstacle" the whole passage appears ridicu-
lous, but only if we read it with a degree of care inappropriate for
the genre.

   Mixing contrasts with syntactic extension, we see source-terms
syntactically/semantically joined with each other even though they
cannot integrate into any familiar schema ("forging ties") or, if they
can, it is an integration which provides a distraction from the intended
meaning ("warm ties") or a contradiction to it ("reopen ties").

Activity 7.8

In the following two examples of unintended humorous mixing, which involves a
contradiction on the source level, and which is simply incongruous?

   1. We are not prepared to stand idly by and be murdered in our beds. (Ian Paisley,
      Tibballs 2006: 512)
   2. I can see the carrot at the end of the tunnel. (Stuart Pearce, Tibballs 2006: 515)

   Comment

   I suppose that in (1) a contradiction is implied since when in bed one
   doesn't stand, one lies. (2) looks like a simple distracting incongruity:
   it is difficult to imagine a consistent schema including carrots and
   tunnels.

(2) is also an example of mixing idioms, *stick and carrot* and *light at the
end of a tunnel*, a kind of idiom malapropism, even more obvious in the
following:

   That's the trouble with directors – always biting the hand that lays the
   golden egg. (Sam Goldwyn, Tibballs 2006: 518)

Activity 7.9

Would you regard the text below as an example of mixing or not? Why?

   Bobby Gould thinks I'm going to stab him in the back. In fact I'm right behind him.
   (Stuart Pearson, Tibballs 2006: 516)

Comment

Stabbing someone in the back and being right behind them are certainly compatible within one schema, the latter being a likely precondition for the former. What makes this a case of mixing is that the second sentence is, by "in fact", placed in a contrastive relationship with the first, as a denial of it. In this special case of mixing, two contrasted schemas at the target level are combined into one reinforcing schema at the source level.

Other humorous quotations of this kind can be contrasted with literalisations. Instead of a metaphorical meaning being consistent with a literal meaning, the source contradicts or is inconsistent with the literal level:

> It's like learning to play golf. Just when you think you've cracked it they move the goal posts. (Adrian Love, Tibballs 2006: 516)

In other cases of "mixing" the metaphorical meaning interacts with its literal context to create a tautology:

> There's going to be a real ding-dong when the bell goes. (Harry Carpenter, Tibballs 2006: 514)

Activity 7.10

As a way of summarising and bringing together the theories on metonymy, metaphor themes, metaphorical extension/mixing and the interplay between the literal and figurative, try to explain this rather complex example.

> Before you criticise someone you should walk a mile in their shoes. That way, when you criticize them you are a mile away and you have their shoes. (Jack Handey, Carr and Greeves 2006: 100)

Some sub-questions might help:

a. What metonymic/metaphoric meaning do we give to the word "before"?
b. What is the ambiguity of "walk a mile in their shoes"?
c. One of the meanings of this phrase is metaphorical: what metaphor theme inherent in the Event Schema or connected with UNDERSTAND/KNOW IS SEE does it exemplify?
d. Which of the two meanings does the second sentence highlight?
e. Does this amount to mixing or extension?
f. What else contributes to the humour here?

Comment

a.   I suppose "before" here means or implies 'to prevent yourself'. Since time is conceptualised as space, and events are associated metonymically with the time at which they take place, "before" refers to a period of time previous to an event, when that event has not yet happened. Somehow the notion of prevention is associated with this time/place of not yet happening.

b.   "Walk a mile in their shoes" has an idiomatic metaphorical meaning 'understand why they are as they are, or experience life from their standpoint'. In the other meaning it is simply a free phrase with a literal meaning.

c.   The metaphorical meaning of this phrase would plug into the metaphor theme STATE IS PLACE: if you put themselves in their place/"shoes" you know what it is like to be in their state. Or it might be connected with OPINION IS PERSPECTIVE: when you are in their shoes you see life from their perspective, appreciate their **stance** and understand why they have their opinions.

d.   The second sentence highlights the non-idiomatic, free phrase, literal meaning.

e.   The second sentence could be a literal extension of the first, but not a metaphorical extension. In fact it looks like a kind of mixing which involves literalisation by the second sentence of the source terms in the first sentence. Of the examples above it approximates most the tautology in the Harry Carpenter example. However, it is not tautologous, but simply spells out an entailment and implication of the literal meaning of the first sentence: if you walk a mile before you criticise someone (stated) and the other person doesn't because you have their shoes (implied) then you are a mile away when you criticise them (entailed).

f.   I suppose part of the humour depends upon the idea that not only can you safely criticise them without provoking a hostile reaction, because you are too far away for them to attack, but you have successfully managed to steal their shoes and are too far away for them stop the theft or retrieve their shoes.

7.6.   *WHAT METAPHORS AND HUMOUR HAVE IN COMMON*

Firstly, it is quite clear from many of the previous examples in this chapter that puns, a form of humorous verbal play, often rely on metaphors. It is no accident that Aristotle discussed puns in the context of metaphor (Attardo 1994: 21). Moreover, just as a metaphorical source forces a ground on the target, so, in some kinds of pun, the first sense forces a connotation on the second sense. For instance, in "news-litter" the connotation of 'litter' (uselessness, waste, etc.) is forced upon the target 'newsletter' (Attardo 1994: 137).

Secondly, both metaphors and humour, at least in the incongruity theory of linguistic humour, involve two schemas or scripts that conflict with each other, which in the case of metaphor we call source and target. In both there will be a tension between the real situation of the utterance (cf. target), and the assertion or reference that contradicts it (cf. source) (Attardo and Raskin 1991: 308). Fonagy mentions the "auto-invalidation of jokes" (Attardo 1994: 187), which is similar to the deliberate and recognisable untruth of a metaphorical assertion.

But, thirdly, as Norrick points out, the humour in the script or schema conflict depends on not just the skewing of one schema with another, but also on finding a good fit between the two at another level (Norrick 1986: 204–5), just as the most appropriate metaphors successfully find grounds to link the source and target, as, for instance, in the Charles Causley "icicles" for dead fingers metaphor. Oring, who claims that successful humour depends upon finding appropriateness in incongruity rather than resolving the incongruity, notes that the difference between definitions and metaphors, on the one hand, and humour, on the other, is that in humour the appropriateness is spurious (Oring 2003: 6).

Fonagy (1982: 64–5) devotes discussion to the similarities between metaphor and jokes. Both necessitate a reaching beyond the most salient or obvious surface meaning of an utterance to discover a solution to an incongruity, beyond the something different that has been uttered to retrieve the something more that is meant. But, and this is a fourth similarity, the meaning of the surface statement has to be in both cases preserved as well as invalidated, otherwise the humorous or metaphorical tension disappears, as it does with inactive metaphors.

The differences that Fonagy notices are that jokes involve a sudden discovery of one definite new meaning, whereas original metaphors are open-ended in their meanings, in the grounds they implicate. Consequently, they have a much higher semantic density than jokes. But we should note that this is only the case for active or original metaphors, like the Charles Causley ones. Conventional metaphors, by contrast, have acquired a second lexicalised meaning and usually a clear two-way ambiguity which makes them more like jokes. This is precisely why this chapter has concentrated on conventional and lexicalised metaphors in Metalude, because these are suitable for puns in the way that original metaphors are not.

Fonagy's point about lexical density brings us to a fifth point. Though jokes may not be as semantically dense as original metaphors, they are still relatively dense due to their evocation of a double schema. Freud refers to this as condensation of meaning through displacement of one schema into another (Attardo 1994: 55). As we explore at length in 11.1 and 11.2, the displacement is an unpredictability that correlates with higher information content (condensation), since information correlates inversely with predictability.

Sixthly, the displacement or unconventional application of the linguistic sign to a new context, in both humour and metaphor, has the effect of *ostranenye*, of making strange (Dorfles, quoted in Attardo 1994: 176). Metaphor, of course, can help us view an object from a different or strange perspective, as though we were seeing it for the first time, without the veneer of habitual use of a more conventional referring term. "He held five icicles in each hand" makes us view cold fingers in a very strange or new light. The effect is not very different from riddles[5] or from this joke:

> A porter was whistling as he walked through the foyer of an exclusive hotel. The manager reprimanded him. "Do you not know it's forbidden for hotel employees to whistle while on duty?" "I wasn't whistling," replied the porter, "I was paging a dog." (Tibballs 2006: 189)

Such ability to renew perception was what Coleridge looked for in poets, and termed "the secondary imagination". Jokes, deliberate humour and original metaphor are, therefore, like poetry, examples of "non-casual speech", an exceptional kind of language (Attardo 1994: 110), though often inserted within the casual speech of conversation (6.4.2).

Seventh, because of their relative density of information, and deliberate artifice, both jokes and metaphors are communicatively risky and can prove problematic in terms of uptake. Sometimes a hearer will insist on taking the serious or literal meaning, even though a non-serious or metaphorical meaning was intended. During the SARS crisis I tried the following joke on a colleague in Hong Kong: "The government is so inconsistent. On the one hand they warn us not to touch other people's hands. And yet they also ask us to join hands in defeating SARS." To which my colleague replied: "They don't mean joining hands literally, you know!" (cf. Norrick 1993: 162). It might well be prudent, therefore, to signal joking or metaphorical intent, to put the humour or metaphor on record rather than off-record. (I have discussed extensively elsewhere (Goatly 2011: chapter 4) the problem of the asymmetry between metaphorical intention and recognition.)

Having explored the similarities and overlaps between metaphor and humour in general, I now wish to shift to a more specific comparison of metaphor and irony. Again, the need for signalling is important in both. Apparently the markers of irony overlap to a large extent with the markers of metaphor. Investigating the markers of written metaphor (Goatly 2011: chapter 6), I identified the same devices (and many more) that Attardo (2001: 119) lists for irony. For instance, explicit verbal process markers like "so to speak, one might say", typography

as in "scare quotes" and "!". I suspect the methods of marking metaphor in speech would also include the following markers of irony:
intonation; slowed speaking, syllable lengthening, pauses; kinesic
markers, e.g. winks, nudges, raised eyebrows.

According to Giora (1995), both jokes and irony violate what she
calls the "**graded informativeness** requirement". That is to say, they
involve marked, unpredictable or unconventional meanings which
imply a sudden jump in informativeness (rather than the more usual
gradient). However, they do so differently. The joke goes from
unmarked meaning to marked meaning, and irony from marked
meaning to unmarked meaning. In other words, with a joke we
normally take the more predictable meaning first and then work
out the second which connects the two schemas. In irony we take
the unpredictable meaning first – the surface meaning of the
utterance – and then are forced to a more predictable unmarked
meaning – often the opposite of the stated marked meaning.
For instance, we first briefly entertain the idea that Sarah Palin was
the best-educated vice-presidential candidate, before finding the
unmarked meaning 'Sarah Palin was the least-educated vice-presidential candidate'. Original or active metaphor is obviously more like
irony, but with conventional metaphor there is the possibility of the
same order of activation as for jokes. So, for example, the Graham
bathroom ad (p. 167), with an immediate preceding co-text mentioning interest-free credit, prompts the conventional metaphorical
meaning of "splash out" ('spend money extravagantly'), the unmarked
meaning, before we register the literal one.

Another similarity Giora sees between original metaphor and irony
is that the unmarked and stated meaning is activated, not ignored.
"With Giora (2003) I question whether adults really skip over the literal
meaning [of an ironic statement] … I start from the thesis that in
prototypical irony what is said and what is meant and especially the
gap between them must make sense" (Kotthoff 2009: 55). Irony,
through opposition between the stated and implied meaning, shares
with metaphor the contrast between what is said and what is
meant. Irony represents the extreme position highlighting difference,
while metaphor necessitates the finding of similarities. Some humorous metaphors might be intermediate, thwarting expectations of
similarity – remember that in the Labour party as product-for-recall
metaphor (7.1) the product cannot be returned, and the voter/
consumer cannot be compensated. Both metaphor and irony are
extreme forms of the phenomenon of meanings changing according
to context that we discovered in *She Picks up your Rubbish* (p. 102).

a. Does irony differ from jokes and metaphor in involving just one schema rather than two?

b. I have suggested, following Giora, that irony is rather like original metaphor because the unmarked meaning is activated first. However, just as metaphors can become conventionalised, so perhaps can ironies. "You are a fine friend" may or may not be ironic, but "a fine friend you are" seems much more likely to be a conventionalised formula for irony. Does this formulaic irony affect which meaning is activated first, and which of the meanings is the unmarked one?

I attempted (Goatly 2011: chapter 5) to develop a theory of irony and metaphor in which there are two types of both. In the kind of irony illustrated above (Sarah Palin etc.), an example of what Simpson calls '**oppositional irony**', you say the opposite of what you are thinking. However, in echoic irony (10.6) you echo what someone else said, again distancing yourself from it. For instance, if my wife says "It's a great day for a walk", we go for a walk and are caught in a thunderstorm, I might ironically echo her by saying on our soaked return "It's a great day for a walk."

There is a second version of metaphor too, so that non-echoic and echoic irony are balanced by non-echoic and "**subjective**" metaphor. Subjective metaphors arise when a speaker expresses a proposition as a sincere assertion or makes a reference that they consider literal. But, though the hearer does not believe it, she nevertheless recognises that the state of affairs described or the reference made resemble the actual state of affairs/entity referred to. For example, you may say "those swallows are flying late into the evening", mistaking bats for swallows. But I, knowing they are bats, can appreciate the grounds for your mistake: zig-zag manner of flight, catching insects, etc.

Finally, the non-factual nature of metaphor, irony and jokes, the suspension of norms of discourse, lend themselves to the development of fantasy or alternative worlds (see Oring 2003: 22ff. for discussion). One kind of metaphor known as the phenomenalistic (Levin 1977) involves an interpretation in which the unmarked meaning achieves a truth within a fictional or fantastic world. For instance, in fables where animals speak, we do not interpret sentences such as "the lion shouted" to mean something like 'the lion roared', as we might with a local metaphor. Instead of changing the meaning of the words to reach an unmarked meaning, we change over to a marked world in which the surface statement could be literally true and unmarked, one in which lions shout. Jokes (and humorous cartoons) often involve similar suspensions of disbelief, in which, for instance, mice can survive being flattened by a steamroller, or cauliflowers answer telephone calls:

> Mr and Mrs Cauliflower received a phone call from the police late one night. "I'm afraid your son has been involved in a bad car crash. Please come to the hospital immediately." They rushed to the accident and emergency unit as quickly as they could. The doctor took them to his office and sat them down. "The good news," he said, "is that your son will survive. But I'm afraid that for the rest of his life he's going to be a vegetable."

Note, by the way, that the punchline is, nevertheless, dependent upon a local conventional metaphor.

Irony, too can take forms similar to phenomenalistic metaphor – using a fictional or unrealistic narrative/drama – in which the ironic voice would be real. Kotthoff gives an example of a pupil taking on the role of an adult telling the student teachers what kinds of Christmas gifts to bring the pupils – saying "No candy" and raising his index finger (Kotthoff 2009: 68).

7.7. DEGREES OF CONVENTIONALITY: SEMANTICS OR PRAGMATICS

We have distinguished conventional (inactive) and original (active) metaphors. Conceptual metaphor theory and the Metalude database are based upon conventional metaphors, as the evidence they adduce or compile comes from already lexicalised metaphorical meanings. But since unconventionality is what distinguishes literal from metaphorical language, there can be no clear dividing line between the literal and metaphorical, and we need the kind of cline illustrated in Table 7.2. Glancing back to the sections on mixing and extension, it seems clear that mixing takes place because there is lack of awareness of the source, and extension takes place when there is such an awareness. Genre might be one factor in this. But another is likely to be the degree of conventionality of the metaphors.

The degree to which metaphors have been conventionalised and lexicalised into the semantics of the language can perhaps be measured, by considering whether the metaphorical statement can be agreed with/denied or questioned.

Activity 7.11

What do you think is the most likely response, (a), (b) or (c) to the following metaphorical statements

1. A committee is an animal with four back legs.
2. Virginity is a frozen asset.

(a) Yes it is. (b) No it isn't. (c) I see what you mean.

Comment

To agree or disagree with active metaphors such as (1) is beside the point, so (c) is much more appropriate than (a) or (b) (Sadock 1979: 54). However, even slightly inactive or familiar metaphors, like (2), are often informative enough to make (a) or (b) appropriate as responses. Because "asset" is an inactive metaphor, the meaning of the modified "frozen asset" is relatively obvious, quite apart from the overtone of sexual frigidity.

By contrast, inactive metaphors are open to agreement, negative questions and "yes/no" questions, as follows:

3. – Stock prices tumbled after 9/11.
   – Yes they certainly did.
4. Didn't stock prices tumble after 9/11?
5. Did stock prices tumble after 9/11?

I would hypothesise that metaphors can be put through the following succession of tests to determine their conventionality: agreement (cf. 3); negative question (cf. 4); yes–no question (cf. 5). The more of these tests they pass the less active and the more conventional they are (Goatly 2011: 37–8).

This cline of conventionality correlates with the distinction between semantics and pragmatics. This distinction might be formulated as follows: the meaning of a sentence (its decoded sense) is the province of semantics, and the meaning a speaker intends to convey by uttering it in context is the province of pragmatics. In active metaphors there is a wide gap between semantic meaning and a speaker's intended meaning. So besides decoding the meaning of the sentence uttered, the interpreter has to access extra information (from background knowledge, knowledge of the genre, and co-textual information) to map the grounds of the metaphor, through a process of pragmatic inference. With inactive metaphors, whose second conventional metaphorical meaning is in the dictionary, the role of pragmatic context is simply disambiguation, as the second semantic meaning has already been lexicalised. Since, presumably, inactive metaphors were active on their first use, the incorporation of their semantics into the lexicon is analogous to osmosis. Frequent similar interpretations in high concentrations on the pragmatic side of the semi-permeable membrane, the pragmatic–semantic boundary, allow migration through to the semantic side, in what has been dubbed "the career of metaphor" (cf. Gentner and Bowdle 2001).[6]

This chapter on metaphor is strategically placed in the book between the chapters on semantics and the next on pragmatics, because conventional and unconventional metaphors are respectively more dependent upon semantics and pragmatics for their interpretations.

7.8. SUMMARY

After placing metaphor in relation to other figures of speech like metonymy, I defined it as unconventional reference or collocation, furnishing terminology for metaphor analysis (target, source, mapping, ground) and demonstrating how it might be applied to metaphor-based jokes. I distinguished innovative and conventional metaphors in order to introduce conceptual metaphor theory, which concentrates on the latter. My database, Metalude, was introduced as a sketch of metaphorical lexical patterns in English, before showing how metaphor-based polysemy and absurdity is exploited in humour, according to metaphor themes CEASE IS STOP, FAILURE/GIVING UP IS BACKWARDS, INTENSITY/EXCITEMENT IS SPEED, DEATH IS A DESTINATION, OPINION IS PERSPECTIVE/ORIENTATION, DECREASE IS FALL, DECREASE IS CUT, SEX IS VIOLENCE. Moreover, the literalisation, extension and mixing of metaphor were shown to be a fecund resource for humour.

Proceeding more theoretically, I compared and contrasted jokes and metaphor in terms of verbal play, schema incongruity, interpretative grounds, surface meaning preservation, open-endedness of interpretation, information density, contextual displacement of the linguistic sign with an effect of strangeness or quasi-plausible absurdity, and communicative risk. I continued by comparing jokes, irony and metaphor, using the concepts of markedness, informativeness, echoicity and fantasy. I ended by locating active and inactive metaphor relative to semantic and pragmatic meaning.

There are many other ways in which metaphor might be related to humour besides those mentioned in this chapter. Draitser (1994), for example, has shown how de-personifying metaphors can be a technique of satire. If metaphor is in many ways similar to humour and irony, this is because script opposition is widespread in discourse, particularly in "creative" genres of discourse. Simpson (2003: 40ff.) points out that it is exploited in the kinds of discoursal deviation common in literature, which may produce foregrounding and schema refreshment (Cook 1994).

> ## Discussion
>
> (1) This chapter suggested a rather crude division between active and inactive metaphors. But a more subtle distinction might be made between those inactive metaphors of which the speaker and hearer are aware and those

which they produce and process without awareness of the underlying metaphor. How might this distinction be useful for explaining the effectiveness of metaphorical puns? Does the awareness of the polysemy, of the metaphorical connection, enhance the humorous effect or not?

(2) It has been traditional to classify verbal humour into two categories: linguistic and non-linguistic. The criterion is whether, as in linguistic humour, the humour is dependent on the particular language, and therefore cannot be translated, as in puns, or whether it depends solely upon the situation and inferencing, as, for example, in the joke about the motorcycle pillion rider (6.4.4). But might metaphorical puns based on metaphor themes that are to some extent universal call into question this neat division? Could you easily translate into another language you know some of the puns of this sort in Section 7.4?

Suggested Readings

- Kövecses (2002) is an introduction to metaphor within the cognitive linguistics tradition, though not necessarily backed-up by lexicographical evidence.
- Semino (2008), by contrast, is in the text-linguistic tradition, taking metaphor as used in discourse as the data for research rather than native speaker intuitions. The book concentrates on the discourses of politics, literature, science and education. Chapter 3 develops the concept of "literalisation" by considering "situational triggering".
- Goatly (2011) attempts a precise definition of metaphor, and a comprehensive introduction to the language in which it is expressed. Chapter 2 is most relevant as far as metaphor themes (root analogies) discussed above are concerned. Chapter 5 is more relevant to irony.
- The author's interactive database *Metalude* is quite good fun to investigate. http://www.ln.edu.hk/lle/cwd/project01/web/home. html; user id <user>, password <edumet6>.
- Simpson (2003: 125–51) explores various metaphorical and metonymic techniques employed in satire.
- Fonagy (1982), Giora (1995) and Attardo (2001) are worth reading for those wishing to explore in more detail the overlaps between irony, jokes and metaphor.

8   Pragmatics: reference and speech acts

The previous seven chapters largely concerned semantics, apart from some passing attention to the interpretation of original metaphor in Chapter 7. Chapters 8 and 9 shift focus to pragmatics, and, following on from Chapter 7, it is worth explaining more about the semantic–pragmatic distinction at the outset.

To recap, a language is a code more or less shared by the members of a linguistic community. Semantics attempts to describe the meanings of this code and the relations between the meanings of the items of the code, as the survey in Chapters 3 to 6 shows. We compose sentences (messages) out of the items in this code, and semantics investigates what the sentences mean. Pragmatics, on the other hand, is about what a speaker means, that is, intends, by the utterance of a sentence in a particular context.

There are three important ways in which semantic meanings differ from pragmatic meanings.[1] Firstly, pragmatic meanings are **non-conventional**: when sentences are uttered in context their conventional meanings may be pragmatically overridden. This means different contexts will produce different pragmatic implications. If I see one of my twenty-year-old students with a Mickey Mouse pencil case and ask "How old are you now?", I imply a criticism of their childish tastes rather than asking a real question as I would if I knew it was their birthday and uttered the same question. Second, pragmatic meanings are **calculable**: they are computed through a process of logical inferencing (see 10.3–5). And, thirdly, implicatures are **defeasible**. If my student replies "I don't want to grow up too quickly", as a response to my implied criticism of her immature taste, I can deny the implied criticism and say "I was only asking your age". Semantic meanings, by contrast, are conventional, less variable according to context, do not need calculating because they are simply decoded, and are non-defeasible: if you make a statement, relying largely on coded meanings, you cannot truthfully claim you didn't express its semantic meaning (Thomas 1995).

8.1.   THE BOUNDARIES OF SEMANTICS AND PRAGMATICS

Decoding the lexis and grammar of a language never conveys the full meaning and intention of the speaker. A friend of mine in northern Thailand applied for a passport and was waiting a long time for it to be issued. When she visited the office to check the progress of her application a Mr X asked for a bribe to expedite it. Indignant, she contacted Mr X's superior accusing Mr X of corruption. A few days later Mr X visited her home demanding she withdraw her accusation. At the end of the conversation he said, "You have two beautiful children. I see them every day on their way to school." Decoding the two sentences indicates little about what Mr X intended to convey by their utterance. We realise that in this context the utterance is unlikely to be intended as a simple assertion, or a compliment, but is most probably a threat. This example illustrates the huge distance between the semantic meaning coded in the sentence and the intended pragmatic meaning of the utterance. No convention in the code of English says "You have two beautiful children. I see them every day on their way to school" means 'Your children will be harmed if you refuse my demand'. To uncover the speaker's thought or intention required considerable pragmatic work. Similarly, no convention stipulates that "icicles" can refer to fingers, in the line from Charles Causley's 'Death of a Poet' (7.2) (Goatly 2011).

However, in other cases utterance meanings become conventionalised or pragmaticised. In many contexts the structure "Will you ... ?" counts as a request rather than a question about the hearer's intention. It now represents two possible sentence meanings to be selected or disambiguated according to context, just as *tumble* represents two possible lexical meanings TUMBLE$_1$ literal ('fall suddenly') and TUMBLE$_2$ metaphorical ('decrease rapidly in amount'). Remember the joke where "I guess" is ambiguous between its literal meaning and as a polite formula for accepting an offer:

> I asked my date what she wanted to drink. She said "Oh, I guess I'll have champagne." I said, "Guess again." (Slappy White, Carr and Greeves 2006: 147)

These examples demonstrate that frequent identical pragmatic interpretations solidify into a more or less coded semantic meaning. This solidification involves de-motivation. With dead metaphors, the motivation, or original meaning of the source, has been lost, for example with *red herring*. We become so used to lexicalised metaphors and phrasal compounds or speech act formulae that, in most genres, we lose awareness of the meanings of their parts. Such de-motivation is the basis for the following joke:

> Why is it that the winner of Miss Universe always comes from earth? (Rich Hall, Carr and Greeves 2006: 17)

8.2. SYMBOL, ICON AND INDEX

Degrees of motivation link to another semantic/pragmatic distinction: that between icons and symbols. **Icons** are signs whose forms (signifiers) resemble in some way the meaning concepts (signifieds) that they convey. The clearest case is onomatopoeia, where, for example, /splæ∫/ supposedly resembles the sound of a splash. **Symbols**, by contrast, are purely arbitrary, depending on apparently unmotivated relationships between form and meaning. Comparing Arabic and Roman numerals clarifies this distinction. In Roman numerals I, II and III are obviously iconic, though the iconicity disappears when one reaches IV and V. Chinese is similar. By contrast, Arabic numerals are more thoroughly symbols, so that 1, 2 and 3 have little if any motivation. In Peirce's basic system there is a third kind of sign, an **index**, that is a sign which points to what it refers to because it is contiguous with it.

A common illustration of the three-way distinction is road signs. The shape of a road sign has an arbitrary relationship with its meaning, as in Figure 8.1. Rectangles give information, triangles warn and circles order or prohibit. These shapes are symbolic signs. But a road sign may have iconic elements within the shape. So a cross within a triangle (Figure 8.2)

Figure 8.1. The symbolic element in road signs

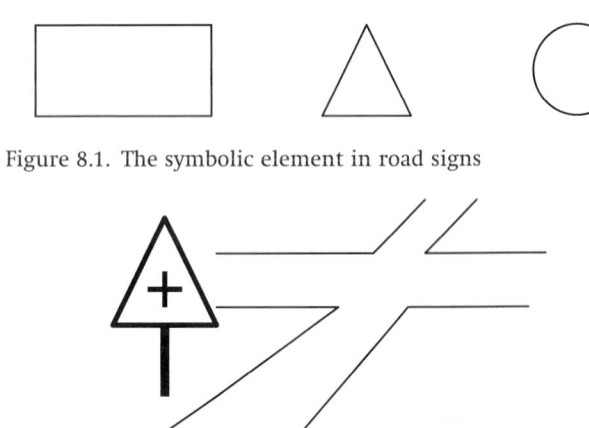

Figure 8.2. Road signs as index, symbol and icon

resembles, in a stylised way, the meaning 'crossroads'. In addition the sign is indexical, as it points to or is contiguous with the crossroads it both refers to and warns about (Fiske 1982).

Activity 8.1

Explain the following blonde joke in terms of icons, indexes and symbols.

A redhead, a brunette and a blonde escape from jail and hide in a barn. The police close in, so the three women each hide in a sack. The police search the barn and, to check each sack, a police officer kicks them as he walks past. The officer kicks the redhead's sack, and the redhead says "Meow!" The officer kicks the brunette's sack, and the brunette says, "Woof, woof." The officer kicks the blonde's sack, and the blonde shouts, "Potatoes!"

Comment

The blonde fails to make the proper distinction between an index and a symbol. The other women make a noise which is an index of the presence of a dog and cat in their respective sacks. The blonde, however, tries to use the linguistic symbol to indicate the presence of potatoes, thereby stupidly giving an index of the presence of a human. Also note that if "meow" and "woof" are conventional signs, as well as indexes, they are icons rather than symbols.

The indexical nature of public notices emphasises the extent to which context (in this case physical, not mental) is important for communication and interpretation of discourse. I used to frequent a village pub called The Plough at Wingfield in Bedfordshire,[2] where a low doorway led from the bar to the restaurant. Over the door was the notice DUCK OR GROUSE. This achieved its double meaning from its physical context above a low lintel, easy to bang your head on, of a doorway to a restaurant where the menu included game birds.

Indexes seem to belong to a different order of classification from icons and symbols, since icons and symbols are mutually exclusive endpoints on a scale, rather like gradable opposites. In fact, indexes are pragmatic in the sense that they relate meanings to the world around them, bridging the divide between Form/Meaning and World (Figure 1.2), whereas symbols and icons are more internal to the sign system and are involved primarily in the Form and Meaning columns, though icons have a secondary relation to their referents as they resemble them.

I mentioned the motivation which distinguishes icons from symbols, and it is partly the desire to (re-)motivate linguistic signs that encourages humour. Why shouldn't *overtaker* and *undertaker* be semantically linked or opposed: "He used to overtake too often and now he's with the undertaker" (Attardo 1994: 157)? We resist the arbitrariness of the linguistic sign:

> Someone once asked Motke Chabad, the legendary wit: "Tell me, Motke, you're a smart fellow. Why is *kugel* called *kugel*?" Motke lost no time in responding. "What kind of a question is that? It's sweet like *kugel*, isn't it? It's thick like *kugel*, isn't it? And it tastes like *kugel*, doesn't it? So why *shouldn't* it be called *kugel*?" (Novak and Waldocks 1981)

The phenomenon of homonymy seems an extension of the arbitrariness of the phoneme to morphemes/words. In which case punning represents a rebellion against it, a pretence of an identity of meaning corresponding to an identity of form (Attardo 1994: 169). This search for motivation suggests permeability in the boundary between form and meaning, columns 1 and 2 of Figure 1.2, as if the form somehow contains the meaning within itself. Such a focus on form, and the imposition of formal/semantic patterns, is an aspect of Jakobson's poetic function, with its patterning at the sub-morphemic or phonetic level. By emphasising the sound iconicity of phonemes as at least contributing to connotation if not sense (Attardo 1994: 157), one denies the arbitrariness of the sounds of morphemes, and thereby also of homonyms.

In the early stages of learning a first or second language there is a tendency to focus on form. For example, English speakers learning Thai tend to progress through links 1 to 4 as they become more proficient (cf. Carter 1987: 156):

1. phonological links with L1: e.g. /kɑːu/ (falling tone) 'rice', and / kɑu/ 'cow';
2. semantic and phonological links between L1 and L2, e.g. /rɪm/ (mid tone) in both English and Thai means 'edge';
3. phonological links in L2: /mɑː/ (rising tone) meaning 'dog', /mɑː/ (mid-tone) meaning 'come', /mɑː/ (high tone) meaning 'horse';
4. semantic and phonological links in L2: /glɑɪ/ (falling tone) means 'near', and /glɑːɪ/ (mid-tone) means 'far'.

Wordplay is perhaps symptomatic of a desire to re-motivate language, to make formal (and semantic) connections as one did when acquiring linguistic competence. Fonagy (1982) talks of the child's refusal of homonymy. He suggests an analogy between this desire to re-motivate language and children's playing hide-and-seek. Meaning seems to be hidden by the arbitrariness of the sign, only to be found later in wordplay or other accidents of motivation. Recently I was delighted when I linked for the first time the long familiar musical term *ostinato*, 'a bass figure repeated throughout a piece of music', with the word *obstinate*.

The kind of wordplay I illustrated in folk-etymology or re-analysis (Chapter 2) is symptomatic of this desire for motivation (Attardo 1994: 154), but the avoidance of taboo reflected meanings is an attempt to avoid it. Taboo is predicated on a motivation which collapses the three WFM columns in Figure 1.2. Mentioning a (taboo) name is supposed to indexically conjure up or even offend its referent (Attardo 1994: 156).[3] It was the reason hunting societies avoided the offensive direct mention of their prey. Bears were referred to euphemistically as *bee wolves* or *honey wolves*, in Germanic and Russian, giving us the glorious Beowulf and Medvedev respectively.

8.3. REFERENCE

When we refer to things in the world there are various semantic relationships between the referring expression, usually a noun phrase, and what it refers to, the referent. **Definite specific reference** points out one specific individual thing/person out of the members of the semantic class represented by the noun, e.g.

> That boy stole my bicycle

The speaker believes that, in context, the hearer is able to identify the specific referent out of all possible ones (boys and bicycles). As indicators of definiteness we use the definite article, pronouns and pronominal adjectives, e.g. *you*, *me* and *him*, *my hamster*, *your wife*, *his goldfish*, as well as demonstrative determiners and pronouns: *this*, *that*, *these*, *those*.

Sometimes only one referent in the context belongs to the semantic class represented by the noun. This **unique reference** employs the definite article.

> The sun was shining on the sea, shining with all its might
> And this was strange because it was the middle of the night.

Despite the existence of other solar systems, in the context of our earth, where most speaking is done, the sun is unique. However, uniqueness often only applies to a local context, so *the car* refers to the family car, and *the post office* to the one nearby.

Sometimes the speaker has a particular referent in mind, without believing the hearer has knowledge of it, or could identify it. In this

Table 8.1. *Varieties of reference*

	Indefinite	Definite
Specific	*I have **a** girlfriend*	***the** tissue is dirty. Use this one.*
		(Unique): *gone to **the** toilet*
Non-specific	*I want **a** drink*	(Generic): ***the** whale is a mammal*

case the speaker will use the indefinite article for **indefinite specific** reference. One test for it is to insert the word *particular* between the indefinite article and the noun without changing the meaning, e.g. "Down the road there's a (particular) house and it's being auctioned by HSBC". On the other hand, indefinite articles can be used without having a particular or specific member of the class in mind, e.g. "Has anyone got a memory stick?" And a test for this **indefinite non-specific** reference is whether the phrase can be altered to *some X or other* without changing the meaning. Often this specific/non-specific distinction is problematic, as the hearer has no access to the speaker's thoughts. For instance if a man says "I want to marry a millionaire", we may be unsure whether he thinks any willing millionaire will do, or he wants to marry the millionaire he has already identified or has a relationship with.

If indefinite articles can be used for specific and non-specific reference, so can definite articles. But non-specific definite articles refer to all the members of the class, the genus, a kind of reference consequently called **generic**, e.g. "The tiger is the only big cat that enjoys swimming". But there are other grammatical means of generic reference, the indefinite article or plural:

> A tiger is the only big cat that enjoys swimming
> Tigers are the only big cats that enjoy swimming

Table 8.1 sums up a simplified version of different kinds of reference.

Activity 8.2

Explain the ambiguity of reference in the following jokes.

1. Somewhere on this globe, every ten seconds, there is a woman giving birth to a child. She must be stopped. (Sam Levenson, Carr and Greeves 2006: 60)
2. This was a mythical beast with the head of a lion and the body of a lion. But the body of *another* lion (Woody Allen paraphrase, Ritchie 2004: 41)

Comment

I suppose after reading the first sentences we take "a woman" and "a lion" to be generic reference. But the second sentences, by using the singular definite pronoun *she* and *another*, not normally used generically, suggest the first indefinite article conveyed indefinite specific reference (cf. Attardo 1994: 133).

It was proposed (1.4) that names have a reference but not a sense. Of course their reference is definite specific, since they ideally identify a unique individual. When word forms are ambiguous between a common noun and a proper noun or name this can be exploited for humour:

Why are soldiers so tired on April 1st? They've just had a 31 day March.
(Tibballs 2006: 39)
I passed Nobody on the road. Therefore, nobody is slower than I am.
(Carroll 1871: 143–4)

When discussing textual meaning (6.3), we noted that co-reference is used to build coherence in a text. But sometimes it is difficult to judge whether two expressions are co-referring or not. The following joke depends upon the reader's assumption that the repeated phrase "a man" is co-referential. The punchline indicates that it is not:

The Five Secrets of a Great Relationship:

1. It is important to find a man who works around the house, occasionally cooks and cleans and who has a job. 2. It is important to find a man who makes you laugh. 3. It is important to find a man who is dependable, respectful, and doesn't lie. 4. It is important to find a man who is good in bed and who loves to have sex with you. 5. It is important that these four men never meet. (Carr and Greeves 2006: 145)

Pronouns are a main referential device and usually specific as well, but it is not always obvious whether a word form is a pronoun or not: "Try our herbal remedies. You can't get better" (UK paper, Tibballs 2006: 494).

Pronouns that share a referent with a noun phrase in the preceding text are called **anaphoric**. Generally the pronoun is assumed to co-refer with the last eligible noun phrase which matches in number and gender, as in the humorous interpretation of this example:

As he uttered the last word he dropped his voice, and she didn't quite catch it.

But not in the following:

If the baby does not thrive on fresh milk, then it should be boiled. (Women's magazine, Tibballs 2006: 491)

In **cataphoric** reference the more explicit text occurs after the pronoun, as intended in the following, though initially we make the more usual anaphoric interpretation.

> For those of you who have children and don't know it, we have a nursery downstairs. (Tibballs 2006: 497)

As in the intended and unintended referents of this announcement, pronouns like *it* or *that* or *this* often have a wider scope of reference than just individual entities or things.

Activity 8.3

Explain the ambiguity in this joke:

> If I said you had a beautiful body would you hold it against me? (Connor Ferris, personal communication)

Comment

The "it" might refer to the beautiful body mentioned in the previous clause, making this a chat-up or seduction line. The second meaning takes the idiomatic meaning of "hold it against me", 'resent it', 'object to it'. The only relevant referent of "it" with this second meaning is the complex proposition 'saying you have a beautiful body'. The meaning would be 'Would you object to my saying you have a beautiful body'.

So pronouns like *it*, *this* and *that* may refer to whole propositions and the actions they convey, or even to whole scenarios or sequences of actions:

> A man walks into a bar carrying an alligator. He says to the patrons, "Here's the deal. I open this alligator's mouth and put my genitals inside. The alligator closes his mouth for one minute, then opens it, and I remove my unit unscathed. If it works, everyone buys me drinks." The crowd agrees. The man drops his pants and puts his privates in the alligator's mouth. The alligator closes its mouth. After a minute the man grabs a beer bottle, and bangs the alligator on the top of its head. The alligator opens wide, and he removes his genitals unscathed. Everyone buys him drinks.
>   Then he says, "I'll pay anyone a hundred dollars who's willing to give it a try." After a while a hand goes up at the back of the bar. It's a woman. "I'll give it a try", she says, "but promise not to hit me on the head with the beer bottle."

Though the more normal use of pronouns is specific definite, the pronoun *you* allows a non-specific, generic meaning, synonymous to *one*, apart from its relative informality:

Activity 8.4

How is the ambiguity of *you* exploited in the following joke?

> Did you know you're eight times more likely to get mugged in London than you are in New York City? It's because you don't live in New York City. (Jimmy Carr, Carr and Greeves 2006: 9)

Comment

We tend to interpret the first *you* as generic or non-specific, though this conflicts with our existing belief that New York is a more violent city than London. This anomaly is explained by the second sentence, where we realise that both *you*s are definite specific references to the addressee.

8.4. DEIXIS

Some word-forms have incomplete meanings unless we know who uttered them (person), when they uttered them (time), or where they uttered them (place). These are **deictics**, from the Greek word **deixis** meaning pointing, or **shifters** because their meaning shifts according to person, time and place of the utterance.

English examples of deixis are

Person	e.g. *I, me, my (you)*
Time	e.g. *tomorrow, yesterday, now*
Place	e.g. *here, there*

With person deixis, obviously *I* refers to the speaker, and its reference changes with the speaker. A previous speaker, if addressed by the new speaker or *I*, will become a *you*. Hence the incongruity of the following: "We were identical twins. One of us drowned. Some think it was Bill, some think it was me" (Mark Twain). With time deixis, *tomorrow* means 'the day after the day of utterance', *yesterday* 'the day before the day of utterance', *today* 'the day of utterance'. Blake tells of a Queensland pub with the sign outside "Free beer tomorrow" (Blake 2007: 52).

Tense markers on verbs are usually time deictic. Past refers to a point of time before the utterance, past perfective to a time even before that past point of time, present continuous to a period of time including the time of utterance, and future to a point or period of time after the time of utterance. However, present simple is not deictic when it makes statements supposed to be true for all time, e.g. "Water freezes at 0°C".

As for place, *here* means 'a place where the speaker is', or 'a place close to the speaker', so what is "here" for the speaker may be "there" for the hearer.

Activity 8.5

How are the first speaker's deictic assumptions reversed by the second speaker in this joke?

"I would go to the end of the world for you." "Yes, but would you stay there?"

Comment

The first speaker seems to assume or imagine that the second is at the end of the world. The second speaker by using "there" disabuses him.

This proximity/distance from speaker distinction is also reflected by *this* and *that*. Further examples are the directions *east* and *west*, which are relative to the place of utterance and *right* or *left*, which can switch according to speaker's and hearer's orientation. If I am facing you what is "right" for me will be "left" for you.

Verb meanings may include the deictic component direction towards or direction away from the speaker: *come* and *bring* entail 'towards the speaker' (though there is dialectal variation). Sometimes *go* and *take* mean 'away from the speaker'. But deixis may be dependent on use: although words like *today* and *here* have deictic meaning built in to them, others like *go* are more variable. In "I went to London yesterday" (said in Manchester) *go* might be deictic (away from the place of speaking), but not in "I went from the Tower of London to the London Eye" (also said in Manchester).

Sometimes speakers imaginatively identify with their speakmate, adopting their perspective or **deictic centre**. On the telephone it's quite normal to say "I'll come to see you tomorrow" even though the movement will be away from the speaker's place of utterance. By contrast, other expressions impose the old colonial powers' deictic centre on the rest of the English-speaking world: *Near East*, *Middle East*, *Far East* are obvious enough, but, surprisingly, Singaporeans refer to Australia as *down under* even though, adopting the Singaporean deictic centre this would refer to Ecuador.

Discussion

If we define deixis in terms of the meaning of an utterance that is not explicit until we know who made the utterance, and when and where, does deixis extend into wider areas of meaning than those exemplified above? For example how might it be connected with various aspects of social meaning (age, dialect etc.), affective meaning and contested terms?

8.5. SPEECH ACTS

"Pragmatic" in its everyday sense relates to the achievement of goals in a practical way, and the technical linguistic field of pragmatics also views language as a purposeful action by the speaker attempting to achieve a certain effect on a hearer. The effect of an utterance, technically its **perlocutionary** effect, may not always be the intended one.

> Experts say you're more likely to get hurt crossing the street than flying, but that doesn't make me feel any less frightened of flying. If anything, it makes me more afraid of crossing the street. (Ellen DeGeneres, Carr and Greeves 2006: 9)

The idea that language is an action of a speaker on a hearer is encapsulated in the label "**speech act**". Using language can be conceived as performing three kinds of acts: uttering the phonemes of words and sentences (**utterance acts**), referring and predicating to produce propositions (**propositional acts**) and attempting to affect a hearer (**illocutionary acts**: e.g. questioning, commanding, informing).

These acts vary independently of each other: "Jan plays" and "Does Jan play?" are identical propositional acts, but different utterance acts (different sounds) and different illocutionary acts, statement and question. "You have two beautiful children" uttered by a director of an upcoming production of *Oliver*, and "You have two beautiful children" uttered by a mafia gangster, are the same utterance acts, the same succession of phonemes, and, providing I am addressed on both occasions, the same propositional act. But they are different illocutionary acts – indirect invitation, and indirect threat. "Mr Jan Martin is a regular player" and "Jan plays" could be the same illocutionary acts, informing, and propositional acts, but their phonemic and formal difference makes them different utterance acts. Finally if "Does Jan play?" refers in one instance to Jan Martin, and in another to Janice Clutterbuck, then, despite being the same illocutionary acts, questions, and the same utterance act, they are different propositional acts (cf. Searle 1969: 22–3).

Speech act theory focuses on utterances as illocutionary acts, and on the intentions that the speaker has, whether or not these intentions

Table 8.2. *Speech acts, propositions and conditions (after Searle 1969: 66–7)*

Speech act	Proposition content	Preparatory conditions	Sincerity conditions	Essential condition
Request	Future act A of H.	H is able to do A. S believes H is able to do A. It is not obvious to both S and H that H will do A in the normal course of events of his own accord.	S wants H to do A.	Counts as an attempt to get H to do A.
Assert	Any proposition p.	S has evidence for the truth of p. It is not obvious to both S and H that H knows (does not need to be reminded of) p.	S believes p.	Counts as an undertaking that p represents an actual state of affairs.
Question	Any proposition or propositional function.	S does not know the answer (if the proposition is true or how to complete the proposition). S believes H knows the answer. It is not obvious to both S and H that H will provide the information at that time without being asked.	S wants this information.	Counts as an attempt to elicit this information from H.
Promise	Future act A of S.	H wants S to do A. S believes H wants S to do A. It is not obvious to both S and H that S will do A in the normal course of events.	S intends to do A.	Counts as an undertaking that S will perform A.

Thank	Past act A done by H.	A benefits S and S believes A benefits S.	S feels grateful or appreciative for A.	Counts as an expression of gratitude or appreciation.
Apologise	Past act A of S.	A was disadvantageous to H, and S and H believe A was disadvantageous to H.	S feels regret for or sorry for regret.	Counts as an expression of regret.
Advise	Future act A of H.	S has some reason to believe A will benefit H. It is not obvious to both S and H that H will do A in the normal course of events.	S believes A will benefit H.	Counts as an undertaking to the effect that A is in H's best interest.
Warn about	Future event or state E.	S has reason to believe E will occur and is not in H's interest. It is not obvious to both S and H that E will occur.	S believes E is not in H's best interest.	Counts as an undertaking to the effect that E is not in H's best interest.
Greet	None.	S has just encountered (or been introduced to) H.	None.	Counts as courteous recognition of H by S.
Congratulate	Some event, act, etc. E, related to H.	E is in H's interest and S believes E is in H's interest.	S is pleased at E.	Counts as an expression of pleasure at E.

are realised in a perlocutionary effect. A speech act and intentional view of meaning runs as follows:

> A speaker S means something by X = S intends the utterance of X to produce some effect in hearer H by means of the recognition of this intention (Grice). And furthermore, if he is speaking literally, he intends this recognition to be achieved through conventional rules linking the expression X with the production of that effect (i.e. code and general rules) (cf. Searle 1969: 49–50).

This definition, in invoking "conventional rules" is, as we shall see, an attempt by Searle to minimise the role of pragmatics which work independent of conventions, or to include pragmatics (inferential communication) within semantics (rule-based coded communication).

8.5.1. Speech act conditions

Preliminary Activity 8.6

Which of the following seem odd to you?

   a. Thank you for coming tomorrow.
   b. I apologise for you doing that.
   c. I apologise for my son doing that.
   d. What will you do when you leave football, Jack – will you stay in football? (Stuart Hall, Tibballs 2006: 514)
   e. Thank you for the chocolates. I couldn't eat them, they were mouldy.
   f. At a Shanghai buffet: we promise to make you fed up.
   g. Advice on a bottle of rum: open bottle before drinking.
   h. A son was born last Monday to Mr and Mrs Charles Johnson. Congratulations, Pete!
   i. Warning at a level crossing: trains going both ways at once.

Interpreting Table 8.2, John Searle suggested that speech acts can be specified according to: the kind of propositional acts that they perform; their preparatory conditions; their sincerity conditions; and their essential conditions.

As far as the propositional act is concerned, the important distinctions are whether it is a past act or future act, whether it is the act of the hearer or the speaker, or whether it refers to an event/state related to the hearer or not. Preparatory conditions concern whether it is obvious or not that the act will be likely to occur, whether p is true, and whether the speaker or hearer have evidence for p, or the ability to perform p. Sincerity conditions involve wanting or not wanting p, believing p, or whether p is in the interest of the hearer. The essential condition is simply part of the convention/rule (according to the speech act definition of meaning above) linking the expression with the effect: such an utterance, with such a propositional content, with the preparatory conditions and sincerity conditions specified, counts, by rule, as having that particular illocutionary force.

Follow-up activity

1. Return to the examples a.–i (p. 208). From the information in Table 8.2 can you account for the oddities that you spotted?
2. Are there any of these sentences which you found perfectly acceptable, but which Searle's theory would appear to disallow?

Comment

1.   (b), (d), (e), (f), (g), (h), and (i) are very anomalous.

   (b) is anomalous because the act A should be the act of S not H. (Though I suppose you could apologise for a requested action that turned out to be pointless, for example writing a reference for a job that you missed the interview for.)

   (d) breaks the preparatory condition on questions: "S does not know the answer" as he already presupposes that Jack will leave football.

   (e) is infelicitous as an act of thanks since the preparatory condition does not apply: "A benefits S and S believes A benefits S". The sincerity condition may nevertheless apply – "it's the thought that counts".

   (f) unintentionally breaks the preparatory condition on promises that the hearer wants the speaker to do A.

   (g) breaks the preparatory condition on advice. It should be obvious to both speaker and hearer that the hearer will do the act in the normal course of events.

   (h) apparently the propositional content matches congratulations – that is, Pete is the father of the child. However, there are doubts about the preparatory condition that the birth was in Pete's interest, or on the sincerity condition that the speaker/writer is pleased about the event.

   (i) breaks one preparatory condition on warnings: I don't suppose the writer has reason to believe this event will occur. The other preparatory and sincerity conditions seem fine: if it does occur it is certainly not in the reader's interest as the chances of avoiding such trains would be relatively low. And it is certainly not obvious to both writer and reader that trains will go both ways at once.

2.   Some of the other examples, (a) and (c), might well be acceptable.

   (a) does not seem anomalous. It just, disingenuously, assumes that the hearer will perform the act, and so thanks can be given in advance (cf. "thank you in advance ...").

(c) although the act apologised for should strictly speaking be an act of the speaker, one can take responsibility for the actions of others closely related to one, especially minors, below the age of responsibility.

The following example from Harold Pinter's *The Birthday Party* makes an interesting play on preparatory and sincerity conditions.

MEG:	Is Stanley up yet?
PETEY:	I don't know. Is he?
MEG:	I don't know. I haven't seen him down yet.
PETEY:	Well, then, he can't be up.
MEG:	Haven't you seen him down?
PETEY:	I've only just come in.
MEG:	He must be still asleep.

Meg's question turns out to be infelicitous in several ways. She may assume that Petey knows the answer, a preparatory condition on questions. However, he doesn't. The other preparatory condition – that Meg doesn't know if Stanley is up – already seems doubtful. Petey, in asking "Is he?", must assume as a preparatory condition that Meg knows the answer to the question she herself has asked. She therefore insists on her own ignorance, "I don't know", which makes her question more felicitous than Petey had assumed. However, without any further evidence she concludes that Stanley is not up and must be asleep. This suggests that, despite her insistence, the preparatory condition on the question, the speaker's ignorance of the answer, may not have applied (Goatly 2008).

Compare this with the anomalous

A:	What's green and yellow and lives in treacle mines?
B:	What?
A:	I don't know.

Joke questions or riddles, like exam questions, are not felicitous questions, because we assume the speaker/examiner knows the answer. The anomaly here derives from the fact that the question fulfils the preparatory condition – the speaker's ignorance of the answer – and is therefore more felicitous than one would expect from a riddle.

Activity 8.7

In the following joke, what kind of speech act do we anticipate the man will make? How is "I beg your pardon" related to this expectation? How does his question relate to the preparatory condition for the expected speech act?

"I beg your pardon," said the man returning to his theatre seat at the end of the interval, "but did I step on your foot when I left?" "Yes, you did." "Oh, good, that means I'm in the right row." (Tibballs 2006: 358)

Comment

We might expect an apology. We are perhaps primed for this by "I beg your pardon" as this is a formula for apologising. But it transpires that the man is apologising for disturbing the other theatre-goer with his question. His question and the answer give us information that the speaker's previous act was disadvantageous or harmful to the hearer. This is what makes us expect an apology.

8.5.2. Categories of speech acts

Searle (1979) developed his theory of speech acts by categorising them according to their relationship between the words and the world.

Assertives commit the speaker to the truth of the expressed proposition, with different degrees of commitment amongst the specific speech acts, e.g. *hypothesise* v. *state* v. *swear* (as in an oath). With

Table 8.3. *Categories of speech acts*

Speech act type	Description	Acts such as	Example
Assertives	Giving information, describing the state of the world	state, inform, swear, remind	'There's a departmental meeting tomorrow'
Directives	Attempting to make the hearer do something	command, request, suggest, plead	'Please type out the agenda'
Commissives	Speaker committing themselves to an act in the future	promise, threaten, vow, volunteer	'Certainly, I'll do it in five minutes'
Expressives	Expressing an inner feeling	thank, congratulate, apologise, condole	'Thank you for doing it so quickly'
Declarations	Changing the state of affairs by declaring something to be the case	umpire scoring, priest marrying a couple, celebrity naming a ship	'We should now start the meeting'

assertives, we assume a state of affairs exists in the world (column 3) and that the speaker fits the words to match the world (cf. *assert* in Table 8.2).

Directives are attempts by the speaker to get the hearer to perform a future action, *A*, with different degrees of force or insistence reflecting the degree of interpersonal vertical distance. For instance, in order of decreasing dominance we have *command*, *request*, *beg* and *pray*. Directives attempt to get the hearer to make the world match the words (the proposition) (cf. *request* in Table 8.2). Speech acts like *dare*, *challenge* and *defy* are difficult to categorise: are they positive directives or prohibitions? *Advise* and *warn* straddle assertives, telling you what is good for you, and directives, attempting to get you to take action for your own benefit.

Commissives commit the speaker in varying degrees to a future act, for example *undertake*, *promise*, *threaten*. They are a commitment that the speaker will make the world match his words (cf. *promise* in Table 8.2).

Expressives express the psychological state in the sincerity condition about a state of affairs specified in the proposition. Examples are *congratulate*, *apologise*, *thank*, expressing attitudes to *p*, such as pleasure, sorrow, gratitude etc. Expressives assume the existence of fit between world and words (cf. *thank*, *congratulate* in Table 8.2).

Declarations, when successfully performed, create a correspondence between the propositional content and reality. Examples are *nominate*, *christen*, *declare war*, *marry*. They depend upon an extra-linguistic institution defining the speaker–hearer roles and the circumstances under which the declaration may be performed. Only the chairperson can officially announce the start of a meeting. To marry a couple I must occupy an institutionally recognised role, e.g. registrar or priest, and law may stipulate the possible venues for the ceremony. No sincerity condition is necessary with declarations. The priest at the end of a christening can't say "I'm sorry ladies and gentlemen, I didn't feel sincere when I performed the ceremony; we will have to repeat it later" (cf. *greet* in Table 8.2).

The contrast between declarations and other kinds of speech act reflects Searle's (1995) distinction between institutional facts and brute facts, with the former radically dependent upon language. In this theory, whether someone is married or not, for example, is regarded as an institutional fact, whereas the level of CO_2 in the earth's atmosphere is a brute fact. But radical philosophers like Foucault and Bourdieu challenge this view. They suggest that acts of linguistic categorisation and labelling are themselves a kind of declaration.

For Foucault, discourse does not describe a pre-existing reality so much as bringing a reality into being. Discourse he defines as "a group of statements that provide a language for talking about – the way of representing the knowledge about – a particular target at a particular historical moment". Physical objects and actions (brute facts) exist independently, but only acquire meaning and become objects of knowledge within discourse. The knowledge discourse creates is linked to power, as, like a declaration, it has the power to make itself true – "all knowledge once applied to the real world has real effects, and in that sense at least, 'becomes true'" (Foucault 1977: 27).

Bourdieu (1991: 134) makes a similar point: "How can one fail to see that a prediction may have a role not only in the author's intentions, but also in the reality of its social realisation ... as a self-fulfilling prophecy". He calls such a prediction "a performative representation capable of exerting a specifically political effect", in other words a declaration. Such declarations are acts of institution that cannot be sanctioned unless they have, somehow, the whole social order behind them. (Only a socially ratified priest can christen.) Similarly, linguistic form and the information it imparts condense and symbolise the entire structure of the social relation from which they derive their existence and efficacy.

> The word or *a fortiori* the dictum, the proverb and all the stereotyped or ritual forms of expression are programmes of perception and different, more or less ritualised strategies for the symbolic struggles of everyday life, just like the great collective rituals of naming or nomination – or, more clearly still, the clashes between the visions and previsions of specifically political struggles – imply a certain claim to symbolic authority as the socially recognised power to impose a certain vision of the social world, i.e. of the divisions of the social world. In the struggle to impose the legitimate vision, in which science itself is inevitably caught up, agents possess power in proportion to their symbolic capital, i.e. in proportion to the recognition they receive from a group (Bourdieu 1991: 106).

8.5.3. Indirect speech acts

The most direct way of performing a speech act is to match it with grammatical mood (see Chapter 5). So assertives are most obviously expressed by declarative clauses: "There are only nine holes on this golf course". Directives are conveyed by imperative mood, "Give me the spanner", except those requesting information, where the typical mood is interrogative, "Who won Wimbledon last year?" Declarations are formulaically first person declarative mood clauses in present simple tense: "I (hereby) declare the new Wanstead Public Library open." ("I hereby pwonounce you man and wife" "And you pwonounce it very nicely, vicar".) Expressives are less easy to match with mood, but may be conveyed by exclamatives, "What a shame it was you failed your exam!" or by first person declarative mood clauses with a mental process verb of affect, "I hate the way Jonathan Ross made that phone call" or its adjectival relational equivalent in (present) simple tense "I'm glad you managed to pass your driving test".

However, speech acts are not always direct; they may lack the neat match between mood and speech act type. For example, directives to action may be achieved by the interrogative or declarative moods: "Would you mind shutting the window?", "I'd like you to see me after class". Directives for information can be achieved by declarative questions with rising intonation rather than interrogative mood:

/
"He went to BIRmingham?"

Indirect statements can be made through questions: "Do you realise that it's already three o'clock?"

Searle (1969; 1975) attempted, unsuccessfully, though interestingly, to extend the idea of conventions to account for indirect speech acts as though they are rule-governed like the rules of the language code. He showed that indirect requests can be made by exploiting conditions on requests.

- Asking about/stating the preparatory condition of ability, e.g. "Can you pass the salt?" "You've got change for a dollar."
- Stating that the sincerity condition obtains, e.g. "I want you to clean the car."

Other indirect directives involve the proposition itself:

- Asking whether H desires or is willing to do the action in the proposition, e.g. "Would you be willing to write a reference for me?"
- Stating that/asking whether there are reasons for doing/not doing the action in the proposition, e.g. *it's better to* or *why not*: "It's better to go on the AI(M) rather than on the M1"; "2 chorus girls discussing what to buy another for her birthday 'Why not buy her a book?' 'No she's already got a book.'"
- Asking whether/stating the propositional content obtains: "Will you stop making that awful racket?"; "You will eat your cereal, won't you?"

Activity 8.8

Explain the ambiguity in an indirect speech act on which this joke depends. What indirect speech act does the writer of the sign intend, and what kind of indirect speech act does the jogger interpret it as?

> After driving all night, a company rep was still far from home as dawn broke. He decided to pull over and catch up on his sleep. Unknown to him he had chosen to park his car on the city's main jogging route. Barely had he dozed off when he was startled by a knock on the car window. It was a jogger. "What's the time?" asked the jogger. "Seven fifteen," said the man drowsily. He tried to doze but soon another jogger knocked on his window. "What's the time?" yelled the jogger. "Seven thirty," said the man, irritated. Again he tried to sleep, but was quickly woken by another jogger hammering on his window. "What's the time?" he screamed. "Seven forty-five," snapped the man. That was the last straw. Taking a pen and paper, he put a sign in his car window saying, "I DO NOT KNOW THE TIME." No sooner had he fallen asleep again than another jogger was pounding on the window, shouting, "Hey, buddy, it's seven fifty-five."
> (Tibballs 2006: 361)

Comment

I suppose the company rep is attempting to indirectly prohibit the asking of questions about the time, by stating that one of the preparatory conditions, the expectation of the hearer knowing the answer, does not obtain. The jogger misinterprets this as an indirect question, because the rep not knowing the time is a preparatory condition for the rep asking a question.

However interesting Searle's observations, pragmatics is not rule-governed in the way he suggests. At one extreme, for example, we simply have hints: "The door is open" might be a very indirect request to shut the door. Moreover, the indirect speech act formulae that Searle identifies are not the only ones, and not all can be related to speech act conditions (Copestake and Terkourafi 2010).

Activity 8.9

The following examples depend, in one of their meanings, upon formulae for signalling speech act types. What are the formulae and what speech acts do they signal?

1. On the door of a Moscow hotel room: "If this is your first visit to the USSR you're welcome to it." (Tibballs 2006: 502)
2. In a New York restaurant: "Customers who consider our waitresses uncivil ought to see the manager." (Tibballs 2006: 499)
3. Never get into an argument with a schizophrenic and say "Who do you think you are?"

Comment

"You're welcome to it (Y)" and "If you think X is bad in some way, you ought to see Y" are both formulae for disparagement of Y, but the latter seems also to mildly challenge a complaint against X. "Who do you think you are?" is a formula for criticising the hearer's pride or pomposity. The last two examples are ambiguous, but the first simply makes a mistake, *welcome to it* rather than *welcome*.

In the area of semantics, despite the fuzziness of meanings, the potential disagreement among speakers with different language experiences about obligatory meaning components, and the dynamic nature of meaning change (6.5), there is some degree of consensus on what the language code means. However, when speakers attempt to express their intentions in context, which is what pragmatics studies, the degree of risk and ambiguity increases dramatically. Plenty of jokes depend upon the ambiguity of utterances as illocutionary acts, that is, the speech act intended by the speaker/writer is unclear and open to misinterpretation.

Question or complaint:
    DINER: Waiter, what's this fly doing in my soup?
    WAITER: Looks like swimming, sir.

Prohibition or hypothetical criticism:
    SEAGOON: Come here, Bluebottle – don't tell me you're a coward.
    BLUEBOTTLE: All right, I won't. But you're bound to hear about it sometime. (Alexander 1997: 58)

Question about speaker's identity or question about hearer's recognition of speaker:
    Andy Williams went to pay a charity visit to an old people's home to cheer up the residents. But he was dismayed that none of the residents seemed to recognise him. Instead they all looked mystified. Finally he went up to one old lady and said, "Do you know who I am?" The old lady whispered, "Don't worry, dear, matron will tell you." (Tibballs 2006: 23)

8.6. *CONVERSATIONAL ANALYSIS*

Conversational analysis (CA) builds on speech act theory. It explores the way different utterances or speech acts relate to each other, and the overall organisational principles of the variety (Levinson 1983). CA was developed by ethnomethodologists, who identify the categories or techniques that members of a society themselves use to interpret and act. There is only space to consider three of the insights from CA here:

Table 8.4. *Preferred and dispreferred seconds in adjacency pairs (after Levinson 1983: 336)*

First part	Second part	
	Preferred	**Dispreferred**
Request	Compliance	Refusal
Offer/Invite	Acceptance	Refusal
Statement	Agreement	Disagreement
Blame	Denial	Admission

the theoretical concept of adjacency pairs, their expansion through pre-sequences, and the related theory of preference organisation.

8.6.1. Adjacency pairs[4]

Adjacency pairs are pairs of speech acts, e.g. greeting–greeting, offer–acceptance, apology–minimisation. They are (i) adjacent, (ii) produced by different speakers, (iii) ordered as first and second parts, and (iv) categorised, so a particular first part requires a particular second or range of seconds, e.g. greetings require greetings, offers require acceptances or rejections, etc. The ordering as a first and second part might be humorously reversed:

> A: Yes I can.
> B: Can you see into the future? (Alexander 1997: 62)

Amongst the range of second parts in adjacency pairs one is preferred by the second speaker, i.e. easier to perform, and one will be dispreferred (Table 8.4, after Levinson 1983: 336).

The dispreferred second can be independently identified as it attracts a number of typical features signalling the relative discomfort of the speaker. These include:

a. prefaces/delays:
   i. markers or announcers of dispreferreds, e.g. *erm, well, so* ...
   ii. pretended agreement before disagreement, e.g. *yes/sure* ... *but/though*
   iii. appreciations (after offers, invitations, suggestions, advice), e.g. *it's nice to be asked* ... *unfortunately* ...
   iv. apologies (after requests, invitations, blame, etc.) *I'm sorry, but* ...
   v. qualifiers, e.g. *I don't know for sure but* ...
   vi. hesitation, self-editing – – *erm, they I mean I*

    b. accounts: careful explanations for why the dispreferred act is
       being done, e.g. *I have to go to the dentist.*
    c. declination component: usually an indirect or softened form of
       refusal, disagreement, admission etc., e.g. *I suppose I might have
       done* (Levinson 1983: 334–5).

For instance:

A:	If you'd care to come and visit a little while this morning I'll give you a cup of coffee	
B:	hehh	*(a) delay by preface (vi): hesitation*
	Well	*(a) preface (i): marker*
	that's awfully sweet of you	*(a) preface (iii): appreciation*
	I don't think I can make it this morning	*(c) declination (softened)*
	.hh uhm I'm running an ad in the paper	*(b) account +*
	and-and uh I have to stay near the phone	*(a) preface (vi): hesitation*

(Levinson 1983: 333–4, quoting Atkinson and Drew 1979: 58)

   In the following joke B's deliberate misinterpretation of the
first speech act by misclassifying it as a statement rather than a
suggestion/indirect request is detected in the inappropriate second
part, *disagreement with*, rather than the more appropriate *compliance/
refusal.*

    A: I feel like a cup of tea.
    B: You don't look like one.

Activity 8.10

How is the underlined utterance in this joke ambiguous as a speech act? And,
according to one of the speech act types it might represent, is it a preferred or
dispreferred second?

   An Irishman wanders into a library and says (1) "Fish and chips, please".
   The librarian says, (2) "Sorry, this is a library."
   The Irishman whispers, (3) "Sorry, fish and chips please". (Carr and Greeves
   2006: 216)

Comment

Presumably the librarian intends this as a refusal, a dispreferred
second to the Irishman's request. As a dispreferred second it has an
apology (a. iv), one kind of preface, and an account (b) for why she
cannot give him fish and chips. However, the Irishman seems to
interpret this as a blame for speaking too loudly, and/or an indirect
request to speak more softly. He responds to the blame with "sorry"

(a. iv), indicating the dispreferred admission; and he responds to the indirect request by compliance – whispering (the repeated request). The exchange can be diagrammed:

Utterance	Adajcency pairs			
"Fish'n chips, please"	request			
"Sorry, this is a library"	refusal	blame	indirect request	
"Sorry, fish'n chips please" whispered		admission	compliance	request

We already discussed the generic structure of jokes from a CA perspective (6.4), but a few further comments are appropriate here. Some kinds of jokes – which in Table 6.6 I labelled optional dialogue with hearer and dialogic rituals, such as question ^ answer, riddles, *knock-knock* jokes – have a three-part structure, rather than being based on adjacency pairs:

– What is the difference between school inspectors and cosmetic surgeons?
– I don't know, what?
– Cosmetic surgeons tuck up your features.

A three-part structure is perhaps associated with sequences of speech acts where the first speaker asks an exam-type question (lacking the preparatory conditions and sincerity conditions on canonical questions) which is why it also appears in classroom discourse (Sinclair and Coulthard 1975). Other jokes have the structure joke ^ laughter (^ evaluation) (Norrick 1993: 23), where optionally the second participant not only laughs but evaluates.

A pattern of joking which disrupts the smooth adjacency pair sequencing is in fact rather common in conversational data and has been called the joke-first sequence (Schegloff 1987). For example:

A: I'm leaving now. Are you coming?   first part
B: No just breathing hard!   [joke
A: You idiot!   response to joke]
B: I'll be ready in a moment.   second part
(after Norrick 1993: 22)

The joke and response constitute an insertion sequence, one of the ways in which adjacency pairs can be extended into larger conversational sequences.

8.6.2. Pre-sequences

Another way adjacency pairs are built into larger structures is through **pre-sequences**, which might include **pre-arrangements**, **pre-requests** or **pre-announcements**. These check on the preparatory conditions for arrangements (e.g. "Are you free this evening?"), requests ("Do you have any hot chocolate?") and announcements ("Have you heard the news about Mike?"), to avoid forcing the hearer to reply with a dispreferred second. Pre-sequence formulae are so frequent they tend to be automatically associated with announcements, arrangements and requests, and consequently function as indirect forms of these acts. For instance, a pre-request can easily be interpreted as an indirect request:

> C: Do you have brownies today?
> S: Sure, here you are.

Pre-announcements are, in theory, designed to test the preparatory condition on assertives, "It is not obvious to both S and H that H knows p". You shouldn't tell people things that they already know.

> A: Have you heard the news about Mike?
> B: No, what happened?
> A: It's terrible news. He was found run over and had to have his leg amputated.
> B: Oh, my God!

However, they seem to have extended beyond this preparatory condition checking, and are often just calls for attention.

> D: I forgot to tell you the two best things that happened to me today.
> R: What were they?
> D: I got an A− on my English test ... and I got a community service award.

Activity 8.11

Use the concept of pre-sequences and dispreferred seconds to discuss this joke.

A man came home with some hot gossip. "Do you know what they're saying?" he told his wife. "They're saying that our janitor has slept with every woman in this apartment block except one!" The wife said, "That must be the girl from number 36 – nobody likes her." (Tibballs 2006: 16)

Comment

"Do you know what they are saying" is a pre-announcement. "They're saying that our janitor has slept with every woman in this apartment block except one!" looks like indirect blame, to which the preferred second would be denial. However, possibly because she interprets it as an indirect question, "Which one has he not slept with?", she does not deny it but replies to this indirect question while also criticising, rather bitchily, the girl from number 36. The implication of this criticism is, of course, that she does not deny the blame but admits it; and, for the recipient of the joke, that she is so bitchy she prefers to cast doubt on another woman's sexual attractiveness than to deny adultery.

There are, of course, speech acts that act as pre-jokes, which, rather like pre-announcements, may have the function of checking whether your speakmates have heard the joke before, or simply be calls to attention, or be a way of framing the joke so that you are allowed an extended turn. "Have you heard/do you know the one about …?" "That reminds me of a joke" "I've got a joke for you" (Norrick 1993; Sacks 1974).

8.7. PROBLEMS WITH SPEECH ACT THEORY AND CONVERSATIONAL ANALYSIS

There are a number of theoretical and procedural problems with speech act theory and speech act analysis. One is that the identification of speech acts is uncertain. This is not in itself a problem since the pragmatic interpretation of utterances is indeed often uncertain. It becomes a problem, however, when the same utterance at a different point in a sequence will be labelled differently. This means that any theory which attempts to expand speech act theory to account for larger stretches of discourse through adjacency pairs, preferred sequences, etc. cannot reliably posit sequencing rules; since there is no independent way of identifying the speech act, the definition and rule become circular (Edmondson 1981; Levinson 1983). For example:

– Can you help me?	Request
– Let me take your bags.	Compliance
– Let me take your bags.	Offer
– Thanks a lot.	Thanks/Acceptance

A second problem, as the last line of the example below shows, is that one utterance can perform two or more speech acts simultaneously (compare Activity 8.10).

A: Are those your clothes lying on the bathroom floor?
B: Yes. Sorry. I'll remove them. (Henry Widdowson, personal communication)

As B's answer shows, A's utterance might simultaneously perform three speech acts: question, hence the answer "Yes", complaint, hence the apology "sorry", and request, hence the compliance "I'll remove them".

8.8.   SUMMARY

I began this chapter by explaining the difference between semantics and pragmatics, while showing that the boundary is permeable. I touched on the index–icon–symbol distinction, discussing the arbitrariness of symbols and how certain types of wordplay try to reduce it. This prepared the way for a simple categorisation of different types of reference according to the specific v. non-specific, definite v. indefinite dimensions, and the general ambiguities of reference as a resource for jokes. The particular kind of variability of reference according to time, place and person known as deixis was then discussed. We moved on to an explanation of Searle's speech act theory, speech act conditions and speech act categories – assertives, directives, commissives, expressive and declarations – highlighting the latter as a potentially more extensive phenomenon according to the discourse theorists Foucault and Bourdieu. During this introduction I exemplified the absurdities possible when speech act conditions are not met, and how indirect speech acts, speech act formulae and, in general, speech act ambiguity are potential pragmatic mechanisms for humour. I went on to briefly demonstrate that speech acts can be combined into larger patterns, to form adjacency pairs and larger sequences, with examples of anomalous humorous sequences. Finally, I raised methodological questions about the categorisation of speech acts and the determination of speech act sequences.

Discussion

What is your opinion on Searle's distinction between brute and institutional facts, compared with Foucault/Bourdieu's idea that even brute scientific facts are somehow decreed as declarations by the powerful (8.5.2)? Is "climate change", for example, a brute fact or institutional fact, or both?

Suggested Readings
- Ding (2010: chapter 4) provides a fuller introduction to the distinctions between index, icon and symbol, and gives interesting examples of how Chinese characters decrease their iconicity over time. He also mentions the re-motivation (re-iconisation) of these signs as a teaching device, which relates to our observations on form–meaning connections at different stages of language acquisition (8.2).

- Langacker (2009) includes an advanced, but fascinating, account of the complexities and ambiguities of distributive reference and how it might depend upon metonymy for its interpretation.
- Searle (1969) introduced the theory of speech acts, and developed it further in Searle (1979) into the different classes of speech acts mentioned in this chapter. These books are a model of clarity, even if his attempt to make pragmatics rule-governed was ultimately in vain.
- Levinson (1983: chapter 6) gives a thorough and thoughtful account of adjacency pairs and pre-sequences in particular, and conversational analysis in general. The present chapter is indebted to his analysis and examples.
- Schegloff (2007) is the best recent account of conversational analysis and of extended sequence organisation.
- Robinson (2006) is relevant to many parts of the present textbook. Chapter 4, which covers speech act theory, and chapter 6, which extends the account of conversational analysis given above, are most relevant to the present chapter. Chapter 3 on performatives [declarations] and pp. 196–202 have important implications for how power is exercised in discourse. His chapter 9, especially the section on allusion, is useful supplementary reading for Chapter 10 of this book.

9 Pragmatics: co-operation and politeness

This chapter extends pragmatics beyond speech act theory (conversational analysis) discussed in the last chapter, by considering two pragmatic theories which sprang from it: Paul Grice's co-operative principle (CP), and offshoots of it, and Geoffrey Leech's politeness principle (PP) or grand strategy of politeness. However, at the outset, we need to explain an important difference between these two principles and Searle's speech act theory.

Searle posited rules to preserve the conventional nature of communication: there would be an agreement between speaker and hearer that such and such a locution meeting such and such conditions should stand for a certain speech act, or what he called "essential conditions" (8.5.1). As we also noted (8.5.3), he claimed this conventionality could extend to indirect speech acts, so, for example, asking about the preparatory conditions for the speech act of request, the willingness or the ability of the hearer to perform the action, can count, by convention, as an indirect request. Grice's theory of communication, and Leech's complement to it, and Relevance Theory that sprang from it (Chapter 10), take a more radical view of communication. Conventions in the form of a code are seldom sufficient to convey a message, indeed, they may not even be necessary. Instead, communication is about a hearer, h, recognising the intention of a speaker, s, in uttering a locution, x. And although coding, the meaning of x, often plays a part, it may vary from the very explicit, such as in a legal document, to the very inexplicit, such as in a poem or in casual conversation. Or, as noted, the pragmatics of communication is about what s means by uttering x rather than simply what x means. To guide this process, rather than positing "rules", which are either observed or broken, Grice and Leech try to discover principles, which are more like guidelines, which may be observed to varying degrees.

9.1. GRICE'S CO-OPERATIVE PRINCIPLE

The philosopher Paul Grice suggested that for society to function communication has to be oriented towards co-operation. Even though humans are not always co-operative, it must be an underlying reference-point for social behaviour. He also suggested that superficially uncooperative utterances may, through implication by the speaker and inference by the hearer, be interpreted as, in fact, co-operative.

According to Grice, conversation, or any other interactive social behaviour, is guided by the **co-operative principle** (CP), which runs thus: "Make your conversational contribution such as is required, at the stage at which it occurs, by the accepted purpose or direction of the talk exchange in which you are engaged." More specifically Grice postulated four maxims:

- a. The Maxim of **Quantity**
  - i. Make your contribution as informative as is required (for the current purposes of the exchange)
  - ii. Do not make your contribution more informative than is required
- b. The Maxim of **Quality**
  Try to make your contribution one that is true:
  - i. Do not say what you believe is false
  - ii. Do not say that for which you lack adequate evidence
- c. The Maxim of **Relation**
  Be relevant
- d. The Maxim of **Manner**
  Be perspicuous:
  - i. Avoid obscurity of expression
  - ii. Avoid ambiguity
  - iii. Be brief (avoid unnecessary prolixity)
  - iv. Be orderly (Grice 1975: 45)

9.2. OBSERVING THE MAXIMS: STANDARD IMPLICATURE

Grice is particularly interested in implicature, the extra meanings we generate from utterances beyond what is actually said. One kind of implicature arises from the assumption that we are observing the maxims. This is called **standard implicature**.

In the case of quality, the implicature is that the sincerity condition applies, e.g.

John swallowed a battery → 'S believes John swallowed a battery'

In the case of quantity the standard implicature is that the statement made is the most informative or strongest that can be made.

I have two children → 'I have only two children'

Although "I have two children" is logically consistent with, indeed is entailed by "I have four children", we normally assume that if I say I have two, I have no more than two.

In terms of relation, the standard implicature would assume that the utterance relates to the present time, place or context of activity. "Did you sneeze?" implicates 'did you sneeze just now here?' and so on. As for manner, the orderliness sub-maxim has the standard implicature that the events related occurred in the order in which they are presented. Although "Julia got a masters degree and went to Yale" and "Julia went to Yale and got a masters degree" are synonymous, standard implicature, equivalent to inserting "then" after "and", suggests they tell different stories.

9.3.   BREAKING THE MAXIMS

We can detect Gricean maxims particularly clearly when they are broken. Consider this answer to a driving-test question:

A: When driving through fog what should you use?
B: Your car.

This obviously breaks the maxim of quantity, as the answer is already AB information, shared by both speakers (6.2). If the following dialogue is gossip about two people you know,

A: John and Peter are seeing a lot of each other nowadays.
B: They're probably sleeping together.
(*John enters the room behind B*)
A: What was that book you wanted to borrow?

B seems to be breaking the maxim of quality by making a statement that B has little or no evidence for. A then breaks the maxim of relation by changing the topic, to avoid offending John, who they were gossiping about.

Puns occurring in conversations often break relation, and disrupt the ongoing interaction. In this example (Norrick 1993: 22–3, 61) Roger's relatively serious talk about dolphins and the name for their social group is disrupted by Jason's pun on "poddy" "party".

> ROGER: And it seems to be a completely egalitarian *band*. There isn't a leader in a dolphin – do they have pods?
> JASON: I don't know what they're called.
> ROGER: Whales are pods. I don't know what dolphins are. *Pod*dies. (1.3) Anyway heh heh. Yeah but I mean –
> JASON: They're poddy animals.
> ROGER: Dheh huh huh.
> JASON: Heh heh heh heh *heh* ha ha ha ha ha ha ha ha.
> ROGER: Oooh. That's – that's like a blow to the midriff, y'know. Huh huh *huh* huh huh.

In fact, one of the functions of conversational joking is to effect a change in topic (Norrick 1993: 24–5). Nevertheless, once a joke has established a new topic, jokes on a similar topic often ensue, for instance one ethnic joke might lead to another (Norrick 1993: 36, 117).

Turning to manner, consider this dialogue where Sheldon is deliberately obscure to prevent bystanders understanding.

> *Leonard is watching a football game with Penny's friends. Sheldon walks in to borrow some toast. He sees Leonard.*

> SHELDON: So Leonard, how goes the mimesis?
> LEONARD: Mimesis?
> SHELDON: You know. Mimesis. An action in which the mimic takes on the properties of a specific object or organism.
> LEONARD: What are you talking about?
> SHELDON: I'm attempting to communicate with you without my meaning becoming apparent to those around you. Let me try again.
> SHELDON: Have the indigenous fauna accepted you as one of their own? Nudge nudge, wink wink.
> LEONARD: Oh I guess so. (*The Big Bang* Series 3 Episode 06)

Puns occurring in conversations often depend upon the pretence that the maxim of manner has been broken by the first speaker: e.g., "Are you coming?" "No, just breathing hard."

Activity 9.1

Which of the above maxims are being broken in the following underlined examples:

1. Weather forecast for tonight: <u>dark</u> (Ross 1998: 3).
2. I'd like to thank you folks for flying with us today. And the next time <u>you get the insane urge to go blasting through the skies in a pressurized metal tube</u>, I hope you'll think of us here at US Airways (Tibballs 2006: 47).
3. And don't forget on Sunday <u>you can hear the two-minute silence</u> on Radio 1 at 11 a.m. (Steve Wright, Tibballs 2006: 511).
4. The secret of a happy marriage is <u>. . .</u>
5. My girlfriend said, "Jimmy, we're at a crossroads in our relationship.

Down one road is hard work and commitment, but ultimately happiness. Down the other road ... well the other road is a dead end." And I said, "That's not a crossroads, that's a T-junction." (Jimmy Carr, Carr and Greeves 2006: 146)

6. On an insurance claim form: "Could either driver have done anything to avoid the accident?" "I could have travelled by bus." (Tibballs 2006: 9)

7. "Why are politicians like golfers?" "They get caught in one bad lie after another."

8. A patient walks into a doctor's surgery and says "Doctor, I think I'm suffering from hypochondria."

Comment

Quantity seems to be broken in (1), (4) and possibly (8): (1), because no new information is given about the night – nights are always dark. (4) is more interesting. It seems to break the maxim of quantity by not giving enough information; but it could equally well be interpreted as a tautology, since a secret, once divulged, is no longer a secret. (8) might be tautologous, too, since, if you believe you are suffering from a disease when you are not, then you must be suffering from hypochondria, and hypochondria is itself a disease. The irony is that if you know you are a hypochondriac then you probably are not, so there is at least a hint of breaking quality here as well.

Quality is clearly broken in (3), which is a logical contradiction. You cannot hear silence, so it must be false.

Relation seems broken in (5) and (6). In the context of a heart-to-heart talk about the future of one's relationship, it seems hardly relevant, at least to the girlfriend, to question the aptness of her metaphors. In (6) the question assumes the relevant context is to do with driving a car, but the answer ignores this relevant context, invoking an alternative context – travelling by bus.

Manner is broken in (2) and (7). (2) looks like a very long-winded way of saying 'choose to fly'. However, like some examples of breaking manner, it appears to break quantity as well, offering the unnecessary information that the aircraft is a tube made of metal and that choosing to fly is insane. (7) is obviously a case of ambiguity. All spoken puns dependent on homonymy/homophony exploit ambiguity.

9.4. WAYS OF BREAKING THE MAXIMS

There are several ways of breaking a maxim, the most important being violation and flouting. Violation is a deliberately covert breach of a maxim, where the speaker conceals the breach from the hearer. It is particularly clear-cut in the case of quality: lies are not intended to be detected. It could also apply to quantity. If there are two topics on the exam paper, presupposition and metaphor, and a student asks the lecturer what topics are on the exam paper, the lecturer might say: "It'll either test you on the semantic–pragmatics distinction, or sense relations, or speech act theory, or types of meaning, or presupposition, or metaphor". This would be giving too much information, or perhaps too little.

Activity 9.2

Which maxim, if any, is violated in the following conversation? How might standard implicature be involved in the miscommunication?

A: Does your dog bite?
B: No.
(*A bends down to stroke the dog and gets bitten*)
A: I thought you said your dog didn't bite.
B: It's not my dog. (Billy Connolly)

Comment

The quality maxim is not strictly broken. But by allowing A's assumption that this is B's dog, because by standard implicature of relation A is referring to the dog in the context, B comes close to violating it.

A more interesting way of breaking maxims is flouting. By contrast with violation, this is an overt breaking of a maxim, which the speaker expects the hearer to detect. For example, saying metaphorically "John is a real bitch" the speaker does not expect the hearer to believe John is a female dog. Because breaking the maxim in a flout is blatant, it assumes that the CP is still in operation and the utterance can be redeemed as co-operative at a deeper level through implicature.

Flouting Quality

George Bernard Shaw to Sam Goldwyn: "The trouble, Mr Goldwyn, is that you are only interested in art, and I am only interested in money." (Alexander 1997: 68) (Irony)
The past is a foreign country; they do things differently there. (Metaphor)
He's so mean he takes the wallpaper when he moves house. (Overstatement)
George Osborne isn't the brightest of finance ministers. (Understatement)

Realising that these statements are breaking the maxim of quality, the hearer finds a meaning which is related to the meaning expressed in the utterance, e.g. "The trouble, Mr Goldwyn, is that you are only interested in money, and I am only interested in art" or "The past is like a foreign country, because in both things are done differently" or "He is extremely mean" or "George is rather stupid".

Flouting Quantity

> Business is business.
> A brother is a brother.

Similarly, the hearer, realising that if "business" and "brother" are given the same interpretation each time they occur the maxim of quantity is being broken, looks for an alternative more relevant interpretation, e.g. 'business is not to be confused with being kind to the poor' or 'a brother is likely to give special favours to a brother' (Sperber and Wilson 1986/1995).

Shaggy dog stories are a species of joke which flout (or perhaps even violate) the maxim of quantity. In one sense they give too much information – spinning out the complicating action (and sometimes the evaluation/orientation) to unnecessary lengths, while never giving the information required to bring a resolution to a narrative (6.4.4).

The Green Light

A teacher who loved hiking went rambling on the Yorkshire moors in the half-term holiday at the end of October. One afternoon the mist suddenly fell and he lost his bearings. After consulting his compass and walking in the same direction for two hours he came to an isolated monastery. He knocked on the door of the gatehouse, and the monks welcomed him in. It was now rather late, so they offered him supper and a cell for the night.

About two in the morning he woke up and saw a green light hovering above his bed. He got up and tried to touch it but it eluded his grasp and eventually seemed to disappear through the wall. In the morning he wondered if he had been dreaming, so he didn't ask the monks about it. The weather had improved, and after a simple breakfast he went on his way.

But when he got home he couldn't get this episode of the green light out of his head. And next October he decided he would return to the monastery to investigate the mystery. This time there was no fog, but the monks were still happy to invite him to supper and to spend the night in the guest cell. Sure enough, at two in the morning he saw the same green light, he pursued it, and, just as he tried to clutch it, it disappeared through the wall. He decided that in the morning he would ask the monks for an explanation.

However, when morning came, in the cold light of day, he began to wonder whether he had been dreaming or hallucinating, and left without asking.

Still, over the next year he couldn't forget his experience and resolved to solve the mystery once and for all. So he re-visited the monastery, was woken by the hovering green light at the same time of night, and saw it disappear through the wall.

In the morning over breakfast he asked the abbot whether he could explain to him an experience he had during the night. The abbot offered to talk to him about it after breakfast. So, the meal over, and grace said, the abbot invited him into his office and enquired about what had happened. "Well, you know I've visited your monastery for the last three years, and you've been good enough to put me up for the night. But every year I've been woken up about two in the morning by this green light hovering in my cell just out of my reach, and when I try to grasp it, it moves away and disappears in the wall. First of all I thought I was dreaming, but the same thing has happened three times, so it can't be my imagination." The abbot went to the door of his office, which was slightly ajar, closed it quietly, and locked it. He uttered these solemn words: "Before I give you an explanation, you must promise me something. Never tell anyone else what I am about to tell you. Will you swear secrecy, a vow of silence?" The teacher-hiker swore he would keep the monastery's secret. And he did.

Flouting Relation

> A: Didn't you think that lecture was boring?
> (Lecturer enters the room)
> B: Shall we go to watch a movie this evening?

A will be led to assume that breaking the maxim of relation (and quantity) is still relevant in terms of social goals (not offending the lecturer). In the following sequence there is a kind of double-flouting of the maxim of relation:

> A: Is Tony Blair really a Tory?
> B: Is the Pope a Catholic?

Catholicism (even though TB converted to it) is not on the surface relevant to the question that is the first part of an adjacency pair. Moreover, another question is not a relevant second part for a first part question. However, relevance can be re-established if A realises that the answer to B's question must be "yes", and that therefore B is implicating an affirmative answer to A's first part question (Norrick 1993: 25).

Flouting Manner

> A: What's Jim doing this Sunday?
> B: Trying to hit three sticks with a red leather ball, or trying to hit the ball as far as he can, or wandering around a green field.

The lack of clarity of B's utterance compared with "playing cricket" nevertheless gives us some extra meaning: B thinks that cricket is stupid. A joke which apparently involves the violation of the maxim of manner, by unnecessary circumlocution, might be regarded as a case of flouting or a clash between quality and manner:

> Pedants rule, OK – or, more precisely, exhibit some of the trappings of traditional leadership. (Alexander 1997: 82)

According to Alexander (1997: 69) jokes appear to flout/violate the maxim of manner: they often depend upon a deliberate creation of ambiguity, which is eventually resolved in the punchline.

Activity 9.3

Consider this humorous exchange from a *Charlie Brown* cartoon (quoted from Alexander 1997: 66):

> LINUS: Do you want to play with me, Violet?
> VIOLET: You're younger than me. (Shuts the door)
> LINUS (*puzzled*):   She didn't answer my question.

Explain how this could be intended as flouting, because its implied meaning is co-operative, but might result in something closer to a violation.

Comment

I suppose Violet expects Linus to supply the background assumption 'Children only play with other children of a similar age', and infer the answer "No". As it is, though Linus registers the breaking of the maxim of quantity, he fails to supply the assumption and make the inference, as the speaker intends when flouting.

Besides violation and flouting there are three minor ways of breaking maxims. **Infringing** occurs because of unintentional inadequacies in the speaker's performance, due to, for example, tiredness, drunkenness, poor command of the language, speaking too softly. Presumably poorly worded headlines are often such performance mistakes, as with the following infringement of the Quantity maxim: "Economist uses theory to explain economy" (Bucaria 2004: 282) or Illustration 2. **Opting out** occurs when the speaker gives reasons for breaking a

此 乃 私 家 地 方
外 人 不 得 內 進
如 有 白 撞
報 警 究 治
PRIVATE PROPERTY
NO TRESPASSING
NO BUM AROUND
聚 龍 居 管 理 處
Parc Royale Estate Management Office

Illustration 2. An example of maxim infringement

maxim, perhaps legal or ethical considerations, or to avoid hurting someone or betraying a source. For instance, in response to a question I might reply "I am not at liberty to say – I was told in confidence." Or, "I'm afraid I'm not allowed to tell you that the source of the rumour was the department secretary, as she swore me to secrecy". Speakers opting out indicate that they are not observing the maxim and give reasons for this uncooperative behaviour. **Suspending** a maxim occurs when it is culturally accepted that precise information or perspicuity will not be forthcoming; for example, actors in the UK think it is unlucky to use the name *Macbeth* and refer to it instead as "The Scottish play", thereby breaking the maxim of quantity (Thomas 1995: 72–8). Presumably euphemisms can be examples of suspension.

9.5. THE CO-OPERATIVE PRINCIPLE AND HUMOUR THEORY

Ever since Grice formulated the CP, humour theorists have shown how breaking Gricean maxims can give rise to various kinds of jokes (see references in Attardo 1994: 272, and Billig 2005: 208).[1] Nash (1985: 117–19), for example, suggests the terms runaround, skid and

googly, for humorous exchanges that are defective in terms of the
co-operative principle.

1. The Runaround, which breaks the maxim of quantity.
   A: Oh, where do you work, Mr Jones?
   B: Oh, you know, at the Town Hall.
   A: And what sort of work do you do there?
   B: Oh, you know, Town Hall work. (Nash 1985: 117)
2. The Skid, which most obviously breaks the maxim of relation, by
   drifting away from the original topic (but also, as a by-product breaks
   the maxim of quantity and maybe manner).
   A: Now, you take the whale, that's just about the oldest fish in the
      ocean.
   B: It isn't a fish it's a mammal. The whale is a mammal.
   A: Well, the Bible says it's a fish. The holiest book in the world says it's
      a fish.
   B: Look, they just didn't know enough in those days. They had a naive
      taxonomy. If it swam in the sea they classified it as a fish. We know
      better now, we know the whale is a mammal.
   A: You're telling me the author of the Bible didn't know what he
      was doing? The Bible? The book you swear on in court?
      (Nash 1985: 117)

Jokes involving presuppositions might depend upon a mental skid –
that is the assumption is so ludicrous it deliberately distracts: "The
duodenum, along with the other so-called organs of speech, has two
functions".

3. The Googly
   A: How would you like to spend seven days in a Thai spa?
   B: I'd love it.
   A: Good, then you can envy me all next week. (cf. Nash 1985: 118)

This breaks the maxim of Manner, through the ambiguity of A's
interrogative – interpreted as an invitation, by B, but a question
for A. Does A's last utterance also break quantity by giving too much
information?

Discussion

Grice seems to assume in his principle that the purposes of
the communication can be agreed upon by all participants.
Does this last joke suggest otherwise? Might there be
asymmetrical purposes in communication? Think of some
examples of your own.

There is clearly a problem in accounting for jokes within a CP framework. Attardo (1994: 173) points out that puns, for instance, are non-communicative. And he and Raskin cite other particular kinds of jokes/humour as violating the CP: quantity, in the case of shaggy dog stories, and in "Do you have the time?" "Yes"; relation, in "How many surrealists does it take to screw in a light bulb?" "Fish"; manner, in the pun "Do you believe in clubs for young people?" "Only when kindness fails"; and quality, in "Why did the Vice-President fly to Panama?" "Because the fighting is over". Because most jokes rely upon implicit meanings, it has been claimed that they involve a deliberate violation of the maxim of quantity, but this may be a by-product of the breaking of manner (i.e. ambiguity) (Attardo and Raskin 1991: 301; Attardo 1994: 272–3; Chiaro 1992: 44, 75).

Because of this "violation" Attardo (1994: 273ff.) sees jokes and humour as forms of non bona fide communication,[2] and I agree that many intrinsically subvert the CP. However, although the initial bewilderment induced by a schema-switch trigger looks like a violation, it might be preferable to regard it as a flout delayed by violation; the breaking of the maxims must be recognised almost immediately, at least within the next couple of turns of the discourse for the joke to work. For example, in the last "googly" joke, B and the reader should realise after A's last utterance that A's first utterance broke manner, and A intends them to do so. This intention is a defining feature of flouts.[3]

As Attardo points out, in terms of interpersonal relationships and entertainment, jokes are still co-operative, bringing about "subversion of the maxims to achieve socially desirable effects" (1994: 287). Banter and playfulness can only be regarded as uncooperative if we adopt a very narrow conception of what cooperative social life is about. Discourse is not simply the efficient exchange of information. This is why the motives for many flouts of the CP can be systematically accounted for by other principles like the politeness principle (9.6 below): uttering "I don't suppose you would have the time to write me a reference", rather than "write me a reference", breaks the maxim of manner by undue prolixity, and quality by disingenuousness; but it implies that the speaker wishes to be polite by making it easier for the hearer to decline.

Nevertheless, there is something especially ludic about jokes when they occur in a conversational context, which is why, like narrative, they are often framed or signalled. Norrick (1993: 143) suggests employing Goffmann's concept of "framing" or Hymes' "key" to account for the shift from more serious to more playful discourse.[4]

Grice's co-operative principle enshrines one kind of expectedness in communication, and the subversion of these kinds of expectedness can be recruited for humour. The principle can and should be related to other kinds of discoursal unexpectedness which are similarly exploited:

> Interpreting the quantity, quality, relevance and manner of utterances functions for Levinson (2000) on the basis of knowing what is normal and can accordingly be expected. Deviations from normal discourse (such as humour or irony) orient the listener to something special. Normality assumptions hold for all sorts of institutionalisations (e.g. activity types, genres, styles and culture-specific formulation conventions). In irony and humour, speakers use implicit meta-communication to make the communicative act comprehensible as something special. (Kotthoff 2009: 52)

9.6. INTERPERSONAL PRAGMATICS: POLITENESS AND THE POLITENESS PRINCIPLE

Grice, and theorists like Sperber and Wilson (1986/1995), who have streamlined his maxims into Relevance Theory, assume the overriding purpose of communication is the efficient exchange of information, or expanding cognitive environments. However, other social and interpersonal aspects of discourse are equally important. We have seen, following Norrick, that humour emphasises the interpersonal (expressive/conative/phatic) and textual (metalingual/poetic) functions more than the ideational or referential (cf. Alexander 1997: 8). As Norrick (1993: 129) puts it:

> Humour seems to have two strikes against it anyway, since it seems to get in the way of the serious business that conversation "ought" to attend to. This bias goes hand in hand with the general cultural conviction that joking and humour are simply not very important ... We joke by habit without realising how our joking works to present a personality, to test for shared attitudes, to identify a common code for our interaction, and generally to keep the conversation moving along so that we can negotiate tasks in a convivial atmosphere.

This even suggests joking in conversation actually changes conversation into less "serious business" after all. Actually, it is doubtful whether pre-genres like conversation could really involve serious business in the first place (6.4.1–2).

In any case, the interpersonal functions of discourse are just as important as the ideational, and often override the efficient exchange of thoughts and information according to Gricean principles. Consider the opening of George Bernard Shaw's *St Joan*.

ROBERT	No eggs! No eggs!! Thousand thunders man what do you mean by no eggs?
STEWARD	Sir, it is not my fault. It is the act of God.
ROBERT	Blasphemy. You tell me there are no eggs and you blame your Maker for it.
STEWARD	Sir, what can I do? <u>I cannot lay eggs</u>.
ROBERT	Ha! You jest about it.
STEWARD	No, sir, God knows. We all have to go without eggs just as you have, sir. The hens will not lay.
ROBERT	Indeed! Now listen to me, you.
STEWARD	Yes, sir.
ROBERT	<u>What am I?</u>
STEWARD	<u>What are you, sir?</u>
ROBERT	Yes: <u>what am I? Am I Robert, squire of Baudricourt and captain of this castle of Vaucouleurs or am I a cowboy?</u>
STEWARD	Oh sir, you know that you are a greater man here than the king himself.
ROBERT	Precisely. And now, do you know what you are?
STEWARD	I am nobody, sir, except that <u>I have the honour to be your steward.</u>
ROBERT	<u>You have not only the honour of being my steward but the privilege of being the worst, most incompetent, drivelling, snivelling, jibbering, jabbering idiot of a steward in France.</u>

The underlined utterances obviously break the maxims of the CP. "I cannot lay eggs" breaks the maxim of quantity; we know this already. Moreover, Robert's two "questions" break the sincerity and preparatory conditions on questions, as he knows the answer and therefore is not seeking information. It does not look as though being Robert's steward is in truth an honour as Robert claims. And finally Robert's insult "you have not only the honour ... in France" breaks the quality maxim, since Robert has no evidence available about the relative merits of all the stewards in France.

Now some of these breaches of the CP occur in order to facilitate the exposition in the opening scene of the play. So, the uninformative at the level of Robert–Steward communication becomes informative at the level of playwright–audience communication: the audience need to know Robert is "squire of Baudricourt and captain of this castle of Vaucouleurs". However, the interpersonal dimension of the character-to-character communication is equally responsible for the uncooperative exchanges. These floutings must be primarily accounted for in relation to status, face and (im)politeness; Robert is trying to humiliate and accuse the Steward, and

Table 9.1. *Combining Leech's grand strategy with the politeness principle*

Constraint	Label for this constraint
Place a high value on O's wants	**Generosity** (in directives and commissives) (a) Minimise benefit to *self* [(b) Maximise cost to *self*]
Place a low value on S's wants	**Tact** (in directives and commissives) (a) Minimise cost to *other* [(b) Maximise benefit to *other*]
Place a high value on O's qualities	**Approbation** (in expressives and assertives) (a) Minimise dispraise of *other* [(b) Maximise praise of *other*]
Place a low value on S's qualities	**Modesty** (in expressives and assertives) (a) Minimise praise of *self* [(b) Maximise dispraise of *self*]
Place a high value on S's obligation to O	Obligation (of S to O)
Place a low value on O's obligation to S	Obligation (of O to S)
Place a high value on O's opinions	**Agreement** (in assertives) (a) Minimise disagreement between *self* and *other* [(b) Maximise agreement between *self* and *other*]
Place a low value on S's opinions	Opinion-reticence (in assertives) Maximise reticence in asserting *self*'s opinions
Place a high value on O's feelings	**Sympathy** (in assertives and expressives?) (a) Minimise antipathy between self and other [(b) Maximise sympathy between self and other]
Place a low value on S's feelings	Feeling-reticence (in expressives) Maximise reticence in expressing *self*'s feelings

the Steward to defend himself. The interpersonal therefore demands attention in pragmatic theory (Goatly 2008: 126ff.).

Indeed, it soon became clear to discourse analysts that floutings or violations of the CP are not random, but depend on the systematic application of other principles to do with social relations. Leech (1983: 132–8), therefore, took up Grice's hint of the need for a **politeness principle** (PP) to complement, or as part of, co-operation, with the six following maxims: Tact, Generosity, Approbation, Modesty, Agreement and Sympathy. Later he incorporated the six maxims into the grand strategy of politeness, adding two more (Leech 2005: 12–17) (Table 9.1). The grand strategy can be formulated thus:

> In order to be polite, S expresses or implies meanings which place a high value on what pertains to 0 (0 = other person[s], [mainly the addressee]) or place a low value on what pertains to S (S = self, speaker).

Activity 9.4

Which maxims of the PP are broken in the following:

a. The "t" is silent as in Harlow (Margot Asquith when her interviewer Jean Harlow repeatedly pronounced the "t" in Margot) (Tibballs 2006: 618).
b. Waiting by the side of the road a fat woman said to a schoolboy, "Sonny, can you see me across the road?" "Of course I can," he said. "I could see you a mile away."
c. A Jew, a Catholic and a Mormon were drinking at the bar after an interfaith meeting. The Jew, commenting on his virility, said, "I have four sons. One more and I'll have a basketball team." The Catholic said, "That's nothing. I have ten sons. One more and I'll have a soccer team." The Mormon snorted. "Big deal! I have 17 wives. One more and I'll have a golf course." (Tibballs 2006: 566)

Comment

(a) looks like an insult – breaking the maxims of approbation. In (b) the boy as a character breaks generosity by not agreeing to the perhaps tactless request of the fat lady, and his response might implicate breaking approbation. (c) obviously breaks modesty.

Discussion

Why is impoliteness a better topic for jokes than politeness?

We can see how these maxims might systematically account for breaking the CP maxims. For example, if someone asks us our opinion of their presentation, and we thought it was poor, we may sacrifice the maxim of quality to the maxim of approbation. Or we might avoid expressing disapprobation by changing the subject, thereby breaking the maxim of relation. And, even though we disagree with someone's statement, we might again sacrifice quality to agreement, and pretend to agree or at least show reticence in disagreeing. We quite often use roundabout and indirect forms when making requests, sacrificing the maxim of manner to tact.

While most of these maxims are self-explanatory, tact and sympathy need more explanation. All other things being equal, in directives one should use grammatical forms which are relatively indirect or allow for optionality, in other words avoid bare imperatives. Consider the following ways of attempting to get a hearer to look after your children:

1. Look after the kids over this Easter holiday.
2. I want you to look after the kids over this Easter holiday.
3. Will you look after the kids over this Easter holiday?
4. Can you look after the kids over this Easter holiday?
5. Could you look after the kids over this Easter holiday?
6. I don't suppose you could look after the kids over this Easter holiday, could you?
7. The kids have their Easter holiday coming up, and we'd like a short break from them.

As we go down the list from (1) to (7) the directives become less direct, ranging through statements of desirability (2), questions about willing-ness (3) and capability (4), hypothetical conditional questions of cap-ability (5), ending with a mere hint (7). They also build optionality into their forms, (3) to (6) being questions, the latter expecting the answer "no" to make the option of refusal easier, and (7) even giving the hearer the option of ignoring that a request has been made. The more indirect they are, the more ambiguous in terms of speech acts, which allows humorous ripostes such as the following: "I wonder if you would shut the door." "Do you? Let me know if you work it out" (Ross 1998: 40).

However, politeness and the imperative are compatible where the action is of benefit to the hearer. So while "Wash my car" is impolite, since compliance is costly to the hearer, the offers "Have a sandwich" or "Take a seat" are, like suggestions and advice, perfectly polite and tact-ful, since they benefit the hearer (Leech 1983: 107–8).

Moreover, high degrees of imposition necessitate tact-ful forms. I might demand you hand in a term paper, and because I am your lecturer this is less of an imposition than ordering you to wash my car – even though the term paper costs more time and effort. This is because a demand for a term paper, unlike an order to wash my car, is something my position as lecturer entitles me to. We also need to factor in the social distance of the speaker and hearer. If the hearer is vertically superior to the speaker and/or the horizontal social dis-tance is medium, the directive requires more tactful forms.

Leech is not very clear about what constitutes sympathy. I suppose it is conveyed by expressive speech acts which claim to share the feelings of the hearer: commiserations, condolences, congratulations and so

on. Perhaps also by questions showing concern for someone's welfare or interest in a topic important to them.

> **Activity 9.5**
>
> How tact-ful are the utterances in this joke, analysed in Activity 7.10? How do they relate to the approbation and sympathy maxims?
>
> > Before you criticise someone you should walk a mile in their shoes. That way, when you criticise them you are a mile away and you have their shoes. (Jack Handey, Carr and Greeves 2006: 100)

> Comment
>
> The first sentence seems to break the tact maxim, since it appears to involve some cost, physical or mental/emotional effort (depending on whether we take the literal or metaphorical meaning). It also uses a relatively direct modal of obligation, *should*, with no optionality built in. However, as the second sentence explains, walking a mile in their shoes will be beneficial to the hearer, as the hearer will have the other person's shoes, and the action is therefore maximising benefit to the hearer and turns out to be perfectly polite. The metaphorical meaning of the first sentence suggests sympathy. The criticising in the second sentence suggests disapprobation.

Leech's PP parallels in many respects Brown and Levinson's politeness theory (1987). However, they highlight the concept of face, the public self-image every member of society wants preserved or enhanced. **Positive face** is the desire to be accepted and valued by one's social group, and relates to the approbation, agreement, generosity and sympathy maxims. **Negative face** is the freedom to be left undisturbed – respect from others for one's freedom of action, and freedom from imposition. Many actions or speech acts threaten others' face, and these are called **face-threatening acts**. The tact and modesty maxims, as well as reticence, are obviously important here, which is why we use the complex grammatical structures involving indirectness and optionality detailed above.

I lack the space for a fuller account of face, but it is worth mentioning because of its explanatory power in humour theory. Firstly, puns, as already noted, tend to be disruptive, breaking the maxim of relation, and therefore threaten negative face (Norrick 1993: 65, 67). On the other hand, humour is a way of making people feel comfortable – avoiding threats to negative and positive face (Brown and Levinson 1987: 124). For instance, punning and irony are, like hints, off record or defeasible/cancellable – that is, one can deny a second humorous or ironic meaning to one's utterance – and their ambiguity can

be a way of saving face and allowing social recovery (Norrick 1993: 63, 151; Chafe 2007: 78–80).[5]

Indeed, humour may be "a socially acceptable means of expressing hostility and criticism" (Bell 2009: 147). Kotthoff (2009: 53) gives an example (slightly modified):

> *Bernd showing his friends, Friederike, Lars, and Annette, academics who are close to 40, around his flat and commenting on the kitchen.*

FRIEDERIKE:	There is only one window.
LARS:	But it is really nice for a young gentleman, you know.
ANNETTE:	Yes, it's sufficient for a young man.
LARS:	For a young "gentleman", your mother always says.

On the surface line 2 is polite. This hides the implicit criticism of the flat, and perhaps disapproval of their mothers' generation for making such sexist distinctions between the relative needs of women and men for a kitchen, and of referring to their generation as "young". Indeed jokes and humour may be less face-threatening ways of conveying messages, flouting quantity and manner maxims in order to mitigate disapprobation. Jokes might be regarded as non bona fide communication if communication is regarded in terms of the most efficient exchange of information, but in their interpersonal function they can clearly be communicative (Oring 2003: 95–6).

9.7. MODESTY, APPROBATION AND BANTER

Modesty and approbation are particularly relevant to aspects of humour theory. First of all, self-deprecatingly modest humour is common, whether using laughter as a means to avoid embarrassment (Chafe 2007: 78) or building solidarity with one's social group by displaying the ability to laugh at oneself. In the following (Norrick 1993: 79) Jason makes an utterance (bolded) implicitly critical about his own weight.

ROGER:	Well, do you want aspirin?
JASON:	Yes. What are they?
ROGER:	These are regular old. Regular, two? Or three?
JASON:	Regular? I'll take three.
ROGER:	At your body weight you'll need three.
JASON:	**Gimme *five*.**
MARGARET:	Huahahahaha.

However, paradoxically, by exhibiting modesty he is thereby making a claim for approbation.

Jokes which target particular outgroups, such as ethnic jokes, presumably involve the breaking of the approbation maxim, implicitly criticising this group, and illustrate aggression theories of humour. On the other hand, ritual insults between good friends express rapport. Leech employs the term "**banter**" in a restricted sense to refer to this phenomenon (1983: 144–5). In Ishiguro's novel *The Remains of the Day*, the butler, Stevens, feels deficient in this (for him, particularly American) aspect of social discourse.

> I remember Mr Simpson, the landlord of the Ploughman's Arms,
> saying once that were he an American bartender, he would not be
> chatting to us in that friendly, but ever-courteous manner of his, but
> instead would be assaulting us with crude references to our vices and
> failings, calling us drunks and all manner of such names, in his
> attempt to fulfil the role expected of him by his customers (pp. 14–15).
> (quoted in Goatly 2008: 169)

For instance, in this snippet of conversation among three undergraduate student assistants in a departmental copying room (Norrick 1993: 62), a pun is used by Judy as banter which superficially insults Arnold:

> ARNOLD: An exact cut. (2.5) Oh no. This one is a little off-center.
> JUDY: That's because you're a little off-center.
> BETH: Heh *heh* he heh.
> ARNOLD: No, it's Tom's print.

Activity 9.6

1. Discuss, using evidence from the dialogue, whether Arnold interprets this as banter, or a more serious criticism.
2. Discuss the role played by metaphor (metaphor themes) in the pun on *off-center*.

Comment

1. Arnold does not respond to Judy's remark in a humorous way. He defends himself by blaming Tom for the literally off-center copy, and thereby indirectly defends himself against the supposedly metaphorical off-centredness which, according to Judy, caused it.
2. The relevant metaphor theme underlying the ambiguity exploited by the pun is MENTAL DISTURBANCE IS IMBALANCE or words to that effect: cf. *unbalanced, off his trolley, mental (dis)equilibrium* etc.

Norrick (1993: 75) sums up Tannen's view of banter:

> By Tannen's paradox of solidarity a verbal attack can signal solidarity,
> because it implies a relationship where distance, respect and power
> count for little. If we can do without the overt trappings of positive
> politeness, and freely poke fun at each other, we must enjoy good rapport.

It follows that some apparently polite behaviour can threaten rapport. This accounts for the stock bantering quips accompanied by polite actions, like "Age before beauty" or "Beauty before intelligence" on ushering someone through a door first (Norrick 1986: 200).

Banter is allowed because, like humour in general, it takes place within a play frame or a non-serious key (or is not bona fide communication). It might be likened to the mock aggression in animal play fighting, which, nevertheless, to achieve its effect, resembles, on the surface, the real thing (Norrick 1993: 147).

9.8. IMPOLITENESS, HUMOUR AND FAILED HUMOUR

Humour may fail for various reasons, the two most important being that the joke is not understood, or, if it is understood, not appreciated (Bell 2009). In Table 6.3 we noted the various options in generic joke structure for uptake, some of which, like mock laughter, indicate understanding without appreciation. These are necessary, as failure to understand a joke threatens the positive face of the hearer, and suggests lack of solidarity or rapport. Since jokes test whether the hearer is on the same wavelength, they are an opportunity to establish and maintain intimacy (Norrick 1993), and if not understood, intimacy is threatened.

Moreover, lack of appreciation of the joke threatens the positive face or shows disapprobation of the teller, and implies that the negative face of the hearer has been threatened (i.e. they have been pointlessly imposed upon), or a lack of generosity has been displayed. Being told a bad joke also threatens the hearer's *positive* face: "Being selected as an appropriate audience for a stupid joke suggests that there is something amiss with the hearer's sense of humour" (Bell 2009: 149). With a bad joke "the behaviour of the joke-teller is not in keeping with the type of relationship that has been implicitly mutually agreed upon. In fact the teller can be seen as lacking in both empathy and respect for her or his hearer" (Bell 2009: 158).

It is not, therefore, surprising that when bad jokes are inflicted on friends the response is often impolite, as Bell (2009: 155–7) discovered. Bad jokes like "What did the big chimney/cup say to the little chimney/cup? Nothing – chimneys/cups can't talk" typically met with face-threatening acts (FTAs) as responses. There were threats to positive face, "Oh shit", some ironic, "Thanks, asshole", "That's a good one", and reprimands for the teller's threat to the hearer's negative face "Um, why did you just tell me that?" "Why do you do this to me?"

Responses that threatened the negative face of the teller even extended as far as shouting and playful hitting – invading personal space. It is also interesting that Bell's study confirmed Wolfson's (1989) findings, that the degree of positive impoliteness correlates with the degree of contact; we take pains to be polite to those with whom we have medium degrees of contact, whereas with intimates (and strangers) we may even deliberately use superficially rude forms.

9.9. SUMMARY

I began by distinguishing Searle's attempt to make pragmatics rule-based from Grice and Leech's principle-based pragmatics, in which inference and the hypothesising of intentions are basic. I surveyed Grice's theory by introducing the co-operative principle and its maxims, showing how standard implicature works when maxims are observed, and how the maxims become apparent when they are broken. Different ways of breaking the maxims are explained, including violation, and especially flouting, where the breaking is intended to be detected and extra meanings inferred. This prepared the way for discussion of the relation of the co-operative principle and humour, and the problem of deciding whether joking counts as co-operative behaviour or is non bona fide, giving arguments for and against. Jokes were shown to systematically break the maxims, and my suggestion was that jokes are usually delayed flouts. Attardo's suggestion that, though ideationally speaking jokes are non-communicative, they are communicatively important on the interpersonal dimension, led in to a discussion of politeness. I introduced Leech's politeness principle, a complement to the co-operative principle, and subsumed this under the "grand politeness strategy" which involves placing a high opinion on the other (hearer) and a low value on self, either in terms of goods and services, opinions, or feelings. Brown and Levinson's theory of face was briefly related to Leech's strategy, in order to show how humour can often threaten the negative face of other conversationalists. Finally the maxims of modesty and approbation were shown to have an ambiguous relation to humour, with self-deprecatory humour on the one hand and banter on the other, while approbation is broken when jokes fail.

Discussion

Make a record of the jokes that you hear in the course of a week. Considering their social context, try to decide what proportion of them

are relatively free-standing attempts to amuse and maintain a
friendly atmosphere, and how many seem to have a purpose beyond
themselves, in terms of making a point, in an argument, for example.
Use this data as a springboard for discussing whether jokes can
have a bona fide or serious purpose as Oring (2003) suggests (see
reading below).

Suggested Readings

- Grice (1975) is obviously a useful place to start. It has been
  claimed that "co-operation" is used in a technical sense in his
  theory, having more to do with the ways that we co-operate to
  create conversation on the basis of human rationality, rather
  than as a principle of human co-operative behaviour in general
  (Davies 2010). In that sense arguments can observe the principle
  without being co-operative in the larger sense. When reading the
  original Grice do you think this is a fair interpretation?
- The universality of Grice's principle, apart from the social situation of conversation among equals, has been cast in doubt. I put
  forward some arguments in Goatly (2008, chapter 6, especially
  pp. 140–3).
- Levinson (2000) is probably the weightiest recent treatment of neo-
  Gricean theory. It is particularly interesting in relation to standard implicatures (or generalised conversational implicature).
- Watts (2003) is an interesting critique of the traditional politeness theories touched on in this chapter. It views (im)polite
  language not as a technical concept realised by an inventory of
  linguistic expressions, but a concept which members of a society
  identify, use and dispute in discoursal and social contexts. Nevertheless, he makes a useful list of potentially polite, or "politic",
  expressions, the kinds of objectified ritual formulae which pass
  without notice. He suggests a theory of politeness based on
  Relevance Theory (see my Chapter 10), which would bridge interpersonal and ideational (propositional) meaning.
- Attardo (1994: 273ff.) is worth reading on the question of whether
  jokes and humour can really count as co-operative bona fide
  communication at all.
- Oring (2003: chapter 7) seems to disagree with Attardo. He gives
  quite convincing evidence that jokes can be used for persuasive
  and other purposes, and even deliberately stored in memory for
  subsequent use in ongoing arguments.

10 Relevance Theory, schemas and deductive inference

We have dealt with four pragmatic theories: speech act theory, conversational analysis developed from it, Gricean pragmatics and his co-operative principle, and Leech's politeness theory. The last two of these, and even more Sperber and Wilson, who developed the pragmatic theory known as Relevance Theory (RT) discussed in this chapter, emphasise that encoding and decoding are seldom sufficient for linguistic communication. Sperber and Wilson argue that the linguistic code may not even be necessary.

For example, imagine I am in Laos in 1974 when the Royal Lao troops and the anti-American Pathet Lao communists are in a power-sharing government. Walking through the countryside, I am detained by communist troops who think I'm American. I studied Russian a long time ago, but can only remember one sentence: "Когда темнеет, мы закрываем шторы" meaning 'when it gets dark we draw the curtains'. I utter this sentence, which convinces the communists I am Russian, and they release me. Although I use language to communicate I am Russian, I only employed an utterance act, not a coded propositional act. If I had, I might have died long ago in a communist mental hospital. Nevertheless, I communicated what I intended (cf. Searle 1969: 44–5).

10.1. PROPOSITIONS, PROPOSITIONAL ATTITUDE AND IMPLICATURE

Sperber and Wilson stress that the semantic output of the lexico-grammar, the result of decoding, is inadequate for communication. Often it is not explicit enough to even provide a propositional form. To reach this propositional form we need to (a) **disambiguate**, (b) **assign reference** to and (c) **enrich** (make less vague) the decoded message. Secondly, decoding doesn't indicate the speaker's attitude to the proposition. And thirdly, it leaves unstated the implicatures of the utterance.

To illustrate the inexplicitness of the propositions conveyed by real utterances, consider the causes of misunderstanding in the following joke.

> Mr and Mrs Harris were desperate for children, after 10 years of marriage. So, as a last resort, they decided to employ the services of a proxy father whom they had never met. On the morning when the sperm donor was due to call, Mr Harris left for work and wished his rather anxious wife good luck.
>
> By chance, that same morning a travelling baby photographer was in the area and called at the Harris's house. Mrs Harris answered the door.
>
> "Good morning, madam,' said the photographer. "You don't know me, but I've come to . . ."
>
> "Yes, I know," she interrupted, "there's no need to explain. Come in. I've been expecting you."
>
> "Really?" said the photographer, thinking his advertising must have paid off. "I must say I have made a speciality of babies."
>
> "That's what my husband and I were hoping," she said. "So where do we start?"
>
> "Well I usually try two in the bathtub, one on the couch, and perhaps a couple on the bed. If we try several different positions and I shoot from six or seven angles, I'm sure you'll be pleased with the results."
>
> "I do hope so," she said nervously. "Can we get this over quickly?"
>
> "In my line of work, I have to take my time," he replied. "It's no good rushing these things. I'd love to be in and out in five minutes, but you might be disappointed."
>
> "That's true," she replied, knowingly.
>
> The photographer opened his briefcase and pulled out a portfolio of baby pictures. "This was done on top of a bus," he explained.
>
> "Wow!" exclaimed Mrs Harris.
>
> "And these twins turned out really well considering their mother was so difficult to work with."
>
> "In what way?" asked Mrs Harris.
>
> "She insisted we go outdoors, so I had to take her over to Hyde Park. People were crowding four deep to watch. It took over three hours to do in all."
>
> By now Mrs Harris was looking decidedly worried.
>
> "Right," he said, "I'll just get my tripod."
>
> "Tripod?"
>
> "Yes, I need the tripod to rest my Canon on."
>
> At which point Mrs Harris fainted. (Tibballs 2006: 54)

Mrs Harris disambiguates, assigns reference and enriches in ways not intended by the photographer. "Shoot", a connector, is three ways ambiguous: the literal meaning, the metaphorical photographic meaning, and the metaphorical sexual meaning. Both metaphorical meanings and the schemas they activate are reinforced by the equally ambiguous homophone "Canon/cannon"/kænən/. The misinterpretation of the reference of "two", "it", "this", and "my Canon" obviously contributes to the humour too. In this particular joke the lack of clarity that prolongs Mrs Harris' misunderstanding largely derives from a lack of specificity of reference, or **vagueness**, that is, when a term is so general (**vertical vagueness**) or its boundaries are so ill-defined (**horizontal vagueness**) it is not clear exactly what is meant: "I have made a speciality of babies", "positions", "results", "these things", "be in and out", "done", "to work with" etc. are examples of vertical vagueness. Mrs Harris might interpret this general vocabulary as euphemistic, since general vocabulary is often used for euphemism, e.g. *thing* 'penis', *do your business* 'shit', etc.

Some jokes seem to exploit this kind of vagueness rather than ambiguity. Most obvious are the "*Do It*" jokes: e.g. "Cheesemakers do it Caerphilly", where the vagueness of the general *do* and *it* lends themselves to sexual innuendo. Or,

> "What do you give a man who **has** everything?"
> "Antibiotics." (Carr and Greeves 2006: 35)

I suppose *have* represents a general meaning which can refer to two different kinds of having: having a possession and having a disease. Exactly when one general meaning splits into two may be difficult to decide: in the pick-up line and rejection "Say, honey, how do you like your eggs in the morning?" "Unfertilised", does *eggs* have different meanings for the man and the woman?

As an example of horizontal vagueness, consider *be going to* in this joke, which refers to a time period in the future with an unspecified boundary:

> A young man goes to his boss. "Excuse me, sir, can I have the afternoon off, my wife's going to have a baby." "Certainly," says the boss, "and good luck."
> When the young man arrives at work next morning, the boss asks him, "Was it a boy or a girl?"
> "Oh, it's too early to tell," replies the young man. "It'll take another nine months."

We can use a modified example from Sperber and Wilson (1986/ 1995: 177–82) to illustrate exactly how propositions are made more explicit, involve a propositional attitude and lead to inferencing. John has prepared supper for Mary, who is sitting in an armchair in the dining room reading the newspaper. John enters, puts a plate of food on the table and says:

It'll get cold.

Firstly we need to **disambiguate** "cold", which can either mean 'low in temperature' as in "ice is cold" or 'experiencing low temperature' as in "I am cold", and "get", 'become' or 'obtain'. Next we need to **assign reference** to "it". Let's assume "it" refers to John's meal rather than the weather or newspaper. Furthermore, we have to **enrich** the proposition. Like "going to" in the joke above, "'ll" is horizontally vague, that is, the limits on the period of future time it indicates are unspecified. In this case we might supply 'very soon' to enrich the proposition. "Cold" is not only ambiguous, but also vague, because it is semantically relative in its meaning (4.4.3); the range of temperature it covers depends on the object to which it applies: compare 'cold' for a meal and 'cold' for water. Disambiguating, assigning reference and enriching in these ways gives a relatively complete proposition: 'Mary's meal will very soon become low in temperature (or reach room temperature)'.

But what is John's attitude to this proposition? If he observes the sincerity conditions on assertions he believes it is true. But suppose the meal is ice-cream. Then he neither believes it nor expects Mary to believe it, which could be a case of oppositional irony, with what is said the opposite of what is thought. Propositional attitude can, of course, be encoded, by the mood and modality systems (5.5): imperatives generally encode the desirability, at least for the speaker, of the propositional act, *yes–no* interrogatives encode doubt about the proposition's truth, etc., both encodings conforming to the speech act conditions on commands and questions.

Sperber and Wilson refer to the above ways of making the proposition explicit (disambiguation, reference assignment, enrichment, establishing **propositional attitude**) as the **development of propositional form** through **explicatures**. But, additionally, decoding the semantic output of the lexico-grammar, even after further explication into a full proposition, indicates nothing about **implicatures**. By saying "It'll get cold", conveying the enriched proposition 'Mary's meal will become low in temperature very soon', John might be communicating 'John wants Mary to come and eat the meal at once'. Implicatures are generated by the interaction of the proposition with contextual information. Mary has information stored in the schema/script of 'eating dinner at home' including the assumption 'John wants Mary to come and eat a meal at the time it is still hot'. This interacts with the developed propositional form to implicate 'John wants Mary to come and eat the meal immediately'.

10.2. WHAT IS RELEVANCE? CONTEXTUAL EFFECTS AND PROCESSING EFFORT

According to RT, information is relevant to you if it interacts with your existing assumptions (beliefs/thoughts) about the world (Wilson and Sperber 1986: 27ff.).

Example 1
You wake up thinking,

> a. If Joseph is taking the choir rehearsal tonight I won't attend choir practice this evening.

You phone up your friend Paul and he tells you

> b. Joseph is taking the choir rehearsal tonight.

From existing assumption (a) and the new information (b) you can deduce further information (c)

> c. I won't attend choir practice this evening.

(b) is relevant because, in the context of (a), it produces new information or **contextually implies** (c).

Example 2
You wake up and you think you remember from an announcement at last week's rehearsal

> d. Joseph is taking the choir rehearsal tonight.

You phone up your friend Paul and he tells you

> e. Joseph IS taking the choir rehearsal tonight.

(e) is relevant because it strengthens an existing assumption. The more assumptions it strengthens, and the more it strengthens them, the more relevant it is.

Example 3
You wake up and you think you remember from an announcement at last week's rehearsal

> f. Joseph is taking the choir rehearsal tonight.

You phone up your friend Paul and he tells you

> g.   Joseph is NOT taking the choir rehearsal tonight.

(g) is relevant in this case because it leads to you abandoning the assumption (f) (which was weaker than (g)).

To sum up, information can be relevant to you in three ways: (1) by creating contextual implications, (2) by strengthening assumptions and (3) by being inconsistent with and thereby eliminating existing assumptions. These are all called **contextual effects**. The greater the contextual effects, the greater the relevance (Goatly 2011: 142ff.).

Activity 10.1

Attempt to spell out the deductive logic involved in understanding the following joke. How does the assumption encoded in the first clause of the sentence, before the colon, interact with the information given after the colon? Which of the assumptions here is eliminated?

> There are three kinds of people: those who can count and those who can't.
> (Carr and Greeves 2006: 10)

Comment
1.   The speaker has said there are three kinds of people: those who can count and those who can't.
2.   Those who can count and those who cannot count are two kinds of people.
3.   If you think two kinds of people are three kinds of people you can't count.
4.   THUS the speaker cannot count.

It is interesting to consider in this contradiction which of the stated assumptions is eliminated: that there are two kinds of people, or that there are three kinds of people. Presumably the latter, because of complementarity of the positive and negative.

The second factor in computing relevance is **processing effort**.

Example 4
You wake up thinking

> h.   If Joseph is taking the choir rehearsal tonight I won't attend choir practice this evening.

Then EITHER you phone up your friend Paul and he tells you

> k.   Joseph is taking the choir rehearsal tonight.

OR you phone up your friend Paul and he tells you

1.   Joseph is taking the choir rehearsal tonight and Maud is taking it next week.

(k) and (l) have the same contextual effects in the context of (h). (k) is more relevant than (l) in this context, however, because (l) requires more processing effort (Sperber and Wilson 1986/1995: 125ff.).

Activity 10.2

How does the extra processing effort element needed show that the question in this QA joke is not optimally relevant:

Q. Why do firemen wear red braces?
A. To keep their trousers up. (Ritchie 2004: 82)

Comment

The extra information conveyed by "red" in the question is irrelevant to the answer. Therefore it involves unnecessary processing effort. Nevertheless, it is, in some way, essential to the joke: we expect that the redness of the braces will be in some way relevant to the answer.

We can summarise the theory so far by providing a comparative definition of relevance (Sperber and Wilson 1986/1995: 153):

Other things being equal the greater the contextual effects, the greater the relevance.
Other things being equal, the smaller the processing effort the greater the relevance.

Or one might wish to present this as a fraction (Goatly 2011: 143):

$$\text{Relevance} = \frac{\text{Contextual Effects}}{\text{Processing Effort}}$$

Clearly the concepts which a language community finds most relevant are encoded as single lexical items rather than as free phrases, because this reduces processing effort. For instance, in popular science we abbreviate the long number 9,460,730,472,580.8 kilometers into the more easily processed compound *light year* (Sperber and Wilson 1986/1995). This influence of relevance on lexicalisation explains the impossibility of guessing riddles for concepts or objects not sufficiently important in a culture to have achieved a lexical status.

- What's green and prickly/hairy and goes up and down?
- A durian/gooseberry in a lift.

"A gooseberry in a lift" has not been lexicalised as a phrasal compound.

Activity 10.3

Look at the following example and decide which of the possible answers is the most relevant, according to the above analysis of relevance:

You think, though you are not sure, that Brussels is in Holland. So you ask Beatrice

A: Brussels is in Holland, isn't it?
B1: I don't think so.
B2: In Belgium.

Comment

B2 is probably more relevant than B1. This is because, although B1 is a more direct answer, Beatrice is apparently not sure. So whether the assumption in her reply is strong enough to eliminate your assumption about Brussels being in Holland is unclear. In B2, through implicature, you can reach an answer to your question:

1. Belgium is a different country from Holland
2. Beatrice has said Brussels is in Belgium
3. THUS Brussels is not in Holland.

Freud has suggested that jokes achieve a mental economy, often, one supposes, by two schemas being instantiated when processing the same text. This is why paraphrasing a joke completely eliminates its humorous effect, and the amount of paraphrase needed is proportional to the humour of the joke (Fonagy 1982: 42–3). But perhaps a sounder claim is that humour depends upon a deviation from the normal degrees of processing effort demanded in discourse (cf. Giora on graded-informativeness, 7.6). Generally the amount of text to be processed might be less than normal. But circumlocution, giving too much text to process, can have equally humorous effects (Attardo 1994: 264), e.g. not calling a spade a spade, but a "metallic blade wedded to ligneous rod, with which the rural swain upturns the sod". The fact that there is an extra degree of processing effort allowed or necessary in jokes, explains the humour in the following:

There were a group of convicts living in a prison on an isolated island off the coast of Australia. In the evenings they would gather around telling jokes. However, the jokes became rather repetitive, especially since very few convicts joined the colony, and the same old jokes were recycled. So, to save time they devised a numbering system, and just saying the number became equivalent to telling the joke.

One day a new convict joined the colony. In the evening the convicts were sitting around telling jokes by numbers: "number 5" followed by laughter; "number 16" followed by laughter, and so on. The newcomer, puzzled, asked the convict next to him what was happening, and learnt about the numbering system. So the new convict decided to try, and at the next opportunity said, "Number 12". This was followed by a prolonged and awkward silence. Embarrassed, he asked his neighbour "What's wrong with joke number 12?" "There's nothing wrong with the joke," he sighed, "it's just the way you told it."

This suggests that in jokes increasing the efficiency of information exchange by reducing processing effort may be unimportant (except in the nonsensical scenario sketched here), and an effective joking style may sometimes sacrifice the brevity mandated by the maxim of manner (9.1).

The above examples of contextual effects grossly oversimplify by assuming we have only a few existing assumptions in our heads. In fact when we communicate there are various assumptions in our short-term memory evoked by the situation and the co-text (see (2) in Figure 10.1), including the generic context. We also have thousands of assumptions stored in long-term memory as factual or socio-cultural knowledge (3). In generating contextual implicatures from an utterance, we activate the **contextual assumptions** which are most relevant.

For example, I wake up thinking

a. If Joseph is taking the choir rehearsal tonight I won't attend choir practice this evening.
b. I've run out of cereal for breakfast.

Paul phones me up and tells me

c. Joseph is taking the choir rehearsal tonight.

I select assumption (a) or (b) for the interpretation of (c) on the basis of relevance: (a) is more relevant than (b) (Goatly 2011: 144).

Therefore, not only is relevance important for gauging contextual implications, but also for activating existing assumptions. This means there are two kinds of **implicature**: contextual implications and contextual assumptions (Sperber and Wilson 1986/1995: 156, 195). The contextual assumptions which we use to derive contextual implications obviously originate in (2) and (3) of Figure 10.1.

1. Knowledge of the language system
2. Knowledge of the context: situation and co-text
3. Background schematic knowledge: factual and socio-cultural.

Figure 10.1. Knowledge sources in interpretation (Goatly 2011: 141, figure 5.1)

10.3. RELEVANCE, DEDUCTIVE LOGIC AND UNDERSTANDING JOKES

The deductive logic of RT is clearly applicable to the pragmatics of understanding humour, in particular jokes (Jodlowiec 1994; Curcó

1996; Ritchie 2004: 7). Consider, for instance, the unintended humour in this notice from a magazine.

> Weightwatchers will be held at the Presbyterian church. Please use the big double doors. (Tibballs 2006: 496)

The unintended inferences can be teased out as follows:

- a.   People attending Weightwatchers are asked to use the big double doors. (stated)
- b.   People attending Weightwatchers are overweight. (background cultural knowledge)
- c.   Overweight people are fat. (factual knowledge, connotation)
- d.   THUS People attending Weightwatchers are fat.
- e.   People who are fat may not be able to get through a single door. (factual knowledge, connotation)
- f.   People attending Weightwatchers may not be able to get through a single door. (from (d) and (e))
- g.   THUS People attending Weightwatchers are asked to use the big double doors because they may be unable to get through a single door.

The background factual and cultural knowledge in premises (b) and (c) interact logically to reach the conclusion in (d). The premises (d) and (e) in turn generate the implicature (f). (f) then becomes an **implicated premise** which interacts with the statement in (a) to create the **implicated conclusion** (g).

One grey area in RT concerns what number and kind of contextual effects are necessary in order to achieve a relevant interpretation (Levinson 1989: 463). For most jokes relevance has a predetermined value, and contexts are expanded until this value is satisfied. This also applies to genres like crossword puzzles and riddles, where we continue accessing contextual assumptions until the solution clicks.

However, relevance might not be a threshold value like this, even in jokes. Relevant information may strengthen assumptions. This indicates that assumptions can be held and implicated conclusions derived with varying degrees of certainty. In some jokes there may be some more subtle possible point beyond just getting the joke, as with good poems, which, when re-read, evoke richer but less certain implicated conclusions. Take, for example, the following joke:

> A grade school teacher was asking the children what their parents did for a living.
> "What does your daddy do for a living?" she asked.
> "My daddy is a doctor," replied Mary.

"And what does your daddy do for a living, Mark?"
"My daddy is a journalist," replied Mark.
"And what about you, James? What does your daddy do for a living?"
"My daddy plays a piano in a whorehouse," replied James.
     The teacher was horrified but thought there must be some explanation for
     the boy's reply. So the next time she saw James' father, she mentioned the
     incident.
     "Well, actually," said the father, "I'm a lawyer. But how can I explain a
     thing like that to a seven-year old?" (Tibballs 2006: 218)

I won't spell out the whole process of deductive logic to illustrate how to
get the joke. The father's account is counterintuitive; one would assume
it is more difficult to explain to a seven-year old what playing a piano in
a whorehouse is than explain what a lawyer does. But perhaps the joke
intends something more subtle than this, to make a metaphorical
comparison between lawyers and whores: both selling their services to
clients without any real commitment (to a relationship or to justice).[1]

     One of the strengths of using RT in explaining the interpretation of
humour is that it employs a form of deductive logic. And many
humour theorists have pointed out the role of absurd or faulty logic
or pseudo-plausibility (Hetzron 1999; Chafe 2007). For instance, the
ambiguity of negation appears to make the following logical:
"Nothing works faster than Anadin. So why bother with Anadin?" Or
the apparent analogical logic of this humour:

     When T. E. Lawrence [Lawrence of Arabia] joined the ranks as private
     Shaw, Noel Coward wrote a letter to him which began: "Dear 338171
     (may I call you 338?)" (Koestler, quoted in Fonagy 1982: 45)

Attardo and Raskin (1991) discuss the logical mechanism essential for
jokes. Though there may be specific kinds of logical mechanism, such
as the analogic just illustrated, RT's deductive logic provides a general,
widely applicable machinery for their interpretation.

     Another advantage of RT over CP is that it dispenses with the quality
maxim. This allows it to cope with fictional, fantastic or unreal worlds,
without this amounting to violation or non bona fide communication.

10.4. THE RELATION OF RELEVANCE THEORY TO GRICE'S THEORY

The notion of relevance, expanding the maxim of relation, seems to
include the maxim of quantity, since it considers the amount of information, or contextual effects, and also the maxim of manner, because
it considers the processing effort involved. Relevance, however, has a
less clear relation to the maxim of quality. Sometimes the processing

effort involved in interpreting a true utterance will be greater than that involved in processing an approximate one, and therefore the less true one will be more relevant (Sperber and Wilson 1986/1995: 233–5). This humorous exchange comes from the grave-digging scene in *Hamlet*:

HAMLET:	What man dost thou dig it for?
CLOWN:	For no man, sir.
HAMLET:	What woman, then?
CLOWN:	For none, neither.
HAMLET:	Who is to be buried in it?
CLOWN:	One that was a woman, sir; but rest her soul, she's dead.
HAMLET:	How absolute the knave is!

Hamlet's last remonstrance could presumably be paraphrased – 'to what an extent this man insists on observing the maxim of quality, at the expense of the maxim of quantity'!

Activity 10.4

A tourist visiting an archaeological site in South America was intrigued by the display of dinosaur bones. She asked a local Indian, who was acting as tour guide, how old the bones were. "Exactly 100 million and 3 years old," replied the Indian. "That's amazing," said the tourist. "How can you be so precise?" "Simple," said the Indian. "A geologist told me they were 100 million years old and that was exactly three years ago." (Tibballs 2006: 360)

Explain the relationship between the maxim of quality and the principle of relevance in the Indian's and geologist's discourse.

Comment

The Indian looks to be a Gricean, expecting by standard implicature that the geologist had given an exact figure three years previously, and proceeding to give an exact figure to the tourist. In fact the geologist was more likely an adherent of RT, thinking that an approximation was more relevant than the exact figure.

10.5. IMPLICATURE AND SCHEMA THEORY

Obviously implicature depends upon accessing existing assumptions, since information is relevant to you if it interacts with your existing knowledge.[2] In this section I explain how the mind stores and organises the background knowledge to be accessed to operate pragmatically in jokes.

This organised storage is in frames, schemas and scripts. These terms are sometimes used interchangeably, but I shall use **frame** to refer to knowledge of objects, **schema** for assumptions about an event or action, and script or **discourse schema** for knowledge of a genre in which language plays an important if not constitutive role.

Schank and Abelson's most famous example is the RESTAURANT (script) schema, which can be detailed as follows:

RESTAURANT (setting)

Props:	tables, chairs, cutlery, food, plates, menu, etc.
Roles:	customer, owner, cook, waiter, (cashier), (captain)
Entry conditions:	customer is hungry, customer has money
Results:	customer has less money, customer is not hungry, owner has more money
Scene 1. Entering:	going in, deciding where to sit, sitting
Scene 2. Ordering:	(asking for menu, waiter bringing menu) choosing, signalling to waiter, giving order, waiter telling cook the order
Scene 3. Eating:	cook giving waiter food, waiter bringing customer food, customer eating food.
Scene 4. Exiting:	customer asking for bill, waiter writing bill, taking bill to customer, (customer tipping waiter), customer going to cashier, paying cashier, leaving restaurant.

This schema also incorporates frames for the props in the schema, and some scenes of the schema will involve language (like ordering, asking for the bill) and are therefore scripts. The point about schemas, scripts and frames is that they are stereotypical. That is to say, once evoked in discourse, the hearer will assume that the typical features of the frame or sequences of events apply. If you say you went to a restaurant and saw Hillary Clinton at an adjoining table, we assume all the other expected features of the restaurant schema, which you don't mention, applied.

Schemas are evoked to make sense of statements that are inexplicit due to the vagueness of lexical items. So in the joke "Mummy, Mummy, I don't like Daddy!" "Then leave him on the side of your plate and eat your vegetables", "like" is vague and we access the most likely schema of family life in which *like* is enriched as 'have affection for', rather than the schema which replaces it at the end of the joke, the meal schema, where it is enriched as 'enjoy eating' (*pace* Chiaro 1992: 15). One reason that jokes don't travel well is gaps in background socio-cultural knowledge or different schemas (Chiaro 1992: 10–11).

Scripts or schemas are concepts which have been exploited in theories of humour, notably the script-based semantic theory of humour (SSTH) first proposed by Raskin (1985) and later developed and modified by Attardo. According to Attardo (1994: 197), "A text can be characterised as a single joke-carrying text if both conditions are satisfied:

  i. The text is compatible, fully or in part, with two different scripts
  ii. The two scripts with which the text is compatible are opposite. (...) The two scripts with which some text is compatible are said to [overlap] fully or in part in this text."

Attardo (1994: 206–7) gives a famous analysis of the following joke using the SSTH framework.

> "Is the doctor at home?" asked a patient in a breathy voice as the doctor's young and pretty wife opened the door.
> "No," she whispered, "come on right in!"

I will quote the whole analysis here, partly to exemplify the theory, partly as a reminder, in brackets, of the concepts of selection restrictions, adjacency pairs, inferencing, and sincerity conditions.

> The first step in the analysis is the listing of all the senses of the words in the text (in other words of all the scripts activated by the text). The second step is the activation of the combinatorial rules that will combine the various scripts according to compatibility (i.e. they will look for words that evoke the same script) and to syntactic and sub-categorisation rules [cf. selection restrictions] ... For example, among the various scripts evoked by the word "is" (from the joke's first sentence) there is a SPATIAL script: among the scripts evoked by "at" there is also a SPATIAL script. Because the two words have the script in common, the combinatorial rules will choose this script as their preferred reading and continue the analysis. The next logical step, which takes place at the same time as the combination of scripts, is the triggering of inferences [implicature]. The reader infers that the second line is meant as an answer to a previous question [question–answer adjacency pair], that the speaker of the first line does not know the answer to the question, and that she/he is interested in knowing the answer to the question [preparatory and sincerity conditions on questions]. By recursively applying the combinatorial rules and the inferencing mechanisms, an interpretation of the entire text is arrived at.
>
>   A semantic reading of the joke can be loosely paraphrased as "someone who was previously treated for some illness inquires about the presence of a doctor at the doctor's place of residence, with the purpose of being treated for a disease which manifests itself by a whispering voice. The doctor's wife (who is young and pretty) answers (whispering as the patient) that the doctor is not at home, and invites the inquirer to enter the house."

The hearer is faced with a puzzle: if the purpose of the patient's inquiry is the desire to be treated for his disease, why is the doctor's wife asking him in anyway [the script-switch trigger or disjunctor], as the doctor is not there and the script for DOCTOR requires physical proximity for examination and treatment of the illness? This situation leads the reader to switch to the NBF [non bona fide] mode and to start looking for a "competing script" (Raskin 1985: 125), i.e. an alternative interpretation of the story.

The reader will then backtrack and re-evaluate the text. The gender of the doctor's wife and her description will be taken into account, as well as the absence of the doctor/husband. This will allow the activation of the LOVER script, which prescribes that an adulterous relationship be acted upon without knowledge of the legitimate spouse. In the light of the LOVER script, the behaviour of the doctor's wife becomes meaningful, i.e. she is taking advantage of her husband's absence to have a secret meeting with another man. The text is thus found to be compatible almost entirely with two scripts (DOCTOR, LOVER), and the scripts are opposed on the SEX/NO SEX basis. Hence it fulfils both requirements of the SSTH and is evaluated humorous (Attardo 1994: 206–7).[3][4]

With this theory in mind we can consider a variety of ways in which schemas (scripts) and frames figure in jokes. The first joke exploits various schemas by cancelling out the stereotypical assumptions associated with them.

My sister had a baby. We would have company over and she'll be there with her breast out, feeding him ... cereal or whatever.
The other day she took me aside and said "Emo, can you baby-sit little Derek while I go to the carnival ... and look for the father?"
I said, "OK". So I'm pushing him through the park, and he's crying ... because I forgot the stroller.
I take him home and I'm trying to rinse out his diaper in the toilet – you ever rinse out a baby's diaper in the toilet? Euch! Anyway ...
I accidentally let go of his foot.
And he's spinning around crying, and I'm trying to get him out with the plunger ... because you can't use Drano, that *hurts* a kid.
(Emo Philips, Carr and Greeves 2006: 133)

The typical schema for breastfeeding is cancelled out by "cereal or whatever". The taking the baby to the park schema has as one of its props a stroller or pram but "I forgot the stroller". The schema for changing a baby's (cloth) diaper has a number of scenes:

(1) baby defecates/urinates in diaper – (2) carer becomes aware of this – (3) carer removes diaper from baby – (4) carer cleans baby – (5) carer puts on new diaper – (6) carer washes out dirty diaper in toilet – (7) carer soaks dirty diaper

Apparently, according to this humorous anecdote, scene (3) does not take place, and the speaker tries to combine (4) and (6). Then there is the schema for removing objects/unblocking a toilet, which does not normally feature a baby as an important object/prop. At least the possible schema of using a powerful chemical to unblock a toilet is rejected!

The following jokes depend upon the information stored in frames, the first in two frames, connected by "neck", the second in one.

> What do blondes and beer bottles have in common? They're empty from the neck up. (Tibballs 2006: 529)

> I'd hate to be next door to Monica Seles on her wedding night. (Peter Ustinov, Tibballs 2006: 652)

The next joke provides frame information, but depends upon how this information could take part in the schema of picking one's nose (if I have understood the joke correctly).

> Why do gorillas have big nostrils? Because they have big fingers. (Tibballs 2006: 34)

In the following, by contrast, the frame for book becomes part of a schema for colouring, either suggesting that these are not typical economics books, or that Reagan doesn't recognise them as such:

> Ronald Reagan has two books on economics, but he hasn't finished colouring the first one yet. (Tibballs 2006: 646)

Other jokes depend upon the coincidence of schemas to create implied similes or metaphors:

> I slept like a baby. I woke up every 3 hours looking for a bottle.

While others draw attention to the fact that not all parts of the source schema can be metaphorically applied to the target:

> If all the world's a stage, where do the audience sit?

Still others posit a hypothetical coincidence of schemas and frames.

> If Michelangelo had been a heterosexual the Sistine chapel would have been painted basic white and with a roller. (Rita Mae Brown, Tibballs 2006: 40)

Here the schema of home-decoration, of which painting walls is part, inter-acts with the frame for heterosexual men and homosexual men, the second being stereotyped as more interested in elaborate colour schemes than the former. These frames are all projected on the schema for Michelangelo, who was homosexual, painting the Sistine chapel in elaborate colourful depictions of the biblical scenes of creation and judgment.

The hypothetical combining of schemas can result in humorous absurdity, as when the frames for toast and cats are combined in the following scenario:

> If toast always lands butter side down, and cats always land on their feet, what happens if you strap toast to the back of a cat and drop it? (Steven Wright, Carr and Greeves 2006: 123)

By far the most common exploitation of schematic information in jokes is when there is schema ambiguity, as in the doctor joke. An action or remark could belong to two different schemas: the actual one less likely than the assumed one.

> A guy walked into a bar and said to the bartender, "I've got this great Polish joke." The bartender glared at him and warned him. "Before you go telling that joke I think you ought to know that I'm Polish, the two bouncers on the door are Polish, and most of my customers are Polish."
>   "OK," said the guy, "I'll tell it slowly." (Tibballs 2006: 58)

In this case the schema intended to be invoked is that of violent objection by members of a minority to a joke targeted at that ethnic minority. But the guy entering the bar interprets it according to an (untrue) stereotypical feature of the Polish frame: mental slowness.

In some cases, like this latter, the interpretation is so unlikely that it might not fit into a schema at all. More technically, the contextually implicated assumption needed to interpret the joke seems initially less relevant or accessible than other possible implicated assumptions.

Activity 10.5

A Scotsman takes all his money out of the bank for a holiday. Once it's had a holiday, he puts it back again.

a. What schema do we use to interpret the first sentence?
b. How do we have to replace this schema after we read the second sentence?
c. How does the second scenario fit our schema or frame stereotype of Scots?
d. How can we use the deductive logic of RT to explain the two interpretations on which the joke depends?

Comment

a.   The schema for going on holiday. Going on holiday involves expenses for travelling and paying for accommodation/food, so presumably the money is taken out of the bank for holiday expenses.

b.   In the second sentence we invoke the unlikely scenario that it is the money that has a holiday rather than the Scotsman.

c.   According to the English ethnic stereotype of the Scotsman frame, one of its features is 'meanness' or at least 'financial prudence' (even after Gordon Brown!). So none of the money is spent.

d.   1. A Scotsman takes all his money out of the bank for a holiday. (stated)
     2. People take money out of the bank to spend. (factual cultural knowledge)
     3. Going on holiday involves spending money on travel/accommodation etc. (factual cultural knowledge)
     4. THUS The Scotsman takes all his money out of the bank to spend on his holiday.
     5. Once it's [the money's] had a holiday he [the Scotsman] puts it [the money] back again. (stated)
     6. Going on holiday involves moving away from your normal location and returning when the holiday is over. (factual, cultural knowledge)
     7. The money has been removed from its normal location (stated in 1) and returned after the holiday. (stated in 5)
     8. THUS the money has had a holiday. (stated in 5)

Impossible schemas may be activated in jokes, especially those which pretend the schema is immune to change over time.

> I think I've worked out how medieval armies broke through the defences of castles. They chose the weakest spot – the gift shop. All a determined enemy had to do was overpower the two old ladies who work there and the whole castle was taken. (Bill Bailey, Tibballs 2006: 39)

Because schemas and frames are ways of storing stereotypical information, they might perpetuate harmful stereotypes by making it necessary for the reader/hearer to invoke them as contextually implicated assumptions (Attardo and Raskin 1991: 301; Norrick 1993: 121). As the stereotypes are not themselves spelt out, just lurking in the background, so to speak, they are less overtly ideological than encoded stereotypes that we saw, for example, with the stupid and helpless American woman (3.6). It is as though the readers/hearers themselves are responsible for the ideological stereotype they provide; however, this is disingenuous, as the joke is carefully constructed with this stereotype in the speaker's mind in the first place. The reader/hearer may not in fact believe the stereotypical contextual assumption invoked, but, still by entertaining it, perpetuates it.

Anyway, here is such a joke, and I hope it is entertaining:

> Ireland's worst air disaster occurred this morning when a small two-seater Cessna plane crashed into a cemetery. Irish search and

rescue workers have recovered 1,826 bodies so far and expect that
number to climb as digging continues. (Carr and Greeves 2006: 199)

One would not expect Polish people, blondes or the Irish to have the
same stereotypes about themselves as the English or Americans do of
them.

Many of the schematically stored contextually implied assumptions
necessary to make sense of jokes are culture specific. Biblical knowledge is necessary to make sense of the following:

> A Jewish father was troubled by his errant son's behaviour and went
> to see the rabbi about it. "I brought him up a Jew, spent a fortune
> on his education and bar mitzvah. Then he calls me to tell me he's
> decided to become a Christian! Rabbi, where did I go wrong?"
> "Funny you should come to me," said the rabbi. "Like you, I too
> brought my son up a good Jew, put him through college – at great
> expense – and then he too came and told me he had decided to become
> a Christian."
>   "What did you do?" the man demanded anxiously.
>   "I turned to God for the answer," replied the rabbi.
>   "And what did he say?" the father pressed.
>   "He said, 'Funny you should come to me . . .'" (Carr and Greeves 2006: 200)

Such allusions to particular (fictional) texts bring us to the topic of the
next section.

10.6.   ECHOIC UTTERANCES AND IRONY

Another interesting element in RT is its discussion of echoic utterances.
The use–mention distinction was introduced (1.2) in the context of the
notational conventions for this book. Sperber and Wilson, in order to
propound a theory of irony, develop this distinction – some utterances
are not the speaker's own because they echo or quote other speakers.
In a book which deals with humour, it is worth discussing and interro-
gating their theory of irony.

For Sperber and Wilson (1986: 237ff.) an echoic utterance is a means
of informing the hearer that the speaker has in mind what X said and
has a certain attitude to it. In the case of proverbs X could be people in
general: "Don't count your chickens before they hatch". But very often
the speaker has a more particular X in mind, as in the following two
cases.

1. J: It's a great day for watching cricket.
   You go to Lord's cricket ground and the weather is beautifully sunny
   M: Indeed, it's a great day for watching cricket.

2. J: It's a great day for watching cricket.
   You go to Lord's cricket ground and there is a thunderstorm
   M: Indeed, it's a great day for watching cricket.

M's utterances are echoic in each case: they inform J that M has in mind what J said, and that M has a certain propositional attitude to it. In the case of (1) this attitude is one of endorsement; and in the case of (2), which is for Sperber and Wilson a prototypical case of irony, the attitude is rejection/disapproval. To spell out the relevant assumptions for the case of (2): if (a)–(d) are a context in which M makes the utterance, then J might well arrive at the ironic interpretation which generates the contextual implicatures (x)–(z):

2. (a) If there's a thunderstorm the weather is no good for watching cricket.
   (b) There's a thunderstorm.
   (c) The weather's no good for watching cricket.
   (d) I (J) said it would be a great day for watching cricket.

   M: Indeed, it's a great day for watching cricket.

The implicatures might be:

(x) M does not believe that it is a great day for watching cricket.
(y) M is echoing my (J's) statement that it would be a great day for watching cricket.
(z) M believes I (J) was wrong to say that it would be a great day for watching cricket.

For a real example look at this dialogue between the brothers Brandon and Ned, about Frank Capra's later films, which Brandon is trying to defend against Ned's charge of didacticism:

BRANDON:	A lot of what he's after in some of these films was this concern about America. And what was going on in the world, and about the little guy, and the depression, and –
NED:	I understand that.
BRANDON:	Y'know.
NED:	I'm in favour of the depression. I think you can [do that]
BRANDON:	[Ha ha] (h) I'm in *favour* of the de*pression* [hahahehehe]
NED:	[Hhaw.] I'm in favour of the little guy, especially in times *like* the depression. (Norrick: 1993: 33)

Notice how Brandon echoes word for word "I'm in favour of the depression", but with extra intonation indicating his lack of belief in the proposition. Also, as if it is direct speech, and this intonation is the equivalent of quotation marks, he maintains the original pronoun "I", keeping Ned as the deictic centre. Moreover, Brandon uses laughter to suggest that he cannot take this over-abbreviated metonymic statement by Ned seriously (Norrick 1993: 38, quoting Jefferson).

One of the problems with irony is that it may not be detected, that is, the attitude to the propositions of the utterance may be misinterpreted. Some comedians, for example, claim not to be sexist or racist even though they tell what, apparently, are sexist or racist jokes, because their propositional attitude is actually one of ironic mockery of the joke's ideology. For instance, if you tell the joke "Why do women have small feet? So they can get closer to the sink", you may be parodying such jokes and targeting their tellers. However, some of the hearers of the joke may take it at face value and revel in its sexism (Ross 1998: 57). Silvio Berlusconi, during a speech to the European Parliament, compared a German MEP to a Nazi concentration camp commandant. In response to the ensuing booing, instead of apologising, he said he regretted his utterance had not been recognised as an ironic joke (Simpson and Mayr 2010: 80, quoting Billig 2005).

Such comedians might claim that their critics had deliberately ignored the ironic distance, as B does in this example adapted from Priego-Valverde (2009: 178).

> *A is a student of linguistics, B and C students of dentistry and D a student of pharmacy. They are discussing potential collaborations for a good dental surgery.*
>
> B: it's complicated, we have to see:
> A: and you're not interested in having a linguist in it?
> B: (*very seriously*) no:: no no
> *general laughter*
> C: a private university uh:::
> A: (*laughter*)
> B: on the other hand a doctor

Apparently B does not wish to switch from a serious discussion of setting up the surgery, as he perseveres by suggesting collaboration with a doctor. It is likely, therefore, that he deliberately pretends not to recognise the humorous voice of A, not wishing to be side-tracked into frivolity.

Metaphor and irony are particularly risky, then, as there is a possibility that the listener will not recognise them, or will pretend not to recognise them. They are off-record, though signalling them (7.6) restricts the possibilities for non-recognition.

10.7.   ECHOIC UTTERANCES, LEVELS OF DISCOURSE AND MULTIPLE VOICES IN TEXTS

Most obviously any quotation of another's speech is a mention rather than a use, and is therefore echoic. As such, like irony, the propositional attitude may not be straightforward: the reporter or echoer may not believe the proposition expressed by the other, and may wish to distance themself from it, signalling this by quotation marks or scare quotes.

There are various ways of representing another's speech: free direct e.g., "'I will come tomorrow'", direct, "John said 'I will come tomorrow'", free indirect, "He would come tomorrow", indirect, "John said he would go the next day", and narrative report of speech act or paraphrase, "Mr John Martin announced his intention of arriving on November 7th". What distinguishes free forms from other forms is the absence of the reporting clause. What distinguishes indirect from direct forms is both the absence of quotation marks to signal the boundary between the two voices, but also the change of deictics (8.4), as the reported voice is assimilated to the deictic centre of the reporter. So, the time deictic tense shifts from present "will" to past "would", the time deictic "tomorrow" changes to "the next day", the person deictic pronoun "I" shifts to "he", and the place deictic "come" to "go".

The possibility of reporting speech draws attention to the fact that discourse in general and jokes in particular can involve more than one level of discourse. Recall the opening of St Joan (9.6). Speech acts that flouted the quantity maxim, or failed to fulfil the preparatory conditions on questions on the character–character level of discourse, in some cases observed the maxims or fulfilled the conditions on the playwright–audience level.

Jokes may be told either on one level of discourse or on two. Reporting unintentional humour as in howlers (student errors), typos, malapropisms etc. maintains a distance between the reporter's voice and the reported voice (Chiaro 1992: 21). More obvious still are narrative jokes. Ritchie (2004: 91–2, 98) surmises that narrative jokes do not have to rely on linguistic ambiguity that forces a re-interpretation, but more on ambiguity of interpretation or understanding. "**Conjecture:** in a narrative joke (*funny story*) if linguistic ambiguity is central to the joke, then it will occur not in the supporting narrative, but only in an utterance by a character in the story (reported directly or indirectly) or in some written material quoted within the story (e.g. a letter, a printed sign)." A good example of this is the narrative about the photographer mistaken for a sperm donor (10.1).

An absurd fictional device sometimes deliberately confounds the levels of reader and character, as when the reader magically becomes a character in the story. In the following joke's variation on this device, the character comes out of the fiction into the world of the narrator, whom he proceeds to hold responsible for his presence:

> A young lady notices from her bed that a strongly built naked black gentleman is climbing through the window. He comes closer and closer, whereupon she exclaims, "What do you want with me?" The stranger answers, "Sorry, it's your dream." (Fonagy 1982: 44)

Echoic utterances can have varying degrees of specificity. Sometimes an echoic/reported utterance may be a stereotypical one associated with a particular schema, script or genre. If used in an inappropriate situation it can provoke humour:

> The opening night of a new play was so bad that the audience started leaving the theatre at the end of the second act. As he got up from his aisle seat, a noted critic raised a restraining hand. "Wait!" he commanded loudly "Women and children first." (Tibballs 2006: 359)

The schema/script opposition is between a play in the theatre and a sinking ship (perhaps suggested by FAILURE IS SINKING).

In a more general case, the echo is of the linguistic or cultural community as a whole, as with proverbs (Attardo 1994: 138). Children not yet fully members of this community may not know all of them and, when questioned, produce novel ones:

> Don't count your chickens . . . eat them.
> A watched pot never . . . disappears.
> Don't bite the hand that . . . looks dirty.
> (Tibballs 2006: 666–7)

Some riddles or proverbs are so well known that they do not even need to be stated in order to be evoked.

> A chicken and an egg were sitting up in bed. The chicken had a smile on its face and the egg looked miserable. Now we know the answer to the riddle.[5]

Other echoic utterances involve more specific famous quotations, which are nevertheless common cultural property. A famous line from a Kipling poem is alluded to in the following: "If you can keep your head when all about are losing theirs, you'll be taller than anyone else." (Tim Brooke-Taylor, Carr and Greeves 2006: 45).

Activity 10.6

How are echoic utterances involved in these jokes?

1. Why did the director of Dignitas cross the road? – To help the patient find the other side. (after Tibballs 2006: 544)
2. Sum ergo cogito. Is that putting Descartes before the horse? (Chiaro 1992: 13)
3. Alas, poor Yorlik – I knew him backwards. (Chiaro 1992: 30)

Comment

1. There are at least two kinds of echoic utterance behind this joke. Firstly it reminds us of the riddle "Why did the chicken cross the road? To get to the other side." In addition, the phrase "the other side" is more generally echoic of spiritualist discourse, where it means 'the afterlife'. The joke also depends upon encyclopaedic knowledge associated with the name of the "Dignitas" clinic, famous for providing assisted suicides to its patients.

2. There is a specific echo of the famous quotation "cogito ergo sum" and we have to know that the author of this quotation was the Frenchman Descartes. There is also an echo of the idiom *to put the cart before the horse*, here given the pronunciation of a Frenchman.

3. The primary echo is from Hamlet's gravedigger scene "alas poor Yorick – I knew him, Horatio", where Hamlet remarks on the unearthed skull of the late court jester. But, since backwards *Yorlik* spells *Kilroy*, there is an additional echo of the graffiti featuring this name "KILROY WAS HERE".

10.8. ECHOES AND ALLUSIONS

Quotation of another well-known text is a kind of allusion. But such allusions may also be achieved by names (though not by numbers – see the convict joke in 10.2).

> Allusions involving proper names are powerful tools for creating a wide range of weak contextual effects because their meaning, in English-speaking cultures, depending on reference rather than their sense [is connotative rather than conceptual]. So names refer to tokens, not types, and the schemas they invoke are particular and individual and consequently much richer than the schemata associated with typed concepts (Goatly 2011: 176).

Alluding to another text through quotation or proper name is particularly effective in compressing information by implicating comparisons between two texts.

But allusion by name may not always be especially successful:

> The beauty of Cup football is that Jack always has a chance of beating Goliath (Terry Butcher, Tibballs 2006: 517).

Perhaps we give Butcher the benefit of the doubt – he may be implicating a comparison not only between underdogs winning cup football and giant killing, but between the Jack and the Beanstalk and David and Goliath narratives.

The humorous value of allusion has been explored by Norrick (1993: 68):

NED:	I keep hearing people call them things like hornets. Let me tell you. That dude was big enough to take off with a payload of about twenty tons.
FRANK:	Well, what do you call it?
NED:	I didn't know what to call it. I had never seen [an insect] that big.
FRANK:	Ever.
	[he he]
NED:	The only thing I could think to [call it–]
FRANK:	[He he] he he Call it "get thee hence".
NED:	Call it "Sir".
BRANDON:	Heh heh *heh* heh hehhehheh.

This alludes to the joke: "What do you call a seven-foot, three-hundred-pound bully armed to the teeth?" "Sir". Allusion can work in several ways in conversational humour. Successfully weaving a familiar expression from a different text or script into a new text gives the childlike pleasure of finding familiar phrases in an unexpected context (Freud 1905). For example, if the custard I made is too thick, trying to pour it out I might say "Out vile jelly" alluding to the phrase used when Gloucester is blinded in *King Lear*. In the Brandon case, though, there happens to be an allusion to another joke, and some of its humour filters through too, including the pun *what do you call?*: 'how do you describe?' or 'how do you address?'. The allusion sets up a kind of metaphorical equivalence between the large bully and the large flying insect. Allusion clearly creates intimacy, because some people may not be acquainted with the original text and the allusion may pass them by. Excluding others makes those who are included closer (cf. Figure 5.2).

10.9.   JOKES: ECHOIC MENTIONS OR USES?

But what about jokes? Setting aside spontaneously occurring puns, which tend to be more context dependent (Ritchie 2004: 109), most jokes in this book are either echoic, quoted from joke books, or, if

I invented them, intended to be echoic – I would like others to quote them. As Ritchie points out, jokes are "typically repeatable in a wide range of contexts" (2004: 15). When quoted, the joke book I took them from is acknowledged, but the compilers of these anthologies can hardly claim them as intellectual property.

Moreover Attardo (1994: 147, 168) has noted the metalinguistic aspects of puns as connectors – the rules of the object language are suspended, to focus, at least momentarily, on the formal similarities (paronyms) or identity (homonyms). Norrick (1993) devotes a whole chapter to the metalingual aspects of joking. It is as though jokes never really engage with a real world in column 3 of Figure 1.2. Treating jokes as prototypical mentions explains the intuition that joking is a non bona fide, bracketed and playful form of communication, where conveying information is beside the point.

However, as Attardo (1994) points out, spontaneous jokes and humour (witticisms, 6.4.6) in the course of conversation might well be original, and can therefore hardly be a mention of a previous use, but rather are put to use themselves. Neither can one regard as mentions original jokes which have never yet been uttered, but which have nevertheless been prepared in the minds of the comedian before their performance. These are canned in the sense of being de-contextualised, but are not mentions when first used in the show.

In addition, even the typical canned jokes, which *are* mentions, may be reworked and modified in a conversational context, with varying degrees of integration into the discourse, just as stock witticisms, also echoic utterances, can be used for greeting or valediction: e.g. "Speak of the devil", "See you later" "Not if I see you first" (Norrick 1993: 28). Oring (2003) cites examples of jokes deliberately stored for use in an argument. So, in any case, we have to consider a cline of cannedness (cf. Norrick 1993: 14). Moreover, the fact that formulaic jokes can be re-worked into novel forms as secondary humour suggests that the novel form is more of a use than a mention ("What's red or green, has a core and is eaten?" "An apple." "Oh, you've heard that one!").

Nevertheless, it is often essential to humour that different voices be detected in the discourse, and that one be identified as less than serious, even echoic. If not detected, the incongruity on which humour depends is lost on the hearer (Priego-Valverde 2009). A contrast needs to be recognised between the use (bona fide communication) and the mention (non bona fide communication), in other words, between a propositional attitude of seriousness/belief, in contrast to a propositional attitude that is less than serious – an invitation to accept the illogical/absurd/fantastic or whatever (Priego-Valverde 2009: 168–9). One of Priego-Valverde's examples, adapted, goes as follows:

> A: no but actually I think it's best if you learn at first in a driving school and then hmm:
> B: (*laughing*) oh, yes, it's clear a driving school is ideal to pass the driving test
> A: yeah but to learn the basics and how to start a car and so on and afterwards we will drive it on a parking lot
> B: (*smiling voice*) we didn't find anything better at that time huh (*laugh*)
> A: (*laugh*) no because actually it is damned hard to teach someone how to start the car, hmm, you see, it's hard to explain

B attributes to A's first utterance a meaning not intended by A, and pretends that A has just said that a good place to learn to drive is a driving school. B pretends to believe it and to believe that A could actually have said something so obvious, to have broken the quantity maxim so blatantly. B's speech here involves three kinds of enunciators (Es), that is, voices/characters: E1 corresponding to a fictitious A who has uttered a truism; E2 corresponding to a fictitious B believing that A's purpose was to state this truism as though it gave new information; and E3, a facetious B laughing about all this. From the ensuing dialogue it is clear that A does not recognise the existence of these fictitious voices nor the facetiousness of B's utterance, and therefore goes on to justify herself. Her final laugh is polite laughter as a concession to B, though she has not understood the nature of B's original double-voiced remark (Priego-Valverde 2009: 172–3).

10.10. SUMMARY

Building on Gricean theory, this chapter gave a detailed account of Relevance Theory. It began by showing how enriching vague expressions, disambiguation and assigning reference are essential to produce an explicit proposition, and how, furthermore, to go beyond this explicit proposition, inferencing is involved in hypothesising the speaker's attitude and implicatures. The chapter proceeded to explain "relevance" as a comparative measure, that is, contextual effects – creating new implications, or strengthening/eliminating existing assumptions – divided by processing effort. The usefulness of the deductive logic of Relevance Theory for humour theory was then demonstrated in analysing several jokes. Comparison was made with Grice's theory, especially the absence of any equivalent to the maxim of quality. The chapter next approached the question of how knowledge is stored in schemas and accessed for implicature, and how this relates to the clash of schemas in incongruity theory. Relevance Theory's treatment of echoic utterances was discussed. I touched on the reporting of speech and the way different levels of discourse operate in narrative jokes, and acknowledged allusion as a rich resource for humour. Finally, I broached the question of whether jokes and irony are echoic mentions or real uses of language.

Discussion

In an earlier chapter on register and genre, we explored the social contexts in which discourse occurs. An early objection to Relevance Theory was that, without a model of social context, relevance becomes a nebulous concept (Clark 1987). Do you think one needs a highly developed notion of social context in order to use Relevance Theory to understand how humour works, or are jokes relatively independent of their context? How might your arguments relate to the question of jokes as mentions or uses?

Suggested Readings

- Sperber and Wilson (1986/1995) is, of course, the canonical account of Relevance Theory. Blakemore (1992) is a more accessible textbook.
- Goatly (2011: chapters 5 and 10) explores how Relevance Theory and genre/register theory might be combined in interpretation, taking metaphor as a case study, including its humorous uses.
- Jodlowiec (1994) and Curcó (1996) are interesting discussions and exemplification of Relevance Theory as a tool for understanding humour interpretation.
- Schank and Abelson (1977) is the classic text on scripts, frames and schemas. Greene (1995) gives a much simpler account of schemas and particular frame theory.
- Raskin (1985) is the foundation text on which the theory of incongruity or script-opposition is based, the opposition between the real and the unreal, the normal and the unexpected or the plausible and implausible. This has an interesting follow-up in Attardo and Raskin (1991), which focuses on developing a model for determining how jokes may be identified as identical or different. Various references to the latter have been made throughout this textbook.

- Bakhtin's theory of dialogism, already mentioned in the suggested readings for Chapter 1, is also relevant to the representation of speech and echoic utterances. Robinson (2003: chapter 4, and 110–23), discussing Derrida on "iterability" and aspects of Bakhtin's theory, suggests that all utterances are to various degrees echoic.

11 Lexical priming: information, collocation, predictability and humour

In Chapter 10 we focused on pragmatic theories which emphasised ideational or conceptual meanings and regarded communication as the efficient transfer or implication of information-bearing propositions. But just as we balanced the ideational/conceptual meaning of semantics in Chapters 3 and 4 with other kinds of meaning in Chapter 5, including the interpersonal, so the last section of Chapter 9 balanced the co-operative principle with the politeness principle. To begin this chapter, I revisit the ideational–interpersonal distinction in the context of information theory and the concepts of entropy and redundancy. The chapter proceeds to discuss collocational predictability as a way of introducing Hoey's theory of lexical priming. Taking a hint from his book, I show that ambiguity (entropy) is much overestimated, and that, indeed, many of the jokes and humorous texts in this book depend upon the overriding of the most obviously primed meanings.

11.1. PREDICTABILITY AND INFORMATION THEORY

As noted earlier (1.5), grammatical/function words carry less information than lexical words because they are more predictable. Technically, information is measured in bits, short for binary digits. One bit of information is carried by a symbol which has 50% predictability, as in binary computer code, notated 0 or 1. A symbol or unit of meaning which is 100% predictable carries no information, and is completely **redundant**. A symbol which is highly unpredictable carries a great deal of information and can be called **entropic**.

We obviously need redundancy in communication for various reasons (Fiske 1982). It is, firstly, a way of identifying errors. Writing a cheque, for example, we give the amount in figures, but, to guard against mistakes we also write the amount in words, repeating information already given (breaking the maxim of quantity). Writing the words fulfils a second function of redundancy: a precaution against noise, that is, anything obscuring the signal. Supposing my handwriting of numbers is unclear with 5s and 6s indistinguishable, or my tears on the cheque for student fees smudge the figure 6. The written version compensates for this noise. Since the words version is longer than the numerical version, and both convey the same information, it must itself be more redundant: *five* uses four symbols and *six* three, whereas 5 and 6 use just one. So, if in doubt, we always check the amount written in words.

Thirdly, redundancy is necessary for overcoming semantic or pragmatic unexpectedness in messages. I have repeated in several publications the radical idea that economic growth in mature economies is economic cancer (Goatly 2000, etc. etc.). I might have to continue repeating it, until others start repeating it in more widely read publications.[1] The markers of dispreferred seconds outlined in Chapter 8 obviously increase the redundancy of the message, suggesting that the preferred second is more expected than the dispreferred, not only with questions and denials, but also with offers and requests.

Fourthly, more interpersonally, redundancy can enhance audience-friendliness and politeness. We saw how phatic functions are realised by tautologies such as "Here we are" or "It's me". Greetings, as adjacency pairs, like "Hello" "Hello" have no information content, only an interpersonal phatic function (though some US fundamentalist Christians prefer the spelling "Hallo"). These polite conventions, making interlocutors feel secure, are part of a pattern of conventional communication which preserves the comfort zone, in contrast to entropic communication which is less comprehensible and might disturb us from our cliché-ridden thought and behaviour. Rituals and liturgies are the most obvious expressions of cultural redundancy. But they are matched by your average folk-song: the redundant words and grammatical structures omitted in the text below can be predicted following the conventions of the genre.

> I gave my love a cherry that has no stones
> ....chicken................b........
> ....ring...................end
> ....baby.........'s not crying
>
> How can there be a...............................
> ....
> ....
> ....
>
> ....when it's blooming it...............
> ....pipping...................
> ....rolling......................
> ....sleeping...................

Paradoxically, the high predictability makes the unpredictable elements much more noticeable. The repetitive formulae found in joke genres may have a similar social comfort and solidarity effect (Attardo 2001: 85).

Headlines are informationally prominent, comprising, with the lead, the summary of the story that follows (van Dijk 1986), and are graphologically foregrounded as well. So it is hardly surprising if they incorporate puns, allusions, metaphors, decomposed clichés seldom found in other parts of news stories. All these devices create an unpredictability, a pithiness, and density of information (Alexander 1997: 96). We noted in Chapter 10 that allusion is a powerful way of achieving multiple contextual effects, which are therefore informationally rich (Bucaria 2004: 280–1).

Such highly entropic texts or text elements run the risk of conveying nothing or being hopelessly ambiguous. Not only headlines, but classified ads, instructions like recipes, internet chat or other texts using abbreviations, filter out redundant features.

> WILLIAM KELLY WAS FED SECRETARY (Bucaria 2004: 293)

Even inserting a 1-bit article *the* before "FED" succeeds in disambiguating.

> Wasp nests destroyed £20. OAPs £15. (*Yours* magazine, Tibballs 2006: 494)

A more redundant version would read "You can have any wasps' nests destroyed by our company for £20, or if you are an old-age pensioner for £15". There was an anecdote in the 1990s about feminists turning up to a WISE conference (Women in Science and Engineering) only to find it was a BNP-organised rally (Welsh, Irish, Scots, English). (Not the Banque Nationale de Paris, but the British National Party.)

In Chapter 7, on metaphor, I introduced Giora's theory of irony and humour, with its interesting relation to information theory. She claims that well-formed discourse observes the graded-informativeness requirement "that each proposition be more (or at least not less) informative than the one that precedes it. A message is considered informative to the extent that it has properties unshared by the previous message, which in turn allow it to reduce possibilities by half" (Giora 1995: 244). As discussed, irony and jokes both violate this requirement. Jokes end with a markedly informative message causing the hearer "to cancel the first unmarked interpretation upon processing the second marked one". So there is no gradual progress in informativeness but "the passage from the least – to the most – informative message is abrupt and surprising" (Giora 1995: 256).

Suddenly high degrees of informativeness may relate to the pleasurable economy of psychical expenditure of jokes.

> If therefore we derive unmistakable enjoyment in jokes from being transported by the use of the same or a similar word from one circle of ideas to another, remote one ... this enjoyment is no doubt correctly to be attributed to economy in psychical expenditure. The pleasure in a joke arising from a "short circuit" like this seems to be the greater the more alien the two circles of ideas that are brought together by the same word – the further apart they are, and thus the greater the economy which the joke's technical method provides in the train of thought. (Freud 1905: 120)

Bergson's three mechanisms of humour – repetition, inversion and interference in a series (Attardo 1994: 58) – can also be interpreted in terms of predictability and information. Repetition decreases information, inversion and interference increase it. I already suggested humour depends upon a mismatch between the normal proportion of text/processing and the amount of information derived (10.2), with shaggy dog stories (e.g. 'The Green Light') at the uninformative extreme (cf. Chiaro 1992: 58).

11.2. COLLOCATION AND PREDICTABILITY

A parallel way of introducing entropy into discourse is to use unusual or unpredictable collocations. Dylan Thomas, transforming the idiom *once upon a time* to "once below a time", surprises us and invites us to explore the metaphor theme POWER IS HEIGHT to implicate our subjection to time's dictates. Introducing the unpredictable so it stands out against the normal background of expectations is called **foregrounding** (see Leech 2008).

The following joke illustrates how internal foregrounding works.

> Two Irishmen were digging a ditch directly across from a brothel. Suddenly a rabbi approaches the front door, glances around and dashes inside. "Ah, will you look at that?" one said to the other. "What's our world coming to when men o' the cloth are visitin' such places?" A bit later, a Protestant minister walks up to the door and quietly slips inside. "Do you believe that?" the workman exclaimed. "Why,'tis no wonder the young people today are so confused, what with the example clergymen set for them." An hour later the local parish priest arrives and quickly enters the whorehouse. "Ah, what a pity," the digger said, leaning on his shovel, "one of the poor lasses must be ill."

The internal foregrounding is obvious here, as the first two clergymen visiting the brothel are condemned for their visits, whereas the third escapes criticism. Externally, however, by the conventions of the narrative joke genre, we expect a deviation in the third episode, so there is no foregrounding. Imagine the ending "Ah what a pity! Even the Catholic clergy, who should be celibate, send the wrong message to our young people about sex". This would be externally foregrounded but internally predictable and backgrounded. Foregrounding relates to one of the logical mechanisms involved in the processing of jokes – the figure–ground reversal (Attardo and Raskin 1991: 305).

An extreme form of collocational predictability can be found in echoic utterances, and we already discussed humour which depends upon less predictable foregrounded variations on them, e.g. "Cleanliness is next to impossible". Any formulaic conventional texts, highly predictable in grammatical (semantic) structure, like the folk song above, are open to subversion: (1) "Give a man a fish and feed him for a day. Teach a man to fish and feed him for life" → (2) "Give a man a fish and feed him for a day. Give a man two fish and feed him for two days" (Thomas Goatly, personal communication). Apparently similar, we have (3) "Build a man a fire and he'll be warm for a day. Set a man on fire and he'll be warm for the rest of his life" (Terry Pratchett, Carr and Greeves 2006: 105). These two variations on the original epigrams differ in terms of foregrounding and predictability. (2) is rather redundant; one only has to multiply the number of fish and the number of days by two to derive the second sentence. However, it is externally foregrounded, something less predictable is expected in such epigrams. (3), by contrast, has the internal unpredictability and foregrounding which (2) lacks. Externally it looks predictable, except that semantically one expects the second sentence to confer benefits on the person mentioned.

Activity 11.1

Explain how predictability and redundancy relate to the following joke.

"How many men does it take to tile a bathroom?"
"I don't know. It depends how thinly you slice them."

Comment

This depends upon two familiar formulaic collocations. The first is a joke formula: "How many men does it take to X a Y", e.g. "How many men does it take to change a light bulb" with answers like "Three. One to hold the ladder, one to hand the bulb up the ladder, and the other to replace the bulb". However, in the genres of do-it-yourself or cookery we often ask questions such as "How many eggs does it take to make omelettes for three people?" or "How many rolls of wallpaper does it take to paper a room 12 feet by 10 feet by 8 feet?", to which the answer is simply a number or quantity. In this particular text we expect the joke formula because humans are mentioned in the first noun slot, rather than ingredients or materials. However the second kind of collocational formula ensues, creating a genre incongruity (Simpson 2003), though the refusal to give an answer, a dispreferred second, is accompanied by an account.

Just as interesting are deliberate attempts to increase entropy and information levels but where the predicted collocations are slightly less formulaic, constituting a range of possibilities.

Activity 11.2

Look at the following texts and predict the most likely collocations to fill the blanks.

1. Smoking is one of the leading causes of _____. (Carr and Greeves 2006: 10)
2. Sex is one of the most wholesome, beautiful and natural things _____ ___ _____. (Steve Martin, Carr and Greeves 2006: 171)
3. In Pierre Elliott Trudeau, Canada has at last produced a political leader worthy of _____ (Irving Layton, Tibballs 2006: 648)
4. "Come back to my place for coffee!" Sorry, I have to study for my _____ test. (Tibballs 2006: 525)
5. I've had more women than most people have _____. (Steve Martin, Carr and Greeves 2006: 173)
6. "If your father could see you now he'd turn over in his _____," said the mother turkey. (Tibballs 2006: 66)
7. Isn't modern technology wonderful? I remember the excitement when we were the first family in our street to have cordless _____.

Comment

Table 11.1 shows the predictable ranges of collocation in the second column and the actual humorous collocation in the third.

In other cases the predictable meaning is cancelled out, not by the collocation, but by the following sentence:

> I can still enjoy sex at seventy-five. I live at seventy six, so it's no distance. (Bob Monkhouse, Carr and Greeves 2006: 174)

Humorous poetry often depends upon rhyme, and the best rhymes combine phonological expectedness with semantic unpredictability. Byron stretches this unpredictability to its limits in a couplet from *Don Juan*:

> But oh! ye lords of ladies **intellectual**,
> Inform us truly – have they not **henpecked you all**?

Table 11.1. *Predictable and unpredictable collocations*

Example	Collocation	
	Predictable redundant	Unpredictable entropic
1	*cancer/heart disease/ etc.*	"statistics"
2	*humans can enjoy/in human life/God gave us*	"money can buy"
3	*the name/ the nation/respect etc.*	"assassination"
4	*maths/biology/driving/law/ etc.*	"blood"
5	*teeth/hairs on their head/had hot dinners/*	"noses"
6	*grave*	"gravy"
7	*telephones*	"pyjamas"

The converse applies where the expectation of a rhyme is defeated, but where, nevertheless, the sense fulfils expectations:

> Roses are red, violets are blue
> I'm schizophrenic and so am I. (Blake 2007: 13)

Rhythm, too, is important in creating fulfilled expectations – except in the humorous verse of Ogden Nash, and in the following:

> Mary had a little lamb
> She also had a duck
> She put them on the mantelpiece
> And let them have a cup of tea.

Moreover, sound patterning contributes to the lexicalisation of humorous collocations, whether compounds – *arty-farty*, *snail mail*, *gender bender*, *greedy guts* – or humorous idiomatic similes – *up and down like a whore's drawers*, or *up and down like a prostitute's pants* (Blake 2007: 64). The sound-patterning makes these more easily remembered than, say, "up and down like a whore's pants".

Advances in lexical computing allow us to calculate the frequency of collocations. Interestingly, the most prevalent lexical word collocations for *joke*, in Wordbanks Online[2] are in descending order:

> *sex, make, like, said, made, just, practical, thought, making, laughing, old, told, little, telling, get, butt, good, laugh, laughed, bad, people, funny, think, time, playing, cracking, big, says, heard, dirty, makes, cracked, cruel, best, crack, private, first, racist, running, yesterday, meant, expense.*

These collocations highlight important aspects of humour theory: the potential creativity of jokes (*make, made, making*); their newness (*old*) and the suddenness associated with their understanding, even if they are packaged or canned (*crack, cracking*); the mental processes necessary for their recognition/understanding (*thought, think*); the importance of response (*laughing, laugh, laughed*), including evaluation (*funny, good, best, bad*); their aggression or victimisation of targets (*butt, racist, expense, cruel*); their echoic/metalingual nature as mentions or quotations (*said, told, telling, says, heard*); their potential for intimacy/ exclusion (*private*); and also their treatment of taboo topics (*sex, dirty*). Perhaps the most significant collocations are *playing* and *just*. The first suggests non bona fide non-seriousness. However, the claim that it is "just a joke" may well be a disingenuous defence against the aggression or disciplining inherent in much joking behaviour (Billig 2005), or its distorted expression of an all too serious and therefore repressed desire (Freud 1905).

11.3. COLLOCATION AND TEXT-LINGUISTICS

Chomsky is probably the most famous linguist alive, and most traditional semantics and pragmatics developed in conjunction with his linguistic theory or bore its influence. His theory had three modules, with syntax central and autonomous, while allowing a place for semantic and phonological modules. Componential feature analysis, selection restrictions, logical approaches to conceptual meaning were all part of the Chomskyan project, or built on it. And Deirdre Wilson (personal communication) sees relevance-theoretic pragmatic theory as a supplement to the Chomskyan tri-modular system. I already voiced some objections and doubts about this traditional approach at the end of Chapter 5. In particular I critiqued it for (1) its outdated objectivism, (2) its failure to deal with vagueness and fuzziness of meanings, (3) the problems it encountered in reaching a consensus among native speakers on the necessary and optional components of meanings, because of (4) its de-contextualisation from co-text and experience of reference to the world, and (5) failure to take into account the dynamic nature of meanings in texts and the meaning changes brought about by them.

An alternative theoretical approach, which might be called text-linguistics, addresses some of these problems. It is associated with linguists like the late John Sinclair, and Michael Hoey with his theory of lexical priming, the focus of the rest of this chapter. This theory adopts a different perspective on the relationship between data and abstractions from Chomsky's, and tries to refrain from imposing analytical categories from the outside until the physical evidence has been examined. The Chomskyan tradition appeals to the intuition/intro-spection of an ideal native speaker as evidence to uncover linguistic and grammatical competence, a set of rules. But the text-linguistic tradition appeals to evidence of actual usage in context, based on an authentic corpus of texts, and investigates probabilities more than rules. Both traditions have their strengths and weaknesses.

The problems of the Chomsky tradition lie mainly in the nature of the evidence. Intuition and introspection are quite often unreliable: what people think they say and what they actually say are often different. Phoneticians long ago showed that informants who claim never to "drop" /h/ in their utterances, routinely do so with pronouns like *he*. But the same applies to our intuitions about grammar. Moreover, corpus data often throws up patterns that we never had intuitions about, for example the fact that *afford* usually occurs with negative polarity. Moreover, different users of the language have different intuitions (as apparent from Lehrer's attempts to discover the semantic components for 'bottle'). And in particular contexts or co-texts grammatical patterns may occur that one's intuitions would rule out.

Chomsky's views on language acquisition are particularly pertinent to this chapter. He argues that there is an innate language instinct, because such is the poverty of data to which infants are exposed they could never derive from it the grammatical rules of their first lan-guage. This theory has been convincingly questioned (e.g. Sampson 2005), and priming theory, within the text-linguistic tradition, claims, on the contrary, that repeated exposure to collocational and other patterns is precisely what enables us to both learn our grammar and use it in an idiomatic way, with a proper feel for the language.

One problem with the text-linguistic tradition is that intuition in any case has to be used for evaluating evidence from corpora. More-over, how large do we have to make corpora before we capture all the generalisations we want? One can make larger and larger maps, but taken to its logical extreme one would simply let the countryside stand for itself. However large a corpus may be, it can never hope to capture more than a fraction of all the text continuously produced in a lan-guage, so that any generalisations from that data are necessarily partial.

For instance, in the first edition of the COBUILD Dictionary, the first to use an extensive computerised corpus for lexicographical purposes, the corpus happened to contain William Golding's *Lord of the Flies*. One of the meanings listed for *maze* was 'confusion' on the strength of the example from that novel "lost in a maze of thoughts". The second edition omitted this meaning, as the corpus was now larger, and this literary example was seen as a "distortion" of normal usage.

This brings us to a second weakness. The nature of the corpus might disguise facts about the world (W) as facts about language (M (F)) (Figure 1.2). For example, the probability of *afford* occurring with negative polarity, e.g. "we cannot afford", could hypothetically be skewed by the fact that newspapers from a time of economic decline constitute a large proportion of the corpus, in which case this "fact" is more a fact about the state of the world than a guide to the possibilities of usage. A related problem is that corpus data of what has actually occurred does not capture the potential for what might occur. One of the strengths and emphases of Chomsky's work is the creativity of language, its potential to form totally original sentences. Sometimes the text-linguistic tradition downplays the creativity of the language user, by suggesting, through uncovering patterns of collocation, that we are more constrained than we believe.

11.4.   LEXICAL PRIMING AND COLLOCATION

Michael Hoey begins his book *Lexical Priming* (2005) with the following examples:

(1)   In winter Hammerfest is a thirty-hour ride by bus from Oslo, though why anyone would want to go there in winter is a question worth considering.

(2)   Through winter, rides between Oslo and Hammerfest use thirty hours up in a bus, though why travellers would select to ride there then might be pondered.

Though both these are grammatical, only (1) sounds natural, because in (2) the collocations are unusual. He therefore suggests that collocation should be a concern of linguistics.

Hoey (2005: 6–7) demonstrates that it is the frequency of normal collocations which make (1) more natural than (2), by presenting collocational frequency data from his own corpus, as in Table 11.2.

His conclusion is that the following collocational sequences are relatively predictable:

> *thirty–hour–ride–by–bus–from*
> *though–why–anyone–would–want–to–go–there*

Hoey explains such collocational patterns in terms of the psychological phenomenon of **priming**. Every word-form, in this

Table 11.2. *Actual collocations and less frequent alternatives*

In + *winter*	507	*through* + *winter*	7
30/thirty + *hour*	35		
bus + *ride*	53		
ride + *hour*	12		
ride + *from*	121		
by^bus	116	*in^a^bus*	15
by^bus^from	7		
though^why	24		
why^ anyone^ would	28	*travellers^would*	13
why^anyone^would/should^want to	23		
want^to^go	355		
want^to^go^there	15		
would want	573	*would select*	21

(Note that ^ means 'followed by'.)

theory, is mentally primed for collocational use. Tabossi explains and illustrates the term as follows:

> When a word is recognised (i.e. its entry becomes activated), activation automatically spreads to entries close to it … This phenomenon, often referred to as lexical priming, is reflected in the shorter time required to identify a target (e.g. *nurse*) when it follows a word (prime) semantically related to it (e.g. *doctor*) (Tabossi 1989: 27).

Highly probable completions tend to be responded to faster than less probable ones, e.g. with decreasing probability "She cleaned the dirt from her shoes/hands/terms" (Tabossi 1989: 28–9).

One could suggest that, much as in theories of ostensive definition where sense is a by-product of reference (4.7, Putnam 1975), so in priming theory, grammar is a by-product of collocation. Moreover, just as grammar varies according to genre (recipe instructions leave out objects, headlines omit articles and finite past tense verbs) so priming is genre specific. For instance, *recent* only primes us for *research* in academic writing and news reports. Hoey sums up:

> The notion of priming … assumes the mind has a mental concordance of every word it has encountered, a concordance which has been richly glossed for social, physical, discoursal, generic and interpersonal context. The mental concordance is accessible and can be processed in much the same way that a computer concordance is, so that all kinds of patterns, including collocational patterns, are available for use (2005: 11).[3]

Notice, moreover, that in this theory, priming can be recursive, so that collocational phrases activate their own primings.

11.4.1. Priming hypotheses

Hoey puts forward the following priming hypotheses. Every word is primed so that it has: (A) collocates; (B) associations with semantic sets, e.g. [NUMBER] ^ *hour* ^ [JOURNEY]; (C) associations with pragmatic functions, e.g. *sixty* is primed to occur with expressions of approximation, *about, around* etc; (D) textual semantic associations, occurring as part of predictable semantic relations, e.g. *sixty* tends to be involved in contrast or as a problem in problem-solution structures; (E) grammatical functions or colligations, e.g. *pondered* is much less frequent as a past participle following *have* (present perfective tense) or *be* (passive), than as simple past tense; (F) association with grammatical categories, e.g. *bully* and *blackmail* tend to fit into the pattern PERSON(S) + BE + *blackmailed/bullied* + *into* + V-ing; (G) textual collocations in terms of cohesion – some words are more likely to form cohesive chains than others; (H) textual colligations which concern positioning in the discourse, e.g. 208 of 307 instances of *sixty* in Hoey's data are in the theme, 200 are the first word of the sentence, 9% are the first word in the text.

The most relevant priming hypothesis for a theory of humour is:

> (I) When a word is polysemous, the collocations, semantic associations and colligations of one sense of the word differ from those of its other senses.

Long before Hoey, John Sinclair (1991: chapter 3) pointed out the statistical correlations between different senses of the same word and their grammar. Different forms of ambiguous words, such as *decline, declined, declining, declines*, tend to correlate with different word classes as in Table 11.3.

Moreover, different meanings tend to correlate with different forms of the lexemes, different grammatical categories and different grammatical structures. *Decline* meaning 'refuse' can be transitive (but no passives occur). 33% of tokens in Sinclair's data are transitive. 43% are

Table 11.3. *Form and word-class correlations for* decline*

	Verbal	Nominal	Adjectival
decline	14	108	0
declined	76	0	0
declining	38	0	26
declines	8	1	0
TOTAL	136	109	26

Table 11.4. *Word-form, voice and tense for* decline* *'refuse'*

'refuse'		
active verb		
75% *declined*		
92% simple past		

followed by infinitive clauses, e.g. *to do so.* Nine "intransitive" clauses with *declined* are text-transitive, i.e. what is declined can be found earlier in the text. In the meaning 'refuse', 75% of tokens are in the form *declined*, and of these 92% are simple past tense (rather than past participle), as in Table 11.4.

By contrast, when the meaning of *declined* is 'become smaller' or 'deteriorate', 50% of the time it occurs in the present perfect tense as past participle.

So typical instances would be:

- I declined the invitation.
- I declined the invitation to spend a holiday with them.
- She invited me, but I declined.
- Standards of English have declined over the years.
- The numbers of students going to Australia have declined.

(Sinclair 1991: 44–51)

Sinclair and Hoey conclude that ambiguity of language in use is a rarity. Compare *He has a problem drinking*, meaning 'finds it difficult to drink', with *He has a problem with drinking/a drinking problem*, usually meaning 'has a problem with alcoholism' (Hoey 2005: 82).[4] As Tabossi puts it:

> One might assume that the dominant meaning of the ambiguity has already achieved activation from context prior to its occurrence, in such a way that, as soon as the word is actually presented, its primed meaning will become available, whereas its subordinate meaning will be inhibited (Tabossi 1989: 38).

Hoey advances the following three sub-hypotheses, that in potential cases of ambiguity:

1. The rarer sense of the word will be primed to avoid the collocations, semantic associations and colligations of the more common sense of the word.
2. Where two senses of a word are as frequent as each other they will both avoid each other's collocations, semantic associations and colligations.

Table 11.5. *Colligation, collocation, association and the meanings of* consequence *(+ and − indicate absolute presence or absence, negative and positive indicate probabilities)*

	Consequence = 'result'	Consequence = 'importance'
Collocation with *any*	−	+
Collocation with *of*	−	+
Colligation with subject and complement	Positive	Negative
Semantic association with LOGIC	+	−
Semantic association with NEGATIVE EVALUATION	+	−
Pragmatic association with DENIAL	−	+
Textual colligation with theme	Positive	Negative

Hoey gives evidence for these two hypotheses with the ambiguous word form *consequence* meaning 'result' or 'importance' (Table 11.5).

3. Where (1) and (2) do not apply the result will be humour, ambiguity, or a new meaning combining the two senses.

The sub-hypothesis (3) is obviously important in explaining humour. Raskin (1985: xiii) points out, for example, that "Deliberate ambiguity will be shown to underlie much, if not all, of verbal humour" (quoted in Ritchie 2004: 40). Ritchie (2004: 94–5) also admits, "The need for there to be a 'most OBVIOUS' reading of any ambiguous forms is also fairly conventional (if not fully understood theoretically)". It is hoped that this chapter goes some way towards explaining this obviousness more theoretically.[5]

11.5. AMBIGUITY, HUMOUR AND THE OVERRIDING OF PRIMING

Simpson (2003), in writing on satire, has already paved the way for developing a theory of humour based upon priming. One of the clearest illustrations of how his theory of satire works is the following:

Olympic Drug Shock
BY OUR OLYMPICS CORRESPONDENT **ANNA BOLIC-STEROID**

THE entire Olympic movement reacted with shock and dismay today after a leading athlete arriving in Sydney was found not to be taking drugs.

"I stupidly thought I could win by sticking to the rules," said the disgraced star. "I now accept that training hard and eating sensibly was not the way to win and that I've let everyone from my pharmacist to my drug dealer down."

(From *Private Eye* 1011; September 2000, p. 22)

Activity 11.3

Since news values the unpredictable, what is paradoxical about the unpredictability in this spoof?

According to Simpson, the priming (set-up) is echoic of a particular discourse schema (genre) with a topic content – i.e. a tabloid news report of illegal drug-taking which brings disgrace on an athlete. This echoic phase is fractured by a dialectic (incongruity) created by the text, engendering an oppositional irony through the use of the unexpected "not" – "was found *not* to be taking drugs" (Simpson 2003: 135–6).

It has long been realised that false-priming or garden-path phenomena are one logical mechanism of humour/jokes (Attardo and Raskin 1991: 306). For instance, consider the joke "Bush has a short one; Gorbachev has a long one; the Pope has one but doesn't use it; Madonna doesn't have one. What is it?" "A second name." We are increasingly primed to think "one" refers to a penis, since a salient association of the Pope is (the profession of) celibacy, and Madonna is a prototypical female.

11.5.1. Linguistic theories of humour theory and ambiguity ▪▪▪▪▪▪

In Chapter 1 I adumbrated an incongruity theory of linguistic humour, introducing the terms set-up, disjunctor and connector, which I resorted to in a fairly superficial way throughout the book. It is time to elaborate a little on verbal humour theory in this final chapter. We consider the General Theory of Verbal Humour (GTVH) (Attardo and Raskin 1991; Attardo 2001), which grew out of the Semantic Script Theory of Humour (SSTH) (Raskin 1985), as well as a more recent development in the same incongruity tradition, Ritchie's (2004) Forced Re-interpretation (FR) Theory of Humour.

Attardo and Raskin (1991: 325) advanced a generative model of humour, diagrammed in Figure 11.1, where the top four elements are content, and the bottom two are tools.

Attardo (2001: 71–4) illustrated this generative model to answer the question "When do two different joke texts actually represent the same joke?" He investigated "light bulb" jokes such as "How many Californians does it take to screw in a light bulb?" "Ten. One to screw it in and nine others to share the experience." This is identified as a

SCRIPT OPPOSITIONS (SO)

LOGICAL MECHANISMS (LM)

SITUATIONS (SI)

TARGET (TA)

NARRATIVE STRATEGIES (NS)

LANGUAGE (LA)

Joke Text

Figure 11.1. A generative model for jokes

light bulb joke by SI, screwing in a light bulb, and NS, question and answer. As for the other elements, the LA has a set wording: a question of the form *How many* + 'person', followed by an answer of this form: 'number', usually *1*, + *to screw in the bulb and* 'number X to do something else'. The target (TA) can be any identifiable social group. The logical mechanism (LM) may vary but will be connected to a stereotypical trait in TA, presumably an implicated premise leading to the implicated conclusion involved in getting the joke. The script opposition, from which all the other elements are ultimately derived, may be smart/ dumb, in many cases, but in others normal/abnormal to include the Californian types.

The connection of this model to the areas of semantics and pragmatics so far covered in this book is clear enough. In earlier chapters (2, 3 and 4) we focused on the conceptual ambiguities of language (LA) at different linguistic ranks, and also social and inter-personal meaning clashes (Chapter 5). In Chapter 6 we discussed at length the generic structures of jokes (NS). LM has been one of my preoccupations, particularly focussed upon in Chapters 10 and 9, where I used the deductive logic of Relevance Theory to illustrate the false logic of jokes.

Such false logic (Nash 1985) or pseudo-plausibility (Chafe 2007) is repeatedly mentioned in humour theory. Attardo and Raskin (1991: 307) make the strongest possible claim for its importance: "Every joke must provide a logical or pseudo-logical justification of the absurdity or irreality it postulates", and they suggest ambiguity, paralogic and analogy as examples of the logical mechanisms involved. A good example is "Suicidal twin kills sister by mistake", which depends upon an analogy between the difficulty the general public would have in distinguishing two identical twins and the difficulty one of the twins has in distinguishing herself from her sister.

As this chapter focuses on text-linguistic notions of priming and collocation, we should highlight observations made in humour theory about the NS/LA, the organisational properties of humour texts. Firstly there is the question of the foregrounding of punchlines. Attardo (2001: 59) recognises that humorous lines are semantically and pragmatically marked in the text, being positioned where they attract attention and are easily retained, with punchlines by definition located in a prominent (final) position appropriate to their informativeness (Manetti 1976). Secondly there is the double cohesion of humorous texts. Using a bottom-up model à la Kintsch, Attardo (1994: 68–9) shows how the isotopies of the text can be created through disambiguation (for instance, by applying selection restrictions on possible meanings) to produce coherence, through redundant or repeated semantic categories (1994: 76). The defining feature of jokes is that they create a variation or opposition of isotopies, a kind of double coherence. This is because humour, according to the theory, has to fundamentally involve Script Oppositions (SO).

Ritchie (2004: 50) takes up a discussion of the dynamism of text structure and its relationship to script/schema opposition, obviously involving priming: "the effect is created (or at least exaggerated) by the temporal sequence and manner in which the scene is described or revealed, with earlier stages of the text establishing expectations to be violated or tensions to be released". But the major element in the Raskin-Attardo and Ritchie models to explore here is incongruity, or script/schema opposition, since ambiguity and its amplification is a main plank of a lexical priming approach to humour.

In Ritchie's Forced Reinterpretation model "the set-up has two different interpretations, but one [SU1], is much more obvious to the audience, who do not become aware of the other meaning, [SU2]. The meaning of the punchline [PL] conflicts with this obvious interpretation, but is compatible with, or even evokes, the other, hitherto hidden, meaning [SU2]. The meaning of the punchline can be integrated with the hidden meaning [SU2] to form a consistent interpretation [I] which differs from the first obvious interpretation" (Ritchie 2004: 59). Furthermore, these elements have the following properties:

OBVIOUSNESS:	SU1 is more likely than SU2 to be noticed by the reader.
CONFLICT:	PL does not make sense with SU1.
COMPATIBILITY:	PL does make sense with SU2.
CONTRAST:	There is some significant difference between SU1 and SU2 (or possibly SU1 and I).
INAPPROPRIATENESS:	I is inherently odd, eccentric or preposterous, or is taboo, in that it deals with matters not conventionally talked of openly, such as sexual or lavatorial matters, or forbidden political sentiments. These differ in terms of which norms are being flouted: those of everyday logic – leading to absurdity – or those of socially acceptable discourse – leading to taboo effects (Ritchie 2004: 61).

Ritchie (2004: 54–5) doubts that the incongruity is ever resolved. Because of the oddness of I, we simply replace one incongruity with another. Crucially, for a priming theory of humour, the contrast in Ritchie's model depends upon prediction. He uses as an example the joke already mentioned: "Isn't modern technology wonderful? I remember the excitement when we were the first family in our street to have cordless pyjamas" (Arnold Brown, Ritchie 2004: 101). Obviously the collocations would predict *phones/telephones*. Ritchie captures this by pointing out that it may be helpful to include details or choose phrasings which support or suggest the 'non-hidden' (more OBVIOUS) interpretation. At the least, nothing in the set-up must draw attention to the 'hidden' interpretation.[6] Ritchie may, however, be going too far when he claims nothing in the set-up must rule out the 'hidden' (less OBVIOUS) interpretation (Ritchie 2004: 104). Priming may more or less do so.

11.5.2. Kinds of ambiguity in jokes and their primings

In this section, which is a kind of climax to this book, I select one or two jokes from each of the main semantic and pragmatic areas covered in the course of this book and investigate, from concordance data, how various kinds of priming relate to the joke.

Speech act ambiguity

> I asked my date what she wanted to drink. She said "Oh, I guess I'll have champagne." I said, "Guess again." (Slappy White, Carr and Greeves 2006: 147).

The question here is what kind of speech act are we primed for, in Hoey's terms, what kind of pragmatic function is *I guess I'll* primed for. Concordance lines suggest an association with either prediction in general or the announcement of an action in the near future by the speaker. The predicted state of affairs may be undesirable.

Prediction

- I don't get to go as much as I'd like, but when I stop playing **I guess I'll** be able to go for the full season.
- "**I guess I'll** just have a family," she said.
- It's been four years now, so **I guess I'll** never really know the truth of what happened out there.

Undesirable prediction/reluctant action

- I'd like a good coonhound, but **I guess I'll** have to settle for a snotty-nosed kid instead.
- **I guess I'll** get used to it.
- **I guess I'll** have to take my chances on the train.
- And then they get to the end and they look around and go, "Well, **I guess I'll** just go back".

Announcement of imminent action by speaker

- His wife came back with the coffee and we thanked her and she looked at our faces and said, "**I guess I'll** get lunch started".
- "Well, then, **I guess I'll** love you and leave you," he said brightly as he put on his coat.
- **I guess I'll** get Angie's skipping-rope out and work out down the basement.
- "**I guess I'll** ride out on a bicycle as fast as I can and look for somebody with a pick-up truck to get me the hell out of here," Bernie Woodall said.

Note too that imminent actions by speakers are associated with material processes "get lunch started", "leave you", "get", "ride out".

Given these general priming patterns, the most obvious pragmatic interpretation of "I guess I'll have champagne" is an announcement of what the girlfriend intends to do immediately, i.e. "have", that is, 'drink' champagne, a material process. This would fit with it being the second part of an offer–acceptance adjacency pair. However, the boyfriend's "Guess again!" undermines these pragmatic associations.

Referential ambiguity and vagueness

> Did you know you're eight times more likely to get mugged in
> London than you are in New York City. It's because you don't live in
> New York City. (Jimmy Carr, Carr and Greeves 2006: 9)

Apparently *you* in the structure *you are^*[NUMBER]*^times^more^likely^to* is
almost always a generic use, referring to people in general, e.g.

- And it is worth bearing in mind that **you are** 13 **times more
  likely to** win £100,000 on the national bingo game than on the
  lottery.
- **You are** 10 **times more likely to** have a fatal crash on a country
  lane than on a motorway.
- We found out that **you are** three-and-a-half **times more likely to**
  respond to Botox if you are not overusing an acute medication.

This phrase, obviously enough, encodes (rather than primes) the
semantics of making a contrast, but in Hoey's terms also primes the
pragmatic function of expressing general meanings, of which generic
you is a part.

However, in many cases, the general reference is made more specific
by adverbials:

- In Canada, where bears occasionally prey on people, **you are**
  67 **times more likely to** be killed by a domestic dog, and 374
  times as likely to be killed by lightning.

This is the case with the concordance line closest to the joke:

- The simple fact is that if you are an adult living in parts of
  Glasgow **you are** three **times more likely** to die tomorrow than
  if you live in Arundel.

This, by the specification of the *if* clause, can much less easily be
transformed into a joke, than the first example:

- And it is worth bearing in mind that **you are** 13 **times more
  likely** to win £100,000 on the national bingo game than on the
  lottery, especially as you never buy a lottery ticket.

Inferential or schematic ambiguity

> My sister had a baby. We would have company over and she'll be there
> with her breast out, feeding him ... cereal or whatever.
>
>   . . .
>
> I said, "OK". So I'm pushing him through the park, and he's crying ...
> because I forgot the stroller.

This joke, depending on inferencing involving the schemas for breast feeding, and taking an infant for a walk in the park, reveals its priming through collocational data. Consider the T-score[7] for collocations of *breast*: *milk* has a T-score of 16.14, and is the fourth most frequent noun collocate after *cancer*, *women* and *risk*. Alternatively, we can focus on the collocations for *feeding*. Suppose we filter the concordance lines for *feed** by looking up to five words left and right ($-5/+5$) for the word-form *breast*. If the resulting filtered lines are re-filtered ($-5/+5$) for *milk*, there are 23 hits, but filtering them for *cereal* gives no hits. There is a strong priming association between *breast*, *feed* and *milk* so that they tend to form a lexical set, reflecting an underlying schema in which 'cereal' plays no part.

Let's now investigate the schema-based inferencing activated by *pushing him through the park*. We can look at the collocational data for the lemma[8] *push**, filtered for the word form *baby* up to 4 places to the right ($+4$). This gives us 56 concordance lines. Eleven of these form the pattern [PERSON] ... *push** (...) *baby* (...) ^ *in* ^ {determiner} (...) ^ *stroller* (4 tokens) | *buggy* (3 tokens) | *carriage* (2 tokens) | *pram* (2 tokens), e.g.

- ... a young woman smoking a cigarette hurried along, pushing a baby in a plaid umbrella stroller.
- A father pushes a baby in a stroller past the arched windows of the Lenape Building ...

According to priming theory we can say that *push** (...) *baby* (...) ^ *in* is primed both for the semantic set association of [PERSON] ^ and ^ [WHEELED-NON-MOTORISED BABY VEHICLE], and for grammatical category association with [PERSON =] SUBJECT/AGENT ^ .... ^ DETERMINER ^ [WHEELED-NON-MOTORISED BABY VEHICLE =] PREPOSITIONAL COMPLEMENT.

The association between 'pushing' and 'baby' and 'stroller' or its synonyms is even higher when *baby* is the premodifier of the wheeled-chair: *stroller* (11) | *carriage* (11) | *buggy* (2) | *pram* (1) as in 25 of the 56 concordance lines, e.g.

- Mrs Pellegrini remembered a cloud of dust as she pushed a baby buggy across the development's dirt roads.
- He was suspicious of everyone, including women pushing baby strollers.

In total these account for 36 out of the 56 lines for the lemma *push* filtered for *baby* up to 4 words to the right ($+4$). This is confirmed by the word sketch data from Wordbanks Online for *stroller*, which gives us 38 instances of *stroller* as the object of *push*, and 41 instances of *stroller* with the noun premodifier *baby*.

Schematic ambiguity

> If we **try several different positions** and I shoot from six or seven angles, I'm sure you'll be pleased with the results.

This is one of the ambiguities in the joke about the photographer mistaken for a sperm donor using natural insemination. When we investigate this phrase, the priming essential to Mrs Harris's mistake is clear-cut. Ten of the twelve concordance hits for this phrase refer to positions of the body during sex (the others refer to football).

- We have **tried different positions**, sexy underwear, candlelight in the room and me talking dirty.
- **Try different positions** and experiment with feathers, silky sheets, silk scarves and eating food off her naked body.
- You should also **try different positions** for oral sex, and asking her what's best is always a good bet.
- She won't **try different positions** – she says the missionary is fine – but I'd like to be a little bit more adventurous in the bedroom.
- Carey tends to **try different positions** if he is not playing to form, and I will be surprised if he does not move away from the Cork man at some stage.

To prime for photography one would be inclined to the phrase *from different positions* which yields these three examples to do with optical viewing angle:

- Try drawing the same tree ... **from different positions**.
- When you see a real landscape it registers as a composite of many images seen **from different positions**, each one reinforcing the other.
- "Parallax" in general refers to the angle through which an object seems to be displaced when viewed **from** two **different positions**.

So here the priming of *try different positions* is extremely effective in misleading the woman up the sex schema garden path. If we regard *different positions* as polysemous and therefore potentially ambiguous, we see that the collocations and more specifically colligations differ: *try* [VERB] *different positions* [OBJECT]; *from* [PREPOSITION] *different positions* [COMPLEMENT]. This confirms Hoey's meta-hypothesis (I) (11.4.1).

Generic ambiguity

Let's consider the earlier example of the *Private Eye* spoof about the shock of an Olympic athlete not taking drugs (11.5). Hoey's hypotheses can't help us much with identifying the priming for a news report in a popular newspaper, as he omits any priming hypothesis about register/genre, perhaps because this would only apply to specialised lexis. Nevertheless, the use of white space, the capitalisation, font size and grammar of the headline, and the minor sentence "By our Olympic Correspondent", including the register-specific noun *correspondent*, are sufficient to prime this genre. It is rather the content of this news report which overrides the priming. The collocation of *athlete**, *take** and *drugs* is well established in news discourse, with thirteen hits, e.g.:

- Bans from two years up to life could be imposed beginning March 1 on managers, coaches or doctors helping **athletes** to **take** performance enhancing **drugs**.
- **Athletes take drugs** so that they are cleared just before a competition.
- Last week the head of the US sports drug agency made the claim **athletes** were **taking** performance-enhancing **drugs** "in all sports, in every country in the world".
- I replied: "I think, potentially, every **athlete** is **taking drugs**."

Olympic filtered (−5/+5) for *shock* gives us eight concordance lines. The most relevant extract is probably:

Games Greek lifter drug shock
WEIGHTLIFTING; ATHENS **OLYMPIC** GAMES 2004, 21 AUGUST 2004

BRONZE medal weightlifter Leonidas Sampanis has failed a drug test ... Two women – Indian lifter Thingbaijam Sanamacha Chanu and Uzbek shot-putter Olga Shchukina – were thrown out after positive drugs tests.

In the context of these primings the "not" of the parody becomes highly unexpected. Paradoxically, since drug taking by athletes appears to be so common, it loses the news value of unexpectedness, and the absence of drug taking in an athlete then becomes unexpected and newsworthy!

As for the last part of the *Private Eye* report "I've let everyone from my pharmacist to my drug dealer down", one could predict something like

> ... he phoned Manly board members yesterday to tell of Walker's drug result ... Walker said ... "I would like to have finished my career in a better way. I **have let down my** family, the Manly fans, my manager Wayne Beavis and the club."

This suggests that, at least in the genre of news reports about athletes/ sportsmen drug taking, *have let down* is primed for an association with the semantic set [MANAGER/TRAINER/FAN/FAMILY] as its Object colligate, rather than [PHARMACIST/DRUG DEALER].

Grammatical ambiguity

> Throwing acid is wrong in some people's eyes. (Jimmy Carr, Carr and Greeves 2006: 44)

Several types of priming are relevant to this joke. Though it may not be exactly ungrammatical to have *throw* + object without a direction adverbial, it is colligationally unusual. Of a hundred-line sample of *throw** in active voice we only have two or three examples outside this pattern, namely:

- If you fail to come up with a word you have to **throw** a dice.
- They'd mess around on the river, **throwing** rocks, playing in the water.

The other exceptions are the technical sporting examples, such as

> He also **threw** an interception and went 1–for–5.

or the metaphorical idiomatic ones

> Ashe could have **thrown** enough dirt to focus official attention.

This grammatical category priming, an expectation of an adverbial following the Object/Goal of *throw**, probably needs activating for the ambiguity to be detected. However, a further collocational/semantic set association helps: *throw* filtered for *acid* (−3/+4), with fifty hits, primes especially for *at/in/into/on* X's *face* (18 lines), but also, minimally, for *in* X's *eyes* (2 lines), e.g.:

- They were then placed in trance and instructed to **throw the acid into the face** of an assistant.
- At about 7.55 pm, two black men called at the address and, after the young woman answered, she had battery **acid thrown in her face**.
- A painter and film producer blinded during a mugging attack in New York – sulphuric **acid was thrown into his eyes**.
- He can have them **throw acid in your eyes**.

This priming makes possible the unexpected meaning 'It is wrong to throw acid into the eyes of some people', which by standard implicature of the maxim of quantity gives us 'it is not wrong to throw acid into the eyes of all people'. In this interpretation "in some people's eyes" is an adverbial of direction modifying "throw acid". But this unexpected meaning has to compete with the equally unexpected interpretation 'In some people's opinion it is wrong to throw acid' with its odd standard implication 'it is not wrong to throw acid in everyone's opinion'.

This latter interpretation with the meaning 'in some people's opinions' is also primed, as observed in the thirty-five lines of concordance data for *wrong* filtered first for *eyes* (−5/+5), and then in *in* (−5/+5). The most common pattern here is negative (16), mostly in the form *can/could do* ^[NEGATIVE] ^*wrong*^*in*^ [PERSON/POSESSIVE] ^*eyes*, (14). But there are also five lines where the polarity is positive:

- He would arrive home furious with me, he would listen to my phone calls and then when I stammered at him or did the slightest thing **wrong in** his **eyes** he would throw cans of beer at me.
- Dietz testified Yates knew her actions were **wrong in** the **eyes** of the law, society and God.
- That relationships outside marriage were completely **wrong in** the **eyes** of the Church.
- What passes for **wrong in** most people's **eyes** is different for what passes as wrong in Parliament.
- "There was no point because it was the chain of command who were, **in** my **eyes**, doing **wrong**."

Cleaning ladies can be delightful. (Ng 2005: 23)

Out of the twenty-two hits we have only one with *cleaning ladies* in theme position followed by a relational process verb such as *to be*.

RUSSIAN **CLEANING** ladies are like cats

Moreover when *cleaning lady*, singular, occurs in theme position it generally has definite and/or specific reference:

- Mrs Annie Maguire, a north London **cleaning lady**, and her family were very unlikely terrorists.
- So I thought well it's quite safe my **cleaning lady**'s upstairs you know.
- I was surprised that my **cleaning lady** ... was also intrigued.
- My **cleaning lady** is not happy.
- My **cleaning lady**, who is from Brazil, is depressed and won't clean my house.
- The **cleaning lady** was a DEA agent working under cover.

On the whole, therefore, *cleaning ladies*, as a phrasal compound, is primed for textual colligation with rheme position in the clause, not theme position, especially when followed by the verb *to be*. I suppose these priming facts are what facilitate treating it as a free phrase meaning 'the act of cleaning ladies', on which the joke depends. In this case we do not override the priming but rely on it to highlight a potential ambiguity.

Decomposition – folk-etymology and ambiguity

Proverbs
Let's consider first the decomposition of proverbs.

> Cleanliness is next to impossible.

The whole proverbial idiom "Cleanliness is next to godliness" is by far the most common in the concordance lines for *cleanliness is next to ___*, in fact fifteen out of twenty times. However, it is interesting that the remaining five lines involve humorous substitutions, including the one we are analysing:

- He is "completely incapable of looking after himself", an animal for whom **cleanliness is next to** impossible.
- **Cleanliness is next to** hilarious in this brush with the reality of TV.
- "**Cleanliness is next to**," Jesus mumbled, sniffing himself, "demonic possession – known as schizophrenia unto the Pharisees."
- **Cleanliness is Next to** Catliness. Like the insane women who love them, cats insist on a clean place to shit.
- 'Cause **cleanliness is next to** freakiness.

Notice that only the first two use an adjective, and thereby plug into the prime *next to* + adjective.

Idioms
> "Listen, honey, you and I were meant for each other."
> "Save your breath for your inflatable date." (Tibballs 2006: 524)

Of the twenty-seven hits for *save your breath* the compound phrase is twenty-four times either the whole clause and/or occurs after the subject. So it is primed for rheme position. For example:

- "**Save your breath**, because I don't love you!"
- "If you're going to tell me about Spud Harvey, **save your breath**."

In these examples the idiomatic meaning is a speech act formula[9] with the pragmatic association of advice against speaking – either a pre-refusal or a pre-empting of an announcement, respectively.

Of the three other lines, two suggest that this idiom had earlier been truncated from the form *save your breath ^ to* infinitive, and the third does not have the idiomatic speech act formula meaning:

- But what did Father used to say about **saving your breath** to cool your porridge?
- I intend to go through with it, Nora, so you may **save your breath** to cool your porridge, as Father used to say.
- That's when I realised that long-distance relationships (or to **save your breath**, LDRs) define our twenty-something generation.

The point of the humorous put down is that it is in theme position and kind of undoes the truncation, though with a prepositional phrase not an infinitive clause, and by doing so allows both the idiomatic and non-idiomatic meaning simultaneously.

Compounds

> My mum's a lollipop lady. By which I mean she has a very long thin body and a big round red sticky head. (Harry Hill, Carr and Greeves 2006: 78)

Collocations of lollipop $(-0/+1)$ give a T-score for *lady* (first lexical item) of 8.31, for *man* (second) 5.15, and for *ladies* (third) 4.12. The vast majority of these mean 'children's road-crossing supervisor' suggesting a phrasal compound. But there is also the relatively high statistical likelihood of *sticks*, *people* and, more to the point, *heads*. Here are the examples of the latter:

- On my back doorstep I have a standard bay on a straight, clean trunk with a rounded **lollipop head**.
- But images of these women are often airbrushed beyond belief and those **lollipop heads** are usually miserable.
- So come on, girls, let's stay fit and healthy but ditch our love affair with the **lollipop heads**.
- Kate, now 29, has always been a champion of curvy women in a world full of size-six **lollipop heads**, but now her own image was becoming more and more muddied.

So we have a weak priming for *lollipop* as a premodifying metaphor whose grounds are the shape of the head and the body, rather than a metaphorical interpretation based on a metonymy: the shape of the top of the pole held by such ladies helping children cross the road. But the strongest collocational priming is clearly exploited in order to be overridden by a metaphorical interpretation.

Pseudo-morphs
Decomposition creating pseudo-morphs also depends upon interesting priming patterns.

> I've got a stepladder. A very nice stepladder, but it's sad that I never knew my real ladder. (Carr and Greeves 2006: 41)

Six out of seven concordance lines have *step-* with the meaning 'related by re-marriage' – "step-daughters", "step-daughter", "step-father (2×)", "step-mum", "step-parents and step- and half-siblings". However, "step-ladder", the other example, is fully lexicalised with the meaning 'a ladder consisting of two sloping parts attached at the top, so that it can be folded or carried', so any subliminal priming by the prefix is ignored. However, the collocation of *know* (...) ^ *my* ^ *real* collocates semantically for [PARENT/NAME], as follows:

- Nobody **knows** who **my real** mom and dad are.
- I don't **know my real** parents.
- I am relieved to know the truth at last but I have no wish to **know** who **my real** father is.
- I was adopted by the most wonderful man but it still affects my life that I don't **know** who **my real** father is.
- Never **knew my real** parents.
- I did not **know my real** name then, so for some years I grew up in a missionary school, just as my father and grandfather had done.
- I don't think anybody really **knows my real** name.

The frequent semantic association with [PARENT] creates an alternative priming which activates the previous priming of *step*, originally suppressed by the lexicalisation of *stepladder*.

Polysemy/Homonymy

> Two birds are sitting on a perch. One says "Can you smell fish?"

Of the eleven hits for *on a perch* all have the meaning 'an area or object above the ground for a bird to rest on' (8), or a widening of that meaning 'a high position occupied by humans' (2), or a metaphorical transfer of that meaning (1). None of these incidences refer to a fish.

- As a hawk landed **on a perch**, the trap would collapse and enclose the raptor in wire mesh.
- I cannot sleep **on a perch**!

This suggests more evidence for hypothesis (I) – the collocations with *on a* all but obliterate the ambiguity.

STOLEN PAINTING FOUND BY TREE

A random sample of a hundred concordance lines from Collins Word-banks Online for *found by* is instructive. First of all we can eliminate the thirteen cases where it precedes nominalisations, e.g.

- More than one married man in St Botolph's has got to places where he wouldn't care to be **found by** being mistaken for the Sheriff in bad light at a distance.

And also eliminate those two cases where it is part of a phrasal compound, e.g.

- Perhaps the propensity to a hangover is evolution's way of pre-venting man from bingeing on alcohol **found *by* chance** in this way.

We are then left with the following semantic sets after *found by*:

> ^ [PERSON] × 83, e.g.
> They told me I might probably get my head broken, and would possibly be **found by** somebody dead in the Cowgate Burn.
> ^ [EQUIPMENT] × 2, e.g.
> ...their bodies were **found by** a mini submarine, still in the wreckage of the helicopter on the seabed.
> ^ [PLACE] meaning 'next to' × 6, e.g.
> WILY Wendy from Romford, Essex, claimed she needed money to pay vet fees for an injured labrador she **found by** the roadside.
> ^ [TIME] meaning 'before' × 4: e.g.
> The second climber was **found by** 8 a.m. and the third was recovered by 10:30 a.m. Friday morning.

On the basis of this sample, the semantic set association for the element following *found by* is more than twelve times as likely to be [PERSON or other AGENT] than [PLACE]. So in this humorous headline we are primed for AGENT after *found by*, but this is incongruous because trees are not usually selected as agents for the process of finding.

Homography

> "Why are disabled parking spaces always empty?"
> "Because people wanting to use them have invalid parking permits."

In cases of the adjective *invalid* /ɪnvælɪd/ used predicatively, X *be invalid* (Table 11.6) or attributively *invalid* ^ noun (Table 11.7) the semantic

Table 11.6. *Word-sketch collocation data for* invalid *(adjective) used predicatively*

Word form	#	T-score	Word form	#	T-score	Word form	#	T-score
patent	19	6.03	**licence**	4	2.97	ruling	3	1.85
referendum	6	4.26	**will**	5	2.78	result	16	1.69
error	12	3.81	**vote**	14	2.73	**contract**	7	1.46
claim	26	3.8	conviction	3	2.5	damage	5	1.46
petition	3	3.71	conclusion	3	2.37	**poll**	3	1.06
constitution	6	3.33	marriage	7	2.05	ticket	3	0.76
election	39	3.08	request	3	2.05	**law**	8	0.51
license	3	3.0	panel	4	1.95	**agreement**	3	0.29

Table 11.7. *Word-sketch collocation data for* invalid *(adjective) used attributively*

[OFFICIAL/LEGAL DOCUMENT/RECORD]			[LOGICAL PROCESS]		
Word form	#	T-score	Word form	#	T-score
passport	8	4.59	comparison	5	3.62
signature	6	4.56	assumption	4	3.3
ballot	11	4.27	perception	3	2.9
entry	15	4.03	argument	3	1.34
key	11	3.88	claim	4	1.1
vote	6	1.51			
ticket	5	1.5			

association is [OFFICIAL/LEGAL DOCUMENT/RECORD], boldened, or [LOGICAL PROCESS].

This means that when we reach "permits" we are forced to back-track by its priming to take this 'not valid' meaning, whereas the set-up, with "disabled", activates the other meaning of the written form. Given the priming established by the set-up, we expect what follows *invalid* to fulfil the semantic prediction for this meaning as a premodifying noun: [PERSON/RELATIVE], or [PAYMENT] or [WHEELED-VEHICLE] (Table 11.8).

Moreover there are seventy-five hits for *disabled* filtered for *parking* (−/+5): none for *invalid* filtered for *parking* (−/+5). So we may reject the 'disabled' meaning even before we reach "permit".

Table 11.8. *Word-sketch collocation data for* invalid *(noun) as premodifier*

[RELATIVE/PERSON]			[PAYMENT]		
Word form	#	T-score	Word form	#	T-score
beneficiary	8	5.93	allowance	15	5.66
pensioner	4	4.46	pension	5	2.49
cousin	4	3.55			
mother	22	2.63	[WHEELED VEHICLE]		
wife	8	1.76	Word form	#	T-score
brother	5	1.61			
sister	3	1.48	carriage	7	4.95
husband	3	0.93	chair	4	1.9

Activity 11.4

Bucaria suggests that the potential humour in the following headline involves double priming:

   STADIUM AIR CONDITIONING FAILS – FANS PROTEST (Bucaria 2004: 289)

Explain how the priming/set up works in a double way here.

Comment

"Stadium" primes for the 'supporters' meaning of "fans", whereas "air-conditioning" primes for the 'a machine for increasing air circulation' meaning. So we identify two disjunctors and connectors. This is a clear case of both meanings being entertained and preserved, not one abandoned, despite the selection restriction violation which, in one interpretation, personifies fans.

11.6.   SOME RESERVATIONS ABOUT PRIMING THEORY AS A THEORY OF HUMOUR

I have sketched priming theory and demonstrated its relevance to a sample of jokes. But it is not without its problems. Firstly, it is doubtful whether all types of humour depend upon the overriding of priming. Take, for instance, the following example of unintentional and humorous ambiguity.

   MARCH PLANNED FOR NEXT AUGUST. (Bucaria 2004: 291, 299)

This seems to be an example needing backtracking, which neither priming, nor for that matter the set-up ^ connector ^ disjunctor model, can account for:

> In the disjunctor ^ connector configuration, it appears that contextual
> pressure fails to disambiguate a clearly parasitical reading, thus
> leading to interesting issues about priming and the relative strength
> of activation of contextually primed meanings and idiomatic ones.
> Certainly the disjunctor ^ connector configuration is strong evidence
> that the meaning not selected by context is nonetheless available to
> the speakers and is not discarded (or at least not completely or not
> immediately). Furthermore, since backtracking requires more effort,
> we can predict that humorous texts with a disjunctor ^ connector
> configuration should be as difficult to process as overlapping
> connector ^ disjunctor configurations, which do require backtracking.
> (after Bucaria 2004: 298. To avoid ambiguity I have replaced Bucaria's
> slashes, /, with carets, ^.)

It may be objected that this is an example of unintentional humour.
But the following is clearly not, yet it too seems to test both the humour
as overriding priming model as well as the connector/disjunctor model.

> It so happens that if there is any institution which is not susceptible to
> any improvement whatsoever, it is the house of Lords. (W. S. Gilbert
> quoted in Kelly (1971: 6), re-quoted in Ritchie 2004: 99)

Quite apart from its relevance to humour theory, priming theory
itself raises many contentious issues. Text is given more prominence
than world (column 3 in Figure 1.2). Clearly the state of the world can
affect linguistic behaviour, as well as vice versa. I already suggested that
afford may be primed to occur with negatives, simply because the corpus
of texts used for computing collocational patterns are made up of
newspapers published in times of economic crisis. Or, more generally,
no news is good news – negativity is a common news value (Galtung and
Ruge 1965). And why is *sixty* so often primed for contrast and part of the
problem in a problem–solution rhetorical structure? This may be to do
with the culture in which sixty has been the normal age of retirement.

Secondly, the psychological reality may be primary, and the linguistic behaviour may follow automatically as a result; that is to say,
psychological coherence is primary and cohesion is simply a by-product. Though, even if this is the case, one can still acknowledge that the
cohesion will reinforce or help produce coherence.

Thirdly, priming theory may not be radical enough. Why take the
word (i.e. orthographic word-form) as the unit? The answer is, of course,
that the computer technology for corpus linguistics can easily identify
orthographic word forms. But only if the orthographic word is the unit
under consideration need one emphasise priming. The concept of
"word" may be a product of literacy (Ong 2002), and we acquire much
of our priming before we learn to read, when words or, at least, their
boundaries are unclear. Overlooking my classmate's diary in primary

school I noticed he had written, *the smorning I got up late* ...; and the following is an attested young child's utterance: *I'm seefing I can do it* (modeled on *see if [seef] you can do it*). Perhaps, then, we could take as the relevant lexicographical unit chunks of language larger than the word, especially in preliterate situations, and genres like newspapers where word-form sequences are produced and processed quickly. Words then become more like phonemes in some genres (news reporting, unscripted conversation, unscripted public speaking). Phonemes become more like morphemes in others (poetry, advertising). This questioning of the orthographic word-form as the invariant unit of lexical analysis, or the morpheme as the basic unit of meaning, would be far more radical than Hoey's theory.

11.7. THEORIES OF HUMOUR AND THE MEANING CONSTRAINTS OF LANGUAGE

There are numerous humour theories (see Martin (2007) for a useful survey). Attardo (1994: 47) suggests three families grouped under the cognitive, social and psychoanalytic (Table 11.9). It might be predicted that I would subscribe to the incongruity theory of humour. However, I actually see incongruity/contrast or the over-riding of priming as a cognitive technique for creating humour rather than an explanation of why humour occurs in society, the functions it serves, and the reason it gives emotional pleasure (Billig 2005: 65). In the short space available I would like to explore the apparently contradictory theories of humour as social control, and of liberation or release, and how these relate to language and meaning.

It is interesting that Attardo lists all the traditional social humour theories with negative names, but the psychoanalytical ones with positive. This contrasts with his discussion of social humour functions. Though these include social control by embarrassment and the communication of social norms by highlighting taboos, arguably negative, most of the functions he lists are positive – play to build social cohesion, ingratiation, creation of common ground, repair (see 6.4, Table 6.1). Indeed, over the past two decades there has been an almost obsessive emphasis on the positive aspects of humour, not only in its psychological (and physiological) effects, but also in terms of its enhancement of social relationships (Billig 2005: 10–34). The already-noted claims that humour generates intimacy (Cohen 1999) or rapport are also found in Hageseth (1988), Du Pré (1998) and Hay (2000). They all stress the empathetic, solidarity and communicative enhancement

Table 11.9. *Families of humour theories*

Cognitive	Social	Psychoanalytical
Incongruity	Hostility	Release
Contrast	Aggression	Sublimation
	Superiority	Liberation
	Triumph	Economy
	Derision	
	Disparagement	

functions of humour, with Attardo himself (1994) suggesting the role of decommitment in softening criticism and mitigating face threats.

Freud's theories of humour can be regarded as a theory of release or liberation from the psychological tension between the subconscious desires or the id, and the control over these by the superego. Freud suggests that much humour targets the sacred, the taboo and the disgusting, because these are normally topics which we repress our feelings about. Humour, then, resembles a temporary carnival, a form of rebellion against normal prohibitions. Jokes may also be ways of expressing aggression, even if our motive remains disguised by humour (Oring 2003: chapter 4). We may believe we are laughing at the technique or incongruity in the humour, whereas in fact we are laughing because the joke indirectly expresses an impulse – it releases a repressed desire in a hidden way (Billig 2005: 155–9).

Earlier Victorian theorists of humour had stressed not only its role in the release and regulation of nervous energy (Spencer 1864), but also its socially rebellious or liberating aspects. Bain (1865), for example, saw the pleasure in degrading persons of dignity as a liberation from the normal constraints which compel us to honour and respect them. Humour might, then, express a rebellion against social order (Billig 2005: 96–8). Heine's joke, as interpreted by Freud, about the poor lottery agent boasting that Baron Rothschild treats him as an equal – in fact quite "famillionairely" – implies a sly criticism of the Baron's patronising condescension. According to Freud, the technique of this joke works by combining two forms *familiarly* and *millionaire*. He calls this "condensation", equivalent to the incongruous conjunction of two opposing scripts or schemas. But the replacement of the first meaning, a compliment about the Baron's friendliness, with an implied criticism of his condescension, amounts to a substitution, involving a speech act ambiguity, and this Freud refers to as "displacement". This looks like a resolution of the ambiguity in one direction rather than another, rather than simply a disjunction.

In previous chapters I suggested that wordplay, the use of homonymic, homophonic and especially paronymic puns, as well as pseudo-morphology, are an attempt at liberation from the language code. In this chapter we have entertained the idea that the primed linguistic and discourse expectations are often overridden by humour, thereby defying convention in an act of creativity. Perhaps the greatest social control we experience is in being taught our first language, which includes acquiring its primings. Language, according to Barthes (1982), is fascist (Billig 2005: 238). It is an imposition on our bodies – our vocal apparatus is disciplined to conform to the phonological standard of our parents' speech community. And we undergo cognitive control when acquiring competence in the higher linguistic ranks extending from morphology right up to primed collocations and register/genre, which demand that we adopt conventions both of form and the relation of form to meaning and categorisation within social contexts. We explored extensively in Chapters 2 and 4, and in the present chapter, how humour might be used to temporarily undermine these conventions.

However, we do not just laugh at intentional attempts to liberate us from the code and discoursal primings. Though we laugh at paronymic attempts to undermine the code, we also target those who are unable to adapt their vocal apparatus (or minds) to its demands. Take the joke:

> VICAR: I hereby pronounce you man and wife.
> BRIDE: And you pwonounce it vewy nicely, vicar.

The inability to pronounce *r* is one reason for the humour here, the bride's failure to adequately discipline her vocal apparatus. But the humour also targets her inability to understand that in this generic context "pronounce" is more likely to mean 'announce that you are'. Moreover, she is apparently unaware that a compliment by the bride on the vicar's speech fails to conform to the generic structure of the wedding service and is an inappropriate speech act.

The fact that, on the one hand, we laugh at ingenious attempts to undermine the discipline of the language code but, on the other, at people's failures to conform to it, underlines the equivocal nature of humour's social functions. It appears to liberate, but it also controls, sometimes cruelly or aggressively. Aggression and cruelty might, after all, be desires of the id which emerge from repression in disguised form in jokes. Bergson (1900), one of the great humour theorists, pointed out this double-sidedness of humour. We laugh at rigidity, using humour to ridicule those who are too conservative to adapt, to free themselves from inappropriately predictable behaviour. Humour is the soul's attempt to overcome the rigidity of the material and the biological, to adapt and spiritually evolve (Bergson 1911). The humorous release from the rigidity of collocation is a main theme of this chapter. And yet, Bergson admits that humour often targets "unsociability", the inability of imperfectly socialised people to conform. Moreover, ironically enough, the response to humour is the rather predictable and rigid bodily response known as laughter, a response beyond our control (Billig 2005: 130–2). A further paradox is that in order to conform to social and linguistic codes we have to adapt, by abandoning our rigidity, for instance our dress and manners, or the mechanical inflexibilities of our infant phonetics – an adaptability that is beyond the best efforts of the bride.

The apparently positive functions of humour, to liberate or enhance solidarity, may, in fact, be disguises of the exercise of power. Holmes (2000) has demonstrated how bosses use joking discourse as a means of social control, especially in nominally egalitarian societies. Humour might be viewed as a coping mechanism or as a means of dealing with depression, but without challenging the (unjust) social systems which cause the depression in the first place. We may well express our aggression towards powerful politicians through humour (rather than, say, throwing shoes or grenades at them), but this does nothing to remove them from power. It's like shadow boxing. The temporary relief of tension, and fleeting sense of liberation, may, like an escape valve on a steam engine, to the contrary, divert and dissipate the pressure for real social or regime change. We may even become so dependent upon these powerful personages for our humour that we develop a fondness for them and allow them, as necessary targets, to exert an extra degree of control. The notion that we are rebelling through humour could be self-deception. Moreover, in the wider context of the economic order of consumer capitalism, humour, originally designed to question the power structures of society, is co-opted and becomes commodified as a consumer product in the form of joke books.

Billig (2005) presents an interesting sociological theory of humour. We become socialised through the threat of embarrassment. And embarrassment derives from situations in which strangers may laugh at us. So, as a child matures, parents use laughter and "teasing", a disguised form of aggressive control, in order to embarrass them, and to signal that they have indulged in inappropriate behaviour (Scheff 1997). The child thereby learns to laugh at others who find themselves in embarrassing situations, or mock them for inappropriate behaviour. Humans are unique in both being laughed at and laughing, in that order. In reproducing ridicule they may take pleasure in the subversion of the social codes, but also take revenge for the laughter previously used to control them by embarrassment. In these circumstances empathy is suspended, "a temporary anaesthesia of the heart" as Bergson puts it (Billig 2005: 43). Billig distances himself from Gofmann's theory that humour is usually a way of saving face and thereby mitigating embarrassment. We may like to think of it as positive and innocent, but much humour is a way of salving our conscience over our aggressive exercise of power.

As an example of the connection between embarrassment, humour and socialisation, Billig (2005: 230ff.) reinterprets Freud's case study of little Hans, whose parents' laughter and the consequent embarrassment disciplined him for looking obsessively at a pretty eight-year-old girl in a hotel restaurant. The adults' laughter brings about repression of Hans' sexual attraction, but it may have more complex origins. It may mask the parents' own sexual attraction to the children, a kind of reverse Oedipus or Elektra complex.

Billig's work explains a great deal of contemporary humour targeting political correctness. Since "political correctness" might be motivated by sympathy for the social groups and minorities who have suffered a history of discrimination, anti-PC jokes are possible only through the suspension of such fellow-feeling. Anti-PC humour therefore becomes the province of neo-conservatism, which tends to construct social disadvantage as a natural result of a Darwinian sociobiology, where the weak deserve to fail and might is right. In fact, it is your fault not only if you are unsuccessful or poor, but also if you are unhappy, a point underlined by theorists who believe humour has positive therapeutic value (Billig 2005: 31).[10] In this way the Right have at their disposal a larger repertoire of the "good" jokes, just as they have more of the "good" metaphors (Lakoff 1996).

11.8. AN AFTERTHOUGHT AND HINT OF A THEORY

It is something of a truism to point out that language and language use is driven by two opposing forces: the centripetal or forces for standardisation, and the centrifugal or forces of variation. If language is fascist, it is so partly by centripetally imposing standards and predictability on language users. Parents, the academy, the educational establishment, the international English as a Foreign Language industry, and copy-editors, among others, attempt to exercise their power by compelling conformity. Priming is clearly a centripetal or standardising force, pushing the language towards conventional collocation and cliché. By contrast, the kinds of humour which override priming, though dependent upon it for their disjunction, can be seen as playful attempts at creativity. Exaggerated as this tension is in these types of humour, such a tension is always present in language. As we have seen, the standardised dictionary semantics of a word are often modified when the word is used in an actual text, which sets up its own local semantic relations. There is a general fluidity of word meanings in real texts, especially in conversation, though countered by redundancy and "graded informativeness".

This variation–standardisation tension is also manifest in the degrees of play, flexibility or loosening of the ties between forms (column 1 of Figure 1.2) and their referents (column 3). Some form–referent bonds are very solid and allow little variation. This is the case with names, where, ideally, a one-to-one relationship exists between form and referent, and changing one's name can be a cumbersome business. One-to-one correspondence applies not only to names for persons, but also ships, planes, novels and the registration numbers of cars. But once we introduce sense, in column 2 (of Figure 1.2), we expand the possibilities for variation in the form–referent relationship. The same form may refer to different referents, and the same referent may be referred to by different forms. The degrees of flexibility vary, of course, according to the genres and sub-genres in which we are operating. Legal documents, the language of air-traffic control, technical and scientific texts use standardised or consistent forms for referring to the same phenomenon, e.g. the forms/formulae for chemicals or the forms used to refer to the different parties to a legal contract. At the other extreme we have literature and poetry, where elegant variation may be de rigueur. However, even here different sub-genres or individual authors use this kind of variation to different degrees – Hemingway, minimally, compared with Henry James.

This literary play in form–(sense)–referent relation is mirrored in the relationships between form and sense in columns 1 and 2. The mere act of literal categorisation by which aspects of reality are forced into classes with conventional lexical item labels, a stable pairing of sense and form, is on the side of standardisation and enables mathematics and the hegemony of quantification. Yet synonymy, like elegant variation, allows different forms to be paired with the same sense, and the converse, homonymy, polysemy and other types of potential ambiguity, allow identical forms to represent different senses, partly undermining this attempt to build order and standards. More radically, innovative metaphor by unconventional reference can eventually bring about changes in sense. Humour seems to be on the side of variation by exploiting ambiguity, making or recording mistakes (paronymy, malapropism, spoonerism, pseudomorphology, decomposition) and generally overriding priming.

In sum, standardisation and predictability is reflected both in form–(sense)–referent pairing, in form–sense(–referent) pairing and in collocational and other priming behaviour. Working against it we have elegant variation, ambiguity through polysemy, homonymy and synonymy, and humour and metaphor, all increasing variation and all potentially creative.

There is a further tension in linguistic and discoursal behaviour between arbitrariness and motivation, which connects, in quite complex ways, with the standardisation–variation tension. Names tend to be arbitrary and unmotivated in their meanings, especially as they avoid column 2 (despite attempts to re-motivate them by buying meaningful number plates or, like one of my students, Sze Ling, calling herself "Ceiling"). Form–sense pairings for lexical items constituted by one simple free morpheme are largely arbitrary, except for the relatively few iconic forms. Variation, whether through elegant variation, synonymy or homonymy draws attention to this arbitrariness. If the same form can be used for different meanings or the same meaning be represented by different forms, this seems even more arbitrary, though less so in the case of polysemy. Similarly, priming, especially collocational priming, appears demotivating – underlining one tendency of language to create semi-fixed phrases, phrasal compounds or idioms in which the original meaning of the individual orthographic words becomes partly irrelevant. By contrast, some linguistic humour through decomposition and false etymology, rather like poetry, pretends or tries to find meaning in sub-morphemic patterns. So we have extremes of genres: conversation and news reports where clichés and predictable collocations abound, with word-forms demoted to the equivalent of a collection of phonemes; and creative and ludic genres which seek out extra levels of motivation.

One of my major academic interests is metaphor, and both humour and metaphor can be creative. However, there is a major difference between them. The latter can be processed in a leisurely way so that the implications of its novel meanings are teased out, whereas jokes, if not all humour, tend to be sudden and instantaneous in their effects. Moreover, metaphor, much more than humour, potentially brings about permanent changes in meaning, even if, paradoxically, these eventually become lexicalised and standardised. But if humour liberates, its liberation is something of a fleeting illusion.

11.9. SUMMARY

After a brief introduction to the technical meaning of 'information' I discussed how redundancy might be useful both interpersonally and ideationally. I proceeded to relate predictability to collocation and other textual patterns. Contrasting Chomskyan linguistics with text-linguistics in the Sinclair–Hoey tradition, in terms of data and the role of intuition and creativity, I went on to explain a recent text-linguistic development, priming theory, which suggests that ambiguity is less common in actual text data than often assumed. I listed the priming hypotheses, drawing special attention to the claim that when the most obvious primed meaning is overridden to create an unusual ambiguity the result can be humorous. Such ambiguities were seen as necessary for the script opposition, incongruity and forced reinterpretation theories of (the mechanisms of) humour. The incongruous overriding of priming was the basis on which I explained a selection of the jokes and humorous examples from earlier in the book, both as a way of testing priming's role in humour, and giving an overview of the areas the book has covered. The chapter ended with a short discussion of the functional theories of humour as either release/liberation or social control, and I attempted to relate these to the undermining of collocational priming. Finally, I brought together a few thoughts on the relationship between humour, language, standardisation v. creativity, and motivation v. arbitrariness.

Discussion

a. Does the fact that humour creatively overrides priming suggest that priming theory and its hypotheses are fundamentally conservative and anti-creative? Is it any less creative than a theory of semantics like Chomsky's that, on the one hand suggests that grammar gives rules for producing an infinite number of different potential sentences, but which on the other rules out as semantically ill-formed sentences like "Colourless green ideas sleep furiously". The latter might, after all, allow a metaphorical or metonymic interpretation. Can you find one?

b. How methodologically sound is the reliance on computer-generated statistical data from the surface of large (often newspaper) corpora, using the orthographic word-form as the key unit? Does this distort the nature of the variability of the textual boundaries of lexemes? Does it ignore the nature of language in use and the contextual contributions to meaning through pragmatics? Does it tell you more about the world than about language as a system of meanings?

c. Corpus stylistics has been seen as having the advantage of giving evidence of how people actually use language, rather than relying on intuitions about how they think they use language. But if corpus linguistics is used to account for priming, which is presumably about the intuitions of native speakers, does this advantage disappear?

Suggested Readings

- Hoey (2005) is an obvious read for anyone interested in a fuller account of lexical priming theory. Sinclair (1991) is an indispensable introduction to corpus linguistics and the use of collocational data, which was instrumental in establishing the tradition on which Hoey builds.

- Attardo (1994), which has been a major inspiration behind this present book, is worth reading in full, but especially relevant for his discussion of the various humour theories touched on very lightly in this chapter, and for his account of the unexpectedness of the disjunctor in joke structure.

- Ritchie (2004) is a more recent development within the script-opposition tradition, elaborating a theory in which the triggering of an unexpected second script forces a reinterpretation of the text.

- Chapter 9 of Billig (2005) elaborates the theory of humour as social control through embarrassment that I sketched briefly above. Chapters 6 and 7 are thoughtful discussions of Bergson and Freud respectively, forming the basis for his own theory. The book is interesting as a whole, and redresses the tendency within humour studies to celebrate humour as a social lubricant and a uniquely human life-enhancing phenomenon, rather than a tool of, or to be used against, the powerful.

Glossary

In order to keep this glossary to manageable proportions, terms already defined in the book are not usually re-defined or explained here. (The definition of such terms is on the page whose number is bolded in their index entry.) The only exception is for terms which recur frequently throughout the book, which are also glossed and exemplified below.

A

Account A reason for not performing the preferred second part of an adjacency pair, e.g. "I have a dental appointment" as a reason for declining an invitation.

Active metaphor, *see* metaphor

Adjacency pair A pair of juxtaposed utterances or speech acts performed by different speakers in a fixed order, such that the occurrence of a particular first part predicts a range of possible seconds, e.g. "I'd like to treat you to lunch today." "Sorry, I don't think I can come, I have to go to the dentist at 1.30." This exchange exemplifies the pair Invitation ^ Refusal. Second part possibilities often consist of a **preferred second** or a **dispreferred second**, the latter identified by symptoms of psychological tension or social awkwardness, suggesting relative difficulty in performing it (not least preferred in a non-technical sense).

Affective meaning Emotional meaning, expressed through words drained of their ordinary conceptual meaning, e.g. *bloody, piss off,* or words with an **affective "spin"** though sharing the same core conceptual meaning, e.g. *help* v. *interfere.*

Affix A (bound) morpheme, attached to a word base to produce a different lexical item, either before as a **prefix**, or after as **suffix**. Suffixation often changes the word-class of the base, e.g. *complete* + *-tion* → *completion.*

Aggression A theory which suggests humour is used as a substitute for violence or as an expression of hostility, usually towards its target.

Agreement, *see* politeness principle

Allusion, *see* intertextuality

Ancillary mode, *see* mode

Antonymy Oppositeness of meaning, not to be confused with meaning opposition in general. Antonyms are generally associated with the meanings of adjectives, verbs and adverbs, e.g. 'alive'/'dead', 'buy'/'sell', 'slowly'/'quickly', which are complementaries, converses, or polar opposites, respectively. But antonymy may be expressed by complementary nouns, e.g. *night/day*.

Approbation, *see* politeness principle

Arbitrariness, *see* motivation

Ascription, *see* qualification

Assertive, *see* speech act

Assignment, *see* qualification

Association, *see* qualification

B

Base, *see* morphology

Bit, *see* information

Blend, *see* derivation

Bound morpheme, *see* morpheme

C

Canned jokes, *see also* witticism   Jokes which are stored in advance and repeated relatively independently of the context of their use, rather than spontaneous innovative jokes/humour arising out of the discourse context.

Classifier, *see* premodification

Coherence   The psychological interpretation of a text to create a consistent schema, mental picture or world. A related concept is **isotopy**. Coherence which depends upon features of the text such as co-referring expressions or sense-relations (synonymy, hyponymy, etc.) is **cohesion**.

Colligation, *see* collocation, and grammatical function priming

Collocation   The (probability of) co-occurrence of word(-forms) in a text. The collocates of a word-form may be computed by concordance programmes which specify the number of words to the left or right to include in the collocational search. **Colligation** is the grammatical connection between collocates, e.g. subject–object, subject–verb, premodifier–noun. The freedom and restriction of collocations varies with words, the **restricted**, e.g. *umbrella*[premodifier] ^ /*stand/group/organisation*, and the fixed, e.g. *rancid* [premodifier] ^ *butter*.

Commissive, *see* speech act

Componential analysis   The attempt to define meanings by dividing them into atoms of meaning or **componential features** in order to show systematic contrasts and relationships, e.g. 'kill' [CAUSE [TO DIE]], 'murder' [+INTENTION, −LEGAL, [CAUSE [TO DIE]]], 'assassinate' [+INTENTION, −LEGAL, [CAUSE [+SOMEONE FAMOUS [TO DIE]]]].

Compound   A lexical item comprising two or more free morphemes. **Word compounds** comprise one orthographic word (including hyphenated forms), **phrasal compounds** more than one.

Conceptual meaning   Synonymous with **ideational** meaning or **sense**. The logical meaning (rather than connotative, affective or social) which depends upon a word-form representing a concept, and which can be investigated through basic logical relations like entailment, inconsistency, tautology, synonymy and hyponymy. It is expressed not just by lexis, but by the transitivity systems of the clause, and is involved in the inferences derived through the (flouting of) the co-operative principle and the deductive logic of Relevance Theory.

Connector   In the incongruity humour theory, the "ambiguous" expression which connects two opposed incongruous scripts, e.g. "Why are soldiers tired on 1st April?" "Because they've just had a thirty-one-day March", "march" is the connector between the schemas for the third month of the year, and long-distance walking in formation.

Connotation   The meaning words acquire though what they refer to, rather than through their logical relationships with the meanings of other words. Connotations may be rather individual, e.g. *swede* may connote 'dinner at home on Wednesdays', the day when my mother always cooked lamb stew with swedes.

Constitutive mode, *see* mode

Contextual effects   In Relevance Theory, the effects on one's mental context of any relevant new information or communication. There are three kinds: strengthening existing ideas; eliminating existing ideas; or generating new ideas. In the dialogue "Is John strong?" "He's an athlete" the reply might convey the information 'John is strong', by interacting with my existing knowledge 'Athletes are strong' through **contextual implicature**. If 'John is strong' is conveyed, this is an **implicated conclusion**, which depends upon the **implicated premise** or **contextual assumption** 'athletes are strong'.

Contextual implicature, *see* contextual effects

Contradiction   A statement that is necessarily false, e.g. "The word-processor ate my cat".

Contrastive stress   A stress used for contrast, by placing the major intonation contour or nuclear tone before the last stressed syllable of the tone unit, e.g. |Why do you like toMATo 'sandwiches|. The nuclear tone falls on "-MAT-", not the last stressed syllable "sand-" , contrasting tomato sandwiches with other kinds of sandwich.

Conversational analysis   An ethnomethodological research paradigm which investigates patterns of discourse from the bottom up using textual data and the categories recognised by ordinary speakers of the language, rather than those imposed by the linguist or analyst. Its preoccupations are the rules governing turn-taking and the sequencing of turns into adjacency pairs and longer sequences.

Co-operative principle   A principle devised by Paul Grice stating that one should make one's contribution to a conversation adequate to its purposes by keeping in mind four maxims: **quality**, making what one says true; **quantity**, giving an adequate amount of information; **relation**, making what you say relevant; **manner**, making what you say clear.

D

Declaration, *see* speech act

Declarative, *see* mood

Decomposition   Splitting word-forms into their constituent parts. The result may be actual morphemes or **pseudo-morphemes**, amounting to a **re-analysis**. Re-analysis may be humorous (as in *wombat* 'a bat for playing wom') or a **folk-etymology** relating loan-words to known existing words or morphemes *asparagus* → *sparrow grass*.

De-contextualisation   The process of abstracting linguistic expressions from the context of use, which may be necessary in order to make generalisations about their meanings.

Definite reference, *see* reference

Defining modification   Modification which defines a subset of the referents of the noun head. For instance in "men who are suffering from prostate cancer [can nowadays often be cured easily]" the postmodifying relative clause defines a subset of men. Not all modification is defining or restrictive: in "the barren desert" "barren" is probably non-defining, since deserts are typically barren so it is unlikely to be distinguishing barren deserts from the non-barren ones.

Deixis   From the Greek, meaning 'pointing', this term covers items whose meaning changes radically according to who is speaking, where, and when, e.g. *I* means 'the speaker' or points to whoever is speaking, *now*, the time they are speaking, *here*, the place where they are speaking.

De-motivation, *see* motivation

Derivation   The process of producing new lexical items from existing lexical items: by a conversion – change of word-class without change of form (e.g. *flow* verb → *flow* noun); or by an affix (e.g. *military* → *militarise* → *demilitarise* → *demilitarisation*); or by a compound (e.g. *doghouse*) or a **blend** (e.g. *smoke* + *fog* → *smog*).

Directive, *see* speech act

Disambiguation   In Relevance Theory, one of the pragmatic procedures sometimes necessary in order to develop the coded meanings of an utterance into a full proposition, e.g. "I met him by the bank" demands the choice from two meanings of "bank", 'slope' or 'financial building'. Priming theory suggests that co-text disambiguates, except where the primed meaning is overridden by humour.

Disjunctor   In the incongruity humour theory, the textual element that triggers a shift from one script or schema to another.

Dispreferred second, *see* adjacency pair

E

Echoic utterances, *see also* metalanguage   One kind of intertextuality, where the wordings of previous texts or utterances are repeated, e.g. allusion, reporting speech, and some kinds of irony.

Effective, *see* ergativity

Elegant variation   Referring to the same referent with varying expressions, e.g. a text referring variously to the same person with "Obama", "The President of the United States", "Barack", "the incumbent of The White House", "the first mixed-race president of the US", "the tall dark gentleman in a suit", etc.

Enrichment, *see* vagueness

Entailment   A semantic relation such that if A X is true then A Y is true, but not vice versa, e.g. "John has a brother" entails "John has a sibling" but not vice versa.

Entropy, *see* information

Epithet, *see* premodification

Equation   The semantic relation in which two noun phrases have an identical referent and may therefore be equated, e.g. "David Cameron, the Prime Minister" or "David Cameron is the Prime Minister" or "The Prime Minister is David Cameron". As the last two examples show, an equation can be reversed.

Ergativity   An alternative model to transitivity for describing the semantic relationships within the clause. Ergative systems apply to a certain class of (material process) English verbs, like *cook, cool, dry* etc. Clauses with these verbs have one or two participants, i.e., just a subject participant, in which case they are labelled **middle**, or subject and object, labelled **effective**, e.g. "the porridge cooled" and "the breeze from the fan cooled the porridge". These verbs are distinct from non-ergative verbs in that the subject participant in the middle version (known as the *medium*), e.g. *the porridge*, becomes the object participant of the effective version, and the subject of the effective version becomes the **instigator**, e.g. "the breeze from the fan", replaces it.

Essential conditions, *see* speech act

Euphemism   The replacement of one expression with another less transparent expression in order to avoid offence or breaking of a taboo, e.g. *restroom* for *toilet*.

Exclamative, *see* mood

Explicature   In Relevance Theory, the making explicit of all the elements of a proposition in order to develop full propositional form. This involves enrichment, disambiguation and reference assignment.

Expressive, *see* speech act

Expressive function   The function of language which focuses on the addresser and the creation of messages expressing the addresser's feelings.

Extended metaphor   A metaphor in which more than one metaphorical lexical item from the same schema or semantic field (the source) is applied in the same text in a consistent way to a parallel literal schema (*the target*). For instance "*The beach* was the bow-stave of a bow and arrow. *The horizon* was a taut wire. *The sun's rays* were arrows." When the metaphorical schemas referring to the parallel literal schema are inconsistent we have **mixed metaphor**, e.g. "I cannot see the carrot at the end of the tunnel", with its incongruous schemas carrot and donkey and light at the end of the tunnel.

F

Face   The public self-image every member of society wants preserved or enhanced. **Positive face** is the desire to be accepted and valued by one's social group, **negative face** the freedom to be left undisturbed – freedom of action, freedom from imposition.

False priming   The stylistic device, also known as the **garden path** effect, by which the expectations set up by the text mislead the reader into activating the "wrong" schema or making irrelevant inferences, often with humorous effect. For instance in "I slept like a baby. I woke up every two hours looking for a bottle", the schema for sound sleep is replaced with the schema for alcohol dependence.

Field   In register theory, the social activity of which language is a part including the purposes and contents of that activity, e.g. the field of automobile advertising is economic, selling and buying of cars.

Finite verb   A verb which carries markers of tense and inflects, if regular, with –*s* in third person present to match a singular subject. In a multi-verb verb phrase in declarative mood the finite verb is always first; e.g. in "The duck does swim", "The ducks do swim", the singular subject "duck" determines the "–s" on "does", "does" and "do" indicate present tense, and begin the verb phrase, and hence are finite verbs.

Flouting a maxim   Breaking a co-operative principle maxim blatantly so the hearer notices the breaking. Flouts lead to an inference which would observe the maxim, e.g. in reply to the question "Is John strong?" the answer "He's an athlete" flouts the maxim of quantity, but, from background knowledge that athletes are strong, 'John is strong' is inferred, which would answer the question affirmatively.

Folk-etymology, *see* decomposition

Foregrounding   Disturbance to the expected discoursal patterns in a text. "Cleanliness is next to *impossible*" disrupts the normal ending "godliness". This is external foregrounding as the expectation is externally determined. But texts set up their own expectations, which may be defeated leading to internal foregrounding, e.g. if the rhyme scheme in the first three stanzas of a poem is ABABAB, and the last stanza uses the foregrounded ABABAA.

Frame, *see* schema

Free phrase   A phrase freely combining two word-forms representing two independent lexical items (e.g. *yellow bird*), to be distinguished from a phrasal compound where two orthographic words represent only one lexical item (e.g. *yellow fever*).

Function word, *see* grammatical word

Fuzzy concepts, *see* prototype theory

G

Garden path, *see* false priming

Generic reference, *see* reference

Generic structure, *see* genre

Generosity, *see* politeness principle

Genitive   The grammatical construction using –'s or *of*, e.g. "John's piano", "the end of the affair".

Genre   A staged purposeful activity recognised by a culture, anything from writing a sonnet to reading a computer manual. In many genres this involves discourse, with a **generic structure**, reflecting the stages of the activity, e.g. a recipe's generic structure – Title ^ Ingredients (^ Utensils) ^ Instructions (^ Preparation Time) (^ Nutritional information) (^ Serving Information) (+ Illustration). A Shakespearean sonnet is in iambic pentameter (an unstressed followed by a stressed syllable five times per line) with a rhyme scheme ABABCDCDE-FEFGG. The relationship between register and genre might be simplified as follows: **register** reflects the social context of field, tenor and mode with linguistic features at the sentence level and below, while genre in addition reflects it with a textual structuring above the level of the sentence (utterance, speech act). Roughly Genre = Register + Structure.

Gradable opposites or polar opposition   A semantic opposition involving gradable adjectives, e.g. "hot" and "cold". The test for gradability is whether comparatives like *more/–er*, or intensifiers like *very, extremely* can modify the adjective.

Grammatical category association   Priming which produces an association of a word with grammatical categories, e.g. *throw** primes for the grammatical structure ^ Object/Goal ^ Adverbial.

Grammatical function or colligational priming   The tendency of a lexical item to occur as a particular grammatical element, e.g. *pondered* is much more frequent as simple past tense than as a past participle.

Grammatical words or function words   A closed set of very frequently occurring words found in any genre or register, whatever its field content. They comprise articles (e.g. *a*), determiners (e.g. *this*), pronouns (e.g. *it, its*), prepositions (e.g. *of*), particles (e.g. *well, not*), auxiliary verbs (e.g. *can, have* as in "I have eaten" not "I have a car"). They contrast with the open set of less frequent **lexical** words which are more sensitive to field contents, comprising nouns, adjectives, main verbs and adverbs.

Grand strategy of politeness, *see* politeness principle

Grapheme   A written mark recognised as a letter in an alphabetic writing system. The exact forms may vary, as in different fonts, e.g. g, ɡ, *g*, **g**, g, *G*, which despite graphetic differences all represent the same grapheme.

Grounds, *see* metaphor

H

Homograph   A written word-form representing two different and unrelated meanings with two distinct spoken forms, e.g. *minute* meaning 'tiny', *minute* 'sixtieth part of an hour'.

Homonym   A word-form representing two different and unrelated meanings where both the written and spoken form are identical, e.g. *rock* 'sway back and forth' or 'large stone'.

Homophone   A spoken word-form representing two different and unrelated meanings with two distinct written forms, e.g. *hare, hair*.

Hyperonym, *see* hyponymy

Hyponymy   The sense relation of inclusion of one meaning inside another: *chair* is the hyponym of *seat*, and *seat* the **superordinate** or **hyperonym** of *chair*. The "a kind of" test, though ambiguous, can be used to detect hyponymy: "A chair is a kind of seat".

I

Icon   A sign that resembles its meaning, as in *splash* or *snort*.

Ideational meaning, *see* conceptual meaning

Idiom   A lexical item comprising more than one word-form, when these individual word-forms in a different context represent complete lexical items, e.g. *kick the bucket*.

Illocutionary act   A speech act such as promising, begging, asking, christening, mourning. To be distinguished from utterance acts which are simply the mouthing of a sequence of sounds, and propositional acts which involve a logical proposition.

Imperative, *see* mood

Implicated conclusion, *see* contextual effects

Implicated premise, *see* contextual effects

Implicature, *see* contextual effects

Inactive metaphor, *see* metaphor

Incongruity theory   The theory that humour arises through the activation of two scripts or schemas which are in **opposition** or incongruous. One schema is activated in the set-up of a joke, and another, less predictable and opposed schema is activated by the disjunctor, while the ambiguous connector activates both schemas.

Inconsistency   The relation between two statements, such that if one is true, then the other cannot be true, and vice versa, e.g. "I am an orphan" is inconsistent with "My parents are both alive".

Index   A sign which points to something in its context, e.g. "gentlemen's toilet" on a door indicates the existence of the gentlemen's toilet on the other side.

Indirect speech act A speech act where the grammatical mood of the clause expressing it doesn't match the act's illocutionary force, e.g. "Can you open the door?" looks like an interrogative mood question, but might be an indirect request to open the door.

Inference The process by which the hearer derives an implied message (implicated conclusion) not explicitly stated in the coded message.

Inflection The addition of suffixes to a stem in order to convey grammatical categories such as tense, aspect, plurality, e.g. *bind, binds, binding, bound*. Unlike derivation, these suffixes do not produce a different lexeme but different forms of the same lexeme.

Information Technically, information is measured by the predictability of occurrence of items in a message. One measure is the **bit** (*binary unit*), the amount of information conveyed by an item with 50% likelihood of occurrence. Totally predictable items are completely **redundant** or uninformative (e.g. the *u* in *queen*), whereas highly unpredictable elements are **entropic** showing **marked informativeness** (e.g. "statistics" in "Smoking is a major cause of statistics").

Informativeness, *see* information

Instigator, *see* ergativity

Interpersonal meaning Meaning primarily concerned with the effect on the addressee and social relationships. It may be expressed by: grammatical moods, designed for the demanding or giving of information or services; modals of obligation and inclination; lexical meanings which express degrees of power, status, contact/familiarity or the expression of emotion; the systems of appraisal; and the pragmatics of politeness.

Interrogative, *see* mood

Intertextuality The ways in which previous texts impinge on later texts. At a more general level, e.g. register or genre conventions, we have interdiscursivity. Reported speech and plagiarism are obvious types of intertextuality, as is **allusion**, where the reference, often by quotation or name, is to another particular text or person.

Intonation, *see* tone

Irony A figure of speech where the speaker draws attention to the gap between the real state of affairs in the world and the proposition the speaker has uttered, by flouting the maxim of quality. **Oppositional irony** simply creates and emphasises this gap, e.g. "Sarah Palin is an extremely well-educated woman", but **echoic irony** is the mention of a previous speaker's utterance, e.g. "As George Bush said of Iraq 'mission accomplished'." Both kinds may express dissatisfaction, oppositional irony with the state of affairs in the world, and echoic irony also with the previous speaker.

Isotopy, *see* coherence

L

Lemma The base form of a word before any (inflectional) suffixes are added to it, especially used when searching corpora, e.g. *finish** is the lemma for locating *finishes, finishing, finished*.

Lexeme, lexical item The relatively abstract concept of a word which lies behind the various word-forms instantiating it, e.g. the lexeme BE is instantiated by *am*, *is*, *are*, *was*, *were*, *being*, *been*. A lexeme has to be defined by meaning, and word-class, as well as the various word-forms that instantiate it.

Lexical word, *see* grammatical words

Lexicalisation The process by which meanings, once derived by pragmatic inference, become fixed and part of the semantics, creating a new lexical item in the dictionary. For instance, initially the word *mouse* used of a computer attachment had its unconventional metaphorical meaning worked out by inference. But, almost immediately, since it filled a lexical gap, it acquired a new fixed meaning listed in the dictionary.

Liberation The humour theory which stresses **release** from inhibition or oppression, whether psychological or social.

Linguistic relativity Whorf's theory that different languages, by using different principles of categorisation and dissection of the continuum of experience, create a reality rather than just describing it, with repercussions for social practice. For instance Thai, classifying siblings primarily by seniority rather than sex, emphasises the importance of seniority in social relationships, and the rights and responsibilities of elder siblings vis-à-vis younger ones.

Logical mechanism According to incongruity and script opposition humour theory, understanding a joke involves "logic", either general logic as in the formalisations of Relevance Theory, or a more specific logical mechanism, for instance, analogy. It may be false or **pseudo-logic**, so any conclusion is itself bizarre or illogical, for instance "suicidal twin kills sister by mistake" in which people's inability to distinguish two identical twins is applied by analogy to one of the twins who cannot distinguish herself from her sister.

M

Malapropism An error in which a word-form is mistakenly used because it is confused with a word with a similar form, e.g. "the allegory [alligator] on the banks of the Nile".

Manner maxim, *see* co-operative principle

Mapping, *see* metaphor

Marked, unmarked The **unmarked** occurrence of a linguistic item is the default option, whereas the marked is the less usual or foregrounded option. For instance, with gradable adjectives *big* is unmarked, and *small* is marked, so that the normal question would be "How big is it?", not "How small is it?"

Marked informativeness, *see* information

Marked theme, *see* theme

Medium, *see* ergativity

Mental process, *see* transitivity grammatical

Mention, *see* metalanguage

Meronymy   A part–whole relation. The meronym is part of another entity, e.g. *pedal* is a meronym of *bicycle*.

Metalanguage   Language used to talk about language, performing Jakobson's **metalingual function**, e.g. *word, answer, question*. Consider "How many syllables are there in *laboratory*?" The word "syllable" is metalanguage and the bit of language being talked about is "laboratory" which is **object language, mentioned** rather than used. The contrast between language mentioned and language used to refer or extend beyond language to the world, is known as **the use–mention distinction**.

Metaphor   Thinking of one thing (A) as though it were another (B) by exploring (X) the ways they are similar or analogous (Y). (A) is the **target**, (B) the **source**, (X) is **mapping** and (Y) is the **grounds**. For example, "The past [target] is a foreign country [source]; they do things differently there [grounds]". Metaphors may be very conventional/**inactive**, with grounds part of a new lexicalised meaning, e.g. *fox* meaning 'cunning person', or they may be original/**active**, where grounds need active mapping, e.g. *icicles* referring to the fingers of a dead man's hand – tapering shape, coldness, stiffness, etc.

Metaphor themes   Intersections of cognitive schemas manifest as patterns of conventional metaphors in the dictionary, e.g. the metaphor theme TRAFFIC IS LIQUID, instantiated by *flow, stream, filter, island, bus bay* etc.

Metonymy   A meaning relation or figure of speech caused by deletion of parts of a message and dependent upon contiguity in experience, e.g. "I drank ~~the contents of~~ two bottles of wine", bottles and their contents being experientially contiguous.

Middle, *see* ergativity

Minimal pair, *see* phoneme

Mixed metaphor, *see* extended metaphor

Mode   In register theory, the role language plays in the socially defined activity taking place. Sometimes it is minimal or **ancillary**, simply facilitating the activity (e.g. ballet lessons), in others it is essential or **constitutive** (e.g. lectures). Mode also distinguishes the medium (spoken or written), scale (dyadic, small group, intra-institutional, mass etc.) and rhetorical function (didactic, persuasive etc.).

Modesty, *see* politeness principle

Mood   The grammatical system related to the interpersonal exchange of information or goods/services, defined linguistically by the presence and order of clausal elements: finite verb (F), subject (S), a *wh*- element (W). "Did (F) the angel (S) give Mary the olive oil?" is **interrogative** mood since finite precedes subject. All interrogatives have finite ^ subject interrogatives except where a *wh*- subject precedes the finite "Who (S/W) gave (F) Mary the olive oil?". "The angel (S) gave (F) Mary the olive oil" is **declarative**, as subject precedes finite. Interrogatives demand

and declaratives give information. "Give Mary the olive oil" is **imperative** with a main verb but no finite. Imperatives demand goods/services. "What wonderful olive oil the angel (S) gave (F) Mary!" is **exclamative** since the *wh-* element is not (part of) the subject but precedes the finite. Moods are grammatically coded and distinct from speech acts which often need to be identified by inference, and the two may not match, e.g. "You went to Harbin?" is declarative in mood, but a question.

Morpheme   The smallest meaningful unit in a language, constituted by one or more phonemes. **Free morphemes** can stand alone as words, whereas **bound morphemes**, like affixes, only form words in combination with other morphemes, e.g. the *un-* in *unhappy*.

Morphology   The study of how morphemes combine to form complex words. Terms indispensable for morphological analysis are: **root** – a form that is not further analysable, the remainder after all other morphemes are removed, e.g. *act* is the root of *reactions*; **stem** – part of the word-form remaining after removing all inflectional suffixes, e.g. *reaction* is the stem of *reactions*; **base** – form to which affixes of any kind can be added, e.g. *react* is the base of *reaction*. All roots and stems are additionally bases.

Motivation, *see also* symbol.   When there is no apparent reason why the forms of a word represent a particular meaning the sign is **arbitrary** or lacks motivation – since in different languages different forms represent similar meanings, e.g. *chien*, *dog*, most linguistic signs are arbitrary. However, many languages have an initial /m/ for the words representing the concept 'mother', *ma* Chinese (and English), *mum*, *mother*, English, *mater* Latin, *mama* Italian, *Mutter* German, *mɛː* Thai, suggesting partial motivation. Perceived motivation distinguishes polysemy from homophony, e.g. metaphorical extension (TRAFFIC IS WATER(FLOW)) motivates *traffic island*. Re-motivation through false etymology may be humorous, e.g. *sparrowgrass*.

N

Negative face, *see* face

Non bona fide communication   The theory that, because humour is not communicative in the normal sense and systematically breaks co-operative principle maxims, it is not serious or sincere.

Nonce word   A word made up spontaneously, which may never be used again or enter the lexicon.

Nuclear tone, *see* tone

Nucleus, *see* tone

O

Object language, *see* metalanguage

Opposition, *see* incongruity theory

Orthographic word   A succession of letters (graphemes) separated by white space or punctuation (but not hyphens) from other letters in a text.

Ostensive definition   Defining meaning through pointing to, showing or making obvious a typical example of a word's referent. Repeated ostension may have a role in language acquisition.

P

Paronym   Words whose spoken and written forms are similar but not identical, e.g. *anglia* and *angular*, often exploited for humour or causing malapropism.

Participant, *see* transitivity grammatical

Perlocutionary effect   The effect of a speech act on the hearer. The intended perlocutionary effect of jokes is presumably laughter or smiling.

Phatic function   The interpersonal function of language when used to (keep) open psychological channels of communication. Phatic greetings like *hi, hallo,* or even *how are you?* have minimal referential function or ideational meaning.

Phoneme   A spoken sound recognised as contrasting with other sounds in a language or dialect in order to contribute to meaning differences. Phonemes as such do not convey meaning, but their contribution to meaning differences is apparent in **minimal pairs**, e.g. *cat/bat, lice/rice, bell/ball*. Second-language learners' problems with phonemic contrasts can make them humorous targets. "'Philately will get you nowhere,' as the geisha said to the amorous stamp-collector."

Phrasal compound, *see* compound

Poetic function   The textual function of language used to create extra layers of discourse patterning, whether phonological (e.g. rhythm and rhyme), syntactic (e.g. repeated syntactic structures), or semantic (e.g. extending metaphors).

Polar opposition, *see* gradable opposites

Politeness principle   Leech's interpersonal complement to Grice's co-operative principle. Its maxims are: **tact** maximising benefit/minimising cost to other; **generosity** maximising cost/minimising benefit to self; **approbation** maximising praise/minimising dispraise of other; **modesty** maximising dispraise/minimising praise of self; **agreement** maximising agreement/minimising disagreement between self and other; **sympathy** maximising sympathy/minimising antipathy between self and other. These were later subsumed under Leech's **grand strategy of politeness** – place a high value on what pertains to the other, and a low value on what pertains to the speaker.

Polysemy   Double or multiple meanings of a word-form, where these are perceived as related, e.g. the polysemy of *mouse* as 'small rodent etc.' and 'computer attachment for moving the cursor etc.' depends upon a metaphorical relation. Contrast homonymy where coincidence of form for two meanings seems arbitrary or unmotivated.

Positive face, *see* face

Pragmatic function   One of the ways in which words are primed, e.g. *sixty* is primed to occur with expressions of vagueness, *about, around.*

Pragmatics (The study of) utterance meaning, how and what a speaker means, i.e. intends, by uttering a sentence in a particular social context and how the hearer interprets that intended meaning. It is distinct from semantic meaning which concerns the meaning of sentences, as messages made up of items of the linguistic code. The main pragmatic theories introduced in this textbook are Searle's speech act theory, Grice's co-operative principle, Leech's politeness principle and Sperber and Wilson's Relevance Theory.

Preferred second, *see* adjacency pair

Prefix, *see* affix

Premodification The use of adjectives and nouns (and quantifiers, articles etc.) before the head of a noun phrase in order to modify its meaning. Premodifying adjectives and nouns divide into **epithets** (indicating a quality), either attitudinal or descriptive, and **classifiers** (designating a subclass), either ascriptive or associative; only ascriptive classifiers can be transformed into equivalent predicative clauses. As follows:

EPITHET		^ CLASSIFIER	
Attitud. ^ Descript.		Ascript.	^ Assoc.
wonderful old		*drystone*	*Lakeland* [walls]

Preparatory conditions, *see* speech act

Presupposition "X presupposes y" means 'if x is true, y is assumed to be true, and if the negation of x is true y is still assumed to be true', e.g. "He looked for John's cat" and "He didn't look for John's cat" both assume "John has a cat".

Priming The theory in psycholinguistics and text-linguistics that when a word is recognised and activated this activation automatically spreads to words nearby. The words and meanings nearby are thereby primed for occurrence when the word is subsequently encountered.

Process, *see* transitivity grammatical

Processing effort One aspect of Relevance Theory, which roughly corresponds to Grice's maxim of manner. The less the processing effort required for adequate contextual effects to be achieved, the greater the relevance; e.g. "9,460,730,472,580.8 kilometers" demands more processing effort than "light year".

Proclaiming tone, *see* tone

Propositional act One kind of act besides the utterance act and illocutionary act performed when making an utterance. The proposition, comprising reference and predication, is a basic ideational or logical construct independent of mood or particular wordings. Thus "Samuel Barber was an American composer" and "Was Barber a US composer?" are the same propositional acts though different wordings or **utterance** acts, and have different illocutionary force as assertive and directive.

Propositional attitude   In Relevance Theory the stance taken towards the explicit proposition of an utterance. The speaker's attitude to the proposition in assertives is one of belief, in directives one of desirability, in metaphor and irony lack of belief, in the latter sometimes belief in the opposite of the proposition stated.

Prototype theory   The idea that members of categories may be more or less central to the category, so membership is a matter of degree, e.g. a teddy bear is a more prototypical toy than a chess set. It connects with the idea that concepts and classes have **fuzzy** boundaries.

Pseudo-logic, *see* logical mechanism

Pseudo-morph, *see* decomposition

Punchline   The element of joke structure occurring towards the end of the joke text and which usually includes a disjunctor triggering a switch from one schema/script to another.

Q

Qualification   A semantic modification where an element is introduced that the speaker believes relevant to the identification/description of an entity. It is distinct from equation where two entities are identified as equivalent, e.g. "John is a teacher" (qualification), "John is the headmaster" (equation, because reversible). There are two kinds of qualification, **ascription** and **association** e.g. (1) *the bottle is blue* and (2) *the blue bottle* (both ascription) can be distinguished from *the ceiling fan*. Ascription may involve **assignment** as in (1), but association may not: **the fan is ceiling*.

Quality maxim, *see* co-operative principle

Quantity maxim, *see* co-operative principle

R

Radial categorisation   A kind of categorisation developing from prototype theory, involving a central case and conventionalised variations on it not predictable by general rule. Unlike in hyponymic structure, in radial structure the central case has a property not shared by the non-central case. For instance, in the semantic relationship between 'mother' (the central case) and 'stepmother' (non-central case), 'stepmother' lacks the feature [GIVES BIRTH TO THE CHILD].

Re-analysis, *see* decomposition

Redundancy, *see* information

Reference   The use of the code elements (form-meaning pairs) in the message, typically noun phrases, to identify or indicate entities in the world beyond language and beyond texts. Indefinite articles make the reference **indefinite**, and definite articles/determiners make it **definite**. Reference may be definite **specific** where the speaker expects the hearer to be able to identify the referent in the context ("my wife"), definite non-specific or **generic** where all members of a class are referred to ("the whale is the largest mammal"), indefinite non-specific referring to any member of the class ("Does anyone have a tissue?") and indefinite specific where the speaker can identify the particular member of the class but doesn't expect the hearer to be able to ("I've got a collie dog").

Referential or representational function   The function of language in which it refers to, describes or represents states of affairs in the world.

Referring tone, *see* tone

Reflected meaning   The meaning association acquired by a word through sharing its form with another lexeme, e.g. *cock* 'male adult chicken' has an association with 'penis', one reason US speakers use the word-form *rooster* instead.

Register, *see also* genre, field, mode, tenor   The semantic relationship between social context and linguistic features of the texts produced in that context. The context can be specified according to the dimensions of field (ideational meanings), tenor (interpersonal meanings) and mode (textual meanings). The closed register/genre of tennis umpiring reflects its field in technical vocabulary, e.g. "let", tenor by using family, not given, names for the players, and its mode in the ancillary role of language and the use of assertives/declarations to describe the game/announce the score.

Relation maxim, *see* co-operative principle

Relativity, *see* linguistic relativity, semantic relativity

Release theory, *see* liberation

Relevance Theory   Sperber and Wilson's pragmatic theory, developed out of Gricean pragmatics. It claims that every act of communication presumes relevance, i.e. that what is uttered will affect the mental context of the hearer, through contextual effects. The degree of relevance depends upon the number of these effects and the amount of processing effort needed to derive them, and can thus be computed as contextual effects divided by processing effort. Contextual effects subsume the Gricean maxims of relation and quantity, and processing effort covers the maxim of manner, but the theory downplays the quality maxim/truth. In addition to Grice's implicature it emphasises the importance of explicature (the making of the message or proposition complete).

Representational function, *see* referential function

Restricted collocation, *see* collocation

Restrictive modification, *see* defining modification

Rheme, *see* theme

Root, *see* morphology

S

Salience, *see also* foregrounding   The degree to which the forms and meanings of a text stand out relative to neighbouring items. Salience relates to predictability – the unpredictable/foregrounded stands out more than the predictable/backgrounded. However, salience may be related to the most likely meaning activated in the context. Often humour is achieved by using the least salient meaning of a connector.

Satiree, *see* satirist

Satirised, *see* satirist

Satirist   A communicative triad proposed by Simpson for explaining satire comprises: the satirist, the **satirised** or **target**, and the **satiree**, to whom the satire is addressed.

Schema   A mental structure where stereotypical knowledge of the world is stored. Though schema, script and frame seem interchangeable in the literature, I use "schema" to refer to knowledge of a stereotypical activity sequence, which includes **frames** for stereotypical knowledge of objects, and may also involve scripts or genres, knowledge of a stereotypical discourse activities. Script or schema or frame opposition is essential for the incongruity on which humour is based.

Scope   The extent over which semantic modification ranges. For instance, "On retirement I came to the end of my career and my real life" is ambiguous in scope. Does the scope of "end of" extend to "my real life" or only extend as far as "my career". In the former case retirement is unhappy, in the latter happy.

Script, *see* schema

Script opposition, *see* incongruity theory

Selection restriction   The semantic restrictions placed on modification, e.g. between subjects and verbs, verbs and objects, or nouns and adjectival premodifiers. So "naked" is restricted to modifying a human body (or perhaps eyes, fire/flames), "assassinate" has to have a famous person as its object, and "die" should take a living thing as its subject.

Semantic relativity   The tendency for gradable adjectives to acquire a less vague meaning relative to the referent of the noun they modify. For instance "cold" in "a cold winter" covers a different range of temperature than it does in "in a cold summer", and "big" premodifying "horse" and "rat" suggests different absolute dimensions.

Semantic set priming   The kind of lexical priming which predicts the semantic categories of a word's collocates or colligates, e.g. *hour* is primed for premodification by number and for the noun head of "journey" and its hyponyms: e.g. [NUMBER] ^ *hour* ^ [JOURNEY]

Semantics   (The study of) the meanings of sentences in so far as this can be decoded from the meanings of grammar and lexis. Semantics depends upon the relatively stable conventional form–meaning pairings of the linguistic code, more or less agreed on by speakers of a language. Semantics answers the question "what does this sentence mean?", pragmatics "what does the speaker of this sentence/utterance mean or intend by uttering it?"

Sense,   *see* conceptual meaning

Set-up   The textual element of joke genre structure preceding the punch-line. In incongruity theory it contains an ambiguous connector whose most obvious meaning is overridden by the disjunctor in the punchline.

Sincerity conditions, *see* speech act

Source, *see* metaphor

Specific reference, *see* reference

Speech act   Also known as illocutionary act. An act which a speaker performs on a hearer through discourse. Speech acts are of various categories: **assertives**, making a statement about the state of the world ("John is blind"); **directives**, an attempt to make the hearer change the state of the world ("pass me my sunglasses, please"); **commissives**, undertakings by the speaker that the speaker will change the state of the world ("I'll visit you tomorrow"); **expressives**, expressing an inner state of the speaker ("I'm glad you passed your exam"); **declarations**, which under the right institutional circumstances automatically change the state of the world ("I hereby name this ship *Bill Clinton*").

Speech act types vary in proposition type, e.g. the proposition in a directive is a future act of the hearer. To be felicitously performed, speech acts must fulfil sincerity and preparatory conditions, thereby jointly meeting the requirements of an **essential** condition. For instance, **preparatory** conditions on questions are that the speaker does not know the answer to the question, the speaker believes the hearer does know the answer to the question, it is not obvious to both speaker and hearer that hearer will provide the information without being asked; the **sincerity** condition is that the speaker wishes to know the answer to the question; and the essential condition is that the act fulfilling these conditions counts as an attempt to elicit information from the hearer.

Standard implicature   An implicature arising from assuming the speaker is observing the maxims of the co-operative principle, e.g. "I've eaten" is interpreted, if observing the maxim of relation, as 'I have eaten recently'.

Stem, *see* morphology

Suffix, *see* affix

Suspending a maxim   One way of breaking a co-operative principle maxim, when it is culturally accepted that precise information or clarity will not be forthcoming. Euphemisms are examples of suspension, as in "he's gone" for "he has just died". Jokes may be too.

Symbol   In Peirce's theory a sign which, unlike an icon, bears no resemblance to its meaning, being completely unmotivated or arbitrary.

Synonymy   Sameness of meaning. Two lexemes are seldom identical on all dimensions of meaning, but may be identical in conceptual meaning, e.g. *aubergine* and *eggplant*, identical in concept, differ dialectally.

T

Tact, *see* politeness principle

Target of humour, *see* satirist

Target, metaphorical, *see* metaphor

Tenor, *see also* register and genre.   In register theory the interpersonal aspect of the social context. Dimensions of tenor include the status or relative power of the discourse participants, their prescribed roles in the activity and their degree of familiarity with each other.

Textual colligations   The priming of word-forms for likely positioning in a text, e.g. *cleaning ladies* usually occurs in rheme position.

Textual meaning   Meanings to do with the distribution of information in a text, its organisation and ordering. It includes aspects of semantics such as generic, paragraph and theme–rheme structure, along with collocational meaning, cohesion and coherence.

Theme   In English the ideational theme, the informational starting point of the clause, is the first grammatical element to occur from among subject, object, verb or adverbial. The remainder of the clause is the **rheme**. For instance "Immediately (theme) Mary swallowed the sweet (rheme)". Placing an element other than subject as theme creates a **marked theme**. It is normal to put old information in the theme and information new to the hearer at the end of the rheme.

Token, *see* type–token distinction

Tone   Tone or **nuclear tone** is the major change in pitch or **intonation** in a stretch of speech. Generally the nuclear tone falls on the last stressed syllable of this unit, the **nuclear syllable**, otherwise it is a **contrastive tone**. English has two main tones – falling (or **proclaiming tone**, signalling information new for the hearer) and fall-rise tone (or **referring tone** signalling information speaker and hearer already share); rise-fall tone and rising tone are respective intensifications of these.

Transitivity grammatical   In Hallidayan grammar the ideational meaning of the clause is expressed through transitivity systems. These involve choosing among five or six **process** types located in the main verb: existential, relational, verbal, material, **mental** or behavioural (intermediate between mental and material). Each process selects for the participants referred to by the subjects, objects or complements of the verb. Adverbial adjuncts are circumstances not participants.

Truth-conditional semantics   An approach to semantics that identifies the meaning of a statement with the conditions in the world that would make it true. For instance, because 'coal is black' is true if and only if coal is black, the meaning 'coal is black' is coal is black. This theory makes language meaning dependent upon the state of the world and is diametrically opposed to the theories of Bourdieu, Foucault and Whorf.

Glossary

Type–token distinction   The distinction between reference to each member of a class separately or to the class as a whole. If I say "there are 245 birds in Hong Kong", I refer to types or species of birds – the total of tokens would be larger, perhaps 300,000+, e.g. 8000 sparrows, 47 black kites etc.

U

Unmarked, *see* marked

Use–mention distinction, *see* metalanguage

Utterance act, *see* propositional act

V

Vagueness, *see also* semantic relativity   An indeterminacy about the boundaries of a meaning. This may be horizontal, so that *be going to/will* are vague about the future time referred to, and *cold* meaning 'low in temperature' is vague about the temperature range involved. Or it may be vertical, using a non-specific word as in "Give me that *thing*". In Relevance Theory vagueness is reduced by **enrichment** as part of explicature.

Violation, *see also* flouting a maxim   Deliberate breaking of a co-operative principle maxim intending that the hearer should not detect this breach. The most obvious maxim to which this applies is quality in the case of lying, but it could, for example, apply to quantity/relevance too – giving people information that they will not need or that will not be relevant to them in the future, as in many education systems.

W

Witticism   A humorous remark made spontaneously in the context of a conversation which relates directly to that conversation. It contrasts with canned jokes, which are remembered and produced, with relatively little relevance to the ongoing conversation.

Word compound, *see* compound

Word-form   The shape of a word in writing and print or its sound in speech. Strictly speaking, as used in this book, it should be the graphemic or phonemic form rather than the graphetic/phonetic variations on that form, e.g. god, God, god, God, GOD, despite their graphetic variations, all comprise the same sequence of graphemes and are therefore the same word-form. The same will be true of words pronounced with different accents.

Z

Zeugma, *see also* selection restriction.   Using a word to modify two or more words when it is conventionally applied to only one of them, or is applied to each with different meanings. E.g. *bring in* and *cut* are applied both literally and metaphorically in "she brought in a bucket of coal and some advice" and my wife's advice "two things should be cut – your toenails and your glossary".

Notes

1 Introduction

1 A related pair of concepts is synthetic and analytic statements. Statements that reach out to give information about the world are synthetic uses, but statements that metalinguistically analyse object language involve analytic mentions.

2 A joke depending upon type–token ambiguity goes: "Heineken aims to eliminate competitors and create a world where there is only one beer left. It would then sell for an extremely high price at auction." The set-up suggests a type meaning, but the punchline insists on a token meaning.

3 In fact the example is more complex than this, since "I Will Not Pass This Way Again" can be interpreted as the name of a song. See later section on reference.

4 The following explanation of this model relies on Goatly 2008: 1–2.

5 I am indebted to Connor Ferris for this diagram introduced when we shared the teaching of a course on Semantics and Pragmatics at the National University of Singapore in 1991–2.

6 For further discussion, see Goatly 2007: chapter 1.

7 Native speakers of the Algonquin language Blackfoot (Niita'wahposin) claim that they seldom use nouns (Goatly 2007).

8 There is experimental evidence for this account in Vaid *et al.* 2003.

9 For a model of how different kinds of humour – satire, parody and puns – might work at different levels of discourse, see Simpson 2003: 76ff.

10 Simpson (2003: 88–9) has already adumbrated this relation by suggesting the set-up may be called a prime, the incongruity a dialectic, and the resolution a synthesis.

2 Meaning in the language system: aspects of form and meaning

1 See Chiaro 1992: 18ff. for further discussion of metathesis.

2 To see the illogicality of this you may refer to: http://www.youtube.com/watch?v=sdgCEmEZc1U

3 Semantics and conceptual meaning of grammar

1 Cases are semantic roles indicted by inflectional suffixes. There are not many in English, but *he* (nominative case), *his* (genitive case) and *him* (accusative or dative case) is an example.

4 Semantics and the conceptual meaning of lexis

1 Whether the poodle has a tail or not!

2 Blake (2007: 69) estimates that there are at least 4,000 homophones and homonyms in current English, as well as 4,000 polysemous pairs capable of exploitation for puns.

3 For more examples consult <http://www.cartalk.com/content/about/credits/ credits.html>

4 **Semantic relativity** should be distinguished from **linguistic relativity**, the theory associated with Sapir and Whorf that the concepts we think are determined by the languages we speak.

5 Attardo (2001: 108) discusses circumlocution and humorous definitions.

6 Barratts is a major builder of mass housing in the UK.

7 Though this assumes that the invention of categories cannot change the world. Foucault, Whorf and Bourdieu (1.4, 8.5.2) thought they can.

5 Personal, social and affective meanings

1 The almost total neglect of non-conceptual meaning in traditional semantics and pragmatics is startling. In Relevance Theory, the need to take into account (coded) textual meaning has surfaced, but other types of meaning are typically brushed aside (e.g. Blakemore 2002: 22–4, 32–6).

2 Much of this section is based on Goatly 2000: chapter 3.

6 Textual meaning and genre

1 It was, of course, extra virgin olive oil.

2 This section is based on Goatly 2000: chapter 1, section 4.

3 Laughter itself may have various social meanings, and may not always occur in this position in the generic structure. For an interesting summary of research, see Billig 2005: 189–92.

4 Alexander (1997) developed a matrix for distinguishing various modes of jokes, according to whether they possessed the components intentional, conscious, benevolent, amusing, light or witty. However, his classification is not generic, as many of his "modes" do not correlate with linguistic structures at the sentence level and below (register) or larger structures of discourse (genre).

7 Metaphor and figures of speech

1 "Apply" covers various pragmatic and semantic relations such as reference, modification, predication and complementation of prepositions.

2 This section and the next draw on and summarise parts of Goatly 2007.

3 http://www.ln.edu.hk/lle/cwd/project01/web/home.html user id = <user>, password = <edumet6>

4 Semino (2008) makes a more delicate distinction between local and global metaphorical extensions.

5 Though for a discussion of the ways in which riddles and metaphors exploit prototypicality differently, see Weiner 1996.

6 Fonagy goes further by suggesting that language itself is "fossil poetry", that, in a sense, it is "only joking". A playful, regressive searching for motivation has moulded language into what it is, partly through joking, but primarily through metaphor (Fonagy 1982: 95).

8 Pragmatics: reference and speech acts

1 A fourth difference, non-detachability, has been suggested, but it is not important for our present purposes.

2 This is not a product placement.

3 Probably this conjuring up of a referent is one reason that euphemisms have to be regularly replaced.

4 This discussion of adjacency pairs, dispreferred seconds and pre-sequences is heavily reliant on Levinson 1983: 332–64.

9 Pragmatics: co-operation and politeness

1 Grice himself quoted the riddling message sent by the British commander Lord Napier to his superiors indicating that he had successfully taken possession of Sindh province in India – *"Peccavi"*, the Latin for 'I have sinned' – which clearly breaks the maxim of manner with humorous intent.

2 Oring (2003: 95–6) contests this, showing how jokes can comment on ideas, themes and situations relevant to the ongoing discourse.

3 The problem with identifying jokes with flouts is that, unlike prototypical flouts, the inferences on which jokes depend (excluding puns and irony) tend not to be defeasible (Attardo, personal communication). The alternative would be to regard these as suspensions, in that, when a joke is told it is culturally accepted that maxims will be broken. However, suspensions are typically associated with conventionalised expressions like "the Scottish play" for *Macbeth*, rather than interpretations made on the fly.

4 Simpson (2003: 165ff.) discusses the validity claims of truth, sincerity and appropriateness as they apply to satire. Chafe (2007) stresses the non-seriousness of humour, that it therefore can be used as a defence against the undesirable, and the fact that laughter is disabling to the extent of preventing action and communication.

5 Simpson (2003: 147) provides an interesting case study of ways in which face-threatening acts are redressed or mitigated in Jonathan Swift's *A Modest Proposal*.

10 Relevance Theory, schemas and deductive inference

1 The question of whether jokes typically demand or intend such extra processing is a somewhat contentious one. For example Oring (2003: 27–40) claims that jokes often convey thoughts of this kind over and above their instant humorous effect. This was, after all, the thrust of much of Freud's work in uncovering the psychoanalytic meanings of jokes.

2 Of course if hearers bring different knowledge to the joke, they may interpret it differently – Oring (2003: 37) furnishes an interesting example – and RT provides a mechanism for spelling out these different interpretations.

3 Simpson (2003: 36) points out that the scripts involved in the opposition are often generic or discourse schemata oppositions, rather than purely cognitive ones, in this case the opposition between the genre of Service Encounter and that of Seduction. Within a different generic context, such as medical soap operas, the cognitive script opposition between DOCTOR and LOVER would be attenuated or disappear.

4 Chafe (2007: 150–1) summarises and critiques Raskin and Attardo's model as being descriptive rather than explanatory.

5 *Come* has a slang meaning 'achieve orgasm'.

11 Lexical priming: information, collocation, predictability and humour

1 I note with some pleasure its appearance in Jonathan Franzen's *Freedom*.

2 The collocational data presented here and later in the chapter was retrieved from Collins Cobuild Wordbanks Online between 20 and 31 August 2010 (http:// 0-wordbanks.harpercollins.co.uk. innopac.ln.edu.hk:80/auth/).

3 Greimas' concept of isotopy (Attardo 1994: 76) is clearly relevant to priming theory, though lack of space precludes discussion here.

4 It might be interesting to look at the collocational data for word-forms which seem to regularly need disambiguation in discourse such that they are often glossed in conversation. The two I have noticed are *funny* and *hot*, which regularly invoke the request for disambiguation such as "funny haha or funny peculiar?" and "hot spicy or hot temperature?"

5 More traditional theories of combinatorial formal semantics, such as Kintsch's construction-integration model, take a bottom-up approach to establishing the coherence of texts (Attardo 2001: 9–14). In this tradition understanding of made-up sentences like "The paralysed bachelor hit the colourful ball" involve "the activation of all the senses of a word and the calculation of inferences, bridgings, etc. to create a textbase (a set of propositions)". In the case of the hypothetical sentence, twelve scripts are activated yielding sixty-four potential combinations. "The integration phase weeds out all the contextually inappropriate propositions and integrates the proposition in a coherent, hierarchically organised textbase" (Attardo 2001: 16, cf. Raskin 1985). This is the kind of bottom-up model that Sinclair and Hoey are arguing against. Jokes give better data for saving models like those of Katz and Kintsch than more serious texts because they deliberately override priming.

6 Cf. my suggestion that nominalisation would be better than the passive in the joke about an agent selling tickets for serial sex with an actress (3.7).

7 There are two ways of computing statistical correlation in Collins Wordbanks-Online. "The Mutual Information score expresses the extent to which observed frequency of co-occurrence differs from what we would expect (statistically speaking). In statistically pure terms this is a measure of the strength of association between words x and y. In a given finite corpus MI is calculated on the basis of the number of times you observed the pair together versus the number of times you saw the pair separately. MI does not work well with very low frequencies – the T-score provides a way of getting away from this problem as it also take frequencies into account. The T-score is a measure not of the strength of association but the confidence with which we can assert that there is an association. MI is more likely to give high scores to totally fixed phrases whereas T-score will yield significant collocates that occur relatively frequently. In most cases, T-score is the more reliable measurement.

   "Consider the example: 'sour and puss'. In the WordbanksOnline corpus, the word form 'sour' occurs 4109 times and there are 254 hits for 'puss' ... 'sour' and 'puss' only co-occur 3 times, this gives this particular collocation a very high MI score [12.01]: i.e. these two words will be very strongly associated. However, the T-score says 'maybe, but we haven't seen enough evidence to be sure that the MI is right!'... [T]he T-score is relatively low: 1.73" (Retrieved from http://0-wordbanks. harpercollins.co.uk.innopac.ln.edu.hk/Docs/Help/statistics.html 11/08/2010).

8 *Lemma* indicated by an asterisked form, is a stem, which allows searching in the corpus for all inflected forms incorporating the stem, e.g. *pushes, pushed, pushing.*

9 See Copestake and Terkourafi 2010 for discussion of such formulae.

10 Martin 2001 has shown that there is little hard evidence for the therapeutic value of humour.

References

Aitchison, J. 2002. *Words in the Mind*. 3rd edition. Oxford: Blackwell.

Akenside, M. 1810. *The Pleasures of Imagination: A New Edition*. London: T. Cadell and W. Davies.

Alexander, R. J. 1997. *Aspects of Verbal Humour in English*. Tübingen: Gunter Narr Verlag.

Alm-Arvius, C. 2009. Opposites attract. Paper delivered at the 2009 Metaphor Festival, University of Stockholm.

Atkinson, J. M. and Drew, P. 1979. *Order in Court: The Organisation of Verbal Interaction in Judicial Settings*. London: Macmillan.

Attardo, S. 1994. *Linguistic Theories of Humour*. Berlin and New York: Mouton.

2001. *Humorous Texts: A Semantic and Pragmatic Analysis*. Berlin and New York: Mouton.

2003. Mif o neprednameronnom iumore. In V. I. Karasik and G. G. Slyščkin (eds.) *Aksiologičeskaja Lingvistika: Igrovoe i Komičeskoe v Obščenii*. Volgograd: Peremena, pp. 4–14.

Attardo, S. and Raskin, V. 1991. Script theory revisited: joke similarity and joke representation model. *Humor* 4-3/4, 293–347.

Attardo, S., Attardo, D. H., Baltes, P. and Petray, M. J. 1994. The linear organisation of jokes: analysis of two thousand texts. *Humor: International Journal of Humor Research* 7-1, 27–54.

Bain, A. 1865. *The Emotions and the Will*. 2nd edition. Harlow: Longmans.

Barthes, R. 1972. *Mythologies,* Selected and Translated from the French by Annette Lavers. New York: Noonday Press.

1982. Inaugural lecture, Collège de France. In R. Barthes *Selected Writings*. London: Collins.

Bauer, L. 1983. *English Word-Formation*. Cambridge: Cambridge University Press.

Bell, N. D. 2009. Impolite responses to failed humour. In Norrick and Chiaro 2009: 143–63.

Bergson, H. 1900. *Le rire: essai sur la signification du comique*. Paris: Felix Alcan.

1911. *Creative Evolution*. New York: Henry Holt.

Billig, M. 2005. *Laughter and Ridicule: Towards a Social Critique of Humour*. London: Sage.

Blake, B. 2007. *Playing with Words*. London: Equinox.

Blakemore, D. 1992. *Understanding Utterances*. Oxford: Blackwell.

  2002. *Relevance and Linguistic Meaning*. Cambridge: Cambridge University Press.

Bourdieu, P. 1991. *Language and Symbolic Power*. John B. Thompson (ed.), Gino Raymond and Matthew Adamson (trans.). Cambridge: Polity Press.

Brazil, D. 1997. *The Communicative Value of Intonation in English*. Cambridge: Cambridge University Press.

Brown, P. and Levinson, S. C. 1987. *Politeness: Some Universals in Language Usage*. Cambridge: Cambridge University Press.

Bucaria, C. 2004. Lexical and syntactic ambiguity as a source of humor: the case of newspaper headlines. *Humor: International Journal of Humor Research* **17**–3, 279–309.

Carr, J. and Greeves, L. 2006. *The Naked Jape: Uncovering the Hidden World of Jokes*. Harmondsworth: Penguin.

Carroll, L. 1871. *Through the Looking-Glass, and What Alice Found There*. London: Macmillan.

Carter, R. 1987. *Vocabulary: Applied Linguistic Perspectives*. London: Allen and Unwin.

  1998. *Vocabulary: Applied Linguistic Perspectives*. 2nd edition. London: Routledge.

  2004. *Language and Creativity: The Art of Common Talk*. London: Routledge.

Chafe, W. 2007. *The Importance of Not Being Earnest*. Amsterdam: Benjamins.

Cheong, Y. Y. 2004. The construal of ideational meaning in print advertisements. In K. O'Halloran (ed.) *Multimodal Discourse Analysis*. London: Continuum, pp. 163–95.

Chiaro, D. 1992. *The Language of Jokes: Analysing Verbal Play*. London: Routledge.

Clark, H. 1987. Relevance to what? *Behavioural and Brain Sciences* **10** (4), 714–15.

Cohen, J. 1979. Metaphor and the cultivation of intimacy. In S. Sacks (ed.) *On Metaphor*. Chicago: University of Chicago Press, pp. 1–10.

Cohen, T. 1999. *Jokes: Philosophical Thoughts on Joking Matters*. Chicago: University of Chicago Press.

Cook, G. 1994. *Discourse and Literature*. Oxford: Oxford University Press.

Copestake, A. and Terkourafi, M. 2010. Conventionalized speech act formulae: from corpus findings to formalization. In P. Kühnlein, A. Benz and C. L. Sidner (eds.) *Constraints in Discourse*, vol. 2. Amsterdam: Benjamins, pp. 125–40.

Coulson, S., Urbach, T. P. and Kutas, M. 2006. Looking back: joke comprehensions and the space structuring model. *Humor* **19**, 229–50.

Coulthard, D. 1985. *An Introduction to Discourse Analysis*. 2nd edition. Harlow: Longman.

Critchley, S. 2002. *On Humour*. London: Routledge.

Croft, W. A. 2001. *Radical Construction Grammar: Syntactic Theory in Typological Perspective*. Oxford: Oxford University Press.

Cruse, D. 1986. *Lexical Semantics*. Cambridge: Cambridge University Press.

Crystal, D. 2001. *Language and the Internet*. Cambridge: Cambridge University Press.

2008. *Txtng the gr8 db8*. Oxford: Oxford University Press.

Crystal, D. and Davy, D. 1969. *Investigating English Style*. Harlow: Longman.

1975. *Advanced Conversational English*. Harlow: Longman.

Curcó, C. 1996. Relevance theory and humorous interpretations. In J. Hulstin and A. Nijholt (eds.) *Automatic Generation of Verbal Humor* (Proceedings of the Twelfth Twente Workshop on Language Technology). Enschede: University of Twente, pp. 53–68.

Davies, B. L. 2010. Grice's co-operative principle: meaning and rationality. In P. Griffiths, A. J. Merrison and A. Bloomer (eds.) *Language in Use: A Reader*. London: Routledge, pp. 23–36.

Ding, E. 2010. *Parallels, Interactions, and Illuminations: Traversing Chinese and Western Theories of Signs*. Toronto: University of Toronto Press.

Downing, A. and Locke, P. 1992. *A University Course in English Grammar*. London: Prentice-Hall.

Draitser, E. 1994. *Techniques of Satire: The Case of Saltykov-Scedrin*. Berlin: Mouton.

Duan, Jie. 2007. *The Discourse of Disease: The Representation of SARS – the China Daily and the South China Morning Post*. Unpublished thesis, Lingnan University, Hong Kong.

Du Pré, A. 1998. *Humour and the Healing Arts*. Mahwah, NJ: Lawrence Erlbaum.

Durkin, P. 2009. *The Oxford Guide to Etymology*. Oxford: Oxford University Press.

Edmondson, W. 1981. *Spoken Discourse: A Model for Analysis*. Harlow: Longman.

Ferris, C. 1993. *The Meaning of Syntax: A Study in the Adjectives of English*. Harlow: Longman.

Fillmore, C. J. 1968. The case for Case. In E. Bach and R. T. Harms (eds.) *Universals in Linguistic Theory*. New York: Holt, Rinehart, and Winston, pp. 1–88.

1982. Frame semantics. In The Linguistic Society of Korea (ed.) *Linguistics in the Morning Calm*. Seoul: Hanshin Publishing Co., pp. 111–37.

Fiske, J. 1982. *Introduction to Communication Studies*. London: Methuen.

Fonagy, I. 1982. He is only joking: joke, metaphor and language development. In F. Keifer (ed.) *Hungarian Linguistics*. Amsterdam: Benjamins, pp. 31–108.

Foucault, M. 1977. *Discipline and Punish*. London: Tavistock Press.

Freud, S. 1905. *Jokes and their Relation to the Unconscious*. Leipzig: Deuticke.

Galtung, J. and Ruge, M. H. 1965. The structure of foreign news. *Journal of Peace Research* **2** (1), 64–91.

Gentilhomme, Y. 1992. Humor: a didactic adjuvant. *Humor* **5-1** (2), 6–89.

Gentner, D. and Bowdle, B. F. 2001. Convention, form and figurative language processing. *Metaphor and Symbol* **16**, 223–48.

Gibbs R. W. 1992. What do idioms really mean? *Journal of Memory and Language* **31**, 485–506.

Giora, R. 1995. On irony and negation. *Discourse Processes* **19**, 239–64.

Goatly, A. 2000. *Critical Reading and Writing*. London: Routledge.

2007. *Washing the Brain: Metaphor and Hidden Ideology*. Amsterdam: Benjamins.

2008. *Explorations in Stylistics*, London: Equinox.

2011. *The Language of Metaphors*. 2nd edition. Abingdon: Routledge.

Goffmann, E. 1981. Footings. In E. Goffmann (ed.) *Forms of Talk*. Philadelphia: University of Pennsylvania Press, pp. 124–59.

Goldberg, Adele. 1995. *Constructions: A Construction Grammar Approach to Argument Structure*. Chicago: University of Chicago Press.

Greene, Judith. 1995. *Language Understanding: Current Issues* (parts I and II). Buckingham: Open University Press.

Grice, P. 1975. Logic and conversation. In P. Cole and J. Morgan (eds.) *Syntax and Semantics 3: Speech Acts*. New York: Academic Press, pp. 41–58.

Groenendijk, J. and Stokhof, M. 1991. Dynamic predicate logic. *Linguistics and Philosophy* **14**, 39–100.

Hageseth III, C. 1988. *A Laughing Place: The Art and Psychology of Positive Humour in Love and Adversity*. Fort Collins, CO: Berwick.

Halliday, M. A. K. 1978. *Language as Social Semiotic*. London: Arnold.

1985/1994. *An Introduction to Functional Grammar*. London: Arnold.

Halliday, M. A. K. and Hasan, R. 1976. *Cohesion in English*. Harlow: Longman.

1989. *Language, Context, and Text: Aspects of Language in a Social-Semiotic Perspective*. Oxford: Oxford University Press.

Halliday, M. A. K. and Matthiessen, C. 2004. *An Introduction to Functional Grammar*. London: Hodder.

Hay, J. 2000. Functions of humour in the conversations of men and women. *Journal of Pragmatics* **32**, 709–42.

Hetzron, R. 1999. On the structure of punchlines. *Humor* **4**, 61–108.

Hoey, M. 2005. *Lexical Priming: A New Theory of Words and Language*. London: Routledge.

Holmes, J. 2000. Politeness, power and provocation: how humour functions in the workplace. *Discourse Studies* **2** (2), 159–85.

Holquist, M. 1990. *Dialogism: Bakhtin and his World*. London and New York: Routledge.

Hudson, R. A. 1995. *Word Meaning*. London: Routledge.

Jakobson, R. 1960. Closing statements: linguistics and poetics. In T. A. Sebeok (ed.) *Style in Language*. Cambridge, MA: MIT Press, pp. 350–77.

Jodlowiec, M. 1994. The role of relevance in the interpretation of verbal jokes: a pragmatic analysis. *Humor* **7**, 87–92.

Kamp, H. and Reyle, U. 1993. *From Discourse to Logic*. Dordrecht: Kluwer Academic Publishers.

Katamba, F. 2005. *English Words: Structure, History, Usage*. London: Routledge.

Kelly, L. G. 1971. Punning and the linguistic sign. *Linguistics* **66**, 5–11.

Koestler, A. 1964. *The Act of Creation*. London: Macmillan.

Kotthoff, H. 2009. An interactional approach to irony development. In N. Norrick and D. Chiaro (eds.) *Humor in Interaction*. Amsterdam and Philadelphia: Benjamins, pp. 49–77.

Kövecses, Z. 2002. *Metaphor: A Practical Introduction*. Oxford: Oxford University Press.

   2005. *Metaphor in Culture: Universality and Variation*. Cambridge: Cambridge University Press.

Kress, G. 1985. *Linguistic Processes in Sociocultural Practice*. Oxford: Oxford University Press.

Labov, W. 1972. *Language in the Inner City: Studies in the Black English Vernacular*. Philadelphia: University of Pennsylvania Press.

Lakoff, G. 1972. Hedges: a study in meaning criteria and the logic of fuzzy concepts. In *Papers from the Eighth Regional Meeting of the Chicago Linguistics Society*. Chicago: Department of Linguistics, University of Chicago, pp. 183–217.

   1987. *Women, Fire and Dangerous Things*. Chicago: University of Chicago Press.

   1993. The contemporary theory of metaphor. In A. Ortony (ed.) *Metaphor and Thought*. Cambridge: Cambridge University Press, pp. 202–52.

   1996. *Moral Politics: What Conservatives Know that Liberals Don't*. Chicago and London: University of Chicago Press.

Lakoff, G. and Johnson, M. 1980. *Metaphors We Live By*. Chicago: University of Chicago Press.

   1999. *Philosophy in the Flesh*. New York: Basic Books.

Langacker, R. W. 1991. *Foundations of Cognitive Grammar, vol. 2: Descriptive Applications*. Stanford: Stanford University Press.

   2009. Metonymic grammar. In K.-U. Panther, L. L. Thornburg and A. Barcelona (eds.) *Metonymy and Metaphor in Grammar*. Amsterdam: Benjamins, pp. 45–71.

Le Page, R. B. and Tabouret-Keller, A. 1985. *Acts of Identity: Creole-Based Approaches to Language and Ethnicity*. Cambridge: Cambridge University Press.

Lecercle, J.-J. 1990. *The Violence of Language*. London: Routledge.

Leech, G. N. 1981. *Semantics: The Study of Meaning*. Harmondsworth: Penguin.

   1983. *Principles of Pragmatics*. London and New York: Longman.

   2005. Politeness: is there an east–west divide? *Journal of Foreign Languages* **6**, 1–30.

   2008. *Language in Literature: Style and Foregrounding*. Harlow: Longman.

Lehrer, A. 1974. *Semantic Fields and Lexical Structure*. Amsterdam: North Holland.

Levin, S. R. 1977. *The Semantics of Metaphor*. Baltimore, MD: Johns Hopkins University Press.

Levinson, S. 1983. *Pragmatics*. Cambridge: Cambridge University Press.

   1989. Review of 'Relevance: Communication and Cognition'. *Journal of Linguistics* **25** (2), 455–73.

Levinson, S. C. 2000. *Presumptive Meanings: The Theory of Generalized Conversational Implicature*. Cambridge, MA: MIT Press.

Lundberg, C. 1969. Person-focused joking. *Human Organization* 28 (1), 22–8.

Lyons, J. 1977. *Semantics*. Cambridge: Cambridge University Press.

Manetti, G. 1976. Per una semiotica del comico. *Il verri* 3, 130–52.

Martin, J. R. 1992. *English Text: System and Structure*. Amsterdam: Benjamins.

    2000. Beyond exchange: appraisal systems in English. In S. Hunston, and G. Thompson (eds.) *Evaluation in Text*. Oxford: Oxford University Press, pp. 142–75.

Martin, J. R. and Matthiessen, C. 1991. Systemic typology and topology. In F. Christie (ed.) *Literacy in Social Processes*. Darwin: Centre for Studies of Language in Education, Northern Territories University, pp. 345–83.

Martin, J. R. and White, P. R. R. 2005. *The Language of Evaluation, Appraisal in English*. London and New York: Palgrave-Macmillan.

Martin, R. A. 2001. Humour, laughter and physical health: methodological issues and research findings. *Psychological Bulletin* 127, 504–19.

    2007. *The Psychology of Humour: An Integrative Approach*. San Diego: Elsevier Academic Press.

Martinet, A. 1960. *Elements of General Linguistics*. London: Faber.

McEnery, T. 2006. *Swearing in English: Bad Langauge, Purity and Power from 1586 to the Present*. Abingdon: Routledge.

Morreall, J. 1983. *Taking Laughter Seriously*. New York: Suny Press.

Nash, W. 1985. *The Language of Humour*. Harlow: Longman.

Ng Ting Fai, John. 2005. *Metaphor as a Resource for Jokes*. Unpublished final year project, Department of English, Lingnan University, Hong Kong.

Norrick, N. R. 1984. Stock conversational witticisms. *Journal of Pragmatics* 8, 195–209.

    1986. Stock similes. *Journal of Literary Semantics* 15 (1), 39–52.

    1989. Intertextuality in humour. *Humor* 2 (2), 117–39.

    1993. *Conversational Joking: Humor in Everyday Talk*. Bloomington: Indiana University Press.

Norrick, N. R. and Chiaro, D. (eds.) 2009. *Humor in Interaction*. Amsterdam and Philadelphia: Benjamins.

Novak, W. and Waldocks, M. (eds.) 1981. *The Big Book of Jewish Humour*. New York: Harper and Row.

O'Mara, D. A., Waller, A. and Todman, J. 2002. Linguistic humour and the development of language skills in AAC. In *Proceedings of 10th Biennial Conference of the International Society for Augmentative and Alternative Communication*. Odense, Denmark.

Oaks, D. 1994. Creating structural ambiguities in humor: getting English grammar to cooperate. *Humour* 7 (4), 377–401.

    2010. *Structural Ambiguity in English*. London: Continuum.

Ong, W. 2002. *Orality and Literacy: The Technologizing of the Word*. London: Routledge.

Oring, E. 2003. *Engaging Humor*. Urbana and Chicago: University of Illinois Press.

Peirce, C. S. 1867. On a new list of categories. *Proceedings of the American Academy of Arts and Sciences* **7**, 1868: 287–98.

Plag, Ingo. 2003. *Word-Formation in English*. Cambridge: Cambridge University Press.

Poynton, K. 1989. *Language and Gender: Making the Difference*. Oxford: Oxford University Press.

Priego-Valverde, B. 2009. Failed humour in conversation. In Norrick and Chiaro 2009, pp. 165–83.

Purdie, S. 1993. *Comedy: The Mastery of Discourse*. Hemel Hempstead: Harvester Wheatsheaf.

Putnam, H. 1975. *Mind, Language and Reality*. Cambridge: Cambridge University Press.

Raskin, V. 1981. Script-based lexicon. *Quaderni di semantica* **2** (1), 25–34.
    1985. *Semantic Mechanisms of Humor*. Dordrecht, Boston and Lancaster: D. Reidel.

Redfern, W. 1984. *Puns*. Oxford: Blackwell/André Deutsch.

Ritchie, G. 2004. *The Linguistic Analysis of Jokes*. London and New York: Routledge.

Robinson, D. 2003. *Performative Linguistics*. New York and London: Routledge.
    2006. *Introducing Performative Pragmatics*. New York and London: Routledge.

Rosch, E. 1975. Cognitive representations of semantic categories. *Journal of Experimental Psychology: General* **104**: 192–233.

Ross, A. 1998. *The Language of Humour*. London: Routledge.

Sacks, H. 1974. An analysis of the course of a joke's telling in conversation. In R. Bauman and J. Sherzer (eds.) *Explorations in the Ethnography of Speaking*. Cambridge: Cambridge University Press, pp. 325–45.

Sadock, J. M. 1979. Figurative speech and linguistics. In A. Ortony (ed.) *Metaphor and Thought*. Cambridge: Cambridge University Press, pp. 46–63.

Saeed, J. I. 2003. *Semantics*, 2nd edition. Oxford: Blackwell.

Sampson, G. 2005. *The 'Language Instinct' Debate*. New York: Continuum.

Schank, R. and Abelson, R. 1977. *Scripts, Plans, Goals and Understanding*. Hillsdale, NJ: Erlbaum.

Scheff, T. J. 1997. *Emotion, the Social Bond, and Human Reality*. Cambridge: Cambridge University Press.

Schegloff, E. 1987. Some sources of misunderstanding in talk-in-interaction. *Linguistics* **25**, 201–18.
    2007. *Sequence Organisation in Interaction: A Primer in Conversation Analysis*, vol. 1. Cambridge: Cambridge University Press.

Searle, J. R. 1969. *Speech Acts*. Cambridge: Cambridge University Press.
    1979. *Expression and Meaning: Studies in the Theory of Speech Acts*. Cambridge: Cambridge University Press.
    1995. *The Construction of Social Reality*. New York and London: Free Press.

Semino, E. 2008. *Metaphor in Discourse.* Cambridge: Cambridge University Press.

Sherzer, J. 1978. Oh! That's a pun and I didn't mean it. *Semiotica* **22** (3–4), 335–50.

Simpson, P. 2003. *On the Discourse of Satire.* Amsterdam: Benjamins.

Simpson, P. and Mayr, A. 2010. *Language and Power: A Resource Book for Students.* London: Routledge.

Sinclair, J. M. 1991. *Corpus, Concordance, Collocation.* Oxford: Oxford University Press.

Sinclair, J. M. and Coulthard, R. M. 1975. *Towards an Analysis of Discourse: The English Used by Teachers and Pupils.* Oxford: Oxford University Press.

Spencer, H. 1864. The physiology of laughter. In H. Spencer, *Essays: Scientific, Political and Speculative.* Second series. New York: D. Appleton.

Sperber, D. and Wilson, D. 1986/1995. *Relevance: Communication and Cognition.* Oxford: Blackwell.

Suls, Jerry. 1972. A two-stage model for the appreciation of jokes and cartoons. In J. H. Goldstein and P. McGhee (eds.) *The Psychology of Humor.* London and New York: Academic Press, pp. 81–100.

Swales, J. 1990. *Genre Analysis.* Cambridge: Cambridge University Press.

Tabossi, P. 1989. What's in a context? In D. S. Gorfein (ed.) *Resolving Semantic Ambiguity.* Berlin: Springer Verlag, pp. 25–39.

Thomas, J. 1995. *Meaning in Interaction.* Harlow, Longman.

Thompson, G. and Hunston, S. 2000. Evaluation: an introduction. In S. Hunston and G. Thompson (eds.) *Evaluation in Text.* Oxford: Oxford University Press, pp. 1–27.

Tibballs, G. 2006. *The Mammoth Book of Jokes.* London: Robinson.

Toolan, M. 1988. The language of press advertising. In M. Ghadessy (ed.) *Registers of Written English.* London: Pinter, pp. 52–64.

Ullmann, S. 1962. *Semantics: An Introduction to the Science of Meaning.* Oxford: Blackwell.

Vaid, J., Hull, R., Heredia, R., Gerkens, D. and Martinez, F. 2003. Getting a joke: the time course of meaning activation in verbal humour. *Journal of Pragmatics* **35**, 1431–49.

Van Dijk, T. A. 1986. News schemata. In C. R. Cooper and S. Greenbaum (eds.) *Studying Writing: Linguistic Approaches.* London: Sage, pp. 151–85.

Vittoz-Canuto, M. B. 1983. *Si vous avez votre jeu de mot à dire. Analyse des jeux de mots dans la publicité.* Paris: Nizet.

Waldron, R. A. 1967. *Sense and Sense Development.* London: Deutsch.

Watts, R. 2003. *Politeness.* Cambridge: Cambridge University Press.

Weiner, E. J. 1996. Why is a riddle not like a metaphor? In J. Hulstin and A. Nijholt (eds.) *Automatic Generation of Verbal Humor* (Proceedings of the Twelfth Twente Workshop on Language Technology) Enschede: University of Twente, pp. 111–19.

Whorf, B. J. 1956. *Language, Thought and Reality.* John B. Carroll (ed.). Cambridge, MA: MIT Press.

Wilson, D. and Sperber, D. 1986. An outline of relevance theory. In H. O. Alves (ed.) *Encontro de Linguistas: Actas*. Minho, Portugal: University of Minho, pp. 19–42.

Wittgenstein, L. 1953/2001. *Philosophical Investigations*. Oxford: Blackwell.

Wolfson, N. 1989. *Perspectives: Sociolinguistics and TESOL*. Cambridge: Newbury House.

Ziv, A. 1979. *L'humour en education*. Paris: Les Editions ESF.

Index

Italicised page numbers indicate the glossary entry for this term. Bold type indicates pages on which definitions of terms appear.